In recent years scientists have become preoccupied with a set of new environmental phenomena, such as global warming, ozone layer depletion, acid rains, fresh water and ocean pollution, desertification, deforestation and the loss of bio-diversity. The crucial and pressing nature of these issues has spawned a new wave of research in environmental economics, the gist of which is reported in this volume.

The volume provides broad surveys of the recent developments of the new economics of the environment and reports the state of the art on a new set of environmental problems, analytical tools and economic policies. The importance of the new approach is that environmental problems are no longer isolated from all other economic dimensions. Throughout the volume they are analysed in an open, generally non-competitive economy with transnational or global externalities. The first part deals with the relationship between the environment, economic growth and technological innovation. The second part analyses the optimal design of environmental taxation, while the third part considers the international dimension of environmental policy.

New directions in the economic theory of the environment

New directions in
the economic theory of
the environment

EDITED BY

Carlo Carraro
University of Venice and FEEM

AND

Domenico Siniscalco
University of Turin and FEEM

CAMBRIDGE
UNIVERSITY PRESS

PUBLISHED BY THE PRESS SYNDICATE OF THE UNIVERSITY OF CAMBRIDGE
The Pitt Building, Trumpington Street, Cambridge CB2 1RP, United Kingdom

CAMBRIDGE UNIVERSITY PRESS
The Edinburgh Building, Cambridge CB2 2RU, United Kingdom
40 West 20th Street, New York, NY 10011–4211, USA
10 Stamford Road, Oakleigh, Melbourne 3166, Australia

© Cambridge University Press 1997

First published 1997

Printed in the United Kingdom at the University Press, Cambridge

Typeset in 10 on 12pt Monotype Times   [SE]

A catalogue record for this book is available from the British Library

Library of Congress Cataloguing in Publication data

New directions in the economic theory of the environment / edited by
    Carlo Carraro and Domenico Siniscalco.
        p.   cm.
    ISBN 0 521 59089 2
        1. Environmental economics. 2. Environmental impact charges.
    3. Environmental policy. I. Carraro, Carlo. II. Siniscalco, Domenico.
    HD75.6 N5   1997
    333.7–dc21
                                                        96–40021
                                                          CIP

ISBN 0 521 59089 2 hardback

Contents

Contributors

Carlo Carraro
Department of Economics, University of Venice, CEPR and
Fondazione ENI E. Mattei

Domenico Siniscalco
Department of Economics, University of Turin and
Fondazione ENI E. Mattei

Andrea Beltratti
University of Turin

David Ulph
Department of Economics
University College, London

A. Lans Bovenberg
CentER, Tilburg University
OCFEB, Erasmus University and CEPR

Michael Hoel
Department of Economics, University of Oslo

Alistair Ulph
University of Southampton

Michael Rauscher
University of Rostock and CEPR

Scott Barrett
London Business School

Hideo Konishi
Department of Economics
Southern Methodist University, Dallas

Michel Le Breton
GREQAM, University of Aix-Marseille and Institut
Universitare de France

Shlomo Weber
Department of Economics
Southern Methodist University, Dallas

Francis Bloch
Department of Finance and Economics
HEC

1 Theoretical frontiers of environmental economics

Carlo Carraro and Domenico Siniscalco

Environmental economics was the subject of a comprehensive research programme in the 1960s and 1970s. This programme dealt with a wide range of issues and policy problems, such as the economics of natural resources, the methods and problems in the correction of externalities, the management of common property goods, the economics of nature preservation. Against this background, suitable analytical tools were provided by the theory of non-renewable and renewable resources; the theory of missing markets; Pigovian taxation and the theory of property rights; the economics of public goods; welfare economics. All in all, the research programme was very successful and in the following decade it gave rise to several textbooks, from Baumol and Oates (1975) to Siebert (1987), Pearce and Turner (1990). At the beginning of the 1990s, no less Partha Dasgupta (1990) was claiming that environmental issues were 'very cold' as topics for analytical investigation and 'dead' as research problems.

In recent years, however, scientists have highlighted a set of 'new' environmental phenomena, such as global warming, ozone layer depletion, acid rains, fresh water and ocean pollution, desertification, deforestation and the loss of bio-diversity (e.g., cf. UNEP (1991)). Some of the above phenomena, such as ozone layer depletion, were newly discovered; some others were known, but attracted new attention, due to their scale and socio-economic implications, such as global warming. In both cases, the new environmental problems entered the agenda of policy makers and became the centre of world-wide debate and a massive diplomatic effort, culminating in the UN Conference on Environment and Development, held in Rio de Janeiro in 1992 (for a discussion, see World Bank (1992), Siniscalco (1992), IPCC (1995)).

The new environmental phenomena have a global scale and for the first time pose a serious threat on the well-being of future generations. Most of all, they share a set of common features: they are closely related to demography, economic growth and industrialisation; they can have a very

1

long-run dimension, affecting future generations as well as the present ones; they have an intrinsic transnational or global dimension, due to nature of the externalities involved; they have important international repercussions through trade and factor mobility. The economists community increasingly recognised that the above common characteristics require new analytical tools and fresh policy analyses (the discussion is summarised in Carraro and Siniscalco (1992)).

The close links between environmental resources and development call for a new viewpoint, which goes under the name of *sustainable development* (Bruntland (1987)). Sustainability, among other implications, requires analysis of the environment as a dimension of socio-economic development, and not as a separate issue, which can be analysed in partial equilibrium or even in isolation from the rest of the economy. Economists, in particular, have to integrate the environment in the theory of growth, with special emphasis on the long run and on the role of innovation and technical progress. And they have to take into account the fact that a substantial part of pollution is produced by firms, which interact in various, not always competitive, market structures.[1]

The global and international dimension of the environmental issues requires an even wider departure from standard analysis. In a world of global externalities, the efficient protection of the environment requires international coordination of environmental policies, and more particularly self-enforcing agreements among sovereign countries. The same applies in a context where costly national environmental policies have important international repercussions through trade and factor mobility, even in the absence of any transnational externality. These two dimensions, in turn, require a shift from the standard literature on government intervention to a literature on negotiations between nations.

Against this background, in the present decade environmental economics have gathered a new momentum, and are now considered a lively and relevant subject, not only on policy but also on analytical grounds. In some cases, the required tools were taken from other areas of economics; in other cases, the analytical requirements provided an impulse for original applications and developments.

Indicators of this new interest in environmental issues and their economic analysis are provided in a recent survey by us on the articles submitted to international conferences and journals on environmental economics (see, Siniscalco (1996)). The survey shows that papers related to sustainable development *and* to the international dimension of environmental policy account for about 40 per cent of the total sample considered and their share is constantly increasing.

The existing new environmental economics literature is not yet systematised in a sufficient way to be reflected in a textbook, but is now an established field of research. For this reason, we believe it is time to take stock and publish a volume containing a coordinated set of surveys. With this aim we asked the best scholars in the field to produce broad reviews of their own specific research areas. Different viewpoints and subjects still need to be developed, but the resulting volume represents a substantial leap forward, *vis-à-vis* similar works, such as the *Handbook of Natural Resources and Energy Economics* or the *Handbook of Environmental Economics*.[2] These volumes, such as the mainstream textbooks mentioned at the beginning of this Introduction, devote little attention to the literature on the new environmental economics but rather represent the up-to-date reviews of the more traditional approach. Such an approach analyses environmental issues in a closed, competitive, full-information economy. We rather propose to analyse them in an open, generally non-competitive economy, with transnational or global externalities. Even when closed-economy issues are analysed the focus is on interactions between trade, industrial and environmental issues and policies, thus stressing the importance of a new approach in which environmental problems are no longer isolated from all other economic dimensions.

Notice that, even if this volume provides a broad survey of the recent developments in the new economics of the environment, we decided not to use the word 'handbook' in the title. We are quite conscious that the material presented herein is still a preliminary study of the problems posed in the recent literature and it is likely to be subject to a rapid evolution which will yield new achievements and results. Therefore, we prefer to see this book as a stimulus to further research. By proposing the state of the art on new environmental problems, analytical tools, and economic policies, the book will provide the right framework upon which further developments can be based. This is going to be particularly helpful in a field, the new environmental economics, in which scholars coming from different fields (international trade, growth theory, industrial organisation, game theory, macroeconomics, labour economics) are joining in their efforts to improve our understanding of complex economic phenomena.

The material presented in this volume can ideally be divided into three parts. The chapters by Andrea Beltratti and David Ulph deal with the relationship between environment, economic growth and technological innovation. These chapters emphasise the link between sustainable development and technical progress as the main way to achieve substantial intergenerational environmental protection. In particular, David Ulph shows how environmental and industrial policies can be adapted to foster firms' technological innovation, whereas Andrea Beltratti analyses how technical progress affects the equilibrium growth path of economies in which environmental concerns must no longer be neglected.

A second set of chapters by Lans Bovenberg and Michael Hoel analyses the issue of the optimal design of environmental taxation. Lans Bovenberg reviews the highly debated problems related to the possible emergence of the so-called 'environment–employment double dividend'. The chapter singles out the conditions under which a joint increase in environmental quality and employment can actually be achieved by an appropriately designed tax policy scheme. Michael Hoel analyses the optimal implementation of environmental taxes at the international level. Should tax rates be coordinated across countries and/or across sectors? How can further additional policy tools, e.g., trade tariffs, be used to achieve the first-best optimal taxation scheme in the presence of countries' heterogeneity?

The third set of surveys, by Alistair Ulph, Michael Rauscher and Scott Barrett, deals explicitly with the international dimension of environmental policy. Alistair Ulph discusses the way in which trade policy can be used to protect the environment and how to reduce the possible negative consequences of environmental policies on trade flows. Michael Rauscher discusses the impact of coordinated and non-coordinated environmental policies (e.g., environmental dumping) on capital mobility. Scott Barrett takes into account all these effects when studying the formation of international agreements to protect the global environment. The analysis of such self-enforcing agreements, carried out in the context of non-cooperative game theory, is important when exploring the possibility of protecting the global environment in the absence of a supra-national institution with the power to design and enforce global environmental policies.

The literature in this area is still developing. Further advances require new developments of the theory of non-cooperative coalition formation. The last two chapters provide the latest results developed by game theorists and also consider applications to environmental issues. In particular, the chapter by Hideo Konishi, Michel Le Breton and Shlomo Weber focuses on games without externalities and discusses the endogenous formation of coalitions for the provision of public goods. The chapter by Francis Bloch complements the previous one by analysing the formation of coalitions in games with both negative and positive externalities. Environmental applications concern international environmental agreements as well as environmental innovation and R&D.

Given the survey nature of the chapters contained in this volume, we do not summarise the articles in detail. We would rather conclude by concentrating on what is missing in the volume and recommend for further reading.

First, the volume ignores the demographic dimension of environmental deterioration, as the topic is very poorly analysed by economists, with very few exceptions (e.g., Baldwin (1995)). This gap should be filled by taking into account the possibility of characterising endogenous population growth as well as migrations.

Second, as an editorial choice, the volume mainly deals with theoretical frameworks, as a good review of empirical work in this area would require a volume by itself. We therefore limit ourselves and recommend further reading starting with Musu and Siniscalco (1996) for data problems, to IPCC (1995) and Carraro and Galeotti (1995) for a review of the existing models. Moreover, we do not deal with applied issues like waste and water management.

Third, the articles of this volume only marginally touch upon some very recent research topics, such as the links between financial markets and environmental protection or the political economy of environmental policy.

Lastly, and most importantly, what is really missing is an integration of the different approaches analysed in the various surveys collected in this volume. But this cannot be done at this stage, and still requires substantial work.

Notes

1 Several recent contributions on the theory of environmental policy when markets are imperfectly competitive are contained in Carraro, Katsoulacos and Xepapadeas (1996).
2 Cf. Kneese and Sweeney (1993), Bromley (1995).

References

Baldwin R. (1995), 'Does Sustainability Require Growth?', in I. Goldwin and L.A. Winters, (eds.), *The Economics of Sustainable Development*, Cambridge, Cambridge University Press.

Baumol W.J. and W.E. Oates (1975), *The Theory of Environmental Policy*, 1st edn, Englewood Cliffs, NJ: Prentice-Hall.

Bromley D.W. (ed.) (1995), *The Handbook of Environmental Economics*, Oxford: Blackwell.

Bruntland Report, World Commission on Environment and Development (1987), *Our Common Future*, London: Oxford University Press.

Carraro, C. and D. Siniscalco (1992), 'The International Dimension of Environmental Policy'. *European Economic Review*, 36, 379–87.

—— (1994) 'Environmental Policy Reconsidered: The Role of Technological Innovation', *European Economic Review*, 38, 545–54.

Carraro C. and D. Siniscalco, (eds.) (1996), *Environmental Fiscal Reform and Unemployment*, Dordrecht: Kluwer Academic Publishers.

Carraro C. and M. Galeotti (1995), *Ambiente, occupazione e progresso tecnico: un modello per l'Europa*, Bologna: Il Mulino.

Carraro C., A. Katsoulacos and A. Xepapadeas (eds.) (1996), *Environmental Policy and Market Structure*, Dordrecht: Kluwer Academic Publishers.

Dasgupta P. (1990), 'The Environment as a Commodity', *Oxford Review of Economic Policy*, 6(1), 51–79.

Intergovernmental Panel on Climate Change (IPCC) (1995), Report, Eleventh Session, Rome, 11–15 December.

Kneese A.V. and J.L. Sweeney (eds.) (1993), *Handbook of Natural Resources and Energy Economics*, Amsterdam: Elsevier Science Publishers.

Musu I. and D. Siniscalco (eds.) (1996), *National Accounts and the Environment*, Dordrecht: Kluwer Academic Publishers.

Pearce D.W. and R.K. Turner (1990), *Economics of Natural Resources and the Environment*, New York: Harvester Wheatsheaf Publishers.

Siebert H. (1987), *Economics of the Environment: Theory and Policy*, 2nd edn, Berlin: Springer-Verlag.

Siniscalco D. (1992), *La Conferenza di Rio de Janeiro: un ambiente per cooperare*, Il Mulino, anno XLI, July–August, 605–18.

(1996) 'Environmental Economics in Europe and the US', Paper presented at the Seventh Annual Meeting of the EAERE, Universitade Nova de Lisboa, 1996.

United Nations Environment Programme (UNEP) (1991), *The State of the Environment*, New York: United Nations.

World Development Report (1992), *Development and the Environment*, The World Bank, Oxford: Oxford University Press.

2 Growth with natural and environmental resources

Andrea Beltratti

1 Introduction

Exploitation of natural resources and environmental assets is a dynamic process, given that utilisation and (spontaneous or induced) regeneration flows affect the quantity and/or the quality of the stock. Optimal exploitation of natural and environmental resources has therefore to be forward-looking, as economic agents need to take into account the consequences of economic activity on the future availability of resources. However, devising optimal exploitation plans is in practice an enormous challenge, due to incomplete information (e.g., about models of the interrelationships among economic and ecological subsystems), genuine uncertainty (e.g., about the possibility of a future climate change or about future environmental policies or technologies) and international links (in the case of uniformly mixing pollutants like CO_2, policies decided by one country in isolation from the international community may not be effective).

Devising optimal exploitation plans is an enormous challenge also in theory. Of course, there are several reasons why it is important to perform a theoretical study of the relationship between economic activity and the use of resources: it may be a source of inspiration for empirical models aimed at building quantitative tools assisting policy makers in the creation of economic and environmental policies (many large-scale econometric models based on optimising agents for studying demand for resources are nowadays based on the assumptions of intertemporal maximisation); it may enlarge the range of phenomena considered by economists, for example to take into account variables that are fundamental to issues of sustainability of growth and its compatibility with the environment, like the laws of thermodynamics and population, and may motivate economists to devote more attention to the analysis of complex systems.

However, such a large reward does not come without a large cost. Economists who wish to study optimal exploitation policies face a very difficult modelling exercise, and are presented with several issues which go

7

beyond the standard difficulties met in studying other economic problems. The effort to model not simply any exploitation policy but a policy which is regarded as optimal in the face of given a certain intertemporal objective function requires sophisticated mathematical instruments. There is not complete freedom in the description of the system: analytical results may be obtained only in small models containing two or three state variables. Economists have in general accepted this methodology, and have studied systems which have been simplified from many points of view, producing a large literature that directly or indirectly is concerned with issues of environment and economic growth. It will be clear in what follows that the particular specification of the model dictates to a large extent the problems that can possibly be discussed with the equations chosen, and this makes many results highly model specific. Indeed, among the many variables which it would be necessary to consider, e.g., physical and human capital, natural capital, reproducible and exhaustible resources, population, one has to make choices in order to solve the models analytically, at the cost of reduced generality and applicability. This has to be kept in mind, especially when it comes to deriving environmental policy implications.

The chapter starts by describing a general reference model, which highlights in a synthetic but unifying form the main issues of growth with natural and environmental resources. While it may be worth waiting until the end of the second section before describing the plan of the chapter in more detail, since at that stage it will be possible to refer to the general reference model, it may be useful to specify immediately what is not considered explicitly in this chapter for reasons of space. First, even though the economic literature on growth and the environment can in some sense be traced back to Malthus, this chapter will be limited to the analytical models that have appeared since the 1970s. Secondly, not all interesting aspects of the main building blocks of these models, that is preferences, productive structure and institutions, will be discussed with equal detail. The space devoted to criteria which are alternative to maximisation of discounted utility will not be as large as this topic deserves; similarly, there will be basically no discussion of models with endogenous population growth. Also, even though typically the existence of environmental resources is connected with ill-defined property rights, requiring various public instruments to internalise some interactions among agents, there will be an emphasis on solutions to planning problems rather than on competitive systems, even though a section will be devoted to a summing up of rules for environmental policy.

2 A reference structure

In order to describe the issues and the variables which will be discussed in this chapter it may be useful to start with a general structure, composed of two blocks describing preferences and technologies.

2.1 Preferences

The preference block is specified as a maximisation of discounted future utilities

$$\max \int_0^\infty e^{-\delta t} u(c,E,p,P)dt$$

where c is the flow of consumption, E is the stock of environmental asset, p is a flow of pollution and P is a stock of pollution.[1] With subscripts denoting derivatives, $u_c > 0$, $u_E > 0$, $u_p < 0$, $u_P < 0$, $u_{cc} < 0$, $u_{EE} < 0$, $u_{pp} < 0$, $u_{PP} < 0$, while the cross-derivatives may have any sign.[2] Before discussing the arguments of the utility function, note that a strictly positive δ is necessary to obtain a finite integral of utilities and to be able to compare alternative policies. δ reflects preference towards the present, and is often taken as representing discrimination against future generations (see Ramsey (1928)). Criteria other than maximisation of discounted utility, such as the Rawlsian criterion and the overtaking criterion, are sometimes recommended to preserve equality of treatment across generations (see Dasgupta and Heal (1979) and Heal (1993) for a general discussion).

The variable c may be interpreted as consumption of a single good or as an index of consumption obtained from different varieties, see Grossman and Helpman (1991). The latter interpretation may be appropriate to represent heterogeneous varieties with decreasing pollution/output ratios, even though a similar description may be achieved by considering heterogeneous intermediate goods in the production function. The other arguments of the utility function usually do not appear all together; the possible choices are whether to include pollution or environmental assets, and whether to consider stocks or flows.

Including flows rather than stocks may not be realistic but simplifies considerably the overall structure. The choice between pollution and environment becomes important in 'genuine' growth models where variables may grow for ever. Solutions with a permanently increasing stock of environment or pollution may not make much practical sense. Indeed it is common to assume an upper bound to the stock of pollution, beyond which the environment loses its role of life-support system. Many different cases may again arise. One can consider the 'original state' as a situation that can only be damaged by human actions, but others may contend that the intervention of humanity can continuously increase the quality of the environment; for example, one may prefer New York City plus some surrounding environmental amenities to amenities without New York City.

A final question regards aggregation: is it meaningful to think of one stock (or flow) of environment when there are many relevant environmental media, like amenities, quality of air and water, and so on? Growth models have to be aggregate in order to preserve analytical tractability, and therefore assuming the existence of one giant stock is in some sense an excusable necessity (this problem will be taken up again in the conclusions). Another way to justify such aggregation is to think of the model as describing a specific phenomenon of interest, e.g., air pollution in a closed economy.

2.2 Technology

The block describing the structure of the economy is composed of a production function and an ecological relation, keeping track of the effects of economic activity on natural and environmental resources. Production is obtained by a function which in general can be written as

$$Y = F(K, H, L, E, r, T, X, w)$$

where K is the physical capital stock, H the human capital stock, L the stock of labour, r a flow of natural resources extracted from a stock of initial dimension S_0 (in the case of exhaustible natural resources there is a total constraint over the planning horizon $\int r_t dt \leq S_0$), T is technological knowledge, w is waste. X is the flow of intermediate goods obtained from a production function

$$X = F_X(K_X, H_X, L_X, E_X, T_X)$$

where the subscript denotes the use of a certain factor of production by the intermediate sector. Constraints on the function F can be of various natures, e.g., one may assume homogeneity of degree one in all the inputs or assume the existence of globally increasing returns to scale. Moreover, various assumptions about the elasticity of substitution may be made, e.g., a constant elasticity lower or larger than one. Technology may be assumed to be constant or exogenously growing or accumulated as a result of accumulation of capital. The same is true of the function F_X; to the extent that some factors of production are a common good, one does not need to distinguish between the inputs to the two functions, e.g., one might plausibly have $F_X(K_X, H, L_X, E, T_X)$.

The description of the production block is completed by the dynamic equation for the stock of capital, $K = Y - c - d$, where d represents a flow of defensive expenditures.

The ecological block can be written as

$$\dot{E} = N(E, r, c, d, w, Y)$$

to take into account the possibility that both consumption and production affect the environment, but that part of produced goods may be used to ameliorate the quality and the quantity of the environment by means of environmental expenditures d. Clearly, technology may affect this function, as the environmental deterioration following production depends on many characteristics of productive processes. The mathematical properties of such a reproduction function may be similar to those of the production function, even though empirical studies are certainly not abundant (see section 7). When natural resources are included as factors of production, one needs a dynamic equation also for their stock

$$\dot{S} = -r$$

Most models of environment and growth contain variations of this basic structure. Some of them concentrate on the use of natural resources and ignore environmental repercussions, while others are mainly concerned with production of pollution as a joint product of economic activity. The earlier literature concentrated on steady states, while recently the emphasis has shifted to techniques appropriate for the study of non-stationary economies, even though part of the natural resources literature, e.g., Dasgupta and Heal (1979), had studied steady-growth solutions with shrinking reserves of exhaustible resources already in the 1970s. Finally, the most recent literature attempts to make growth endogenous by explaining the process of accumulation of the stock of knowledge.

The first part of this chapter (sections 3 and 4) will concentrate on natural resources which do not enter the utility function. Section 3 analyses what happens when the structure of preferences is hidden behind the assumption of an exogenously given savings rate, concentrating attention on the structure of the production function, especially in terms of importance of exhaustible raw materials relative to other reproducible factors like capital. Section 4 incorporates such a structure in an optimising framework, contrasting growth with maximising consumers and growth with rule-of-thumb policies to highlight the possibility that a sustainable process of permanent production is stopped by optimal savings decisions.

The second part will concentrate on models of environmental assets, where scarcity of natural resources is not a concern. In the context of models with a steady state (section 5) one can derive comparative statics results about the importance of various parameters (e.g., the rate of time preference) for determination of steady-state equilibria. Models with permanent and endogenous growth (section 6) assume conditions which are necessary for a permanently growing economy and discuss optimality of growth under these conditions, as well as the environmental policies which are necessary to implement optimal growth.

Section 7 discusses applications of the theoretical structure. Section 7.1 considers some policy rules that are suggested by the theoretical models as a result of the comparison between centralised and decentralised solutions; 7.2 discusses the connection between theoretical models and stylised facts, while 7.3 is concerned with the recent debate about sustainability of growth. The conclusions discuss future research possibilities.

3 Exogenous economic growth with natural resources

At the analytical level, much can be said by simply analysing the production structure of the economy, especially if one assumes exogenous rates of technical change and of savings. Even though these assumptions are extreme and have been relaxed in the most recent literature (see section 4), many interesting phenomena can be studied under this framework, especially issues connected with the physical possibility of production given initial stocks of capital and labour and a finite amount of resources.

In the standard Solow model there is a production function $F(K,L)$ and a constant savings rate s. The rate of change of production over time is $\dot{Y}=F_K\dot{K}+F_L\dot{L}$, where $F_K=\dfrac{\partial F}{\partial K}$, etc. The model can be reformulated in ratio form $x\equiv\dfrac{K}{L}$ to obtain $\dot{x}=sf(x)-nx$, where n is the exogenous rate of growth of population and $f(x)\equiv F(x,1)$, so that $F(K,L)=LF(K,1)=Lf(x)$, $F_K=f_x$ and $F_L=f-xf_x$. The existence and stability properties of a steady state depend on the assumptions about the production function, see Solow (1956). The various cases can be described starting from a general CES representation

$$F(K,L)=\left[\beta K^{\frac{\sigma-1}{\sigma}}+(1-\beta)L^{\frac{\sigma-1}{\sigma}}\right]^{\frac{\sigma-1}{\sigma}}$$

where $0<\beta<1$ is a distribution parameter and $\sigma\geq0$ is the elasticity of subtitution between the two factors. The following table, from Dasgupta and Heal (1974), shows the connection between inputs and output for various levels of elasticity

	$F(K,0)$	$\lim_{x\to\infty}f_x$	$\lim_{x\to\infty}\dfrac{f}{x}$	$\lim_{x\to\infty}(f-xf_x)$	$\lim_{x\to\infty}f$
$\sigma=1$	0	0	0	∞	∞

$0 \leq \sigma \leq 1$	0	0	0	$(1-\beta)^{\frac{\sigma}{\sigma-1}}$	$(1-\beta)^{\frac{\sigma}{\sigma-1}}$
$\infty > \sigma > 1$	>0	ρ	ρ	∞	∞

where $\rho \equiv \beta^{\frac{\sigma}{\sigma-1}}$ is the (asymptotically) constant marginal productivity of capital, reached as $x \to \infty$ when $\sigma > 1$. In such a case the marginal product of capital is asymptotically constant; labour becomes inessential and the rate of growth of output becomes equal to the rate of growth of capital. If the savings ratio is large enough, then the economy may grow forever. In the Cobb–Douglas case with unitary elasticity of substitution, the output–capital ratio decreases over time and permanent growth is not possible. Only technological progress may produce permanent growth even in a Cobb–Douglas economy. Unity is therefore the borderline case separating growing from stagnating economies.

Stiglitz (1974) considers the Cobb–Douglas case with exhaustible resources, where $Y_t = K_t^{\alpha_1} L_t^{\alpha_2} r_t^{\alpha_3} e^{\tau t}$, τ being an exogenous rate of technical progress. In the presence of natural resources there is an important choice problem about what proportion of the stock should be used at a given point in time. The fundamental optimality condition can be obtained either from the first-order conditions of the maximisation problem of producers (see section 4.2 for the derivation) or from an intuitive reasoning based on a no-arbitrage requirement of equality among rates of return in the production of capital and extraction of exhaustible resources, yielding

$$F_K = \frac{\dot{F}_R}{F_R} \tag{1}$$

known as the Hotelling condition.[3] Only if this equality is satisfied there will be no incentive to move resources from one economic activity to the other.

Stiglitz shows that, contrary to what happens lacking natural resources, the rate of growth depends on the savings rate. More importantly from the point of view of this chapter, a necessary and sufficient condition for a constant level of consumption with no technical change and no population growth is that the share of natural resources be less than the share of capital, that is $\alpha_3 < \alpha_1$. If population growth is positive, the condition for a constant level of per-capita consumption is that the ratio of the rate of technical change to the rate of population growth must be greater than or equal to the share of natural resources.

Such an inequality is assumed by Hartwick (1974), who modifies the assumption of a constant savings rate by considering instead a total amount of savings (and investment) equal to the rent obtained from natural resources, that is $F_r r$. When this rule is applied to the rate of change of production over time together with the Hotelling condition (1), one obtains

$$\dot{Y}_t = F_{rt} \dot{r}_t + \frac{\dot{F}_{rt}}{F_{rt}} F_{rt} r_t = \frac{d(F_{rt} r_t)}{dt}$$

This, together with the identity $\dot{Y}_t = \dot{c}_t + \dot{K}_t$ and the rule $\dot{K} = F_r r$, implies that the rate of change of production is equal to the rate of change of investment, so that the rate of change of consumption is equal to 0.

3.1 An evaluation

The contribution of this class of models is valuable: it clarifies the technological circumstances under which the economy can survive in the long run even in the case when exhaustible resources are essential to production and at the same time providing a simple rule of thumb which can be interpreted in terms of keeping constant an extended definition of capital, equal to the sum of the (utility value) of physical and natural capital. It will be seen in section 7 that such a rule can be extended to the case when environmental assets themselves are considered as a stock of natural capital.

Assuming large substitutability between finite and reproducible factors amounts to ignoring issues related to the laws of thermodynamics, since substitutability makes the resource constraint virtually ineffective in the long run. On the other hand, considering low substitutability is a shortcut for taking into account physical limitations, as emphasised by Georgescu-Roegen (1975), according to whom the limits to production will be eventually reached after a secular struggle between attempts at recycling raw materials and the laws of thermodynamics, preventing 100 per cent efficiency in recycling.

4 Optimising models of growth with natural resources

A limitation of the models considered in the previous section is the assumption made about savings behaviour. One can instead consider an economy with optimising agents based on the Ramsey–Cass–Koopmans (RCK) version of the growth model where, rather than being a constant fraction of output, consumption is the outcome of intertemporal optimisation decisions. This section starts with the case of a fixed stock of natural resources and no capital accumulation (the spaceship earth) but exogenous technical progress. The model is then extended to incorporate capital accumulation.

4.1 Fixed natural resources, no capital accumulation

The cake-eating model is the crudest way to take into account the effects of finiteness of resources on growth; it shows that, lacking technical progress, natural resources are the ultimate constraint to growth. The problem consists of deciding the flow of consumption of a non-renewable stock of resources over an infinite horizon in order to maximise discounted utility. Krautkraemer (1985) augments the version considered by Dasgupta and Heal (1974) to incorporate technical progress

$$\max \int_0^\infty e^{-\delta t} u(c_t) dt \tag{2}$$

$$\dot{S}_t = -r_t \tag{3}$$

$$c_t = r_t e^{\tau t}$$

$$c_t \geq 0, \; S_0 \text{ given}$$

where $u(.)$, is assumed to be monotonically increasing, strictly concave, twice differentiable everywhere with $\lim_{c \to 0} u'(c) = \infty$. The exogenous rate of technical progress τ can be interpreted as a synthetic way to model an economic system which can, over time, obtain increasing amounts of consumption goods from natural resources. The model can be considered as a very stylised description of an economic system that cannot escape a constraint on the total amount of resources.[4]

In this model, technical progress is necessary to ensure a continuous increase in the flow of consumption. Also, the stock of natural resources is necessarily depleted in the long run. To prove these, form the Hamiltonian $H = u(c_t) - \lambda_t c_t$ and derive the necessary conditions

$$\lambda_t = e^{\tau t} u_{ct} \tag{4}$$

$$\dot{\lambda} = \delta \lambda_t \tag{5}$$

The standard method to turn the first-order conditions into an equation describing the rate of growth of consumption is the following: (a) differentiate equation (4) with respect to time $e^{\tau t} u_{cc} \dot{c} + u_c \tau^{\tau t} = \dot{\lambda}_t$ and (b) use (5) to obtain

$$g_{ct} = \frac{\tau - \delta}{\eta} \tag{6}$$

where $\eta \equiv -\dfrac{c u_{cc}}{u_c} > 0$ is the elasticity of marginal utility. Equation (6) shows that the rate of growth of consumption is related to the difference between the rate of technical progress (in the more elaborate description of the economy that includes production the place of technical progress will be taken by the marginal productivity of capital) and the rate of time preference.

From (5), prices grow at the rate of time preference. There is asymptotic depletion of the initial stock in the sense that $\lim_{t \to \infty} S_t = 0$, even though there is never complete depletion in finite time.

4.2 Fixed natural resources with capital accumulation

Introducing production and capital accumulation may change in a substantial way the growth possibilities of the economy. In Dasgupta and Heal (1974) the structure of the economy is enriched by considering a production function which is assumed to be increasing, strictly concave, twice differentiable and homogeneous of degree one

$$\dot{K}_t = F(K_t, r_t) - c_t \tag{7}$$

The Hamiltonian, $H = u(C_t) + \lambda_{1t}[F(K_t, r_t) - c_t] - \lambda_{2t} r_t$, generates the necessary conditions

$$\lambda_{1t} = u_{ct} \tag{8}$$

$$\lambda_{1t} F_{rt} = \lambda_{2t} \tag{9}$$

$$\dot{\lambda}_{1t} = (\delta - F_{Kt}) \lambda_{1t} \tag{10}$$

$$\dot{\lambda}_{2t} = \delta \lambda_{2t} \tag{11}$$

Defining[5] $x = K/R$ and writing the elasticity of substitution between the two factors as $\sigma = -[xf\, f_{xx}]^{-1}[f_x\,(f - xf_x)]$, one obtains from the first-order conditions

$$g_x = \frac{\sigma f}{x}$$

showing that the rate of growth of the capital–resource ratio is equal to the product of the elasticity of substitution and the average product per unit of fixed capital. The former gives an indication of the ease with which substitution can be carried out, and the latter can be regarded as an index of the importance of fixed capital in production. Thus, the easier it is to substitute, and the more important is the reproducible input, the more one wants to substitute the reproducible resource for the exhaustible one.

Using the previously described method to turn the first-order conditions into an equation describing the rate of growth of consumption, one obtains

$$\eta g_c = F_K - \delta \tag{12}$$

showing that the rate of growth of consumption depends on the wedge between the marginal productivity of capital (equal to the interest rate) and the pure rate of time preference, which gives agents an incentive to postpone consumption also taking into account the utility costs of intertemporal transfers of resources, related to the elasticity of marginal utility. As accumulation of capital proceeds, the interest rate decreases. As pointed out by Dasgupta and Heal, permanent growth is possible with a high elasticity of substitution, that is

$$\sigma < 1 \qquad \sigma > 1, \rho > \delta$$

$$\lim_{t \to \infty} C = \lim_{t \to \infty} K = \quad 0 \qquad \infty$$

$$\lim_{t \to \infty} g_C = \lim_{t \to \infty} g_K = \quad 0 \qquad \frac{\rho - \delta}{\eta}$$

where ρ is the asymptotic marginal productivity of capital. When $\sigma > 1$ it is possible to substitute out the exhaustible resource with capital, and keep the economy growing as long as the asymptotic marginal productivity of the reproducible factor is larger than the rate of time preference. When $\sigma \leq 1$ instead the interest rate decreases with capital accumulation to the point that no further incentive to savings is provided.

4.3 An evaluation

This class of model highlights the fundamental interaction between production structure and preferences in determining growth. While the economy could be kept alive in the long run in the case of a fixed savings rate or of an exogenously imposed savings rule even in the Cobb–Douglas case, it is shown here that this is not an optimal outcome given a positive rate of time preference and maximisation of discounted utility. A large substitutability is necessary (but not sufficient) to keep the economy growing in the long run.

Lacking exogenous technological progress, permanent growth can only come from permanent accumulation of capital that may counterbalance exhaustion of the natural resource. It is important to notice that such a continuous substitution implies a permanent modification of productive processes, motivated in market economies by the continuous increase in the price of natural resources.[6]

While this substitution process may well be produced by an unrestricted competitive system without public intervention, the substitution possibilities implicitly inherent in the growth solution may or may not be considered realistic. Continuously substituting natural resources in the production function may not be feasible beyond a certain point, even though economic history has shown a remarkable change in the structure of production, moving away from primary goods and shifting to the use of less and less natural resources.

5 Environmental and natural resources

The most recent discussion has been cast around environmental assets in their role of life-support system, and in their use for the benefit of the present and future generations. The question can be framed in the following way: if one considers environmental assets as a stock of natural capital (in a manner which is compatible with recent proposals of macroeconomic accounting, see section 7), and if economic activity affects such capital (e.g., negatively by discharging wastes into the environment or positively through preventive environmental expenditures), can one find new limits to development that are due not to the physical impossibility to produce, but rather to an excessive use of resources which are necessary for life? Also, even if such dangerous limits are not met, is the use of (sometimes irreversible) environmental assets compatible with intergenerational equity?

The second question has been briefly touched upon in discussing Hartwick's rule which, producing a constant level of consumption over an infinite horizon, can be considered as an example of intertemporally just policy. More generally, the discussion of fairness to future generations requires an analysis of the criteria which are used to decide optimal paths, especially those that are alternatives to maximisation of discounted utility, like the Rawlsian max–min criterion and maximisation of steady-state utility. Such alternative criteria have been explored in the context of various descriptions of the economy, see Asako (1980) and Solow (1956). The reader is referred to Dasgupta and Heal (1979) for a general discussion.

The first question is instead the focus of this section. Given the wide variety of existing contributions, the discussion tries to provide a unifying framework by considering a general model with environmental assets and defensive expenditures of which several others are particular cases. In this section only steady state solutions are considered, while non-stationary solutions are the subject of the next section. Such a distinction did not make much sense in the model with exhaustible natural resources, whose finite stock requires non-stationary solutions. Here instead one can in principle think of a steady state where the use of environmental resources is counterbalanced by an increase that may be either spontaneous or due to defensive expenditures.

5.1 A model with pollution and defensive expenditures

This subsection starts with a model derived from that of section 2, including the stock of environment E in the utility function. In the stylised framework of this section there are again two factors of production, capital and labour, but labour is exogenously fixed. Capital accumulation is therefore described by

$$\dot{K}_t = F(K_t, L_t) - c_t - d_t \tag{13}$$

where d represents defensive expenditures. Excluding the flow of natural resources from the production function makes the model amenable to analysis of steady states, as it is now possible to conceive a situation where the factors of production are constant and output is also constant.

The stock of pollution increases naturally according to a function $N(E,d)$ where $N(0,d) = N(E,0) = 0$ and $N_d > 0$, $N_{dd} < 0$. If such a function is logistic (for a given level of defensive expenditures), then N_E can have any sign, depending on which side of the curve the economy finds itself in.[7] Consumption depletes the environment, so that

$$\dot{E}_t = -c_t + N(E_t, d_t) \tag{14}$$

Clearly, other specifications would be possible, e.g., one in which defensive expenditures directly enter the utility function in their role of improving the services offered by the stock of environmental assets. The point that is made with such specification is that economic activity may deplete the environment but at the same time create resources which can restore the damage. In (14) it is even possible that defensive expenditures prevent the damage from taking place. In other cases one may think that defensive expenditures can partially rebuild a stock which has been depleted. The Hamiltonian $H = u(c,E) + \lambda_1[F(K) - c - d] + \lambda_2[-c + N(E,d)]$ generates the first-order conditions described in the appendix, also discussing existence and stability of solutions. In a steady state, the following relations hold

$$u_c - \lambda_1 - \lambda_2 = 0 \tag{15}$$

$$-\lambda_1 + \lambda_2 N_d = 0 \tag{16}$$

$$\delta = F_K(K,L) \tag{17}$$

$$\delta\lambda_2 = u_E(c,E) + \lambda_2 N_E(E,d) \tag{18}$$

$$F(K,L) = c + d \tag{19}$$

$$c = N(E,d) \tag{20}$$

According to the equations describing the steady state, the stock of capital is a function of the rate of time preference and technology, while the division of production between consumption and defensive expenditures depends on their productivity and on preferences. Defensive expenditures are larger the more tilted towards the environment are preferences and the larger is the marginal productivity. Shadow prices are implicitly defined in a standard way.

A number of published papers are closely connected to such a structure. Keeler, Spence and Zeckhauser (1974) consider a special case with a linear abatement technology, corresponding to

$$\dot{E}_t = -c_t + N(E_t) + \gamma_0 d_t$$

where γ_0 is a constant. Now the optimisation problem has to consider explicitly the lower bound $d \geq 0$, as nothing would prevent the mathematical solution from requiring a negative level of defensive expenditures. Two cases have to be taken into account, in which alternatively $H_d = 0$ and $H_d < 0$. In the second case (the Murky Age) there is no defensive expenditure, and comparatively larger levels of capital, production and consumption. Van der Ploeg and Withagen (1991) also show a negative relationship (across steady states) between the level of capital and environmental concern.

An interesting issue is about the comparative static relationship between the rate of time preference and the stock of environment. In the Murky Age case where $d = 0$ it is possible to show that the sign of the relationship is crucially dependent on the sign of the derivative N_E. By equating (19) and (20) and by considering the resulting equation together with (17) one finds two equations that can be differentiated to give

$$dE = \frac{F_K}{N_E F_{KK}} d\delta$$

which is positive (negative) if N_E is negative (positive). Musu (1993) considers $N_E < 0$ and finds that a forward-looking society will have a lower steady-state stock of environment than a society which is more concerned with current than future utilities. Beltratti, Chichilnisky and Heal (1994) consider the logistic reproduction function also including the environmental stock into the utility function, and find the same result after showing that the 'negative-slope side' of the logistic function is the one that gives rise to a stable equilibrium.[8] Musu (1993) also considers the more general case where $d > 0$, and shows that a lower rate of time preference may increase environmental quality if productivity of defensive expenditures is large enough to counterbalance increased pollution connected with larger capital stocks.

The model of Tahvonen and Kuuluvainen (1993) allows for substitution between consumption and pollution in the utility function, $U(c,P)$, and between capital and emissions e in the production function, $F(K,e)$. Here the environment is directly depleted by production activities; such a specification, due to Brock (1973), can be considered as a reduced form of a more general model of production and cleaning, where firms may use factors of production to limit the negative consequences of production, and there is, if they choose to employ factors this way, a negative relationship between the level of production and environmental quality. Tahvonen and Kuuluvainen (1993) discuss stationary solutions of this model, showing that at least one steady state exists if $\lim_{k \to 0} F_K(K,e) > \delta \forall e > 0$ (that is if the marginal productivity of capital is bounded below for a stock equal to zero) and that the steady state is unique (and a local saddle-point) if $U_{cP}(c,P) \leq 0$. Uniqueness also holds if the rate of discount is small enough.[9]

5.2 An evaluation

These models are useful in clarifying the indirect channels according to which economic activity may affect welfare. By considering the negative environmental consequences of production and by admitting the possibility of devoting a share of production to activities which restore the environment, they achieve a much deeper level of understanding of the costs and benefits of economic growth. The crucial role of the rate of time preference in discriminating future generations and in determining the long-run ratio between capital and environmental stocks is also clearly brought into the picture.

However by concentrating mainly on comparative statics analyses of the steady state, these models miss a few points which can only be properly considered in a situation of permanent growth. Such an issue may be of interest in itself, to explore the logical possibility of permanent growth with environmental resources, and/or to analyse the requirements that have to be imposed on the system to show such persistence of growth, i.e., constant or increasing returns to scale in the sector which eliminates waste, or in the context of an exploration of the parameters that are more important to ensure compatibility of growth and environmental quality.

6 Endogenous economic growth with environmental resources

The main goal of the growth literature of the 1980s is to explain growth, rather than assume it. This is especially important for policy analysis: claiming that technical progress is the engine of growth is by itself not very helpful if one does not explain which factors affect such a progress. Endogenous growth models, see references included in Sala-i-Martin

(1990), Grossman and Helpman (1991), Romer (1994), provide explanations at various levels; some models offer little more than a mathematical formalisation consistent with permanent growth with no substantial economic explanation of what microeconomic factors cause growth, while other models are quite explicit as to the relevant engines of growth.

The most recent models of growth with environmental assets differ mainly in their assumptions about the productive structure of the economy, and cover the various cases that have been analysed in the literature, that is constant returns to scale to one factor, constant returns to scale to all factors, increasing aggregate returns to scale, production function with new varieties of intermediate goods. The review is not exhaustive but will concentrate on a few prototype papers.[10] Before discussing these models it is however useful to consider early attempts at tackling the problem of permanent growth in a model with environmental assets.

6.1 The relevance of natural resources for permanent preservation

Krautkraemer (1985) extends the model of Dasgupta and Heal (1974) to consider a resource entering both the production and the utility functions.[11] This is a shortcut to allow preferences to determine environmental quality, even though the resulting model may be applicable to few cases, since a natural resource that enters as a flow in the production function would not be likely to enter as a stock in the utility function, while an environmental amenity would be unlikely to be so important to be one of the two factors included in the production function. The Hamiltonian of the model is

$$H = u(c,S) + \lambda_1[F(K,r) - c] - \lambda_2 r$$

By following the steps outlined in the previous sections one finds the dynamic equations for consumption and the capital–resource ratio

$$g_c = \frac{F_k(K,r) - \delta - r\left(\dfrac{u_{SC}}{u_C}\right)}{\eta}$$

$$g_x = \sigma(x)\frac{f(x)}{x} + \frac{\left(\dfrac{u_S}{u_c}\right)}{x^2 f''(x)}$$

These equations show that in the general case of a CES production function it is not possible to obtain a stationary solution, either for the original variables or for some transformation of them. Krautkraemer uses an argument based on bounds to show that even in the presence of an amenity value of the environment, it may be optimal to deplete in the long run when the marginal utility of the stock is finite for a zero stock. In the more general case of infinite marginal utility the solution prescribes a stock decreasing towards a finite value $\bar{S}>0$.

The environment is preserved only if preferences are sufficiently tilted towards the environment, and if there is enough substitution in production between the flow of resource and the stock of capital (the situation with high elasticity of substitution considered by Dasgupta and Heal). Depletion of the environment may be a necessary cost that society is willing to pay to obtain larger and larger amounts of consumption goods. Even more importantly, permanent preservation is possible only if the marginal productivity of capital is bounded below. Only in that case may society choose whether to preserve or not. On the other hand, the model also points out that preservation, when optimal, takes place by means of an increasing shadow price of the environment, which reflects increasing marginal utility as the stock is depleted. It is not clear what institutional setting may implement this, given the lack of markets for transacting environmental resources.

An important criticism of the model, from the point of view of analysing the compatibility of economic growth with the environment, is that under the circumstances giving rise to permanent growth, there is either no compatibility or no long-run trade-off between production of goods and the stock of environment; in one steady state the environment is exhausted and consumption can tend to zero or remain positive, while in the other steady state it is possible to have a permanently positive rate of growth of consumption with no exhaustion of the environment, as production may take place with a minimum stress on environmental resources.

6.2 Permanent growth and pollution

6.2.1 Constant returns to scale with one factor of production

Michel and Rotillon (1992) consider a model with a linear production function, $Y_t = \gamma_3 K_t$. Production increases the stock of pollution since $\dot{P}_t = \gamma_4 Y_t - \gamma_5 P_t = \gamma K_t - \gamma_5 P_t$. Given a utility function of the form $u(c,P)$, the effect of production on pollution becomes a negative externality to the extent that producers ignore their effects on welfare when taking their decisions about capital accumulation and production. The Hamiltonian is

$$H = u(c,P) + \lambda_1(\gamma_3 K - c) - \lambda_2(\gamma K - \gamma_5 P)$$

The standard necessary conditions for optimality lead to an equation describing the rate of growth of consumption in the general case of the non-separable utility function

$$\eta g_c + \eta_P g_P = (\delta - \gamma_3) + \gamma \frac{\lambda_2}{\lambda_1}$$

where the elasticity of marginal utility of consumption $\eta = \frac{cu_{cc}}{u_c}$ and the elasticity of marginal utility of consumption with respect to pollution $\eta_P = \frac{pu_{cP}}{u_c}$ are assumed to be constants. In order to solve the model it is necessary to impose restrictions on the utility function. Michel and Rotillon show that with a separable utility function the optimal private (decentralised) solution entails positive growth (if the marginal productivity of capital is larger then the rate of time preference), while permanent growth is not optimal in the social solution, as it is possible to find a unique steady state for the model.[12] These results hold even more strongly when the marginal utility of consumption decreases as pollution rises, while, in the case when the marginal utility of consumption rises with the level of pollution, then it may be socially optimal to achieve permanent growth. The result, formally shown in the context of two examples provided in the paper, is intuitively clear: if a larger stock of pollution increases the marginal utility derived from a given flow of consumption, it may be optimal to grow in the long run, and live in a world extremely polluted and with large consumption.

6.2.2 Aggregate increasing returns to scale

In a variant of this model amended to make the emission–production ratio a function of technological knowledge produced by a second economic sector, Xepapadeas (1994) shows that permanent growth may become optimal without excess pollution (see also Michel (1993) in the context of an overlapping generations model) if technology allows to decrease the emission–production ratio towards zero. The economy is characterised by aggregate increasing returns to scale and two types of capital, one used in the production sector and the other in cleaning activities.

The structure of the economy is composed of an equation describing the impact of economic activity on pollution

$$\dot{P}_t = n\gamma(k_H, K_H)F(k_Y, K_Y) - \gamma_5 P_t$$

where n is the number of firms, k_H is the stock of capital of the representative firm producing goods aimed at decreasing the pollution–output ratio, $nk_H = K_H$, k_Y is the stock of capital of the representative firm producing goods for consumption and capital accumulation, $nk_H = K_H$, and $\gamma(.,.)$ is now a function rather than a constant as in the previous model. It is assumed that there are increasing returns to investment in abatement capital in a certain range above which there are decreasing returns to scale. It is also assumed that the utility function is separable in consumption and pollution, and that there is an upper bound of pollution above which survival is not possible.

Xepapadeas confirms that permanent growth is not optimal with a constant pollution–emission ratio, and also shows that if the economy starts with an initial endowment of capital in the abatement sector that is large enough to place the economy in the regions of increasing returns to scale, it may be possible to find a steady state with a lower pollution–output ratio or even a path of permanent growth where the pollution–output ratio decreases towards zero (the ecological paradise also considered by Michel (1993)).

6.2.3 A two-sector model with constant returns to scale

In Bovenberg and Smulders (1995) the environment, entering both the utility and the production functions, is a renewable resource depleted by a flow of pollution originated by a Brock-type production function. There are two constant returns to scale sectors: sector Y produces the final good by means of capital and pollution, while sector H produces a public good, to be interpreted as general knowledge, increasing the pollution–production ratio

$$Y = A_Y(E)F(K_Y, Z_Y)$$

$$\dot{h} = A_H(E)G(K_H, Z_H)$$

where $K_Y + K_H = K$, $Z_Y + Z_H = Z \equiv hp$, are capital and a flow of effective pollution, given by the product between the flow itself p and a productivity-enhancing stock of general knowledge. The two factors are both essential to production and E is a stock of natural capital providing a positive externality to production. It is therefore assumed that the flow of pollution P becomes more and more productive as the stock of knowledge increases over time. This continuous increase in the effective stock of pollution is necessary to keep the economy growing while respecting environmental quality. Indeed, given a dynamic equation for the evolution of the stock of natural capital of the type $\dot{E} = N(E, p)$, Bovenberg and Smulders consider the case where $\dot{E} = 0$, which implies a 'sustainable' flow of pollution determined by the regeneration ability of the environment. Even with this sustainability requirement[13] the economy can keep growing so long as the two factors (physical capital and knowledge) are increased as a result of optimal choices of agents. In order to ensure that the growth rate is constant, a number of assumptions have to be made on the relevant functions like a constant elasticity of intertemporal substitution and a unitary elasticity of substitution between environmental amenities and consumption of produced goods.

The authors use the structure to analyse various issues, among which are the transitional dynamics following a shock to the flow of pollution. In order to do that, they first transform the initial model into a specification based on stationary variables, and then linearise it. In applying the methodology to a negative shock to pollution, they show that there may be a non-monotonic approach to the new equilibrium on the part of some variables, and they also point out the crucial importance of the specification about the role of the environment in the economy: an increase in the environmental standards necessarily hurts long-run growth if the environment has only an amenity value, but this is not true if it represents a relevant factor of production. The latter condition is unlikely to hold in practice for advanced economies, but may be of interest to agricultural economies or in cases in which pollution is so heavy as to damage productivity of factors, see, e.g., Margulis (1992) on the Mexican case.

6.2.4 Varieties of consumption goods

Finally, to complete the spectrum of applications of endogenous growth model to environmental issues, one should mention the models of Romer (1990) and Grossman and Helpman (1991), which are those with the richest economic structure among the ones used to explain growth. The main agents are profit-maximising firms, which innovate by introducing new varieties of goods into the economic system. Research and development is subject to initial fixed costs, but yields a stream of future cash flows which make innovation profitable in equilibrium. The description of the productive structure of the economy is in terms of the following two equations

$$Y_t = X_t^\eta K_t^\beta L_t^{1-\eta-\beta}$$

$$X_t = \left[\int_0^{n_t} x(i)^\alpha di \right]^{\frac{1}{\alpha}}$$

where $x(i)$ is the quantity of variety i of an intermediate product and n_t is the number of varieties existing at time t (generally evolving according to constant returns to scale to allow for permanent growth). In equilibrium $x(i)=x$ and therefore $X_t = n_t^{\frac{1}{\alpha}} x_t$ and $Y_t = n_t^{\frac{\eta}{\alpha}} x_t^\eta K_t^\beta L_t^{1-\eta-\beta}$.

Verdier (1993) (see also Hung, Chang and Blackburn (1993)) extends the model to analyse a situation where variety matters not only for the production function but also for environmental pressure. Intermediate goods differ in terms of emission–output ratios, which are optimally chosen by firms at the initial stage of research and development. In order to develop a new product with an emission–output ratio equal to eq_i, a firm has to use an amount $\dfrac{a(eq_i)}{n_t}$ of labour, where n_t is the number of products already developed at time t. The flow of profit from production of good i is affected by an emission tax. The solution to this maximisation problem yields the monopolistic price for good i, $p(i)=\dfrac{w+ek_iT}{\alpha}$, which is then used to compute the present discounted value of profits from undertaking research and development (R&D). Given this value, the firm decides whether to engage in R&D and at what level to set the emission–output ratio. From the solution it is possible to derive the effect on growth of alternative policies of taxation and regulations. Taxation may benefit growth to the extent that resources are free to be allocated to the R&D sector (presumably in practice this effect is likely to be very small), and technological standards are more harmful than emission taxes to economic growth.

6.2.5 An evaluation

The importance of this group of papers is to pose in clear and dynamic terms the issue of optimality of permanent growth when environmental assets are damaged by production. The productivity of the abatement sector becomes crucial for determining the trajectory of the economy. When it is not possible to decrease the emission–output ratio, growth becomes optimal only under restrictive, and perhaps implausible, conditions on the utility function. When there are increasing or constant returns to scale it is instead feasible and perhaps optimal to keep pushing the level of production at higher and higher levels. In Bovenberg and Smulders this happens because technology allows a continuous increase in the physical productivity of pollution that decreases the actual pollution–output ratio, while in Xepapadeas technology directly allows a reduction in the latter. In some sense the model by Verdier provides a rich microstructure to the assumption made by Xepapadeas.

The papers therefore provide a clear clue about empirical research; the goal should be to assess, perhaps with case studies, the possibility of achieving constant or increasing returns to abatement. All the issues that have been discussed before in connection with the use of natural resources and the possibility of permanent recycling should also be considered.

This line of research is also useful in discussing the meaning of sustainability, and its relationships with optimality, even though in effect the models keep the impact of environmental dynamics in the background. By imposing the equivalence between sustainability and no time change in the stock of natural capital, the environment is eliminated from the analysis, also in order to obtain a useful reduction in the number of state variables. This equating of sustainability with the ecological paradise may however be considered a bit too extreme.

7 Applications

Theoretical models may be useful along several dimensions. Firstly, by providing a synthetic description of some key elements, they can shape the way of thinking about an economic problem. Secondly, they may help by pointing out which empirical evidence should be looked at in order to evaluate the costs and benefits of specific situations. Thirdly, they can sometimes be 'tested' against data sets to suggest along which directions theories can be improved and/or used to obtain quantitative evidence necessary for deciding policies.

This final section is aimed at discussing some applications of the previous framework along the three dimensions that have just been outlined. In terms of relevance to a specific problem, the theory is 'tested' against the issue of sustainability of growth: can theory clarify the meaning of sustainability and suggest instruments for implementing it? In terms of connections with statistical analyses, the recent discussion on the existence of an environmental Kuznets curve is considered. Before these, a short section looks at the policy implications of the models.

7.1 Policy rules

The chapter has used the fiction of a competitive planner knowing the structure of technology and preferences, and devising policies able to internalise all the externalities. The difference between such solutions and those emerging from a decentralised market is already large in the case of productive externalities like those emphasised by the recent endogenous growth literature, but is even more important when environmental assets are taken into account, as in practice there are no market prices for such goods and services. The main use that can be made of the models from a policy point of view is therefore to suggest ways to correct market incentives to have agents plan their actions with a proper judgement of the external effects they create.

The suggestions from growth models all point at taxes and subsidies that accelerate capital accumulation to internalise aggregate increasing returns to scale. However, there are also useful indications about the consequences of imposing stricter environmental standards, e.g., Bovenberg and Smulders (1995) examine the reaction of the economy to a tighter environmental policy.

Perhaps the new (policy) points that are made by these models is that taxing the environment is not necessarily harmful to growth when the latter is endogenous, and that providing incentives to economic growth may not necessarily destroy environmental resources. In the model of Verdier (1993), for example, a tax on polluting activities may increase the rate of growth by freeing labour resources that can be employed in the research sector. In Bovenberg and de Mooij (1993) there may be positive effects from a tax on polluting activities due to the role of the environment as a fator of production. Another interesting issue has to do with environmental standards, that have always been considered as inefficient policy instruments. Verdier (1993) shows that for severe pollution targets, standards may dominate taxes, as the latter may induce a rate of economic growth which is so large as to imply an excessive amount of emissions. A common prescription of the models is the necessity to strengthen the role of the abatement sector, and this requires a policy of taxes and subsidies which may be fairly involved in practice.

Of course the practical relevance of these results depends on matters that can only be decided on at an empirical level, even though at the current stage one doubts that for most economies the role of the research and development and environmental sectors is enough large to strongly affect growth.

7.2 Stylised facts

The models imply that: (a) lacking technical change, the prices of minerals and energy sources should be increasing over time, and (b) the association between environmental quality and economic growth is strongly dependent on the amount and the productivity of abatement expenditures. A significant empirical literature has reviewed (a), and a recent literature has been concerned with (b).

7.2.1 Natural resources

Exhaustibility of natural resources has been the object of many empirical studies, and of a few discussions about appropriate measurement, see Dasgupta and Heal (1979) and Fisher (1979). Even though answers are not univocal, it seems that most authors conclude that scarcity of raw materials is not a significant problem for economic growth in the foreseeable future. The two key elements are substitutability on the one hand, see, e.g., Dasgupta (1993), and energy on the other. Substitutability is important, as already mentioned before, to the extent that market prices may convey to producers and consumers the right signals about relative scarcity. Energy is equally important, as one implication of the laws of entropy is that it is always possible to use materials from lower quality ores if increasing amounts of energy are available. It follows that if energy were unlimited, it would always be possible to extract raw materials from sources of decreasing quality.

In practice, even though substitutability is not perfect, and energy sources are finite, the consensus among scientists seems to suggest that there are no imminent problems, also due to continuous technological improvements. Such an impression in general comes more from analyses of scenarios about future demand and supply than from direct estimates of substitution elasticities obtained from production functions. This is useful to avoid the problems connected with estimating aggregate elasticities of substitution, see Fisher, Solow and Kearl (1977), even though subjective margins increase dramatically when it comes to measuring alternative scenarios by using different methodologies.

7.2.2 Environmental resources

Currently, depletion of natural capital and pollution are perceived to be obstacles to growth which are more relevant than those connected with exhaustible resources. Available empirical evidence on this is scant; only recently there have been empirical studies by Grossman and Krueger (1993), Grossman (1994), Selden and Song (1994), Holtz-Eakin and Selden (1992), Hettige, Lucas and Wheeler (1992), Shafik (1994) and Xepapadeas and Amri (1995). The common methodology consists of fitting a (usually cubic) polynomial to the relationship between per-capita income and various indicators of environmental degradation or quality. The data come from different countries at different points of time.

For example Grossman and Krueger (1994) use data assembled by the Global Environmental Monitoring System (GEMS) to examine the relationship between the level of a country's per-capita income and various environmental indicators. They find no evidence that environmental quality deteriorates steadily with economic growth. In many cases, economic growth brings an initial phase of deterioration followed by a subsequent phase of improvement of environmental quality; this empirical finding is summarised by an 'environmental Kuznets curve' (EKC) of the standard bell-shaped variety.

These empirical findings are more or less common to the other empirical studies, with some caveats: (a) the positive relationship between quality and income is less clear in the case of public goods which have mainly an amenity value and do not directly affect human health and (b) in the case of CO_2 the relationship disappears in terms of emissions, presumably because of the influence of population.

The EKC resembles the early Phillips' curve in its status of a stylised fact in search of an interpretation. On the positive side one may think that societies may be or are willing to devote more attention to environmental quality as the amount of available resources increase sufficiently. For example some clean technologies may be used only at high levels of income, or the large fixed costs connected with building adequate infrastructures can only be borne by rich counries, or there may be a shift in preferences towards the environment. Another possibility is that the abatement techology improves with production. See Beltratti (1995) for an attempt at generating the EKC from the transitional dynamics of endogenous growth models, and Selden and Song (1995) for an analysis based on a steady-state model.

Of course there is nothing automatic in this path, especially given the public nature of the environment, which requires the actions of the public decision makers to coordinate private agents either through taxation and spending or by means of more severe regulations, the costs of which can be borne more easily at higher levels of income. Therefore even the positive interpretation does not suggest the irrelevance of environmental policy. Jorgenson and Wilcoxen (1989) for example find that, in the US case, environmental regulation has been an important contributor to the growth slowdown.

On the negative side, see Saint-Paul (1994), it can be contended that the decrease in the pollution–output ratio that goes with the increase of income is mainly due to relocations of dirty industries to less-developed countries which are more willing to stand the pollution costs of industrial production. This possibility, compatible with the empirical evidence of Hettige, Lucas and Wheeler (1992), who have shown the existence of an upward long-term trend in industrial emissions, both relative to GDP and relative to manufacturing output, especially for lower-income countries, raises the question of the continuation of the path for the world as a whole.

If the stylised facts described here do represent the outcome of a path which implies an increasing amount of resources devoted to environmental protection as the economy grows, there is some hope that a solution to a few environmental problems, which, given absence of market prices cannot come from price elasticity of demand, will be the outcome of large income elasticity of demand for environmental services.

7.3 Sustainability of growth

The Brundtland Report (World Commission (1987)) popularised the concept of sustainable growth, defined as growth that 'meets the needs of the present without compromising the ability of future generations to meet their own needs'. Attempts at studying sustainability in a formal context are due to Solow (1986) and Maler (1991), who use the framework of an infinite horizon maximisation problem, and point at different reasons why growth may not be sustainable in a competitive economy (see Toman, Pezzey and Krautkraemer (1995) for a review of this literature).

Within the realm of deterministic models one can understand the lack of sustainability partly as an institutional problem, as most environmental phenomena are related to externalities of various kinds. Market failures are therefore connected with such externalities as pointed out by early important contributions by Ayres and Kneese (1969) and D'Arge and Kogiku (1973), given the inevitable tendency of economic production to generate waste and other residuals. This is particularly important for environmental resources which are part of the utility function and are not traded in the markets. Policies derived on the basis of a utilitarian model with a positive rate of time preferences are also likely to be biased against sustainability, see Heal (1995) and references therein.

Given the difference existing between centralised and decentralised solutions, and given the necessity of using taxes and subsidies in order to fill the gap between the two, what is the characteristic of sustainable policies? Some of the papers considered in this chapter have shown that such policies should aim at keeping constant an index of capital stocks including natural capital. This is a generalisation of Hartwick's rule which allows the economy many different ways to trade off capital stocks of different kinds. A decrease in the stock of environment might be associated with an increase in the stock of human capital. As long as compensations take place humanity is simply transforming the relevant parts of the environment and not depleting it; as a consequence there is no decrease in the utility that future generations can obtain from the bequest which is left from current generations. Presumably, the larger the relevant definition of capital and the substitution possibilities, the easier it is to make the economy sustainable in the long run. Substitutability among factors becomes again the key to growth, this time interpreted in a more general sense as a growth in utility. Constancy or even increase in the stock of total capital is however not a sufficient condition for sustainability under the discounted utilitarian criterion, see Asheim (1994).

Unfortunately there are few estimates of substitutability among the environment and other factors of production or the environment and other consumption goods; as was pointed out before, there are few hopes of isolating the cases for which substitutability is large enough, especially starting with macroeconomic data.

Environmental accounting may be an important practical step towards sustainability, as pointed out by Solow (1993). The System of Environmental and Economic Accounts (SEEA) proposed by the UN

(1993) is based on reclassification of expenditures already belonging to the national accounts as an estimate of environmental expenditure, and on an enlargement of physical information about the state of the environment, which should be multiplied by appropriate shadow prices to obtain information comparable with the other which is incorporated in the system of national accounts.

In estimating these prices, the problem of the absence of markets for most environmental goods emerges again. A few of the proposals based on estimates obtained from contingent valuation or from replacement costs are directly connected with the models described before. Replacement cost is the measure needed to bring the stock of environment back up to some predetermined level. However the physical target cannot be set in an 'objective' way, given the previously discussed substitution possibilities. The target must be set on the basis of a political judgement. In some sense therefore one is back at the starting point: worries about the environment are mainly originated by absence of market prices, but a proper evaluation of environmental policy should be based on the same prices that one is trying to estimate.

8 Conclusions and directions for future research

Natural and environmental resources are key factors in thinking about long-run growth. They can become limiting factors, especially because externalities connected with their commonality of use may add institutional problems to technological constraints. This concluding section tries to mention directions for future research.

Currently, worries in industrialised countries are particularly related to environmental resources, and to the possibility that economic growth may damage them to the point of decreasing, rather than increasing, welfare. Recent research analyses how environmental protection can be compatible with economic growth, even though this happens more by assumption about functional forms than by empirical and technological evidence. A drawback of such research, from the point of view of environmental policy, is the small number of state variables in the dynamic system under consideration and the strong restrictions chosen to obtain closed-form solutions. Small dimensions are certainly useful to provide sharp theoretical results but are too simple to provide realistic implications.

One direction for the future would therefore consist of models of economic and ecological systems which are not necessarily assumed to grow in a balanced way. Given that, lacking such assumptions, analytical solutions become more difficult to obtain, it may be worth going all the way and shift the emphasis towards large-scale models which can be simulated and estimated by combining econometrics and knowledge of physical systems. To the extent that various blocks of the model, e.g., pollution, population growth and production, interact in non-linear ways, the case for abandoning the study of small-case systems for policy purposes is even stronger. If it is impossible to understand well the weather with a few state variables, why should it be possible to understand the indefinite future of the world economy on the basis of a two-variable model?

A second direction for future research, entirely compatible with the one that has just been outlined, is population dynamics, whose rate of growth is generally (when population is considered at all) a positive exogenous constant. This is clearly not very satisfying, and even more so when the issue under consideration is depletion of environmental assets. There is evidence that poor areas with large populations deplete environmental assets at a faster rate than developed areas. Also, large population growth brings about problems of industrialisation and of use of natural resources, along with the emission of CO_2 into the atmosphere. These problems require serious and urgent policies, about which economists have little to say without a theory of population dynamics.

Third, there is a real need for a better theory of technological innovation. This is a key parameter which is often taken as exogenous. Endogenous growth models push the explanation a little bit further, but the relevant economic variables need to be cast in more precise terms. Human capital is an appealing but too aggregated a concept. There is a need to understand more about the origin of technical progress, and about how to effectively increase the productivity of the resources spent on research and development, both in general and in environmental fields. Technical progress may affect the notion of substitutability among factors for which substitutability is relevant to determine whether sustainability is feasible: current estimates refer to a static measure, but the key variable is the rate of change of this parameter over time.

Fourth, most models are deterministic, even though some problems are stochastic. At a conceptual level, the very problem of sustainability of growth could be considered in terms of a model involving uncertainty, perhaps connected with the level of economic activity (see Heal (1990) and Nordhaus (1993)). Also, the hypothesis of known and constant preferences over an infinite planning horizon might be considered simplistic (see Beltratti, Chichilnisky and Heal (1993) for a model with stochastic preferences and a connection with the literature on environmental options). This development is not unrelated to the others, especially to models with stochastic endogenous technical change. One may notice that in this case the natural resources literature has again anticipated other contributions (see for example the second part of Dasgupta and Heal (1974) and Dasgupta,

Heal and Pant (1980)), even though many difficult analytical problems remain to be solved to increase the applicability of this line of research to other environmental issues.

Appendix

This appendix contains analytic material relevant to the model with defensive expenditures described in section 5.1.

The Hamiltonian $H=u(c,E)+\lambda_1[F(K)-c-d]+\lambda_2[-c+N(E,d)]$ generates the first-order conditions

$$u_c-\lambda_1-\lambda_2=0 \tag{21}$$

$$-\lambda_1+\lambda_2N_d=0 \tag{22}$$

$$\dot\lambda_1-\delta\lambda_1=-\lambda_1F_K \tag{23}$$

$$\dot\lambda_2-\delta\lambda_2=-u_E-\lambda_2N_E \tag{24}$$

plus the dyamic equations (13) and (14) in the text, and the transversality conditions

$$\lim_{t\to\infty}e^{-\delta t}\lambda_1K=0 \tag{25}$$

$$\lim_{t\to\infty}e^{-\delta t}\lambda_2E=0 \tag{26}$$

Proposition 1: Equilibria are the solutions to the following equations

$$N(E,d)+d=F(K)$$

$$\frac{u_C}{u_E}=\frac{1+N_d}{\delta-N_E}$$

Proof: Equation (17) determines the optimal level of capital, call it K'. Equations (19) and (20) then determine possible combinations of E and d that satisfy the technological restrictions, that is

$$N(E,d)+d=F(K') \tag{27}$$

Equations (21), (22) and (18) can be written in a compact way as

$$\frac{u_E}{u_C}=\frac{\delta-N_E}{1+N_d} \tag{28}$$

that can be rewritten as

$$m(E,d)=n(E,d)$$

For a given $d=d_1$, $m(E,d_1)$ is a decreasing function of E. This is clear if the utility function is separable, since in that case u_C is constant while u_p is decreasing. If $u_{cE}>0$ the slope is even larger, since low (high) values of E decrease (increase) the value of u_c. Only if u_{cE} is strongly negative, that is

$$u_{cE}<\frac{u_c(u_{EE}+u_cN_E)}{u_E}-u_{cc}N_E,$$ can m become an increasing function of E; such a case will be excluded from the analysis. Moreover, for each given E, the function is increasing in d if $u_{cE}=0$, and may be increasing or decreasing if $u_{cE}>0$.

For a given d_1, $n(E,d_1)$ is an increasing function of E if $N_E<0$ and $N(E,d)$ is separable in its two arguments. In that case N_E becomes more and more negative as E increases, and N_d stays constant. The same is true even if N is not separable but the interaction between d and E is not too strong. n is increasing in d if the direct effect of the increase in d on its marginal productivity of capital is stronger than the effect on the marginal productivity of the stock of environment, that is if $N_{dd}>\dfrac{N_{Ed}(1+N_d)}{N_E-\delta}$.

Under the conditions for which m is decreasing and n increasing, there is a unique value of E for each d that solves (28). When u_{cE} is not large the described equilibrium represents a negative relationship between E and d, that is a function $E(d)$, with $\dfrac{dE}{dd}<0$. Such a function can now be used in (27) to yield $N(E(d),d)+d=F(K)$, a function in d. The slope of such a function is $\dfrac{\partial N}{\partial E}\dfrac{dE}{dd}+\dfrac{\partial N}{\partial d}$. The equilibrium is unique if the slope is always positive. Once d is determined it is possible to use (27) and (28) to find the values of the other variables.

Assuming separability of the arguments both in the production and in the utility functions, to show that the steady state is a local saddle-point one has to analyse a system with four differential equations. Inverting (21) and (22) one obtains

$$C=f[\lambda_1+\lambda_2]$$

where $f_{\lambda_1}=f_{\lambda_2}<0$, and

$$d=g(\lambda_1,\lambda_2)$$

where $g_{\lambda_1}<0$ and $g_{\lambda_2}<0$.

The linearised system

$$\dot{\lambda}_1 = -\lambda_1 F_{KK} K \tag{29}$$

$$\dot{\lambda}_2 = \delta\lambda_2 - u_{Ec} f_{\lambda_1}\lambda_1 - u_{Ec} f_{\lambda_2}\lambda_2 - u_{EE}E - \lambda_2 N_{EE}E - \lambda_2 N_{Ed}d - N_{E\lambda_2} \tag{30}$$

$$\dot{K} = F_K K - f_{\lambda_1}\lambda_1 - f_{\lambda_2}\lambda_2 - g_{\lambda_1}\lambda_1 - g_{\lambda_2}\lambda_2 \tag{31}$$

$$\dot{E} = -f_{\lambda_1}\lambda_1 - f_{\lambda_2}\lambda_2 + N_E E + N_d g_{\lambda_1}\lambda_1 + N_d g_{\lambda_2}\lambda_2 \tag{32}$$

can be rewritten as

$$\dot{\omega} = \Psi\omega \tag{33}$$

where $\omega' = (K, E, \lambda_1, \lambda_2)$. For a local stability analysis one needs the determinant of ψ

$$|\psi| = -\lambda_1 F_{KK}|M|$$

where $M = \begin{bmatrix} 0 & -f_{\lambda_1} - g_{\lambda_1} & -f_{\lambda_2} - g_{\lambda_2} \\ N_E & N_d g_{\lambda_1} - f_{\lambda_1} & N_d g_{\lambda_2} - f_{\lambda_2} \\ Y_1 & 0 & Y_3 \end{bmatrix}$, where $Y_1 = -u_{EE} - \lambda_2 N_{EE} > 0$ and

$Y_2 = \delta - N_E > 0$. After some algebraic manipulations one finds

$$|\Psi| = -\lambda_1 F_{KK}(f_{\lambda_1} N_E Y_2 + N_E Y_2 g_{\lambda_1}) - (1 + N_d)Y_1 f_{\lambda_1}(g_{\lambda_2} - g_{\lambda_1}) > 0$$

To complete the stability analysis one needs to compute $\Omega = |M_1| + |M_2| + 2|M_3|$, where

$$M_1 = \begin{bmatrix} F_K & -f_{\lambda_1} - g_{\lambda_1} \\ -\lambda_1 F_{KK} & 0 \end{bmatrix}$$

$$M_2 = \begin{bmatrix} N_E & N_d g_{\lambda_2} f_{\lambda_2} \\ Y_1 & Y_2 \end{bmatrix}$$

$$M_3 = \begin{bmatrix} 0 & -f_{\lambda_2} - g_{\lambda_2} \\ 0 & 0 \end{bmatrix}$$

It follows that

$$\Omega = -f_{\lambda_1}\lambda_1 F_{KK} - g_{\lambda_1}\lambda_1 F_{KK} + N_E Y_2 - N_d g_{\lambda_2} Y_1 + f_{\lambda_2} Y_1 < 0$$

By lemma 1 of (61), these are sufficient conditions for stability.

Notes

I thank Carlo Carraro, Geoffrey Heal, Ignazio Musu and Domenico Siniscalco for conversations and useful comments on a previous version of this paper. Correspondence to: Andrea Beltratti, Department of Economics G. Prato, University of Torino, Corso Unione Sovietica 218 bis, 10134, Torino, Italy. Fax +39 11 6706062. Email address: beltratti@econ.unito.it

1 In the rest of the chapter notation will be introduced incrementally, so that one should keep track of the meaning of the symbols for the pages that follow.
2 It will be seen that the sign of the cross-derivative is often crucial to evaluate optimality of growth in a polluted economy.
3 See Dasgupta and Heal (1979) for a discussion of the ability of competitive markets to set the initial price at the level which just exhausts the available supply along the optimal path, that is the ability to follow a dynamically efficient rule.
4 See the remarks of the previous subsection on the laws of thermodynamics.
5 Equation (1) is obtained by differentiating equation (9) with respect to time and by using (10).
6 Along a growth path the shadow price of the natural resource satisfies the Hotelling rule and grows at a rate equal to the interest rate.
7 The logistic production function involves technical difficulties caused by non-convexity, see Withagen and Toman (1995) and Tahvonen and Withagen (1995).
8 By maximising steady-state utility Chichilnisky, Beltratti and Heal (1995) obtain a Green Golden Rule where the stock of environment is set at the utility-maximising level, and show that in general the actual level of environment in a competitive system will be lower than the Green Golden Rule level.
9 A model with three state variables is considered by Tahvonen and Kuuluvainen (1991), that adds a renewable resource to their model (1993).
10 See Smulders (1994) for a discussion of a few variants of models of endogenous growth with environmental assets.
11 Barrett (1992) compares the specification of Krautkraemer with that of Fisher, Solow and Kearl (1977) pointing out that in the former the benefits from the stock of resources are related to the rate at which the environment is depleted, while in the latter development benefits flow from the stock of the resource in its developed state but not from the rate of development.
12 Withagen (1995) confirms this result, also showing that when abatement is possible optimal growth is positive but not necessarily balanced.
13 See Musu (1995) for a similar definition of sustainability.

References

d'Arge, R.C. and K.C. Kogiku (1973), 'Economic Growth and the Environment', *Review of Economic Studies*, 40, 61–77.

Asako, K. (1980), 'Economic Growth and Environmental Pollution under the Max–min Principle,' *Journal of Environmental Economics and Management*, 7, 157–83.

Ashiem, G.B. (1994), 'Net National Product as an Indicator of Sustainability', *Scandinavian Journal of Economics*, 96, 257–65.

Ayres, R.U. and A.V. Kneese (1969), 'Production, Consumption and Externalities', *American Economic Review*, 59, 282–97.

Baldwin, R. (1993), 'Does Sustainability Require Growth?', in I. Goldin and L.A. Winters (eds.), *The Economics of Sustainable Development*, Cambridge University Press.

Barrett, S. (1992), 'Economic Growth and Environmental Preservation', *Journal of Environmental Economics and Management*, 23, 289–300.

Beltratti, A. (1995), 'Can a Growth Model with Defensive Expenditures Generate an Environmental Kuznets Curve?', Paper presented at the Workshop on Designing Economic Policy for Management of Natural Resources and the Environment, 12–13 May, Venice.

Beltratti, A., G. Chichilnisky and G. Heal (1993), 'Preservation, Uncertain Future Preferences and Irreversibility', *Nota di Lavoro 59.93*, Milan: Fondazione ENI Enrico Mattei.

—— (1994), 'Sustainable Growth and the Green Golden Rule', in I. Goldin and L.A. Winters (eds.), *The Economics of Sustainable Development*, Cambridge University Press.

Bovenberg, A.L. and R.A. de Mooij (1993), 'Environmental Tax Reform and Endogenous Growth', mimeo.

Bovenberg, A.L. and S. Smulders (1995), 'Environmental Quality and Pollution-Augmenting Technological Change in a Two-Section Endogenous Growth Model', *Journal of Public Economics*, 57, 369–91.

Brock, W.A. (1973), 'A Polluted Golden Age', in V.L. Smith (ed.), *Economics of Natural and Environmental Resources*, chapter 25.

Chichilnisky, G., A. Beltratti and G. Heal (1995), 'The Green Golden Rule', *Economics Letters*, 49, 175–9.

Daly, H.E. (1991), *Steady State Economics*, 2nd edition, Washington, DC: Island Press.

Dasgupta, P. (1993), 'Natural Resources in an Age of Substitutability', *Handbook of Natural Resources and Energy Economics*, vol. III, edited by A.V. Kneese and J.L. Sweeney, Elsevier.

Dasgupta P. and G. Heal (1974), 'The Optimal Depletion of Exhaustible Resources', *Review of Economic Studies, Symposium on the Economics of Exhaustible Resources*, 3–28.

—— (1979), *Economic Theory and Exhaustible Resources*, Cambridge University Press.

Dasgupta, P., G. Heal and A. Pant (1980), 'Optimising R&D Expenditure in the Development of Resource Substitutes', *Applied Mathematical Modelling*, 4, 87–94.

Fisher, A. (1979), Measures of Natural Resource Scarcity', in V. Kerry Smith (ed.), *Scarcity and Growth Reconsidered*, Resources for the Future, Baltimore and London: Johns Hopkins University Press.

Fisher, F.M., R.M. Solow and J.M. Kearl (1977), 'Aggregate Production Functions: Some CES Experiments', *Review of Economic Studies*, 44, 305–20.

Georgescu-Roegen, N. (1975), 'Energy and Economic Myths', *Southern Economic Journal*, 41, 347–81.

Grossman, G. (1994), 'Pollution and Growth: What Do We Know?', in I. Goldin and A. Winters (eds.), *The Economics of Sustainable Development*, Cambridge University Press.

Grossman G. and E. Helpman (1991), *Innovation and Growth in the Global Economy*, Cambridge, MA: MIT Press.

Grossman G.M. and A.B. Krueger (1993), 'Environmental Impacts of a North-

American Free Trade Agreement', in P. Garber (ed.), *The US–Mexico Free-Trade Agreement*, Cambridge, MA: MIT Press.

(1994), 'Economic Growth and the Environment', National Bureau of Economic Research Working Paper, No. 4634.

Hartwick, J.M. (1974), 'Intergenerational Equity and the Investing of Rents from Exhaustible Resources', *American Economic Review*, 67, 972–4.

Heal, G.M. (1985), 'Depletion and Discounting: a Classical Issue in the Economics of Exhaustible Resources', American Mathematical Society, Proceedings of Symposia in Applied Mathematics, vol. 32, 33–43.

(1990), 'Interactions Between Economy and Climate: A Framework for Policy Design Under Uncertainty', in R.E. Just and N. Bockstael (eds.), *Commodity and Resource Policies in Agricultural Systems*, Berlin, Heidelberg and New York: Springer, pp. 196–212.

(1993), 'The Optimal Use of Exhaustible Resources', *Handbook of Natural Resources and Energy Economics*, vol. III, edited by A.V. Kneese and J.L. Sweeney, Elsevier.

(1995), 'Interpreting Sustainability', *Nota di Lavoro 1.95*, Milan: Fondazione ENI Enrico Mattei.

Hettige H., R.E.B. Lucas and D. Wheeler (1992), 'The Toxic Intensity of Industrial Production: Global Patterns, Trends and Trade Policy', *American Economic Review*, 82, 478–81.

Holtz-Eakin, D. and T.M. Selden (1992), 'Stoking the Fires? CO_2 Emissions and Economic Growth', National Bureau of Economic Research Working Paper, No. 4248.

Hung, V., Chang P. and K. Blackburn (1993), 'Endogenous Growth, Environment and R&D', in C. Carraro (ed.), *Trade, Innovation and Environment*, Kluwer.

Jorgenson D.W. and P.J. Wilcoxen (1989), 'Environmental Regulation and US Economic Growth', Harvard Institute of Economic Research Discussion Paper, No. 1458.

Keeler E., M. Spence and R. Zeckhauser (1974), 'The Optimal Control of Pollution', *Journal of Economic Theory*, 4, 19–34.

Krautkraemer, J.A. (1985), 'Optimal Growth, Resource Amenities and the Preservation of Natural Environments', *Review of Economic Studies*, 52, 153–70.

Maler, K. (1974), *Environmental Economics: A Theoretical Inquiry*, Baltimore and London: Johns Hopkins University Press.

(1991), 'National Accounts and Environmental Resources', *Environmental and Resource Economics*, 1, 1–15.

Margulis, S. (1992), 'Back-of-the-Envelope Estimates of Environmental Damage Costs in Mexico', Policy Research Working Papers, World Bank.

Michel, P. (1993), 'Pollution and Growth towards the Ecological Paradise', *Nota di Lavoro 80.93*, Milan: Fondazione ENI Enrico Mattei.

Michel, P. and G. Rotillon (1992), 'Pollution's Disutility and Endogenous Growth', mimeo, Université Paris I.

Musu, I. (1993), 'Sustainable Economy and Time Preference', *Structural Change and Economic Dynamics*, 5, 81–6.

(1995), 'Transitional Dynamics to Sustainable Economic Growth', mimeo, University of Venice.

Nordhaus, W.D. (1993), 'Rolling the "Dice": An Optimal Transition Path for Controlling Greenhouse Gases', *Resource and Energy Economics*, 15, 27–50.

Ploeg, F. v.d. and C. Withagen (1991), 'Pollution Control and the Ramsey Problem', *Environmental and Resource Economics*, 1, 215–36.

Ramsey, F. (1928), 'A Mathematical Theory of Saving', *Economic Journal*, 38, 543–59.

Romer, P.M. (1990), 'Endogenous Technological Change', *Journal of Political Economy*, 98(2), S71–S102.

(1994), 'The Origins of Endogenous Growth', *Journal of Economic Perspectives*, 8, 5–22.

Saint-Paul, G. (1994), 'Trade Patterns and Pollution', *Nota di Lavoro 40.94*, Milan: Fondazione ENI Enrico Mattei.

Sala-i-Martin, X. (1990), 'Lecture Notes on Economic Growth (I)', National Bureau of Economic Research Working Papers, Nos. 3563 and 3564.

Selden, T. and D. Song (1994), 'Environmental Quality, and Development: Is There a Kuznets Curve for Air Pollution Emissions?', *Journal of Environmental Economics and Management*, 27, 147–62.

(1995), 'Neoclassical Growth, the J Curve for Abatement, and the Inverted U Curve for Pollution', *Journal of Environmental Economics and Management*, 29, 162–8.

Shafik, N. (1994), 'Economic Development and Environmental Quality: An Econometric Analysis', *Oxford Economic Papers*, 40, 757–75.

Solow, R.M. (1956), 'A Contribution to the Theory of Economic Growth', *Quarterly Journal of Economics*, 70, 65–94.

(1974), 'Intergenerational Equity and Exhaustible Resources', *Review of Economic Studies, Symposium on the Economics of Exhaustible Resources*, 29–45.

(1986), 'On the Intergenerational Allocation of Natural Resources', *Scandinavian Journal of Economics*, 88, 141–9.

(1993), 'An Almost Practical Step Towards Sustainability', *Resources Policy*, 19, 167–72.

Smulders, S. (1994), *Growth, Market Structure and the Environment*, Hilvarenbeek.

Stiglitz, J. (1974), 'Growth with Exhaustible Natural Resources: Efficient and Optimal Growth Paths', *Review of Economic Studies, Symposium on the Economics of Exhaustible Resources*, 123–37.

Tahvonen, O. and J. Kuuluvainen (1991), 'Optimal Growth with Renewable Resources and Pollution', *European Economic Review*, 35, 650–61.

(1993), 'Economic Growth, Pollution and Renewable Resources', *Journal of Environmental Economics and Management*, 24, 101–18.

Tahvonen, O. and C. Withagen (1995), 'Optimality of Irreversible Pollution Accumulation', mimeo.

Toman, M.A., J. Pezzey and J. Krautkraemer (1995), 'Neoclassical Economic Growth Theory and "Sustainability"', in D.W. Bromley (ed.), *Handbook of Environmental Economics*, Cambridge, MA: Blackwell.

United Nations (1993) *Integrated Environmental and Economic Accounting*, New York: United Nations.

Verdier, T. (1993), 'Environmental Pollution and Endogenous Growth: a Comparison between Emission Taxes and Technological Standards, in C. Carraro and J.A. Filar (eds.), *Control and Game-Theoretic Models of the Environment*, Boston: Birkhauser.

Withagen, C. (1995), 'Pollution, Abatement and Balanced Growth', *Environmental and Resource Economics*, 5, 1–8.

Withagen, C. and M. Toman (1995), 'Cumulative Pollution with a Backstop', mimeo, Resources for the Future, Washington, DC.

World Commission (1987), *Our Common Future*, New York: Oxford University Press.

Xepapadeas, A. (1994), 'Long-Run Growth, Environmental Pollution, and Increasing Returns', *Nota di Lavoro 67.94*, Milan: Fondazione ENI Enrico Mattei.

Xepapadeas, A. and E. Amri (1995), 'Environmental Quality and Economic Development: Empirical Evidence based on Qualitative Characteristics', *Nota di Lavoro*, Milan: Fondazione ENI Enrico Mattei.

3 Environmental policy and technological innovation

David Ulph

1 Introduction

There has been a very considerable surge of interest in recent years on the question of how various types of environmental policy will affect incentives to innovate. There have been two main strands of concern underpinning this work.

The first is prompted by the concern that environmental policies operate by correcting the distortions introduced by having unpriced externalities. Since the major externalities of concern arise from pollution, this typically means that when goods and services are traded at their true price they become more expensive, leading to a reduction in output of those activities and a re-allocation to others. While this is precisely what these policies are intended to achieve, the question arises as to whether the amount of re-allocation might be reduced if the introduction of such policies spurred firms to innovate in order to discover new cleaner technologies which had lower levels of emissions. The question therefore arises as to just how effective environmental policies are in generating new innovation.

Early work on this question by, for example, Downing and White (1986) Magat (1979), Malueg (1989) and Milliman and Prince (1989), explored the effectiveness of a number of different environmental policies. However this literature suffered from a number of weaknesses. The focus was purely on the polluting activities of firms, and the interaction between this and the product market was poorly developed. Indeed the product market was typically taken to be perfectly competitive. Finally innovation was modelled as an activity taking place under perfect certainty and with full information.

The first two of these features are at odds with two crucial and related features of the economics of innovation: that R&D is undertaken for strategic reasons in order to gain some advantage in the product market; and that R&D typically introduces a significant fixed cost to firms, which in turn serves to make product markets imperfectly competitive. The more recent literature has taken on board this strategic aspect of innovation within a setting of imperfect competition, and it is this literature which will be the main focus of this chapter.

However, the bulk of this literature has maintained the assumption of perfect certainty and full information. More recent contributions by, for example, D. Ulph (1994) have modelled R&D as a stochastic process, while, for example, Carraro and Topa (1995) and Cadot and Sinclair-Desgagne (1996) have considered more explicitly the issue of incomplete information.

The second main concern lying behind this upsurge of interest has been the recognition that the possible disruptive effects of introducing environmental policies become most acute in an open-economy international setting, for now the fear is that countries which operate tougher environmental policies than others will suffer a loss in real income as production relocates through both trade and the physical relocation of plants to countries with more lax environmental policies. This prompts concern that, in the absence of international cooperation, the freeing up of trade will lead to environmental dumping – the uniform reduction by all countries in the toughness of their environmental policies. This raises two issues. The first again is whether the potentially disruptive effects of environmental policies on resource re-allocation might be significantly mitigated through the encouragement these policies give to innovation. The second is whether environmental dumping will indeed take place when strategic innovation becomes a consideration. It has been suggested that countries might now have incentives to set environmental policies which are excessively tough in order to spur the firms in their country to innovate ahead of rivals and so gain market advantage. This has become known as the 'Porter hypothesis', following the article by Michael Porter (1991) which articulated this possibility. The bulk of the recent literature has examined the effects of environmental policy on innovation within this international context.[1]

Now the whole issue of trade and the environment, including the links with innovation, have been surveyed in chapter 6 in this volume by A. Ulph (1996b). So the aim of this chapter is as follows. In Section 2 I will examine the question of how environmental policies affect the incentives of firms to innovate in the context of models where there is perfect certainty and full information. The class of models is in fact what is known in the strategic innovation literature as non-tournament models – see, for example, Beath, Katsoulacos and Ulph (1995) for an extensive discussion and survey of this literature. I will develop the analysis in the context of a single closed economy in which all firms face the same policies. This section will considerably unify and extend the existing literature in two ways. All the arguments will be developed for general functional forms, whereas much of the literature has relied on special functional forms. Using this more general approach it is possible to better understand what drives the results of particular papers. Secondly, I endogenise the number of firms whereas much of the literature focuses on the case where the number of firms is fixed – usually at two.

While the analysis is developed for a closed economy, I will show how it can be easily reinterpreted in the context of an open economy, and that in terms of the major qualitative positive predictions, there is in fact no loss of generality in considering a closed economy.

In section 3 I will examine how environmental policies affect innovation in the context of models where there is uncertainty and incomplete information. The class of models considered here is what is known as tournament models.

All this discussion will follow the bulk of the literature by concentrating on process innovation, where R&D brings in new cleaner technologies. In section 4 I will briefly consider how environmental concerns by consumers may put pressure on firms to innovate, by introducing more environmentally friendly products – even in the absence of explicit environmental policies.

Section 5 offers conclusions and suggestions for future research.

At this point it may help to anticipate one of the conclusions in order to explain one of the features of this chapter, which is that the approach is purely positive. That is I will focus entirely on the issue of how environmental policies affect the level of innovation rather than on the optimal design of policies. There are two reasons for this. The first is that the question of policy design in an international context is already well surveyed in the chapter by A. Ulph (1996b). The second is that, for a closed economy, the optimal design of policy is inadequately developed, and it would go way beyond the scope of this chapter to remedy this defect. The point is that there are three types of market failure at work when we consider the question of innovation and the environment.

The first is the conventional market failure associated with externalities. The second is the conventional *static* market failure associated with imperfect competition – typically output is too low, prices too high, and there is excessive entry. The third aspect of this market failure, which has only recently received serious attention, is the *dynamic* market failure surrounding R&D and innovation. This arises fundamentally from the public-good nature of knowledge as being expensive to produce but cheap to reproduce. This gives rise to a complex set of questions.

(i)   How many firms should engage in R&D?
(ii) What information should they share (a) with each other, (b) with other non-innovating firms?
(iii) How much R&D should each of the innovating firms do?

Now a partial solution to some of the market failures associated with

R&D is the creation of a system of property rights, the most obvious one being patent protection. The problem with this is that it typically gives too much protection and prevents socially beneficial sharing of information. This distortion of the information-sharing aspects of R&D generates consequent distortions on the decisions about the amount of R&D being done. Thus we know that, in non-tournament models, each firm typically does too little R&D, but there is excessive duplication of R&D. However in tournament models each firm undertakes too much R&D. Again, a useful reference on these points is Beath, Katsoulacos and Ulph (1995).

For these reasons a lot of the focus of technology policy is now on arrangements like research joint ventures (RJVs) as ways of correcting the distortions of the patent system by promoting more information sharing. The difficulty now is that we have only a very limited understanding of how well these perform, mainly because, with the exception of the recent paper by Katsoulacos and Ulph (1996), the literature on RJVs treats the amount of information sharing as exogenous.

I therefore think that even without the complications induced by taking on environmental market failures, we are far from having a complete understanding of policy design towards R&D. Simply including an R&D subsidy alongside an environmental tax as an additional policy instrument (as is done in some of the literature) is very far from being a satisfactory analysis of policy design.

For this reason I have eschewed questions of policy design, but leave it as an important research question, to think about the combined design of environmental and technology policy.

2 Non-tournament models

The idea here is that there are many possible research paths that a firm can pursue. These paths have two crucial characteristics. The first is that they are sufficiently similar that a given amount of R&D spent on one path produces the same amount of progress as would have been obtained had that R&D been spent on another path. So, in terms of the underlying R&D technology, these paths are perfect substitutes. On the other hand, these path are sufficiently different that a discovery made on one path can be so distinguished from discoveries made on other paths that they can be independently patented, and so give the discoverer the exclusive right to use the new technology. Thus in this class of models patents can protect firms against costless imitation by rivals, but not against costly innovation by rivals.

The basic model we will consider in this section goes as follows. There are n firms producing a homogeneous product. The inverse demand for this is given by the function

$$p=f(X), f'<0$$

where p is price, $X=nx$ is aggregate output, and x is output per firm. Each firm has constant unit costs of production

$$c=b+te(z)$$

where b is a constant reflecting costs in terms of labour and raw materials, etc., t is the emissions tax, and e represents emissions per unit of output. This latter is assumed to depend on the amount, z, spent on R&D to produce a cleaner technology. The function $e(.)$ is assumed to satisfy the conditions

$$\forall z \geq 0, \ 0<e<\infty; \ e'<0; \ e''<0 \tag{1}$$

So emissions are lowered by R&D but can never be completely eliminated. There are diminishing marginal returns to R&D.

In addition to the (endogenous) fixed costs z each firm is assumed to have additional fixed costs $F>0$. This might be associated with other forms of R&D.

The profits of a typical firm which has spent z on R&D and has produced output x when all the other firms have chosen output, $\bar{x}$, is then given by

$$\pi(x,z;\bar{x},t,n,F) \equiv x[p(x+(n-1)\bar{x})-(b+te(z))]-z-F \tag{2}$$

The basic equilibrium notion is that of a Nash equilibrium, so each firm chooses output and R&D taking as given the output and R&D choices of all other firms.

The majority of models in the literature focus on the case where the number of firms is fixed (usually at two), and also consider the case where the nature of the game is that firms first choose R&D and then choose output (usually in a Cournot fashion). This gives rise to strategic considerations in the choice of R&D. However, in order to get insights into the sequential equilibrium, I want to begin by considering the case where firms choose output and R&D simultaneously and so there are no strategic R&D motives. This makes it easier to see some of the essential comparative static structures of the results. I will then consider the sequential equilibrium.

In both cases I will go beyond much of the existing literature by endogenising the number of firms.

2.1 The simultaneous equilibrium

Here R&D and output are chosen simultaneously. We can think of this as being a two-stage equilibrium. In stage 1 firms enter the market. Then in stage 2 firms choose output and R&D simultaneously, and we get a Nash equilibrium in R&D and output.

2.1.1 The **short-run** (stage 2) equilibrium

Here the number of firms, n, is fixed.

From (1) it is straightforward to see that, assuming symmetry, the first-order conditions characterising this short-run symmetric equilibrium are

$$m(x;n) \equiv f(nx) + xf'(nx) = b + te(z) \tag{3}$$

$$-txe'(z) = 1 \tag{4}$$

Equation (3) is just the familiar condition that marginal revenue equals marginal cost. For later purposes make the conventional assumptions that marginal revenue is decreasing in both output and the number of firms so $m_x < 0$, $m_n < 0$.

Equation (4) says that the marginal gain from a unit increase in R&D equals the marginal cost. The marginal gain from an increase in R&D is the product of three terms: (i) $(-e'(z))$ which is the marginal reduction in emissions per unit of output from a unit increase in R&D; (ii) the emissions tax rate, t; (iii) the level of output, x. It is easy to see from (4) that, *holding output constant*, an increase in the emissions tax, will certainly lead to an increase in R&D, z, because it increases the marginal gain from R&D. For later purposes, it is useful to note that by differentiating (4) with respect to t this *constant output effect*, denoted dz, is given by

$$dz \equiv -\frac{e'}{te''} < 0 \tag{5}$$

Let $\tilde{x}(t,n)$, $\tilde{z}(t,n)$, denote the stage 2 equilibrium values of output and R&D – i.e., the solutions to (3) and (4). We are interested in the comparative static effects of an increase in t. So differentiate (3) and (4) totally with respect to t and we get

$$\frac{\partial \tilde{x}}{\partial t} = \frac{t\tilde{x}[(e')^2 - e.e'']}{\Delta} \tag{6}$$

and

$$\frac{\partial \tilde{z}}{\partial t} = \frac{e'(\tilde{z})[te(\tilde{z}) + \tilde{x}m_x]}{\Delta} \tag{7}$$

where $\Delta = -[txe''m_x + (te')^2]$ and standards conditions on stability of the equilibrium require this to be positive.

The intuition behind these results is as follows.

Whether an increase in the tax causes output to rise or fall, will depend on its effect on unit costs. There are two effects: holding R&D constant an increase in the tax causes costs to rise; but it also encourages firms to do more R&D and this lowers costs. Looking at the overall effect we have

$$dc = e(z) + t.e'(z).dz = \frac{[e.e'' - (e')^2]}{e''}$$

where the last step comes from substituting (5). So costs rise (output falls) if and only if $k(\tilde{z}) \equiv e(\tilde{z}).e''(\tilde{z}) - [e(\tilde{z})]^2 > 0$.

As discussed in Ulph (1994) and in Ulph and Ulph (1996), the value of k depends crucially on the nature of the function $e(.)$. Thus, in particular, if:

(i) $e(z) \equiv e_0 \exp(-\alpha.z)$, then $e(.)$ satisfies (2) for all non-negative z. For these values of z, $k(z) \equiv 0$, and so costs and output are unaffected by the tax;

(ii) $e(z) \equiv e_0(1 + z)^{-\alpha}$, then $e(.)$ satisfies (2) for all non-negative z. For these values of z, $k(z) > 0$, and so costs rise and output falls with the tax;

(iii) $e(z) \equiv e_0(1 - \alpha.z)^2$, then, provided, $0 \leq z > \frac{1}{\alpha}$, $e(.)$ satisfies (2). For all these values of z, $k(z) < 0$, so costs fall and output rises with the tax.

Since the usual presumption would be that taxes increase costs, we will refer to (ii) as the *conventional case*. The functional form given in (i) is that used by Simpson and Bradford (1993). For other functional forms, the sign of $k(z)$ will vary depending on the particular value of z, and so it will be more difficult to obtain unambiguous results. In particular, this is true for the model considered by Katsoulacos and Xepapadeas (1996) where $e(z) = e_0 - \alpha.\sqrt{z}$.

Turning to the effect of an increase in the tax on the amount of R&D, we see that there are two effects. First there is the *direct* effect that, *other things equal*, an increase in the tax raises the marginal benefit from environmental innovation and so encourages each firm to do more R&D. On the other hand there is the *indirect* effect that, *other things equal*, an increase in the tax raises costs which reduces output and hence the incentive to undertake cost-reducing R&D.

This can be seen more formally by noting that the term in square brackets in the numerator of (7) contains two terms, one positive and one negative. However, we can get a bit more insight into this result by letting

$$\sigma \equiv \frac{te(\tilde{z})}{b + te(\tilde{z})}, \text{ and } \epsilon = -\frac{\tilde{x}m_x}{m} > 0$$

denote, respectively, the fraction of variable costs attributable to environmental taxes, and the elasticity of marginal revenue. Then, using the first-order condition (3), we can rewrite (7) as

$$\frac{\partial \tilde{z}}{\partial t} = \frac{[b + te(\tilde{z})][e'(\tilde{z}).(\sigma - \epsilon)]}{\Delta} \tag{8}$$

So we see that provided $\sigma < \epsilon$ and environmental taxes account for a sufficiently small fraction of variable costs then an increase in environmental taxation will indeed have the effect of encouraging firms to do more R&D. Since empirically environmental costs do account for a small fraction of costs, we can conclude that in most realistic cases an increase in the tax will indeed cause firms to do more R&D.

It is straightforward to check that since an increase in the number of firms shifts down each firm's marginal revenue curve, this reduces the equilibrium output of each firm. This in turn lowers the marginal gain from R&D and so reduces the equilibrium R&D per firm. Thus $\frac{\partial \tilde{x}}{\partial n} < 0; \frac{\partial \tilde{z}}{\partial n} < 0$.

Having understood the nature of the short-run equilibrium, let us turn now to:

2.1.2 Stage 1 (**long-run**) equilibrium
Let

$$\tilde{\pi}(t,n,F) \equiv \tilde{x}[f(nx) - (b + te(\tilde{z}))] - \tilde{z}F$$

denote the stage 1 profits per firm when all firms choose the Nash equilibrium levels of output and R&D.

Assume that the equilibrium number of firms, $\tilde{n}$, is pinned down by the zero-profit condition

$$\tilde{\pi}(t,\tilde{n},F) = 0 \tag{9}$$

To obtain the comparative static results, differentiate (9) totally with respect to t to obtain

$$\frac{d\tilde{n}}{dt} = \frac{\tilde{\pi}_t}{\tilde{\pi}_n} \tag{10}$$

where

$$\tilde{\pi}_n = \frac{\partial \tilde{\pi}}{\partial n} = (n-1).\tilde{x}.f'(n\tilde{x}).\frac{\partial \tilde{x}}{\partial n} + \tilde{x}^2 f'(n\tilde{x});$$

$$\tilde{\pi}_t = \frac{\partial \tilde{\pi}}{\partial t} = (n-1).\tilde{x}.f'(n\tilde{x}).\frac{\partial \tilde{x}}{\partial t} - e(\tilde{z}).\tilde{x}$$

The first terms in these expressions arise from the fact that changes in t and n will affect *every* firm's output, yet each firm has made its profit-maximising choice of output on the assumption that everyone else's output remains constant.

If we look at the expression for $\tilde{\pi}_n$, then the first term is positive while the second is negative. However a necessary condition for local stability of the equilibrium is that $\tilde{\pi}_n < 0$, and we will assume this to hold.

Turning to the expression for $\tilde{\pi}_t$, the second term is the *direct* effect of the tax on a firm's profits, and (as we would expect) is negative. The first term captures the *indirect* effect of the tax increase through its effect on the output of all the other firms in the industry. This is non-positive if $\dfrac{\partial \tilde{x}}{\partial t} \geq 0$, ($k \geq 0$), and so reinforces the *direct* effect. However for the conventional case where $k > 0$, the tax causes other firms to reduce their output, and so this indirect effect is going to be positive, since firms gain when their rivals reduce their output. The overall balance between the two effects is difficult to establish at this level of generality. However it is straightforward to show that if $\dfrac{(e')^2}{e.e''} > \dfrac{1}{n} . \dfrac{Xf''}{f'}$, then $\tilde{\pi}_n < 0 \Rightarrow \tilde{\pi}_t < 0$. This will certainly be true if $f'' \leq 0$, or if we are dealing with a very competitive industry (large n).

So we can take it that in a wide class of cases $\tilde{\pi}_t < 0$, and so, from (10), $\dfrac{\partial \tilde{n}}{\partial t} < 0$.

From our analysis of the short-run (stage 2) equilibrium, we know that this long run effect of higher taxes leading to reduced entry will increase the equilibrium output per firm, and so increase the incentive to undertake R&D. Nevertheless there remains the possibility that an increase in the environmental tax will increase a firm's profits (and so increase entry) through its beneficial effect on restricting the output of rival firms.

So the broad conclusion from this analysis of the simultaneous equilibrium is that there are no general analytical results showing that in both the short run and long run an increase in the environmental tax *necessarily* leads to an increase in innovation to bring in more environmentally friendly technologies. In both the short run and the long run there are *direct* effects of the tax increase which certainly lead to higher R&D spending. However in both cases there is also an *indirect* effect which arises from the fact that the tax can raise each firm's costs and so restrict their equilibrium output. In the short run this directly reduces the incentive to undertake cost-reducing innovation. Now this reduction in output also has the beneficial consequence that the output of rival firms is reduced. However, in the long run this promotes more entry, which again lowers equilibrium output and reduces the incentive to undertake cost-reducing innovation.

Nevertheless, we have also seen that in a wide class of empirically relevant cases the direct effects will dominate, and that an increase in the environmental tax will generate more environmental innovation both in the short run and in the long run.

Having thus understood the simultaneous equilibrium, let us turn to the analysis of the sequential equilibrium.

2.2 The sequential equilibrium

Here we think of there being a three-stage game. In stage 1 firms enter. In stage 2 firms choose their R&D, and then in stage 3 firms choose output (in a Cournot fashion).

2.2.1 The output game (stage 3)

This is just a conventional Cournot oligopoly equilibrium, so we can just use results from conventional theory. Suppose then that, as a result of previous decisions, one firm enters this game with unit variable costs c, while the $n-1$ remaining firms have unit costs $\bar{c}$.

Let $x(c,\bar{c};n)$, $\bar{x}(c,\bar{c};n)$, denote, respectively, the Cournot equilibrium outputs of the first firm, and of each of the remaining $n-1$ firms. These functions can be assumed to satisfy the following conditions

$$x_c < 0; \ x_{\bar{c}} > 0; \ \frac{d}{dc} x(c,c;n) \equiv x_c + x_{\bar{c}} < 0; \ \bar{x}_c > 0$$

Thus each firm's output is increasing in its own costs, but decreasing in the costs of the rivals. However own effects dominate cross effects in the sense that an increase in the costs of all firms, assuming they initially have the same costs, reduces each firm's output.

Let $\pi(c,\bar{c};n)$ be the operating profits of the first firm in the resulting Cournot equilibrium. Then this satisfies the conditions

(i) $-\pi_c = x - x.f'[x(n-1)\bar{x}].\bar{x}_c < 0;$

(ii) $\pi_{\bar{c}} > 0; \ \frac{d}{dc} \pi(c,c;n) \equiv \pi_c + \pi_{\bar{c}} < 0;$ (11)

(iii) $\pi_{cc} > 0; \ \pi_{c\bar{c}} < 0; \ \frac{d}{dc} \pi_c(c,c) > 0;$

(iv) $\pi_n < 0; \ \pi_{cn} > 0$

Expression (11(i)) reveals that the marginal gain from a reduction in unit variable costs is made up of two terms. The first is output – which is just the marginal gain we saw above in the simultaneous equilibrium. But now there is a second term which reflects the gain to the firm from having all the other firms reduce their output when it manages to lower its costs. This captures the *strategic* incentive for firms to innovate.

Expression (11(ii)) tells us that an increase in the costs of rival firms increases a firm's profits. However a uniform increase in the costs of all firms (assuming that they initially have the same costs) reduces profits – so the own effect dominates the cross effect.

Expression (11(iii)) captures the requirement that each firm's profits are a convex function of its own costs. So the marginal incentive for a firm to lower its costs is greater the lower its costs already are. This is because the lower its costs currently are the higher is its output, and, from (11(i)), this increases the incentive for cost reduction (*ceteris paribus*). By analogous reasoning, an increase in the costs of rival firms also increases the incentive for a firm to lower its costs. However, once again a uniform increase in the costs of all firms (assuming that they initially have the same costs) lowers the marginal incentive to reduce costs, as the own effect dominates the cross effect.

Finally from (11(iv)) we learn that an increase in the number of firms reduces both the profit per firm and the marginal gain from lowering costs.

2.2.2 The R&D game (stage 2)

Here a typical firm takes as given the R&D, and unit variable costs of rival firms, and chooses its own R&D, z, to

$$max \ \pi[b+te(z),\bar{c}] - z \qquad (12)$$

The first-order condition characterising a symmetric equilibrium is

$$\{-[\pi_c(b+te(z),b+te(z);n)]\}.[-t.e'(z)] = 1 \qquad (13)$$

This just says that the marginal benefit of a unit increase in R&D should equal the marginal cost. The marginal benefit is the product of two terms. The first is the marginal gain from a reduction in costs; the second is the marginal reduction in costs brought about by a unit increase in R&D.

Let $\tilde{z}(t,n)$ be, as before, the equilibrium level of R&D per firm. To obtain the comparative static effects of an increase in the environmental tax, differentiate (13) totally with respect to t, and we get

$$\Delta > \tilde{z}_t = [\pi_c.e'] + \left[t.e'.e.\frac{d}{dc}\pi_c \right] \qquad (14)$$

where $\Delta = -\left\{ \pi_c te'' + (te')^2 \frac{d}{dc}\pi_c \right\}$ and standard second-order and stability conditions require that $\Delta > 0$. From the right-hand side of (14) we see that, as before, there are two effects of the tax increase. The first is that it increases the effectiveness of R&D in lowering costs and this leads to an increase in R&D. On the other hand it raises costs (*ceteris paribus*) and this lowers the marginal value of reducing costs (essentially because it lowers output).

To get a sense of how these two factors might balance out, notice that we can rewrite (14) as

$$\Delta.\tilde{z}_t=[\pi_c.e'].[1-\sigma.\eta] \tag{15}$$

where, as before, $\sigma=\dfrac{t.e}{b+t.e}$ is the share of environmental costs in variable costs, and $\eta\equiv-\dfrac{c}{\pi_c}.\dfrac{d}{dc}\pi_c>0$ is the elasticity of marginal profits with respect to costs. We see therefore that, given the fact that σ is typically small, it is likely to be the case in practice that an increase in environmental taxes will indeed encourage firms to spend more on R&D.

We now want to know the overall effect of a tax increase on costs. So let

$$\tilde{c}(t,n)\equiv b+t.e[\tilde{z}(t,n)]$$

and we have

$$\tilde{c}_t=e(\tilde{z})+t.e'(\tilde{z}).\tilde{z}_t=\dfrac{[-t.\pi_c].[e.e''-(e')^2]}{\Delta}$$

So, just as before, whether, overall, costs rise or fall with the tax rate will depend on the nature of the function $e(.)$, and in particular on the value of $k(\tilde{z})$.

Finally it follows immediately from (11(iv)) and (12) that an increase in the number of firms lowers R&D per firm, i.e., $\tilde{z}_n<0$, and consequently increases costs per firm, i.e., $\tilde{c}_n>0$.

Having understood stages 2 and 3, we can now turn to

2.2.3 The entry game (stage 1)

The story here is exactly analogous to that in stage 1 of the simultaneous model.

Let

$$\Pi(t,n)\equiv\pi[\tilde{c}(t,n),\tilde{c}(t,n);n]-\tilde{z}(t,n)-F$$

be the profits made by a firm when the tax rate is t and the number of firms is n.

Notice that

$$\Pi_t=\dfrac{d\pi}{dc}.\tilde{c}_t-\tilde{z}_t \tag{16}$$

and

$$\Pi_n=\dfrac{d\pi}{dc}.\tilde{c}_n+\pi_n-\tilde{z}_n \tag{17}$$

From $(11(ii))$ $\frac{d\pi}{dc}<0$. While we cannot say anything in general about the sign of $\tilde{c}_t$, we know that in the *conventional case* $\tilde{c}_t>0$. Similarly, we know that in a wide class of empirically relevant cases $\tilde{z}_t>0$. So, from (16) we can take it that typically, though not generally, $\Pi_t<0$. In (17), we know that $\tilde{c}_n>0$; $\pi_n<0$; $\tilde{z}_n<0$. While this makes the overall sign of (17) ambiguous, it is a condition for local stability of the equilibrium that $\Pi_n<0$. Recalling (10) we can therefore conclude that typically, though not generally

$$\frac{d\tilde{n}}{dt}<0$$

Hence the long-run effect of a tax increase is to reduce entry, which stimulates R&D.

We therefore see that the analysis and conclusions of the sequential entry model are very similar to those of the simultaneous entry model. While the introduction of the additional strategic investment motive will change the quantitative predictions of the model, it has very little impact on the qualitative predictions.

2.3 Extensions and connections to the literature

Having set out this very general approach, it is now easy to connect this analysis to the existing literature, much of which relies on particular functional forms which are just special cases of this general analysis.

2.3.1 Extension to an international setting

As pointed out in the introduction, much of the literature has been concerned with the link between trade, innovation and environmental policy. In that context it has been natural to operate with models in which firms are located in different countries and so each firm faces a potentially different tax rate (at least when governments act non-cooperatively). In terms of the previous analysis this makes very little difference, for all that happens is that the total derivatives $\frac{d\pi}{dc},\frac{d}{dc}\pi_c$ that appear in the various expressions above just get replaced by partial derivatives π_c, π_{cc} respectively. But since these have exactly the same signs as the total derivatives, no qualitative results are changed. In particular, we have already noted that some of the results in Katsoulacos and Xepapadeas (1996) are just special cases of the results obtained here.

One issue that does arise in this international context is how the tax rate levied in one country affects the R&D done in another. As the formulation of the individual firm problem in (12) makes clear, this can happen only through the effects of the tax rate on costs of the firm within that country. As we have seen repeatedly this is governed entirely by the nature of the function $k(z)$. Thus Simpson and Bradford's (1993) conclusion that the tax rate in one country has no effect on the R&D in the other depends crucially on the fact that they assume that the function $e(.)$ is negative exponential, and so $k(z)=0$.

2.3.2 Other forms of R&D

So far it has been assumed that the only R&D that a firm undertakes is that involved in lowering emissions. Ulph and Ulph (1996) consider a more general framework in which firms may undertake two forms of R&D – one which lowers emissions e, and one which reduces the other element of costs, b. They show that all the qualitative comparative static predictions are exactly as set out above for the case where there is only environmental R&D. This is not surprising, for all that drives the comparative static results are marginal conditions. If a firm undertakes more than one type of R&D it will carry them out until the marginal returns are equalised. But then, at the margin, it is indifferent to which type of R&D it changes, and all its behaviour will be exactly the same as if it chose only one type of R&D – the environmental R&D.

One case which is a little different from the above analysis is that contained in A. Ulph (1992, 1993a and b) where the only form of R&D that firms undertake is that to lower the other component of costs, b. But then there can be no *direct effects* of taxes on R&D, and everything will be driven by the *indirect effects* of the environmental tax on a firm's costs. Thus, from what we have done before, we know that a higher environmental tax will lower the amount of R&D that each firm does, and will consequently unambiguously drive up its costs – which is precisely what A. Ulph (1993 a and b) finds.

2.3.3 Other instruments

Although the literature has predominantly focused on taxes as instruments there has been some analysis of the use of other instruments.

Amongst others, A. Ulph (1992, 1996a) and Ulph and Ulph (1996) consider the use of standards, whereby firms are required to keep total emissions below some level E. Notice that in this case a tougher environmental policy is associated with smaller values of E. The analysis and conclusions can be briefly sketched.

If these standards are to be effective in changing behaviour, they must operate to limit firms' output below the level that would otherwise be profit maximising. Firms therefore have incentives to introduce a new technology which allows them to lower emissions per unit of output and so expand output. So define

$$\pi(x,\bar{x}) \equiv x\left[f\left(x+(n-1)\bar{x}\right)-c\right]$$

as the operating profit of a firm when it produces output x and all the other firms produce output $\bar{x}$. Assume that, over the range of outputs in which we are interested

$$\pi_x > 0; \ \pi_{\bar{x}} < 0; \ \pi_{xx} < 0; \ \frac{d}{dx}\pi(x,x) \equiv \pi_{xx} + \pi_{x\bar{x}} < 0$$

Each firm chooses R&D taking as given the R&D, and hence output, of all other firms. A typical firm therefore chooses z to

$$\max \ \pi\left[\frac{E}{e(z)},\bar{x}\right] - Z$$

It is easier to work with the function $\phi(z) \equiv \dfrac{1}{e(z)}$, which is assumed to be strictly increasing and strictly concave. Then the first-order condition characterising a symmetric equilibrium is

$$\pi_x[E\phi(z),E\phi(z)].(E\phi'(z)) = 1 \tag{18}$$

The interpretation of (18) is exactly analogous to that of (13).

We are interested in whether a tougher environmental policy (lower E) encourages more R&D. Differentiate (18) totally with respect to E and we get

$$\Delta.\left(-\frac{dz}{dE}\right) = (-\pi_x.\phi') + \left[E.\phi.\phi'.\left(-\frac{d}{dx}\pi_x 1\right)\right] \tag{19}$$

as before we can take it that $\Delta > 0$. The first term on the RHS of (19) is the *direct effect* of the tougher policy, and is *negative*. The intuition is straightforward: lowering emission levels reduces the effectiveness of any reduction in emissions per unit of output in increasing output. The second term on the RHS of (19) is the *indirect effect* of the policy and is *positive*. Again the intuition is straightforward. Toughening the policy lowers output and so makes it more valuable to find ways of increasing output.

So introducing this alternative policy turns round the signs of the direct and indirect effects of the policy, although the logic remains essentially the same as in the case where tax was the instrument. Once again the overall effect of the policy is ambiguous.

2.3.4 Differentiated products

So far the analysis has been confined to the case where the product is homogeneous and product market competition takes the form of Cournot competition. There is no problem at all in extending the analysis to the case of differentiated products. Provided the resulting profit function satisfies all the conditions in (11) then all the conclusions about R&D competition continue to hold.

Allowing for differentiated products also introduces the possibility that product market competition might now take the form of Bertrand competition. This form of competition is explored by Barrett (1994) and A. Ulph (1996a) amongst others. Ulph (1996a) shows that the broad qualitative conclusions about the effect of taxes on R&D in the stage 2 game are precisely the same whether the nature of competition is Bertrand or Cournot. This conclusion is derived in the context of a model using particular functional forms, where taxes unambiguously stimulate greater R&D.

More generally, it was pointed out above that, provided the profit function derived from the stage 3 game satisfies all the properties (11), then all the conclusions in the earlier stages will continue to hold. Given that, even then, we could not get sharp predictions about the effects of policy on R&D, it is hard to see that switching the nature of product market competition is going to change the general predictions of the model.

2.3.5 Spillovers

An issue that has not been considered in the above analysis is that of innovation spillovers. Katsoulacos and Xepapadeas (1996) allow for these. Intuitively the introduction of such a spillover will have two effects. On the one hand it has the *direct effect* of lowering the marginal gain from innovation since firms will realise that the R&D they do will lower their rivals' costs – at least to some extent. On the other hand it has the *indirect effect* that for any given amount of R&D spending by each firm the total amount of cost reduction will be greater, hence each firm's output will be greater, and this will increase the incentive for further cost reduction. It is therefore not surprising that even with their special functional forms Katsoulacos and Xepapadeas find it hard to sign the effect of the spillover parameter on R&D – though numerical simulations suggest it is negative (reflecting the dominance of the direct effect).

3 Tournament models

Here the idea is that there is effectively just a single research path which firms can pursue. Assume that this research leads to the discovery of some new technology which lowers emissions of some pollutant. Continue to assume that whoever makes a discovery has access to an infinitely lived and completely effective patent. Then whichever firm first makes a discovery will be the sole firm that is able to take advantage of this new technology.

Accordingly the nature of R&D competition now takes the form of a race to be the first to innovate.

There are a number of ways of modelling such a tournament, the following approach is that which is now most commonly adopted. Fuller details of all the ideas are set out in Beath, Katsoulacos and Ulph (1995).

Assume that there are just two firms involved in the race. Discovery of the new technology is a stochastic process in which at any instant of time the probability of discovery by either firm (conditional on neither having discovered before) depends solely on the flow rates of R&D done by each firm at that time. Moreover the rate of arrival of discovery is a Poisson (constant hazard) process where the hazard rate depends on the flow level of R&D done by each firm. Given these assumptions we can assume that each firm chooses a constant flow level of R&D expenditure and hence a constant hazard.

Assume that the level of emissions of the old and new technology are, respectively, e_0 and e_1, $e_0 > e_1 > 0$. Hence unit costs with the old and new technologies are, respectively, $c_0(t) = b + te_0$; $c_1(t) = b + te_1$, $c_0(t) > c_1(t)$ $\forall t > 0$.

Let $\pi[c, \bar{c}]$ denote, as before, the operating profits of a firm whose unit costs are c, while those of the rival firm are $\bar{c}$. Using this definition we can therefore let $\pi^w(t) = \pi[c_1(t), c_0(t)]$; $\pi^\ell(t) = \pi[c_0(t), c_1(t)]$; $\pi^0(t) = \pi[c_0(t), c_0(t)]$ denote, respectively, the operating profits of the firm that succeeds in making the discovery – the winner; the operating profits of the firm that fails to make the discovery – the loser; and the operating profits of each of the two firms prior to the discovery being made.

It turns out to be easier to work with hazard rates as the control variables. So let z now denote the hazard rate chosen by a typical firm, and let $\gamma(z)$ be the flow level of R&D that this firm needs to undertake in order to generate this hazard. Assume that

$$\gamma(0) = 0; \text{ and, } \forall z \geq 0, \gamma'(z) > 0; \gamma''(z) > 0$$

So the marginal R&D cost of increasing the hazard rate is positive and increasing.

Finally assume that both firms can borrow and lend at the rate of interest $r > 0$.

Then the·expected present value of profits of, say, firm 1, is

$$V(z_1, z_2; t) = \frac{z_1 \dfrac{\pi^w(t)}{r} + z_2 \dfrac{\pi^\ell(t)}{r} + \pi^0(t) - \gamma(z_1)}{z_1 + z_2 + r}$$

Each firm chooses its hazard rate to maximise the expected present value of profits, taking as given the hazard rate chosen by the other firm. It is then relatively easy to show that the essential determinant of the Nash equilibrium hazard rate/R&D is the *competitive threat*

$$G(t) \equiv \pi^w(t) - \pi^\ell(t)$$

To understand how the tax affects the equilibrium level of R&D, we therefore need to know how it affects the competitive threat. An increase in the tax will reduce profits for both the winner and the loser, the question is whether the effect is greater for the winner or for the loser. Once again there are two offsetting effects. The *direct effect* is that, precisely because the winner has the new technology, its costs are increased less by the tax increase than are those of the loser. However the *indirect effect* is that because the winner has a greater output than the loser, its profits are more affected by any given increase in costs. In principle the competitive threat can either rise or fall with an increase in the tax. One clear, but extreme, case where the competitive threat will definitely fall with an increase in the tax, is that where the cost difference between winner and loser is so great that the loser is driven from the market. In this case the competitive threat is just the profit of the winner, and this definitely falls with an increase in the tax.

More generally, the competitive threat will fall when the difference in market share between winner and loser is sufficiently large and rise when the share difference is small. Three factors will determine which of these cases arise: (i) the extent of the improvement in technology; (ii) the size of the tax; (iii) the nature of demand, and hence the importance of cost differences in determining market share.

While, as before, we may take the view that environmental costs are a relatively small share of total costs, nevertheless the nature of the market may still be such that relatively small differences in costs have large effects on market share, so we cannot quite so easily rule out the possibility that the tax will reduce the competitive threat and hence the incentive to innovate.

Example Suppose that the inverse demand curve is

$$p = a - X$$

Let $\alpha = a - b$. Then, in order for the loser to have positive market share, it is necessary that

$$\alpha > t(2e_0 - e_1) \tag{20}$$

On the other hand

$$\frac{dG}{dt} = 3(e_0 - e_1)\alpha - t(e_0 + e_1) \tag{21}$$

so

$$\frac{dG}{dt} < 0 \Leftrightarrow \alpha < t(e_0 + e_1)]$$ (22)

For these two conditions to hold simultaneously we need

$$t(2e_0 - e_1) < \alpha < t(e_0 + e_1)$$ (23)

This implies $e_1 > \frac{e_0}{2}$, so the new technology should not in fact be too great an advance on the old one, but, once that condition is met the remaining restriction implied on (23) is on how the difference between the choke price a and the principal component of unit costs, b, relates to both the tax rate and the emission levels.

Thus an increase in the emissions tax can causes R&D to fall, even if environmental costs are a small part of overall costs.

So the general conclusion that we reach from this analysis is that, while the effects of taxes on R&D is subject to exactly the same two types of effects working in opposite directions that we encountered in the analysis of non-tournament models, we cannot rule out the possibility that higher environmental taxes might indeed discourage R&D by appealing to the fact that environmental costs are just a small part of total costs. This is because what matters now in determining R&D is profit differences rather than profit levels, and so the competitiveness of the market also has a part to play in determining the effects.

3.1 Extensions and connections with the literature

A number of extensions of this analysis have appeared in the literature.

3.1.1 Extension to an international setting

Once again we can think of this as arising when each firm is located in a different country, and so faces a potentially different tax rate. This is the approach taken by Ulph (1994). However, as in the case of non-tournament models all we have to do is to replace total derivatives of profit functions with partial derivatives. Once again this does not affect the qualitative comparative static results.

3.1.2 Other instruments

Cadot and Sinclair-Desgagne(1996) consider the use of standards, but in the context of a rather different model from that set out above. Here we can take it that the two firms are in different countries. One firm has actually discovered and adopted the new technology – perhaps under pressure of tighter standards in that country. The firm in the other country can now adopt the new technology, albeit at a cost, which is assumed to be sufficiently large that it would not immediately adopt the new technology. The government in that country therefore faces a dilemma. It can either enforce tough standards which will force the firm to adopt the new technology, but will also impose very large adoption costs. On the other hand if it delays the imposition of standards the firm will do nothing and the game will start over again next period with no progress towards the new technology. Cadot and Sinclair-Desgagne show that a desirable incentive scheme involves the government threatening to impose tough standards randomly, with the probability of tough regulation being introduced falling as the firm makes progress in improving its emissions.

Carraro and Topa (1995) consider a similar problem of the design of emission taxes and adoption/innovation subsidies to promote the optimal adoption of some new technology, but here there are two firms involved, and they make strategic decisions as to when to adopt. The adoption decision by any firm involves trading off the fixed costs of switching to a cleaner technology against the savings in emissions taxes. But the size of the fixed costs depend on the date at which the technology is adopted. They show that it is optimal to have diffusion – firms do not adopt simultaneously. Carraro and Soubeyran (1996) extend this analysis to the case where there are many firms/plants.

The issue of adoption is also addressed by Requate (1994) who also examines the role of tradable permits in inducing adoption.

4 Product innovation

So far we have operated under the assumption that, in the absence of government policy, firms would have no incentive to respond to environmental concerns, and hence no incentive to innovate. However consumers may have an interest in the environmental properties of the products they consume, so the normal forces that drive firms to differentiate their products could lead them, or at least some of them, to improve the environmental characteristics of their products. There has been little systematic analysis of this issue, so in this section I will briefly review a couple of contributions.

4.1 Energy efficiency

The first is by Conrad (1995). He considers the case where, quite plausibly, consumers are interested in the energy efficiency of the goods they buy. He considers the case where the goods in question are consumer durables, so, if they buy one at all, each consumer just buys one unit of this good. Let q

denote the producer price of energy, and assume that the government imposes an energy tax t. Then the consumer price of energy is $p_e = q + t$, and the effective cost to a consumer of buying a good with purchase p and with energy efficiency e is

$$C(p,e;p_e) \equiv p + p_e.e \tag{24}$$

The energy efficiency of a product depends on the amount of R&D, z, undertaken by a firm via the function $e(z)$ which satisfies all the conditions specified in (1). Firms can choose both the price of their product and its energy efficiency. Firms therefore have two routes by which they can lower the effective consumer cost of their product and so increase its demand – they can cut the price or they can invest in making their product more energy efficient. The cost implications of these different routes are very different. Cutting the price incurs forgone revenue, whereas increasing energy efficiency incurs additional fixed costs.

A key factor in determining the balance between these two alternatives is clearly the consumer price of energy, which will be positive even if the tax rate is zero. An important insight which this model therefore offers is that firms may have incentives to undertake energy-saving R&D even in the absence of any explicit government policy.[2]

The question is how changes in the energy price affect both the energy efficiency of products, e, and their price, p.

Conrad considers two cases. The first is that where there is a single monopoly producer. Aggregate demand depends on the effective cost to the consumer of buying the good. Conrad shows that

(i) whether an increase in the energy price raises or lowers the energy efficiency of the product depends on the difference between the elasticity of demand and the share of energy in total consumer costs – compare with (8);

(ii) whether or not the equilibrium price p, rises, depends on whether or not the total energy cost of the product rises, which in turn depends on the value of $k(z)$ – compare with (6).

In other words this model effectively replicates all the results we learned from the case of process innovation in section 2. A moment's reflection reveals that this is because it really does not matter whether it is the firm or the consumer that has to bear the energy costs. In other words we could think of the firm as charging the consumer a price C and meeting the energy costs itself. In terms of consumer demand and firm profits, this changes nothing.

Conrad goes on to consider the case of duopoly where the products of the two firms are implicitly differentiated by some factor other than energy efficiency. Here he considers two subcases: (a) firms choose prices and energy efficiency levels simultaneously; (b) firms act strategically, choosing efficiency levels in one stage, and then prices in the next. Once again the results effectively duplicate those for the case of process innovation surveyed in section 2.

So the important insight we gain from this analysis is that if the 'environmental' characteristic which consumers care about is reflected only in the effective cost they incur in consuming the product, then the analysis of product innovation is formally identical to that of process innovation. This suggests that if we are to get new insights into how consumer pressure might lead firms to innovate in order to produce more environmentally friendly products then we have to model consumers as caring directly about the characteristics of the goods they purchase, and to this approach we now turn.

4.2 'Green consumerism'

There has recently been an upsurge of interest in applying the conventional theory of product differentiation to analysing consumer demand for environmentally friendly products. The idea is that goods differ in a number of characteristics amongst which might be the level of emissions associated with their production or consumption. We could plausibly suppose that the environmental friendliness of a product is a characteristic which consumers care about directly in just the same way as they care about any other characteristic. However the existing literature adopting this approach has operated in a static framework and has not explicitly addressed the innovation issues.

A model which considers innovation explicitly is that of Owen and Ulph (1994). Here goods differ in two characteristics. Although their analysis is general we could interpret one of these characteristics as being the environmental friendliness of the product as reflected, say, in the reciprocal of the level of emissions per unit of output. Consumers differ in the absolute and relative weights they attach to these two characteristics in determining their view of the quality of any good that is on offer. There are two firms, and they can spend R&D on improving either or both characteristics. Owen and Ulph allow for the possibility that there might be economies of scope which mean that there might be cost advantages to pursuing both types of product improvement rather than specialising in just one.

The firms have to decide how much product improvement they should undertake in each of the two characteristics. If they both specialise and each improves just one (though obviously different) characteristic then they are never involved in pure price competition. If they both try to improve both characteristics then they run the risk that they both come up with identical products, in which case price competition would eliminate operating profits. On the other hand one of them might come up with a 'superproduct' which dominates the other in both dimensions. Owen and Ulph explore how the equilibrium outcomes vary with factors such as the degree of economies of scope.

This model clearly has the property that consumer pressure could lead firms to reduce emissions even in the absence of a tax.

As indicated, the model is not set up explicitly in the context of environmental concerns, and an obvious research question therefore is to explore the impact of environmental taxation within such a model.

However while this approach to modelling green consumerism offers useful insights an important objection is precisely that it treats environmental attributes just like any other, and, in particular, does not explain why consumers might care about this attribute. At the very least one would think that consumers' degree of concern ought to relate to the severity of the pollution problem. More fundamentally, green consumerism is clearly a response to the market failure created by the externality, and one therefore has to address all the questions involved in modelling why consumers would rationally choose not to free-ride. One approach to this is contained in Ulph (1995), and there is an interesting research agenda in trying to integrate this with the innovation questions.

There is therefore considerable scope for further work on product innovation.

5 Conclusions

In this chapter I have surveyed and synthesised the recent literature on environmental policy and innovation in which a full account has been taken of how both environmental policy and the nature of the technology affect product market competition.

There is a rather simple common structure underlying all the various models, and this shows that there are two effects of environmental policy on innovation. The *direct effect* is to alter the effectiveness of R&D in lowering costs. However the *indirect effect* of the policy is to change the value to the firm of lowering costs. These effects go in opposite directions, though the sign depends on the nature of the policy instrument. An environmental tax has a positive direct effect and negative indirect effect, whereas standards have a negative direct effect and positive indirect effect. These conclusions are very general and do not depend greatly on the nature of either product market competition or R&D competition. However the balance between the two effects does depend on the nature of R&D competition. So in non-tournament models it will typically be the case that higher environmental taxes will stimulate R&D, whereas in tournament models the balance between the effects depends sensitively on the competitiveness of the product market.

There are two major directions for future research.

The first is policy design. The current discussion of policy design pays insufficient attention to the fundamental market failures, and to the range of policy instruments needed to address these. In particular more care is needed in thinking separately about the amount of R&D that is to be done and the amount of information that is to be shared. Some recent work on research joint ventures could be usefully extended to the case of environmental innovation.

The second is to look more carefully at product innovation and in particular at modelling how factors like green consumerism might put pressure on firms to innovate, even in the absence of government policy.

Notes

Financial support from Fondezione ENJ. E. Mattei is gratefully acknowledged.
1 See, for example, Barrett (1994), Carraro and Siniscalco (1992, 1994), Katsoulacos and Xepapadeas (1996), Simpson (1995), Simpson and Bradford (1993), A. Ulph (1992, 1993a, 1993b, 1996a, 1996b), A. Ulph and D. Ulph (1996), D. Ulph (1994).
2 However care must be taken in interpreting this result. It does not really mean that this investment is in any sense environmentally friendly. For if there were no externalities associated with energy consumption and, if its price correctly reflected its scarcity, then firms would just be responding to normal market signals to conserve scarce resources. There would only be an issue of environmental friendliness if there were any otherwise unpriced externalities which the tax was trying to correct.

References

Barrett, S. (1994), 'Strategic Environmental Policy and International Trade', *Journal of Public Economics*, 54, 325–38.
Beath, J., Y. Katsoulacos and D. Ulph (1995), 'Game-Theoretic Models to the Modelling of Technological Change', in P. Stoneman (ed.), *Handbook of the Economics of Innovation and Technological Change*, Oxford: Basil Blackwell, pp. 132–81.
Cadot, O. and B. Sinclair-Desgagne (1996), 'Innovation under the Threat of Stricter Environmental Standards', in C. Carraro, Y. Katsoulacos and A. Xepapadeas (eds.), *Environmental Policy and Market Structure*, Dordrecht: Kluwer, pp. 131–41.
Carraro, C. and D. Siniscalco (1992), 'International Competition and Environmental Innovation Subsidy', *Environmental Resource Economics*, 2, 183–200.

(1994), 'Environmental Policy Reconsidered: The Role of Technological Innovation', *European Economic Review*, 38, 545–55.

Carraro, C. and A. Soubeyran (1996), 'Environmental Policy and the Choice of Production Technology', in C. Carraro, Y. Katsoulacos and A. Xepapadeas (eds.), *Environmental Policy and Market Structure*, Dordrecht: Kluwer, pp. 151–80.

Carraro, C. and G. Topa (1995), 'Taxation and Environmental Innovation', in C. Carraro and J. Filar (eds.), *Game-Theoretic Models of the Environment*, Boston: Birckauser.

Conrad, K. (1995), 'Energy Tax and R&D Competition: The Case of Energy Efficient Consumer Durables', University of Mannheim Discussion Paper, 531–95.

Downing, P.B. and L.J. White (1986), 'Innovation in Pollution Control', *Journal of Environmental Economics and Management*, 13, 18–29.

Katsoulacos, Y. and D. Ulph (1996), 'Endogenous Information Sharing and Technology Policy', CEPR Discussion Paper, No. 1407.

Katsoulacos, Y. and A. Xepapadeas (1996), 'Environmental Innovation, Spillovers and Optimal Policy Rules', in C. Carraro, Y. Katsoulacos and A. Xepapadeas (eds.), *Environmental Policy and Market Structure*, Dordrecht: Kluwer, pp. 143–50.

Magat, W. (1979), 'The Effects of Environmental Regulation on Innovation', *Law and Contemporary Problems*, 43, 4–25.

Malueg, D.A. (1989), 'Emission Credit Trading and the Incentive to Adopt New Pollution Abatement Technology', *Journal of Environmental Economics and Management*, 18, 297–300.

Milliman, S. R. and R. Prince (1989), 'Firm Incentives to Promote Technological Change in Pollution Control', *Journal of Environmental Economics and Management*, 17, 247–65.

Owen, R. and D. Ulph (1994), 'Racing in Two Dimensions', *Journal of Evolutionary Economics*, 4, 185–206.

Porter, M. (1991), 'America's Green Strategy', *Scientific American*, 168

Requate, T. (1994), 'Incentives to Innovate under Emission Taxes and Tradeable Permits', Discussion Paper, University of Bielefeld.

Simpson, R.D. (1995), 'Optimal Pollution Taxation in a Cournot Duopoly', *Environmental and Resource Economics* (forthcoming).

Simpson R.D. and R.L. Bradford (1993), 'Taxing Variable Cost: Environmental Regulation as Industrial Policy', *Journal of Environmental Economics and Management* (forthcoming).

Ulph, A. (1992), 'The Choice of Environmental Policy Instruments and Strategic International Trade', in R. Pethig (ed.), *Conflicts, and Cooperation in Managing Environmental Resources*, Berlin: Springer-Verlag.

(1993a), 'Environmental Policy and International Trade when Governments and Producers Act Strategically', *Journal of Environmental Economics and Management* (forthcoming).

(1993b), 'Strategic Environmental Policy, International Trade and the Single European Market', in J. Braden, H. Folmer and T. Ulen (eds.), *Environmental*

Policy and Political Integration: The European Community and the United States, Edward Elgar.

(1996a), 'Strategic Environmental Policy', in C. Carraro, Y. Katsoulacos and A. Xepapadeas (eds.), *Environmental Policy and Market Structure*, Dordrecht: Kluwer, pp. 99–127.

(1996b), 'Environmental Policy and International Trade – A Survey of Recent Economic Analysis', chapter 6 in this volume.

Ulph, A. and D. Ulph (1996), 'Trade, Strategic Innovation and Strategic Environmental Policy – A General Analysis', in C. Carraro, Y. Katsoulacos and Xepapadeas (eds.), *Environmental Policy and Market Structure*, Dordrecht: Kluwer, pp. 181–208.

Ulph, D. (1994), 'Strategic Innovation and Strategic Environmental Policy', in C. Carraro (ed.), *Trade Innovation, Environment*, Dordrecht: Kluwer.

(1995), 'A Theory of Green Consumerism', mimeo, University College, London.

4 Environmental policy, distortionary labour taxation and employment: pollution taxes and the double dividend

A. Lans Bovenberg

1 Introduction

Environmental policy is traditionally analysed assuming that pollution externalities are the only market failures. In recent years, however, policy makers have increasingly recognised the importance of interactions between environmental policy and other policies aimed at addressing non-environmental distortions. In particular, the revenues from pollution taxes can be used to cut other, distortionary taxes. In conducting such an environmental tax reform, governments may reap a 'double dividend' – not only a cleaner environment but also non-environmental benefits associated with lower distortionary taxes (see e.g., Pearce (1991), Pezzey (1992), and Repetto et al. (1992)). Governments in Europe are particularly concerned about the adverse impact of high levels of distortionary labour taxation on employment and labour supply. Some analysts claim that a shift from labour towards environmental taxation may help to boost employment by encouraging employers to substitute labour for polluting inputs (including energy). Moreover, lower levels of labour taxation might stimulate labour supply.

The non-environmental dividend can be defined in various ways.[1] This chapter focuses on the non-environmental dividend in terms of higher levels of employment. However, in addition to employment, other economic variables, such as transfers and profits, may directly impact overall welfare. Therefore, at several places, the chapter refers to changes in these non-environmental variables also as dividends.

The rest of this chapter is organised as follows. Section 2 develops a simple general equilibrium model to explore the employment and welfare effects of an environmental tax reform, i.e., raising environmental taxes and using the revenues to cut labour taxes. Due to the presence of a distortionary labour tax, a decline in employment produces a first-order loss in welfare (section 3). Section 4 reveals that an environmental tax reform reduces employment. Intuitively, even though public spending remains constant, an environmental tax reform raises the overall tax burden – the so-called tax burden effect. In particular, the private sector incurs additional abatement costs in order to expand the supply of the public good of the environment. The associated higher tax burden is entirely borne by workers, as general equilibrium effects cause the real wage to drop. Hence, an environmental tax reform replaces an *explicit* tax on labour by a higher *implicit* tax on labour. With workers thus paying for the cleaner environment, employment declines.

Section 5 deals with the optimal level of pollution taxes. It reveals that the presence of distortionary taxes may reduce optimal environmental taxes below the Pigovian level. Intuitively, a marginal reduction of pollution taxes below their Pigovian level alleviates the tax distortion in the labour market.

The chapter then proceeds by exploring whether various real-world complications may upset the two major results derived in sections 4 and 5, namely, first, that an environmental tax reform fails to produce a non-environmental dividend in terms of higher employment and second, that, in the presence of distortionary taxes, the optimal environmental tax is lower than the Pigovian tax. Section, 6 elaborates on the feedback of environmental benefits on the labour market. It reveals that the employment impact of an environmental tax reform depends on the specific features of the public environmental good. To illustrate, if the environment is a public *capital* good rather than a public *consumption* good, the environmental benefits accrue in the form of higher wages, thereby raising labour supply. In this case, the *net* tax burden (i.e., the balance between, on the one hand, the abatement costs, and, on the other hand, the benefits in the form of a higher labour productivity) may fall rather than rise.

Sections 7 and 8 demonstrate how an environmental tax reform can shift the tax burden away from workers towards those outside the labour force, the so-called tax shifting effect. Section 7 focuses on pollution taxes on consumption. Here, the employment dividend comes at the cost of a negative dividend, namely a drop in the living standards of those dependent on transfer incomes. Section 8 deals with pollution taxes on intermediate inputs and shows how these taxes can also be shifted by labour – in this case to the owners of other factors of production.

Section 9 incorporates involuntary unemployment due to a rigid and too high consumer wage in a model with a non-labour production factor. Hence, it analyses the interaction between three market imperfections: not only pollution externalities and distortionary taxes, but also rigid wages due to malfunctioning labour markets. If the profit tax on the non-labour production factor is less than 100 per cent, the introduction of a pollution tax yields a triple dividend, i.e., increases in environmental quality, employment and profits. Hence, in contrast to the outcome in section 7, an employment dividend does not require a drop in non-labour incomes. The reason is that the initial tax system is suboptimal from a non-environmental point of view. In this case, the net tax burden effect is negative because the non-environmental efficiency gains associated with a move towards an optimal tax system from a non-environmental point of view more than offset the rise in the tax burden due to additional abatement costs.

Section 10 investigates optimal taxation if the tax system faces the three-fold task of raising public revenues, reducing involuntary unemployment and internalising pollution externalities. It is shown that a marginal environmental reform boosts employment if the initial tax system is optimal from a non-environmental point of view. However, profits decline. Moreover, large increases in pollution taxes harm employment, especially in the long run and in small open economies in which non-labour factors are mobile internationally.

Section 11 provides a microeconomic foundation for involuntary unemployment and wage formation in the form of a labour market model with search and hiring costs. Within this framework, the tax burden can be shifted towards those collecting unemployment benefits. Shifting the tax burden in this way reduces the tax burden on employment in the formal sector. Moreover, it moderates consumer wages by weakening the bargaining position of workers by making the outside option of workers less attractive.

2 The model

Production is described by a constant returns to scale production function $F(NL,X,R)$ with aggregate labour (the product of the number of households, N, and per-capita labour supply, L), a 'clean' intermediate good (X) and a 'dirty' intermediate good (R) as inputs. Firms maximise profits under perfect competition and thus equalise the marginal product of each factor to its user cost

$$F_{NL}(1,X/NL,R/NL)=w_p \tag{1}$$

$$F_X(1,X/NL,R/NL)=1+t_X \tag{2}$$

$$F_R(1,X/NL,R/NL)=1+t_R \tag{3}$$

where t_X and t_R stand for the taxes on clean and dirty intermediate inputs, respectively. w_p represents the producer wage, while a subscript denotes a partial derivative with respect to a particular variable. The last two first-order conditions yield the demands for the two intermediate inputs conditional on the level of employment:

$$X=NLx(1+t_X;1+t_R); \quad R=NLr(1+t_X;1+t_R) \tag{4}$$

Substituting (4) into (1), we find the producer wage in terms of t_X and t_R

$$w_p=\Omega(1+t_X;1+t_R) \tag{5}$$

where

$$\frac{\partial\Omega}{\partial(1+t_x)}=-\frac{X}{NL}; \quad \frac{\partial\Omega}{\partial(1+t_R)}=-\frac{R}{NL} \tag{6}$$

Output can be used for public consumption (G), for demand for clean or dirty intermediate inputs and for household consumption of a 'clean' and 'dirty' consumption good (per-capita consumption is denoted by, respectively, C and D). Hence, commodity market equilibrium is given by

$$F(NL,X,R)=G+X+R+NC+ND \tag{7}$$

We normalise units so that the constant rates of transformation between the five produced commodities are unity.

Environmental quality, E, deteriorates with the quantity used of dirty intermediate and dirty consumption goods

$$E=e(R,ND) \quad e_R,e_{ND}<0 \tag{8}$$

Private decision makers ignore environmental externalities.

The representative household faces the following budget constraint:

$$C+(1+t_D)D=wL \tag{9}$$

where t_D denotes the tax on dirty consumption and w is the after-tax wage rate. The household maximises utility $u(C,D,1-L,G,e(R,ND))^2$ subject to the household budget constraint (9). This yields

$$u_c=\lambda \tag{10}$$

$$u_D=\lambda(1+t_D) \tag{11}$$

$$u_{(1-tL),}=\lambda w \tag{12}$$

where λ represents marginal utility of income.

The government budget constraint amounts to

$$G=t_X X+t_R R+t_D ND+t_L wNL \tag{13}$$

We assume (without loss of generality) that the clean consumption commodity is untaxed. The labour tax rate t_L is an *ad valorem* on wages ($w_p=w(1+t_L)$).

3 Welfare effects of tax reforms

The welfare effects of a revenue-neutral change in the tax mix (i.e., a change in taxes such that $dG=0$) are derived by taking the total differential of utility

$$du=u_cdC+u_DdD-u_{1-L}dL+u_Ee_RdR+Nu_Ee_{ND}dD \qquad (14)$$

Substituting (10), (11) and (12) into (14), we can write

$$\frac{du}{u_c}=dC+(1+t_D)dD-wdL+\frac{u_Ee_RdR}{u_C}+\frac{Nu_Ee_{ND}dD}{u_C} \qquad (15)$$

Taking the total differential of goods-market equilibrium (7) and substituting (1), (2) and (3), we find

$$Nw_pdL+t_XdX+t_RdR=NdC+NdD \qquad (16)$$

Using (16) to eliminate dC from (15), we arrive at

$$\frac{du}{u_c}=wt_LdL+\left[t_D-\frac{Nu_E(-e_{ND})}{u_C}\right]dD+\left[t_R-\frac{Nu_E(-e_R)}{u_C}\right]\frac{dR}{N}+t_X\frac{dX}{N} \qquad (17)$$

Equation (17) shows the welfare impacts associated with the changes in labour supply, input demands and consumption. The first term on the right-hand side of (17) stands for the distortionary effect in the labour market, which is regulated by the pre-existing tax on labour income. If the existing tax rate on wage income is positive, an expansion of employment raises welfare. Intuitively, at the margin, the social benefits of employment exceed the social opportunity costs because, with the tax on labour, the marginal product of labour exceeds the marginal opportunity cost (the value of forgone leisure). In particular, the additional production from one additional unit of labour not only compensates the worker for giving up leisure but also yields tax revenue. Hence, by strengthening the economic base of the public sector, employment yields a public benefit to society over and above the compensation to the private supplier of labour.

The next two terms on the right-hand side of (17) correspond to the effects on the environmental margin. The welfare impact of a marginal increase in the demand for dirty goods amounts to the difference between, on the one hand, a tax term, which measures the social benefits of additional tax revenue due to a wider revenue base, and, on the other hand, the marginal social damage from pollution. If the pollution levies t_D and t_R are initially zero, a marginal reduction in the demand for the dirty commodity enhances overall welfare by reducing the adverse pollution externalities.

In the 'first-best' case, in which there is no need to finance public spending through distortionary taxation (i.e., if $t_L,t_X=0$), the optimal values of t_i,

$i=D,R$ simply correspond to the Pigovian taxes. These taxes fully internalise the adverse external effects of pollution:

$$t_D=\frac{Nu_E(-e_{ND})}{u_C}; \ t_R=\frac{Nu_E(-e_R)}{u_C} \tag{18}$$

Substituting (18) into (17), one finds that in this first-best case, the beneficial environmental effects associated with less dirty consumption (e.g., $[Nu_E(-e_D)/u_C]dD$) exactly offset the adverse welfare effects due to an erosion of the tax base (e.g., t_DdD). In the absence of distortionary labour taxation, incremental changes in employment do not affect welfare because the social opportunity costs of these transactions exactly offset the social benefits at the margin.

For the more general case where distortionary taxes are present, we can diagnose the effects of tax changes by rearranging expression (17):

$$\frac{du}{u_C}=-\frac{u_E}{u_C}\left[N(-e_{ND})dD+N(-e_R)\frac{dR}{N}\right]$$
$$+\left[wt_LdL+t_DdD+t_R\frac{dR}{N}+t_X\frac{dX}{N}\right] \tag{19}$$

The first term at the right-hand side of equation (19) corresponds to the welfare effect of changes in environmental quality. The last term in square brackets stands for the impact on the tax base. This tax-base effect represents the 'gross' distortionary costs (i.e., the costs before netting out the environmental benefits) of the tax-induced changes in the allocation of resources; it represents the consequences of a different tax mix for the efficiency of the tax system as an instrument to raise revenue. In particular, an erosion of the tax base indicates that the tax system becomes less efficient as a revenue-raising device as higher marginal tax rates are required to collect the same amount of revenue.

The tax-base effect can also be written as the change in real private (after-tax) income enjoyed by households, dY^D, by taking the total differential of the government budget constraint (13) (with $dG=0$) and using (5) and (6) and $w_p=w(1+t_l)$

$$wt_LdL+t_DdD+t_R\frac{dR}{N}+t_X\frac{dX}{N}=Ldw-Ddt_D=-dY^D \tag{20}$$

We can employ expression (19) to examine the double-dividend argument: the two 'dividends' are represented by the two terms in square brackets in equation (19). The tax-base effect corresponds to the non-environmental dividend of environmental taxes. If the double dividend hypothesis were to hold (small), environmental taxes would not only raise environmental quality, but also, by expanding the base of the distortionary labour income tax, would reduce the tax burden on private incomes. In this way, pre-existing distortions in the labour market would make pollution taxes more attractive.

4 An environmental tax reform: effects on employment and welfare

Consider now a situation where the government raises the pollution taxes on household consumption and intermediate inputs. Let the policy change be revenue neutral: here the government keeps the budget in balance by adjusting the tax rate on labour. The tax rate on clean intermediate demand is assumed to be zero (i.e., $t_X=0$). Utility is given by $u=u(M(Q(C,D), 1-L),G,E)$. Hence, private goods are (weakly) separable from public goods G and E. Environmental quality and public consumption thus do not directly affect private demands. The subutility function Q aggregating clean and dirty consumption into a composite consumption good is homothetic. Hence, in the absence of environmental externalities, a uniform tax on clean and dirty consumption is optimal (see, e.g., Auerbach (1985, section 6.1)).

To find the general equilibrium effects of the pollution tax on dirty consumption, t_D, on employment, one first derives $(u_D/u_C)=(1+t_D)$ from (10) and (11). Taking the total differential, we find

$$\tilde{C}-\tilde{D}=\sigma_H \tilde{t}_D \tag{21}$$

where $\tilde{t}\equiv dt_D/(1+t_D)$. For other variables, $a\sim$ stands for a relative change. σ_H represents the substitution elasticity between clean and dirty consumption in the subutility function $Q(C,D)$. In deriving (21), we have used the assumption that, in private utility, leisure is weakly separable from the produced commodities C and D. Under these separability assumptions and homotheticity of the subutility function $Q(C,D)$, the first-order conditions for optimal household behaviour can be written as $u_Q/u_{1-L}=p_Q/w$, where p_Q is the ideal consumer price index of the consumption basket Q. Taking the total differential of this first-order condition and using (21) and the total differential of the household budget constraint (9), we find

$$\tilde{L}=V(\sigma_V-1)\tilde{w}_R \tag{22}$$

$$\tilde{C}=\tilde{L}+\tilde{w}_R+(1-\alpha_C)\sigma_H \tilde{t}_D \tag{23}$$

$$\tilde{D}=\tilde{L}+\tilde{w}_R-\alpha_C\sigma_H \tilde{t}_D \tag{24}$$

where σ_V stands for the substitution elasticity between leisure (i.e., $1-L$) and composite consumption, $\alpha_C\equiv C/wL$ is the share of non-polluting consumption in overall household consumption and $\tilde{w}_R\equiv\tilde{w}-\tilde{p}_Q$ represents the relative change in the real after-tax wage.

To find the impact of the pollution tax on intermediate inputs, we derive from the second part of (4)

$$\tilde{R} = \tilde{L} - \sigma_F \tilde{t}_R \tag{25}$$

where $\tilde{t}_R \equiv dt_R/(1 + t_R)$ and

$$\sigma_F \equiv -\frac{\partial r}{\partial t_R} \frac{(1 + t_R)}{r} \tag{26}$$

We can write goods market equilibrium (16) as (with $t_X = 0$)

$$w_L \tilde{L} + \theta_R w_R \tilde{R} = (1 - \theta_L) w_L [\alpha_C \tilde{C} + ((1 - \alpha_C)/(1 + t_D)) \tilde{D}] \tag{27}$$

where $\theta_i \equiv t_i/(1 + t_i)$, $i = L, R$ and w_L and w_R represent the production shares of labour and dirty intermediate inputs in production, respectively. Substituting (22), (23), (24) and (25) into (27) (with $t_X = 0$), we arrive at

$$\tilde{L} = \frac{\beta_L}{\Delta} [-\theta_R w_R \sigma_F \tilde{t}_R - \theta_D \alpha_C (1 - \alpha_C) w_L (1 - \theta_L) \sigma_H \tilde{t}_D] \tag{28}$$

where

$$\Delta \equiv S - \beta_L T \tag{29}$$

$$S \equiv (1 - \theta_L) w_L (1 - \theta_D (1 - \alpha_C)) \tag{30}$$

$$T \equiv w_L \theta_L + \theta_R w_R + \theta_D (1 - \alpha_C) w_L (1 - \theta_L) \tag{31}$$

where $\theta_D \equiv t_D/(1 + t_D)$ and $\beta_L \equiv V \sigma_V - V$ stands for the uncompensated wage elasticity of labour supply. The latter elasticity is positive if the substitution effect dominates the income effect, i.e., if the substitution elasticity between leisure (i.e., $1 - L$) and composite consumption, σ_V, exceeds unity. We assume that the labour-supply curve is indeed upward sloping, as most empirical studies yield positive estimates for the elasticity.[3]

Consider the effects of introducing small environmental taxes in an equilibrium without any such prior taxes (i.e., $t_D = t_R = 0$). This policy change does not affect employment, although the revenues from the pollution taxes allow for lower taxes on labour (see equation (28)). The reason is that the incidence not only of the labour taxes but also of the pollution taxes falls on labour. Substituting pollution levies for labour taxes amounts to substituting implicit taxes on labour for explicit taxes on labour.[4]

This can be illustrated with the introduction of a pollution tax on dirty consumption. The wage rate that affects the incentives to supply labour is the real after-tax wage (i.e., the wage not only after labour taxes but also after (indirect) consumption taxes). The wedge between the before-tax and real after-tax wages is widened not only by the distortionary tax on labour but also by the pollution tax on consumption. Given the constraint of revenue neutrality, the higher pollution tax exactly offsets the effect of a lower labour tax on the overall wedge between the before- and after-tax wages.

Labour bears also the burden of a pollution tax on dirty inputs. This tax reduces the demand for polluting inputs, thereby reducing labour productivity and thus the before-tax wage. If the initial pollution tax is zero, the adverse effect of the lower before-tax wage on the after-tax wage is exactly offset by the positive effect of lower taxes on labour income.

In order to gain some insight into the effects of large pollution levies, we now turn to the case in which environmental taxes are raised from an initial equilibrium in which environmental taxes are positive (i.e., t_D, $t_R > 0$). In this case, an increase in the pollution tax reduces employment.[5] The negative effect on employment is due to a decline in the real after-tax wage, which erodes the incentive to supply labour. The negative effect on the real after-tax wage comes about because the lower tax rate on labour income does not fully compensate workers for the adverse effect of the pollution levy on their real after-tax wage. This incomplete offset is due to the erosion of the base of the environmental taxes. In particular, the increase in environmental taxes causes private agents to reduce their demands for polluting goods. If the initial pollution tax rates are positive, these behavioural effects erode the base of the environmental taxes. The associated adverse implications for public revenues imply that the government is not able to reduce the tax rate on labour sufficiently to offset the adverse effect of a higher pollution levy on the real after-tax wage. The resulting lower income from an additional unit of work reduces labour supply and thus employment.

These results reveal that, as an instrument to finance public spending with the least costs to after-tax wages, environmental taxes are less efficient than a broad-based labour tax. This applies to the taxes on dirty consumption and the taxes on dirty intermediate inputs. In contrast to a labour tax, pollution taxes on dirty consumption 'distort' the composition of the consumption basket.[6] Furthermore, taxing gross instead of net output by levying pollution taxes on inputs in production 'distorts' the input mix into production. These 'distortions' enhance environmental quality but at the same time reduce the real after-tax income from work. Whereas the environmental benefits are public and thus independent of private behaviour, the costs depend on the amount of labour supplied. Indeed, by enhancing environmental quality, pollution taxes expand the overall supply of public goods, thereby raising the overall tax burden as measured by the burden of the provision of public goods on private incomes. This additional tax burden corresponds to the abatement costs. These compliance costs associated with environmental protection are 'hidden' in the sense that they are not reflected in higher tax revenues collected by the government.

Indeed, if the government adopts pollution taxes for environmental objectives, the private sector in effect supplies the public good of the environment. The costs and benefits of environmental protection thus do not appear in the government budget.

The term between square brackets in (28) represents the additional tax burden associated with a cleaner environment. The costs of a cleaner environment depend on two elements: First, the initial pollution levies and, second, the substitution elasticities between clean and dirty commodities.

The initial pollution taxes measure the marginal abatement costs. Without prior pollution taxes, reducing a marginal unit of pollution comes free. However, the higher the initial pollution taxes are, the larger the marginal costs of increasing environmental quality become. In particular, higher initial environmental taxes intensify the adverse revenue effects associated with the erosion of the base of these environmental taxes. Hence, while small environmental taxes impose only small abatement costs, large pollution taxes tend to impose a substantial burden on private incomes.

Whereas the initial tax rates determine the costs associated with each unit of reduced pollution, the substitution elasticities between clean and dirty commodities affect the magnitude of the reduction in pollution. The larger these elasticities are, the larger the improvement in environmental quality, and thus the overall costs associated with the additional supply of this public good. Thus, a fundamental trade-off exists between, on the one hand, beneficial environmental effects and, on the other hand, favourable employment effects. The more successful environmental policy is in improving the quality of the environment, the higher the overall tax burden and thus the less likely an expansion of employment becomes. Indeed, if a pollution levy is successful in changing behaviour, it does not generate much revenue, thereby reducing the scope for reducing distortionary taxes on labour.

Armed with the general equilibrium effects on employment, we can now return to expression (17) for the welfare effects of marginal tax changes. By harming employment, pollution taxes narrow, rather than widen, the tax base. Accordingly, the gross distortionary costs of pollution levies *cum* lower labour taxes are positive and the double dividend hypothesis fails. Moreover, by eroding the base of the labour tax, environmental taxes exacerbate pre-existing tax distortions. Hence, the larger the magnitude of pre-existing tax distortions, the lower is the attractiveness of revenue-neutral pollution taxes in the sense that their gross distortionary cost will be higher. In particular, in the presence of a distortionary tax on labour, welfare would rise if the government marginally reduced the environmental tax below its Pigovian level (and, at the same time, raised the tax on labour, t_L, to offset the revenue losses).[7]

This is a typical second-best result. The theory of the second best teaches that, in a world with remaining distortions, introducing an additional distortion (i.e., reducing the environmental tax below its Pigovian value) may not necessarily reduce overall efficiency. Intuitively, the introduction of the distortion may alleviate the remaining distortions. This is exactly what happens when environmental taxes are reduced below their Pigovian level in a world with tax distortions. In particular, by raising employment, lower environmental taxes alleviate the distortions due to an excessively low level of employment.

Oates and Swabb (1988) also highlight the interaction between environment policy and tax distortions. They demonstrate that, from the viewpoint of global efficiency, communities that require high distortionary taxes on mobile capital should set relatively lax environmental standards. This would serve to offset the distortions introduced by the taxes on capital.

The second-best argument suggests that a cleaner environment is an expensive commodity if a large public sector requires high distortionary taxes. Indeed, expression (28) reveals that an important determinant of the adverse employment effect is the size of the public sector, which is closely related to the term T in the denominator Δ of the reduced form for employment (see expression (31)). A larger revenue requirement implies that an environmental tax yields a larger adverse effect on employment. The reason is that a fall in employment reduces revenues from pre-existing labour taxes and environmental taxes more substantially if these taxes are high. Hence, environmental taxes become less effective instruments for raising additional revenues and thus allow for a smaller decline in explicit tax rates on labour.

5 Optimal environmental taxes

This section uses the model presented in section 2 to derive explicit expressions for the optimal environmental taxes. The government maximises household utility subject to the government budget constraint and decentralised optimisation by firms and households. Private commodities are separable from public goods.[8] Accordingly, the government adopts its four tax instruments (t_L, t_D, t_X, t_R) to optimise

$$NV((1+t_D), w, G, e(R, ND)) + \mu[t_L wNL + t_D ND + t_X X + t_R R] \qquad (32)$$

where V represents indirect utility and μ denotes the marginal disutility of raising one unit of public revenue.

To find the optimal tax rates, we use $w = w_p/(1+t_L)$ and substitute (4) and (5) into (32) to eliminate w, X and R. Maximising with respect to t_L, we find the following first-order condition (after dividing through by $-Nw/(1+t_L)$)

80   **A. Lans Bovenberg**

$$(\lambda-\mu)L+\mu\left[t_D\frac{\partial D}{\partial w}+(t_Lw+(X/NL)t_X+(R/NL)t_R)\frac{\partial L}{\partial w}\right]$$

$$+Nu_Ee_{ND}\frac{\partial D}{\partial w}+(R/NL)Nu_Ee_R\frac{\partial L}{\partial w}=0 \tag{33}$$

where we have used Roy's identity $\frac{\partial V}{\partial w}=\lambda L$. Define

$$t_D^E\equiv\frac{Nu_E(-e_{ND})}{\mu} \tag{34}$$

$$t_R^E\equiv\frac{Nu_E(-e_R)}{\mu} \tag{35}$$

Substitution of (34) and (35) into (33) yields

$$(\lambda-\mu)L+\mu\left[(t_D-t_D^E)\frac{\partial D}{\partial w}+t_Lw\frac{\partial L}{\partial w}\right]$$

$$+\mu[(X/NL)t_X+(R/NL)(t_R-t_R^E)]\frac{\partial L}{\partial w}=0 \tag{36}$$

The first-order condition for maximising (32) with respect to t_X is given by

$$\mu\left[X+t_XNL\frac{\partial x}{\partial t_X}+(t_R-t_R^E)NL\frac{\partial r}{\partial t_X}\right]+\frac{\partial\Omega}{\partial(1+t_X)}\mu NL=0 \tag{37}$$

where we have used (34), (35) and (36). Substitution of (6) yields

$$t_X\frac{\partial x}{\partial t_X}+(t_R-t_R^E)\frac{\partial r}{\partial t_X}=0 \tag{38}$$

In an analogous way, we derive the first-order condition for t_R as

$$t_X\frac{\partial x}{\partial t_R}+(t_R-t_R^E)\frac{\partial r}{\partial t_R}=0 \tag{39}$$

Combining (38) and (39), we find

$$t_X=0 \tag{40}$$

$$t_R=t_R^E=\left[\frac{Nu_E(-e_R)}{u_C}\right]\frac{1}{\eta} \tag{41}$$

where $\eta\equiv\mu/\lambda$ stands for the marginal cost of public funds (MCPF). Substitution of (40) and (41) into (36) and the first-order condition for t_D yields

$$(\lambda-\mu)L+\mu\left[(t_D-t_D^E)\frac{\partial D}{\partial w}+t_Lw\frac{\partial L}{\partial w}\right]=0 \tag{42}$$

$$(\lambda - \mu)D - \mu\left[(t_D - t_D^E)\frac{\partial D}{\partial t_D} + t_L w \frac{\partial L}{\partial t_D}\right] = 0 \tag{43}$$

Optimal taxes on intermediate goods

Expression (40) reveals that the clean intermediate inputs should not be subject to any tax. Hence, in the absence of environmental externalities, net rather than gross output should be taxed. This is an application of the well-known optimality of production efficiency derived by Diamond and Mirrlees (1971). They demonstrated that, if production exhibits constant returns to scale,[9] an optimal tax system should not distort production. Intuitively, a tax on intermediate inputs is borne by the only primary factor of production, i.e., labour, and thus amounts to an implicit labour tax. From a revenue-raising point of view, the implicit labour tax is less efficient than an explicit tax on labour; whereas both taxes distort labour supply by reducing the consumption wage, only the input tax distorts the input mix into production.

In contrast to the tax on clean inputs, the tax on dirty inputs, t_R, is positive as long as households value environmental quality (i.e., $u_E > 0$; see expression (41)). The term between square brackets at the right-hand side of (41) corresponds to the textbook Pigovian tax (see (18)). The Pigovian tax is optimal only if the marginal cost of public funds, $\eta \equiv \mu/\lambda$, equals unity. A unitary MCPF indicates that public funds are not scarcer than private funds (as is the case if lump-sum taxes and subsidies are available or labour supply is completely inelastic). However, in a second-best world without lump-sum taxation, the MCPF typically differs from one. Indeed, the MCPF term in (41) reveals how second-best considerations affect optimal environmental taxation. In particular, the higher the MCPF is, *ceteris paribus*, the smaller becomes the optimal environmental tax.

The reason for the inverse relationship between the MCPF and the optimal environmental tax is as follows. The government employs the tax system to simultaneously accomplish two goals: raising revenues and internalising environmental externalities. If public revenues become scarcer, as indicated by a higher marginal cost of public funds, the optimal tax system focuses more on generating revenues and less on internalising pollution externalities. The conflict between raising revenues and protecting the environment exists because an environmental levy reduces pollution by encouraging taxpayers to avoid taxes. Tax avoidance not only reduces pollution but also makes it necessary to levy higher distortionary taxes to finance public spending. Accordingly, the larger the government's revenue needs are (as indicated by a higher marginal cost of public funds), the less the government can afford tax differentiation aimed at environmental protection.

Indeed, the optimal pollution tax balances the social costs of pollution against the social benefits from additional tax revenues. Therefore, the higher the social value attached to tax revenue, the higher the marginal social costs of pollution have to be to justify a given environmental tax.

High estimates for the marginal efficiency costs of the existing tax system (i.e., the MCPF) have been used in support of pollution taxes (see, for example, Pearce (1991) and Oates (1991)). Such arguments are misleading because they ignore the costs of environmental taxes in terms of exacerbating pre-existing tax distortions. These additional costs of environmental taxes are likely to be especially large if the marginal efficiency costs of the existing tax system are substantial. Therefore, the higher the efficiency costs of the existing tax structure, the higher the environmental benefits need to be in order to justify the additional costs of environmental taxes in terms of a less efficient mechanism for financing public spending. Thus, high estimates for the efficiency costs of existing taxes weaken rather than strengthen the case for environmental taxation (see also Bovenberg and Goulder (1996)). Indeed, as a public good, the environment directly competes with other public priorities.

Optimal taxes on consumption

The optimal tax on dirty consumption consists of two parts (see also Sandmo (1975), Auerbach (1985) and Bovenberg and van der Ploeg (1994b)). The first part, t_D^E, corrects for the environmental externality (use (34) with $\eta = \lambda/\mu$ and $\lambda = u_C$)

$$t_D^E = \left[\frac{N u_E(-e_D)}{u_C} \right] \frac{1}{\eta} \tag{44}$$

This term looks very similar to (41). It amounts to the Pigovian tax divided by the MCPF. The second part of the optimal pollution tax on consumption, $t_D^D \equiv t_D - t_D^E$, is the distortionary (or revenue-raising) component of the tax on polluting consumption. Together with the optimal labour tax, the optimal level of this distortionary component is determined on the basis of the familiar Ramsey formulas for raising revenues with the lowest costs to private incomes (see (42) and (43)). To illustrate, if (as assumed in section 4) clean and dirty consumption are weakly separable from leisure and if utility is homothetic, uniform taxation of clean and dirty goods is optimal from the point of view of raising revenues with the smallest burden on private incomes. Here, the optimum involves equal distortionary components of the two taxes on consumption. In this model, uniform distortionary taxes on consumption are equivalent to taxes on labour; the optimum is thus characterised by zero distortionary taxation of consumption.

Accordingly, the only non-zero component of the optimal tax on dirty consumption is the externality-correcting part (44) (i.e., $t_D^D=0$ and $t_D=t_D^E$). In this particular case, the MCPF can be written with the aid of (42) as

$$\eta=[1-t_L\beta_L]^{-1} \tag{45}$$

The MCPF thus exceeds unity if, first, the uncompensated wage elasticity of labour supply, β_L, is positive and, second, Pigovian taxes do not suffice to finance public consumption so that the distortionary tax on labour, t_L, is positive. These results are consistent with the literature on the MCPF surveyed in Ballard and Fullerton (1992). For public spending that is separable from consumer's choice on leisure and consumption, this literature finds that distortionary labour taxes raise the marginal costs of public spending above unity if the uncompensated wage elasticity of labour supply is positive. Combining (41), (44) and (45), one finds that the same condition on this uncompensated elasticity determines whether distortionary labour taxes raise the marginal cost of (the collective good of) environmental protection above its social benefit.

6 The environment as a public consumption and a public capital good

The model above assumes that the environment is a public consumption good that enters the utility function in a weakly separable way. As a direct consequence, the improved quality of the environment (i.e., the 'excess benefit' of an environmental tax reform or the 'green' dividend) does not affect the labour market. In principle, however, a cleaner environment could impact the labour market through two channels.

First, it affects labour supply if environmental quality enters household utility in a non-separable fashion. In particular, environmental quality may be complementary to leisure as a cleaner environment is likely to make leisure more enjoyable. In that case, the environmental benefits reduce labour supply, thereby strengthening the adverse employment effects associated with higher abatement costs.

In a similar way, the literature on the costs of ordinary (i.e., non-environmental) public goods in the presence of distortionary taxation has shown that the way a particular public good enters utility affects the marginal costs of financing such a public good. In particular, Atkinson and Stern (1974), Wildasin (1988) and Ballard and Fullerton (1992) explore the conditions under which distortionary taxation crowds out public spending by raising the marginal cost of public funds above unity (i.e., the marginal costs of public funds in a first-best economy with lump-sum taxes). For a public good that is separable from consumer choices on leisure and consumption, this literature finds that distortionary labour taxes raise the marginal costs of such a public good above unity if the uncompensated wage elasticity of labour supply is positive. However, if a public good is not separable but instead is a perfect substitute for private consumption, the sign of the compensated rather than *un*compensated elasticity governs the effect of distortionary taxes on the marginal costs of the public good (see Wildasin (1984)). Since compensated wage elasticities exceed uncompensated ones, such a public good is more expensive compared to a public good that enters utility in a separable way. Similarly, if environmental quality were a perfect substitute for private consumption, pollution taxes would become more costly than they would be with weakly separable environmental quality.

The second channel through which the green dividend could impact the labour market is through the positive effect of a higher environmental quality on productivity and thus the demand for labour. To illustrate this effect, let production, Y, be given by

$$Y=a(E)F(NL,X,R) \tag{46}$$

By entering production as an input, a cleaner environment acts not only as a public *consumption* good but also as a public *capital* good. For example, in agriculture, production benefits from a better quality of the soil and the air. Furthermore, less air pollution is likely to improve health and morale, thereby boosting labour productivity. Slowing down global warming avoids productivity losses in agriculture and other climate-sensitive sectors.

With the positive productivity effects of a cleaner environment, the left-hand side of the linearised equation for equilibrium on the commodity market (27) becomes

$$\frac{a'(E)}{a(E)}[e_R R\tilde{R}+e_{ND}ND\tilde{D}]+\omega_L\tilde{L}+\theta_R\omega_R\tilde{R} \tag{47}$$

Employing this expression and following the same steps as in deriving (28), we arrive at

$$\tilde{L}=\frac{\beta_L}{\Delta_p}\left[-\frac{\bar{t}_R}{1+t_R}\omega_R\sigma_F\tilde{t}_R-\frac{\bar{t}_D}{1+t_D}\alpha_C(1-\alpha_C)\omega_L(1-\theta_L)\sigma_H\bar{t}_D\right] \tag{48}$$

where

$$\Delta_p\equiv S_p-\beta_L T_p \tag{49}$$

$$S_p\equiv(1-\theta_L)w_L\left[1-\frac{\bar{t}_D}{1+t_D}(1-\alpha_c)\right] \tag{50}$$

$$T_p\equiv\theta_L\omega_L+\frac{\bar{t}_R}{1+t_R}\omega_R+\frac{\bar{t}_D}{1+t_D}(1-\alpha_c)\omega_L(1-\theta_L) \tag{51}$$

$$\bar{t}_R \equiv t_R - (-e_R)a'(E)F; \ \bar{t}_D \equiv t_D - (-e_D)a'(E)F \tag{52}$$

The two terms between square brackets in (48) can be interpreted as the *net tax burdens* of the two pollution taxes, i.e., the excess burdens associated with the additional abatement costs net of the 'excess benefits' of a cleaner environment in terms of higher productivity. If the environment is a public *consumption* good, all residents benefit from higher environmental quality – irrespective of the amount of labour supplied. Whereas the excess burden (i.e., the abatement costs) is borne privately by those who supply labour, the excess benefit is thus public. If the environment is a public *capital* good, in contrast, the benefits associated with a cleaner environment accrue in the form of a higher productivity of labour. Hence, residents with the highest supply of labour benefit most. Both the benefits and costs thus accrue privately. The net effect of a reduction in pollution on the tax burden depends on the net balance of excess costs (i.e., the first terms at the right-hand sides of (51) and (52)) and excess benefits (i.e., the second terms at the right-hand sides of (51) and (52)).

The expression for the optimal tax rate on dirty inputs becomes (see also Bovenberg and van der Ploeg (1997))

$$t_R = \left[\frac{Nu_E(-e_R)}{u_C} \right] \frac{1}{\eta} + (-e_R)a'(E)F \tag{53}$$

Compared with the case in which the environment is a pure consumption good (see expression (41)), the optimal pollution tax incorporates a term representing the adverse effect of pollution on productivity in addition to a term correcting for the consumption externality. In contrast to the first term for the consumption externality, the second term corresponding to the production effect does not involve the marginal costs of public funds.

Bovenberg and de Mooij (1997) derive an expression similar to (53) in an endogenous growth model. In this model, income taxes reduce the return on saving, thereby distorting capital accumulation. It is shown that the optimal pollution tax lies below its Pigovian level if the environment enters utility as a public consumption good. In the context of the model of the labour market developed here, the Pigovian tax on dirty inputs, t_R^p, is given by

$$t_R^p = \left[\frac{Nu_E(-e_R)}{u_C} \right] + (-e_R)a'(E)F \tag{54}$$

A comparison of (53) and (54) reveals that the Pigovian tax exceeds the optimal tax (as $\eta > 1$ if t_L, $\beta_L > 0$, see (45)). Intuitively, if the environment enters utility, the net tax burden is positive at the Pigovian tax level (i.e., $t_R^p - (-e_R)a'(E)F = Nu_E(-e_R)/u_C$). Hence, cutting the pollution tax from its

Pigovian level raises employment (see (48) and (51)), which is too low from a social point of view because of tax distortions. Whereas a marginal cut in the pollution tax below its Pigovian level exerts only a second-order effect on the environmental distortion, it implies a first-order reduction in the tax distortion. Hence, such a tax cut boosts welfare.

If the environment acts only as a public capital good and hence does not enter utility (i.e., $u_E=0$)), the net tax burden is zero at the Pigovian level (i.e., $t_R^p-(-e_R)a'(E)F=0$). Accordingly, a marginal reduction of the pollution tax below its Pigovian level does not affect employment (see (48) with $\bar{t}_R=0$) and thus does not impact the labour-tax distortion. Hence, the Pigovian tax is optimal.

This section has illustrated that, to assess the employment effects of an environmental tax reform, in principle one should explore the feedback on the economy of a higher supply of the public good of the environment. Similarly, when analysing the employment effects of a higher level of ordinary taxation, one should take into account the employment effects of the public expenditures that are financed by the additional tax revenues. The overall impact of a larger public sector on employment may well be favourable if the additional tax revenues finance public investments that substantially boost labour productivity. However, if income transfers rather than public investments are raised, labour supply is likely to fall on account of the positive income effect associated with these types of spending. In that case, the expenditure side exacerbates the adverse employment effects of the higher level of taxation. Most macroeconomic models exploring the consequences of an environmental tax reform abstract from feedback of environmental benefits on economic decisions. In particular, they ignore the impact of environmental benefits on both labour demand and labour supply. This is a valid assumption only if the environment does not enter production and enters households' utility function as a consumption good in a weakly separable way.

7 Taxes on consumption: tax shifting and non-labour incomes

The previous sections assumed that households receive only labour income. This section explores the impact of an environmental tax reform if some households consume out of non-labour income. In particular, it is assumed that there are two types of households. The first type, which will be called the 'active' household, relies entirely on labour income. The second type, the 'inactive' household, finances its consumption exclusively out of transfer incomes provided by the government. Higher taxes on consumption reduce the purchasing power of the inactive households because transfers are fixed in terms of the producer prices of the consumption goods.

Transfers are not subject to the tax on labour income. The relative changes in the demands for the two commodities (23) and (24) become

$$\tilde{C}=(1-\phi)(\tilde{w}_R+\tilde{L})-\phi(1-\alpha_C)\tilde{t}_D+(1-\alpha_c)\sigma_H\tilde{t}_D \tag{55}$$

$$\tilde{D}=(1-\phi)(\tilde{w}_R+\tilde{L})-\phi(1-\alpha_C)\tilde{t}_D-\alpha_c\sigma_H\tilde{t}_D \tag{56}$$

where ϕ denotes the share of non-labour income in aggregate household income (after labour taxes). Abstracting from pollution taxes on intermediate inputs, we arrive at the following expression for employment:

$$\tilde{L}=\frac{\beta_L}{\Delta_T}[1-\theta_D\alpha_C(1-\alpha_C)w_L(1-\theta_L)\sigma_H+\phi S(1-\alpha_C)]\tilde{t}_D \tag{57}$$

where

$$\Delta_T\equiv(1-\phi)S-\beta_L T_T \tag{58}$$

$$T_T\equiv\theta_L\omega_L(1-\phi)+\omega_L\phi+\theta_D(1-\alpha_D)\omega_L(1-\theta_L)(1-\phi) \tag{59}$$

In the absence of transfer income, expression (28) reveals that an environmental tax reform does not affect employment if the initial pollution tax is zero. If transfers are positive, in contrast, such a reform boosts employment (see (57) with $\theta_D=0$). The reason is that, unlike the case without non-labour income, the government is able to more than compensate workers for the real income loss due to a higher environmental tax. Intuitively, contrary to the labour tax, the environmental tax is not only borne by labour but also by non-labour incomes. Hence, the tax reform redistributes income from those receiving non-labour income (who pay the higher tax on dirty consumption but are not compensated with either lower labour income taxes or higher nominal transfers) towards those collecting labour income. As a direct consequence, real wages – and thus labour supply – rise. Accordingly, better environmental quality is accompanied by a higher level of employment, thereby alleviating the labour-market distortion due to the labour tax.

With positive initial pollution taxes (i.e., $\theta_D>0$), the overall impact on employment occurs through two channels. The first channel, represented by the first term in square brackets in (57), is the tax *level* effect discussed in section 4. This effect reduces employment. It operates only if the initial pollution tax is positive: only in that case does a cleaner environment require real resources at the margin.

The second channel through which an ecological tax reform impacts employment is what we call the tax *shifting* effect. This channel, represented by the second term in square brackets in expression (57), involves redistribution of income between labour and non-labour incomes. Through this channel, an environmental tax reform can raise employment if it redistributes income away from non-labour incomes to labour income. This suggests that the government typically faces a trade-off between efficiency and equity. Indeed, in terms of our model, the government can raise employment only if it cuts the real value of transfers. If the government would raise transfers to maintain the real purchasing power of these transfers after the introduction of a pollution tax, the employment impact of the higher labour taxes required to finance the additional transfers would exactly offset the positive employment effect of the tax shifting effect (see Bovenberg and de Mooij (1994b)). Accordingly, the double dividend can be reaped only at the cost of a negative dividend, namely, more inequity as the pollution tax on consumption reduces the real value of transfer income and therefore decreases welfare of the inactive household. Indeed, the government generally does not need to use environmental taxes to achieve the efficiency gains that are associated with a different income distribution due to lower transfers. In terms of the model analysed here, the government can reap these efficiency gains more directly by cutting public transfers, by subjecting these transfers to the labour income tax, or by replacing a tax on labour income by a broad-based tax on consumption.

The overall effect on employment depends on the balance between, on the one hand, the tax *level* effect, and, on the other hand, the tax *shifting* effect. Employment increases only if the tax shifting effect exceeds the tax level effect. In that case, the cleaner environment is entirely paid for by those outside the labour force.

8 Taxes on production: tax shifting and non-labour production factors

The previous section focused on pollution taxes on consumption and showed that these taxes do not need to be implicit taxes on labour income if some households consume out of non-labour income. This section deals with pollution taxes on intermediate goods and shows that labour may escape also part of the burden of these taxes. In particular, other factors of production may share the burden of these taxes with labour. In that case, replacing labour taxes by pollution taxes on intermediate inputs may involve a tax shifting effect away from labour towards other production factors, thereby benefiting employment.

To formalise this effect, assume that, rather than a clean intermediate input, a clean non-labour production factor enters production. Dirty consumption goods are abstracted from. Hence, equilibrium on the goods market is given by

$$F(NL,H,R)=G+R+NC \tag{60}$$

where the production function, F, exhibits constant returns to scale in its three arguments. H stands for the non-labour production factor,[10] which is assumed to be in fixed supply.[11] Profit maximisation gives rise to the following linearised demand equations:

$$\tilde{L}=\tilde{H}-\epsilon_{LL}\tilde{w}_p-\epsilon_{LR}\tilde{t}_R \tag{61}$$

$$\tilde{R}=\tilde{H}-\epsilon_{RR}\tilde{t}_R-\epsilon_{RL}\tilde{w}_p \tag{62}$$

where ϵ_{ij}, $i=L,R$ stands for demand elasticity of input i with respect to the producer price of input j. To obtain a better understanding of what determines the own- and cross-price elasticities of factor demand, appendix A considers three types of separable production functions in turn. Table 4.1 summarises the results for the various elasticities.

Table 4.1. *Separability in production and factor demand elasticities*

	Case (i) $Y=F(Q(L,H),R)$	Case (ii) $Y=F(Q(R,H),L)$	Case (iii) $Y=F(Q(L,R),H)$
ϵ_{LL}	$\sigma_{LH}(1-\omega_R)/\omega_H$	$(\sigma_L+\sigma_{RH}\omega_L\omega_R/\omega_H)/$ $(1-\omega_L)$	$(\sigma_{LR}\omega_R+\sigma_H\omega_L/\omega_H)/$ $(1-\omega_H)$
ϵ_{LR}	$\sigma_{LH}\omega_R/\omega_H$	$\sigma_{RH}\omega_R/\omega_H$	$[(\sigma_H/\omega_H)-\sigma_{LR}]\omega_R/$ $(1-\omega_H)$
ϵ_{RR}	$(\sigma_R+\sigma_{LH}\omega_L\omega_R/\omega_H)/$ $(1-\omega_R)$	$\sigma_{RH}(1-\omega_L)/\omega_H$	$(\sigma_{LR}\omega_L+\sigma_H\omega_R/\omega_H)/$ $(1-\omega_H)$
ϵ_{RL}	$\sigma_{LH}\omega_L/\omega_H$	$\sigma_{RH}\omega_L/\omega_H$	$[(\sigma_H/\omega_H)-\sigma_{LR}]\omega_L/$ $(1-\omega_H)$
$\epsilon_{LL}-\epsilon_{RL}$	σ_{LH}	$(\sigma_L-\omega_L\sigma_{RH})/(1-\omega_L)$	σ_{LR}
$\epsilon_{RR}-\epsilon_{LR}$	$(\sigma_R-\omega_R\sigma_{LH})/(1-\omega_R)$	σ_{RH}	σ_{LR}
ϵ_D	$\sigma_{LH}\sigma_R/\omega_H$	$\sigma_{RH}\sigma_L/\omega_H$	$\sigma_{LR}\sigma_H/\omega_H$

Note:
$\epsilon_D\equiv\epsilon_{LL}\epsilon_{RR}-\epsilon_{RL}\epsilon_{LR}>0$. For the definitions of σ's, see Appendix A.

Income from the fixed factor, which we refer to as profits, is given by

$$\Pi=F(NL,H,R)-w_pL-(1+t_R)R \tag{63}$$

where Π denotes pre-tax profits. The government levies a profit tax, τ. Higher wage costs and pollution taxes reduce after-tax profits according to

$$(1-\tau)\tilde{\Pi}=(1-\tau)[-\omega_L\tilde{w}_p-\omega_R\tilde{t}_R] \tag{64}$$

where $\tilde{\Pi}=d\Pi/Y$.

The household sector consists of two types of households: those of the first type ('labourers') supply labour but do not collect profits. The households of the other type ('capitalists') receive profits but do not participate in the labour market. Equating labour demand from (61) to labour supply from (22), we can solve for wages, employment and the demand for the polluting input in terms of the two tax rates (i.e., the labour tax and the pollution tax). In particular, employment is given by

$$\tilde{L} = \beta_L \tilde{w} = -\alpha[\epsilon_{LL}\tilde{t}_L + \epsilon_{LR}\tilde{t}_R] \tag{65}$$

and

$$\tilde{R} = -\left[\epsilon_{RR} - \frac{\epsilon_{LR}\epsilon_{RL}(1-\alpha)}{\epsilon_{LL}}\right]\tilde{t}_R - \alpha\epsilon_{RL}\tilde{t}_L \tag{66}$$

where

$$\alpha \equiv \beta_L/(\beta_L + \epsilon_{LL}) \tag{67}$$

Substituting these results in the following government budget constraint

$$(1-\tau)[\omega_L\tilde{t}_L + \omega_R\tilde{t}_R] + \theta_L\omega_L\tilde{L} + \theta_R\omega_R\tilde{R} + (\theta_L-\tau)\omega_L\tilde{\omega} = 0 \tag{68}$$

we can solve for reduction in the labour tax allowed for by an increase in the pollution tax

$$\tilde{t}_L = -\frac{\Delta_R}{\Delta_F}\tilde{t}_R \tag{69}$$

where

$$\Delta_R \equiv \omega_R(1-\tau) - \alpha\theta_L\omega_L\epsilon_{LR} - \theta_R\omega_R\left[\epsilon_{RR} - \frac{\epsilon_{LR}\epsilon_{RL}(1-\alpha)}{\epsilon_{LL}}\right]$$
$$- (\theta_L-\tau)\omega_L(1-\alpha)\frac{\epsilon_{LR}}{\epsilon_{LL}} \tag{70}$$

$$\Delta_F \equiv \alpha[\omega_L(1-\tau) - \theta_L\omega_L\epsilon_{LL} - \theta_R\omega_R\epsilon_{RL}] + (1-\alpha)\omega_L(1-\theta_L) \tag{71}$$

We assume that in the initial equilibrium the economy is on the upward-sloping parts of the Laffer curves for both the labour tax and the resource tax. Hence, the additional public revenues generated by a higher pollution tax allow for a cut in the labour tax rate. For the Laffer curves to slope upwards, the public sector should not be very large, i.e., the initial tax rates (τ, t_L and t_R) should not be too large, so that an erosion of the tax bases yields only relatively minor adverse effects for public revenues.

To uncover the effects of environmental tax reform on employment, substitute (69) into the expression for employment given by (65), and use $\omega_L\epsilon_{LR} = \omega_R\epsilon_{RL}$ to obtain

$$\tilde{L} = \alpha[(1-\tau)(\epsilon_{LL} - \epsilon_{RL}) - \theta_R\epsilon_D]\omega_R\tilde{t}_R/\Delta_F \tag{72}$$

The first term in the square brackets on the right-hand side of (72) stands for the shifting of the tax burden away from labour to the fixed factor. This tax shifting effect, which is positive,[12] exerts a positive impact on employment. The second term in square brackets on the right-hand side of (72) represents the additional tax burden associated with the costs of a cleaner environment. This tax burden effect adversely affects employment. As discussed in section 4, the magnitude of the tax burden effect depends on the initial tax rate.

Employment expands if and only if the tax shifting effect dominates the tax burden effect. In that case, the fixed factor, rather than employment, pays the additional tax burden associated with a higher quality of the environment. In particular, employment expands if the initial tax on resources is zero (i.e., $\theta_R=0$) and profits are not fully taxed away ($\tau<1$). With a zero initial pollution tax, a marginal increase in environmental quality is free so that the tax burden effect is zero. However, if profits have already been fully taxed away,[13] an environmental tax reform cannot shift the burden to (non-existing) after-tax profits. Hence, employment never expands as long as the initial pollution tax is non-negative.

To shed more light on how the production structure impacts the employment effects of an environmental tax reform, appendix B analyses the employment consequences for the three separable production functions discussed in appendix A. This analysis reveals that a necessary condition for employment to rise is that the after-tax income from the fixed factor can bear a large share of the tax burden. This requires a small rate of profit taxation and a large production share of the fixed factor, $\omega_H=I-\omega_L-\omega_R$. Moreover, for employment to rise, resources and the fixed factor must be poor substitutes. With poor substitution, the fixed factor bears a large part of the additional tax burden on resource use. In contrast to the fixed factor, labour should be a good substitute for resources in order for an employment dividend to occur. Intuitively, a large elasticity of substitution between resources and labour causes substantial substitution away from resources and towards labour if resources become more expensive relative to labour. Indeed, if labour is a better substitute for resources than the fixed factor is, the substitution effect of the tax reform dominates the (negative) output effect so that the demand for labour expands.

9 Involuntary unemployment

The previous sections assumed a well-functioning labour market in which the wage rate cleared the market. However, in Europe, the interest in the double dividend issue originates mainly in the existence of widespread involuntary unemployment. Bovenberg and van der Ploeg (1994c) analyse the consequences of an environmental tax reform in a model with involuntary unemployment due to a rigid and too high consumer wage. In other respects, the model they adopt is similar to that used in section 8 except that households are identical. Hence, each household collects income from both labour and the fixed factor. The budget constraint for each household is given by

$$C = wL + (1 - \tau)\frac{\Pi}{N} \qquad (73)$$

The presence of a labour market distortion affects the welfare analysis. In particular, the change in welfare expressed as a fraction of national income becomes

$$dU/u_C Y = \omega_L(\theta_L + s)\tilde{L} + \omega_L(\theta_R - p)\tilde{R} \qquad (74)$$

$$p \equiv \frac{Nu_E}{u_C(1 + t_R)} \qquad (75)$$

$$s \equiv \frac{w - w^*}{w_p} \qquad (76)$$

Hence, an increase in employment yields a first-order welfare gain not only because of the tax distortion θ_L, but also because of the gap, s, between the actual consumer wage, w, and the reservation wage, w^*. The reservation wage corresponds to the wage at which households would be willing to work. The wedge between the actual consumer wage and the reservation wage can be interpreted as a virtual tax on labour. This virtual tax increases if the gap between the market wage and the reservation wage expands and thus provides a measure of the distortion in the labour market due to wage rigidities.

In analogy to the labour-market distortion, the other non-tax distortion in the model (i.e., the pollution externality) can be modelled as a (negative) virtual tax. In particular, p (defined in (75)) can be interpreted as a virtual subsidy on polluting inputs on account of no price being charged for the associated environmental damages.

By substituting after-tax profits (64) and the government budget constraint (68) into (74) and using $\tilde{w} = 0$, one can write the welfare effect in an alternative way

$$dU/u_C Y = s\omega_L\tilde{L} - p\omega_R\tilde{R} + (1 - \tau)\tilde{\Pi} \qquad (77)$$

The three terms on the right-hand side of (77) represent the threefold task of the tax system. First, to reduce involuntary unemployment (the first term); second, to combat pollution (the second term); and, third, to raise revenues with the least cost to profits (the third term). Bovenberg and van der Ploeg (1994c) use expression (77) to decompose welfare into three dividends: the employment dividend (which they call the 'pink' dividend), the environmental dividend (the 'green' dividend) and the profit dividend (the 'blue' dividend).

The solution for employment is very similar to that in (72)

$$\tilde{L}=[(1-\tau)(\epsilon_{LL}-\epsilon_{RL})-\theta_R\epsilon_D]\omega_R\tilde{r}_R/\Delta_u \tag{78}$$

where $\Delta_u \equiv (1-\tau)\omega_L - \theta_L\omega_L\epsilon_{LL} - \theta_R\omega_R\epsilon_{RL}$. Expression (72) yields expression (78) by setting α equal to 1. Intuitively, a fixed consumer wage implies that labour supplied to the market is effectively infinitely elastic with respect to the consumer wage. Hence, $\alpha \equiv \beta_L/(\beta_L+\epsilon_{LL})$ approaches unity.

The reduced-form expression for after-tax profits is given by

$$(1-\tau)\Pi=(1-\tau)\omega_R\omega_L[\theta_L(\epsilon_{LL}-\epsilon_{RL})-\theta_R(\epsilon_{RR}-\epsilon_{LR})]\tilde{r}_R/\Delta_u \tag{79}$$

If the initial tax rates on labour and resources are zero, an environmental tax reform does not affect profit income. As we assume that the own price elasticities exceed the cross-price elasticities (i.e., $\epsilon_{LL}>\epsilon_{RL}$, (see footnote 12)), an environmental tax reform raises profit income if initially only the tax on labour is positive. Conversely, if the economy starts off with a high pollution tax (θ_R large) and a low tax rate on labour, an environmental tax reform depresses profit income (as $\epsilon_{RR}>\epsilon_{RL}$)[14]. Intuitively, the tax structure that maximises profit income and thus minimizes the burden of taxation on profit income involves positive tax rates on both labour and resource use. Expression (79) reveals that the profit-maximising tax structure is given by

$$\theta_L/\theta_R=(\epsilon_{RR}-\epsilon_{LR})/(\epsilon_{LL}-\epsilon_{RL}) \tag{80}$$

Hence, the relative tax burden on labour varies inversely with the elasticity of labour demand ϵ_{LL} and positively with the own price elasticity of resource demand ϵ_{RR}. In accordance with the familiar Ramsey principle, the government should thus levy the heaviest taxes on relatively inelastic tax bases.

If the initial equilibrium features only a positive tax on labour (i.e., $\theta_L>0$, $\theta_R=0$), an environmental tax reform typically yields a triple dividend as it boosts employment (see (78)), profit income (see (79)) and environmental quality. Intuitively, minimising the burden of taxation on income from the fixed factor requires that the government spread the tax burden over both labour and resources (see (80)). The social objectives of stimulating employment and reducing pollution strengthen the case for a higher tax on resources and a lower tax on labour.

This case shows that the scope for a double dividend increases if the initial tax system is suboptimal from a non-environmental point of view. In that case, the non-environmental welfare gains associated with a move towards a non-environmental optimum can finance the costs associated with a cleaner environment. In other words, the decline in the excess burden due to the non-environmental efficiency gains more than offsets the rise in the excess burden due to the additional abatement costs. Accordingly, the overall effect on the tax burden (on non-environmental income) becomes negative. As a direct consequence, an improvement in employment does not necessarily require redistributing income away from non-labour incomes.

The suboptimality of the initial tax system creates the possibility of a free lunch, i.e., raising environmental quality without reducing private incomes. In practice, tax systems may indeed be far from optimal. To illustrate, applied general equilibrium models of the US economy suggest that, compared to taxes on labour income, taxes on capital income tend to produce larger marginal efficiency losses. The most direct way to improve the efficiency of the tax system as a revenue raising device would be to finance a cut in capital taxes with higher taxes on labour. However, if the government does not want to adopt labour taxes, it can use environmental taxes that are primarily borne by labour.[15]

In the context of the model outlined here, the mix of factor taxation is inefficient from a non-environmental point of view. In particular, the two factors are labour and the fixed factor. Since the fixed factor is in fixed supply, a 100 per cent profit tax would be optimal. If such a tax is excluded, the government may be able to adopt the pollution tax as an indirect instrument to tax the fixed factor. A tax on the polluting input is an effective instrument to tax the fixed factor, if, compared to labour, the polluting input is more complementary to the fixed factor (i.e., the $\epsilon_{LL} - \epsilon_{RL}$ is large compared to $\epsilon_{RR} - \epsilon_{LR}$).

The welfare effects associated with a suboptimal initial tax system do not necessarily make environmental tax reforms more attractive because the burden of the environmental tax may well fall on the factor that is taxed excessively high rather than excessively low. Intuitively, environmental taxes may exacerbate rather than alleviate these inefficiencies.[16] In the framework of our model, this occurs if, compared to labour, the polluting input is a better substitute for the fixed factor. In that case, the labour tax rather than the pollution tax is the best instrument to indirectly tax away profits.

The suboptimality of the initial tax system raises the issue why governments have not reformed their tax systems to deal with these inefficiencies. Indeed, the case for such a tax reform is independent of environmental concerns. However, political and distributional constraints may prevent the government from making the tax system more efficient. Only by employing environmental taxes to generate the revenues to eliminate particularly inefficient taxes, can the government formulate a 'package deal' that creates the social consensus needed to eliminate particularly inefficient taxes. In other words, environmental taxes act as the lubricating oil that allows a tax reform to eliminate particularly 'bad' taxes.

10 Optimal tax rates and involuntary unemployment

The government selects the optimal tax rates on labour and dirty inputs to maximise overall welfare, $U=U(C,1-L,E)=u(M(C,1-L),E)$. By substituting the household budget constraint, we can write the objective function as

$$U=u\{M[wL(w(1+t_L), (1+t_R))+(1/N)(1-\tau)\Pi(w(1+t_L),$$
$$(1+t_R)), 1-L(w(1+t_L), (1+t_R))]; E[R(w(1+t_L), (1+t_R))]\} \quad (81)$$

The government maximises (81) subject to a given consumer wage (w) and taking account of the government budget constraint

$$t_L NwL[w(1+t_L), (1+t_R)]+t_R R[w(1+t_L),$$
$$(1+t_R)]+\tau\Pi(w(1+t_L), (1+t_R))=G \quad (82)$$

The first-order conditions for the optimal tax rate on labour and on resources are:

$$\epsilon_{LL}(\theta_L+s/\eta)+\epsilon_{LR}(\theta_R-p/\eta)=(1-\tau)\left(1-\frac{1}{\eta}\right) \quad (83)$$

$$\epsilon_{RL}(\theta_L+s/\eta)+\epsilon_{RR}(\theta_R-p/\eta)=(1-\tau)\left(1-\frac{1}{\eta}\right) \quad (84)$$

where we have used $\dfrac{\partial R}{\partial w_p}=\dfrac{\partial L}{\partial(1+t_R)}$. This yields the optimal tax rates on the use of labour and resources[17]

$$\theta_R-p/\eta=(1-\eta^{-1})(1-\tau)(\epsilon_{LL}-\epsilon_{RL})/\epsilon_D \quad (85)$$

$$\theta_L-s/\eta=(1-\eta^{-1})(1-\tau)(\epsilon_{RR}-\epsilon_{LR})/\epsilon_D \quad (86)$$

The optimal resource tax rate rises with the environmental externalities (as measured by the virtual pollution subsidy, see expression (85)), while the optimal labour tax rate declines with the virtual labour tax caused by a rigid consumer wage (see expression (86)). Hence, the resource tax acts to offset the implicit subsidy on pollution due to environmental externalities (p), while the labour tax offsets the virtual tax due to rationing of labour supply. The optimal 'distortionary' components of the resource and labour tax rates are given by, respectively, θ_R-p/η and θ_L+s/η. These distortionary components measure the wedges between the social benefits and social costs of the two inputs. They thus amount to the sum of the explicit tax rates (i.e., θ_R and θ_L) and the implicit taxes due to non-tax distortions (i.e., $-p/\eta$ and s/η). The implicit taxes are divided by the marginal costs of public funds, η, in order to measure these taxes in terms of tax revenues.

The expressions for the optimal tax rates may be used to explore the consequences of an environmental tax reform starting from an initial equilibrium based on particular evaluations of the non-tax distortions s and p. In particular, by using expressions (85) and (86) to eliminate θ_R and θ_L from (78) and (79), we find for employment and profits

$$\tilde{L}=[(1-\tau)(\epsilon_{LL}-\epsilon_{RL})-p\epsilon_D]\omega_R\tilde{i}_R/\Delta_u^0 \tag{87}$$

$$(1-\tau)\tilde{\Pi}=-[(\epsilon_{LL}-\epsilon_{RL})s+(\epsilon_{RR}-\epsilon_{LR})p](1-\tau)\omega_R\omega_L\tilde{i}_R/\Delta_u^0 \tag{88}$$

where $\Delta_u^0=w_L[1-\tau+s\epsilon_{LL}-p\epsilon_{LR}]$. If the initial tax system serves only revenue objectives and is not concerned with either employment or the environment (i.e., $p=s=0$), an environmental tax reform boosts employment (if $\tau<1$). Profits are unaffected. However, profits decline if the initial tax system is concerned not only with minimising tax distortions but also with correcting non-tax distortions (i.e., with pursuing other social objectives besides revenue raising so that p and s are positive). Intuitively, society pays for these social objectives in the form of a lower level of after-tax profits.

Moving away from labour towards pollution taxation continues to produce a double dividend (i.e., a rise in both employment and environmental quality) if the existing tax system cares only about employment and revenue raising (i.e., $s>0$, $p=0$). However, this double dividend comes at the price of a negative dividend, namely a fall in profits.

If the initial tax system accounts for environmental objectives (i.e., $p>0$), employment may decline. Intuitively, a further tightening of environmental policy is costly if society attaches a positive priority to environmental quality in the initial equilibrium. Hence, the tax burden effect (i.e., the second term in square brackets at the right-hand side of (87)) is positive. This effect causes employment to decline if the production share of the fixed factor is small (implying that the term ϵ_D is large), the profit tax rate is large, substitution between labour and resources is difficult (implying that the term $\epsilon_{LL}-\epsilon_{RL}$ is small), and substitution between the fixed factor and resources is easy (implying that the term ϵ_D is large, see table 4.1). In that case, the costs associated with a cleaner environment cannot be shifted towards non-labour incomes. Hence, employment rather than the fixed factor pays the costs associated with a cleaner environment.

11 Unemployment and endogenous wage determination

Sections 9 and 10 assume that consumer wages are fixed exogenously. Bovenberg and van der Ploeg (1994d), in contrast, endogenise the process of wage determination within a labour-market model with hiring and search costs. These search and hiring costs imply a rent on job matches. Wages are the outcome of a bargaining process between workers and employees about the distribution of these rents.

Bovenberg and van der Ploeg (1994d) incorporate the labour-market model in a small open economy. Shifting the tax burden to a fixed factor is excluded because the only non-labour input, capital, is assumed to be perfectly mobile internationally. Hence, capital can escape the tax burden by moving abroad. However, just as in section 7 of this chapter, the tax burden can be shifted to those collecting transfer incomes. In the context of the search model, the transfer recipients are those who receive unemployment benefits because they are not employed in the formal sector. As in section 7, lower unemployment benefits raise labour demand by reducing the need to raise labour taxes to finance these benefits. However, in the search model, lower unemployment benefits raise employment through another channel, namely the process of wage determination. In particular, less generous unemployment compensation induces workers to moderate wages as a less attractive outside option weakens the bargaining position of workers.

Section 7 showed how higher pollution taxes on consumption can redistribute income away from transfer recipients to workers. Bovenberg and van der Ploeg (1994d) argue that pollution taxes on intermediate inputs may have the same distributional effects if those not employed in the formal sector (the 'unemployed') receive not only unemployment benefits but also incomes from activities in the informal sector. These activities are not subject to the labour tax so that the unemployed escape the burden of the labour tax. However, they may bear some of the burden of the pollution tax. In particular, a pollution tax on intermediate goods, by reducing labour productivity in the formal sector, also hurts incomes in the informal sector. An environmental reform thus substitutes a tax that is in part borne by the unemployed (i.e., the pollution tax) for a tax that is entirely escaped by the unemployed (i.e., the labour tax). The resulting shift in the tax burden away from the employed in the formal sector towards those who are not employed in the formal sector corresponds to yet another form of the tax shifting effect. This tax shifting effect, which makes the outside option of workers in the formal sector less attractive, induces these workers to moderate wages, thereby benefiting employment in the formal sector.

The tax level effect, representing the abatement costs associated with a cleaner environment, typically hurts employment. However, the drop in employment is generally less dramatic compared to the case with fixed consumer wages (see sections 9 and 10). If consumer wages are fixed, workers shift the higher tax burden entirely towards employers by raising wage costs, thereby harming labour demand. In a model of endogenous wage determination, in contrast, employers and employees typically share the tax burden. Workers absorb a large share of the additional tax burden in terms of lower after-tax wages if income during unemployment is strongly indexed to wages. In fact, with full indexation of unemployment incomes and zero utility of leisure in unemployment, workers bear the entire burden of the decline in labour productivity due to a higher tax rate on intermediate inputs. Accordingly, these taxes do not affect wage costs per unit of output and thus leave unemployment unaffected. Intuitively, with full indexation of monetary incomes and no non-monetary income from leisure, incomes during unemployment decline proportionally with incomes in the formal economy. Hence, the threat point of workers worsens, inducing workers to accept lower after-tax wages.

The overall effect on employment depends on the net impact of the tax burden and tax shifting effects. Even if the increase in the tax burden is large, employment may rise if workers accept a large drop in their disposable income. An environmental tax reform succeeds in moderating wages if it makes work in the formal sector more attractive compared to being unemployed. With endogenous wage determination, therefore, a higher tax burden associated with a cleaner environment does not necessarily result in a higher level of unemployment. Intuitively, workers and the unemployed may absorb the costs of the cleaner environment in terms of lower after-tax wages rather than an increased risk of becoming (or staying) unemployed.

12 Conclusions

This chapter indicates that the employment effect of environmental tax reforms depends on the so-called tax *burden* and tax *shifting* effects. Three factors determine the tax burden effect: first, the abatement costs associated with a higher supply of the public good of the environment; second, the beneficial effect of a higher environmental quality on productivity; and, third, the efficiency effect of making the tax system more or less efficient from a non-environmental point of view.

The tax shifting effect allows an environmental tax reform to boost employment by shifting the tax burden away from workers to those outside the labour force. In particular, environmental taxes may succeed in shifting the tax burden to those on transfer incomes. Whereas such a scenario may boost employment by moderating wages, it is likely to be unattractive from a distributional point of view. Distributional issues are at the heart of the double dividend issue: without distributional concerns, taxes would not need to be distortionary, as governments could freely use lump-sum taxation to meet their revenue needs. In designing environmental tax reforms, governments typically face a trade-off between equity and efficiency. In particular, the revenues from pollution taxes can be used only once: either to compensate the poor or to reduce distortionary taxes.

The tax burden can be shifted to others besides those collecting transfer incomes. In the short run, an environmental tax reform may shift the tax burden to capital. However, in the face of international capital mobility, taxing capital on a sustainable basis is likely to require international coordination on a global level. Another option, not discussed in this chapter, is to shift the tax burden to foreigners. In particular, if explicit tariffs are excluded, pollution taxes may raise non-environmental national welfare by acting as an implicit optimal tariff. However, most countries are too small to wield substantial market power on world markets. In most cases, countries importing fossil fuels need to cooperate to gain sufficient market power to shift the burden of higher fuel taxes by reducing world-market prices of these commodities.

The analysis has revealed that an environmental tax reform does not necessarily raise employment, as the ultimate incidence of pollution taxes may largely fall on labour. Moreover, high distortionary labour taxes generally do not make pollution taxes more attractive – even though the revenues from pollution taxes can be employed to cut labour taxes. The reason is that pollution taxes typically exacerbate pre-existing tax distortions.[18]

If pollution taxes raise employment, the boost in employment typically comes at the cost of a negative dividend (e.g., a less equitable tax system). Only if the initial tax system is suboptimal from a non-environmental point of view (e.g., due to low taxes on a factor in fixed supply or in the absence of optimal tariffs) may the double dividend come free, i.e., without damaging other non-environmental priorities. Intuitively, the welfare gains associated with moving towards a more efficient system from a non-environmental point of view may finance the improvement in environmental quality. The case for reform is independent of environmental concerns. It is not always clear, therefore, why environmental policy would succeed in moving the system closer to the non-environmental optimum where other policies have failed. By employing instruments directly addressing the non-environmental inefficiencies, the government can typically reap the non-environmental efficiency gains more directly than by using pollution taxes. Indeed, if the government aims for two objectives, the target principle implies that in principle the government should employ two instruments. One policy is aimed at improving the quality of the environment (i.e., the pollution tax) and the other policy at raising employment (e.g., shifting the tax burden away from labour to non-labour incomes).

Appendix A Three separable production functions

A.1 Resources separable

If resources are separable from the other production factors, the production function may be written as $Y=F(Q(H,L),R)$ where the subproduction function $Q(.)$ features constant returns to scale. Profit maximisation yields $Q_L/Q_H=w_P/p_H$ or $\tilde{L}-\tilde{H}=\sigma_{LH}(\tilde{p}_H-\tilde{w}_P)$, where $\sigma_{LH}\equiv \mathrm{dlog}(L/H)/\mathrm{dlog}(Q_H/Q_L)$ stands for Allen's elasticity of substitution between L and H. Using $\omega_H\tilde{p}_H+\omega_L\tilde{w}_P+\omega_R\tilde{i}_R=0$ to eliminate $\tilde{p}_H$, we obtain $\epsilon_{LL}=\sigma_{LH}(1-\omega_R)/\omega_H\geq 0$ and $\epsilon_{LR}=\sigma_{LH}\omega_R/\omega_H\geq 0$. Symmetry yields $\epsilon_{RL}=\sigma_{LH}\omega_L/\omega_H\geq 0$.

Profit maximisation yields also $F_R/F_Q=(1+t_R)/p_Q$ or $\tilde{R}-\tilde{Q}=\sigma_R(\tilde{p}_Q-\tilde{i}_R)$, where σ_R denotes the elasticity of substitution between Q and R in $F(.)$ and p_Q represents the ideal price index for the composite labour-resource input, Q. Using the expression $(1-\omega_R)\tilde{Q}=\omega_L\tilde{L}+\omega_H\tilde{H}$ with $\tilde{H}=0$ and $(1-\omega_R)\tilde{p}_Q=\omega_L\tilde{w}_P+\omega_H\tilde{p}_H=-\omega_R\tilde{i}_R$ to eliminate $\tilde{Q}$ and $\tilde{p}_Q$, we obtain $\epsilon_{RR}=(\sigma_R+\sigma_{LH}\omega_L\omega_R/\omega_H)/(1-\omega_R)=0$.

Without substitution between labour and the fixed factor ($\sigma_{LH}=0$), the own- and cross-price elasticities of labour demand are zero and labour demand is thus completely inelastic ($\tilde{L}=\tilde{H}=0$). In addition, the demand for resources does not respond to changes in the producer wage ($\epsilon_{RL}=0$).

A.2 Labour separable

If labour is separable in production, i.e., $Y=F(Q(R,H),L)$, the derivation of the own- and cross-price elasticities of factor demand follows the same procedure as in subsection A.1. Table 4.1 contains the results, where σ_{RH} denotes the elasticity of substitution between R and H in the subproduction function $Q(.)$ and σ_L represents the elasticity of substitution between L and the composite capital-resource input Q. Hence, as long as substitution between resources and the fixed factor is feasible (i.e., $\sigma_{RH}>0$), labour and resources are cooperant production factors (i.e., ϵ_{LR} and ϵ_{RL} are positive). Without substitution between resources and the fixed factor ($\sigma_{RH}=0$), the demand for resources is completely inelastic.

A.3 Fixed factor separable

If the fixed factor is separable, we have $Y=F(Q(L,R),H)$. A similar procedure as in subsection A.1 yields the factor demand elasticities presented in table 4.1, where σ_{LR} stands for the elasticity of substitution between L and R in the subproduction function $Q(.)$ and σ_H denotes the elasticity of substitution between the fixed factor and the composite labour-resource input. With this specification, resources and labour are non-cooperant factors of production, i.e., ϵ_{LR} and ϵ_{RL} are negative, if the production share of the fixed factor (ω_H) is large, substitution between the labour-resource composite and the fixed factor is difficult (σ_H is small), and substitution between labour and resources is easy (σ_{LR} large).

Appendix B Employment effects with separable production functions

This appendix analyses the employment effect of an environmental tax reform for the three separable production functions introduced in Appendix A by substituting the various elasticities contained in table 4.1 into the term in square brackets in (72).

B.1 Resources separable

$$\tilde{L} \propto (1 - \tau - \theta_R \sigma_R / \omega_H) \sigma_{LH} \tag{B1}$$

If substitution between resources and value added Q is easy (i.e., σ_R large), the profit tax rate and the initial resource tax rate are large, and the production share of the fixed factor (ω_H) is small, then employment falls. However, employment rises if the burden of environmental tax reform is mostly borne by the fixed factor. This is the case if substitution between resources and value added is difficult, profit and resource tax rates are small and the fixed factor accounts for a large production share.

B.2 Labour separable

$$\tilde{L} \propto (1 - \tau)\sigma_L - [(1 - \tau)\omega_L + \theta_R \sigma_L (1 - \omega_L) / \omega_H] \sigma_{RH} \tag{B2}$$

An employment dividend is more likely to occur if substitution between resources and the fixed factor is difficult (i.e., σ_{RH} small), the initial tax rates on resources and profit income are small, and the production share of the fixed factor is large. In that case, environmental policy is cheap (because of the small initial tax rate on resources), while the costs can be absorbed by the fixed factor (because of a large production share ω_H, a small elasticity σ_{RH} and a small profit tax rate τ). Also, easy substitution between labour and the composite of resources and the fixed factor (i.e., σ_L large) makes a rise in employment more likely.

B.3 Fixed factor separable

$$\tilde{L} \propto (1 - \tau - \theta_R \sigma_H / \omega_H) \sigma_{LR} \tag{B3}$$

Employment rises if the initial profit tax rate and the initial tax rate on resource use are small, substitution between the fixed factor and the labour-resource composite is difficult (i.e., σ_H small), and the production share of the fixed factor is large. In that case, the increase in employment is particularly large if substitution between labour and resources is easy (i.e., σ_{LR} large).

Notes

The author would like to thank Larry Goulder and Ruud de Mooij for helpful comments on an earlier draft. Financial support from Fondazione ENI E. Mattei is gratefully acknowledged.

1 See Goulder (1994) for definitions of various notions of the 'double dividend'.
2 The number of hours available for work has been normalised at unity.
3 See, e.g., Hausman (1985).
4 For a more extensive analysis of this issue, see Bovenberg and de Mooij (1994a, 1994b).
5 See expression (28). Recall that we assume that the uncompensated wage elasticity of labour supply, β_L, is positive.
6 The word 'distort' is in quotes to acknowledge the notion that the change in resource allocation may be justified once environmental benefits are taken into account.
7 The importance of pre-existing distortionary taxes in the labour market suggests that a partial equilibrium analysis, which ignores these distortions, can be highly misleading.
8 In contrast to section 4, this section does not necessarily assume that leisure is weakly separable from produced consumption goods.
9 Under decreasing returns to scale, production efficiency continues to be optimal as long as a 100 per cent profit tax is available.
10 This factor can be interpreted as capital, land or natural resources.
11 The assumption of fixed supply simplifies the analysis considerably. A more general model allowing for elastic supply of the non-labour factor would yield similar results.
12 The term $\epsilon_{LL} - \epsilon_{RL}$ is always non-negative for cases (i) and (iii) contained in table 4.1 and described in Appendix A. However, this term may be negative for case (ii) in table 4.1, i.e., if labour is separable from the other production factors. In particular, it is negative if, compared to labour, resources are a much better substitute for the fixed factor (i.e., σ_{RH} large relative to σ_L) – see table 4.1. We rule out this possibility and thus assume $\epsilon_{LL} - \epsilon_{RL} > 0$.
13 A 100 per cent profit tax is, in fact, optimal, because the fixed factor is in inelastic supply. Hence, an employment dividend can occur only if monitoring problems preclude a 100 per cent profit tax (see Atkinson and Stiglitz, 1980, pp. 467–8). In that case, a resource tax acts as an indirect tax on the fixed factor.
14 Table 4.1 provides expressions for the term $\epsilon_{RR} - \epsilon_{LR}$ for the three separable production functions. It indicates that this term is generally positive. Only if labour is a better substitute for the fixed factor than resources, may $\epsilon_{RR} - \epsilon_{LR}$ be nega-

tive. In this latter case, the labour tax is a better instrument for environmental protection than the resource tax. We assume that this is not the case, so that $\epsilon_{RR} - \epsilon_{LR} > 0$. This condition always holds for cases (ii) and (iii) in table 4.1 and for case (i), if σ_R exceeds $\omega_R \sigma_{LH}$ – see table 4.1.

15 See Goulder (1994) for an extensive discussion of this issue.

16 The numerical general equilibrium analysis in Bovenberg and Goulder (1997) suggests that inefficiencies in the initial US tax system may make carbon taxes less rather than more attractive.

17 Only demand elasticities feature in the expressions for the optimal tax rates. Supply elasticities do not enter because the fixed consumer wage implies that the supply of labour is in effect infinitely elastic. If the consumer wage were to depend on the level of involuntary unemployment, the optimal tax rates would depend not only on demand elasticites but also on supply elasticities.

18 Goulder (1994) calls this the 'tax interaction' effect. Parry (1994) refers to it as the 'interdependency' effect and shows that this effect typically dominates the efficiency gains due to the reduction in distortionary taxes, which he calls the 'revenue tax recycling' effect.

References

Atkinson, A.B. and N.H. Stern (1974), 'Pigou, Taxation and Public Goods', *Review of Economic Studies*, 41, 119–28.

Atkinson, A.B. and Stiglitz (1980), *Lectures on Public Economics*, London: McGraw Hill.

Auerbach, A.J. (1985), 'The Theory of Excess Burden and Optimal Taxation', in A.J. Auerbach and M.S. Feldstein (eds.), *Handbook of Public Economics* 1, Amsterdam: North Holland.

Ballard, C.L. and D. Fullerton (1992), 'Distortionary Taxes and the Provision of Public Goods', *Journal of Economic Perspectives*, 6(3), 117–32.

Bovenberg, A.L. and R.A. de Mooij (1994a), 'Environmental Levies and Distortionary Taxation', *American Economic Review*, 94(4), 1085–9.

(1994b), 'Environmental Taxation and Labour-Market Distortions', *European Journal of Political Economy*, 10(4), 655–84.

(1997), 'Environmental Tax Reform and Endogenous Growths.' *Journal of Public Economics*, 63(2), 207–37.

Bovenberg, A.L. and F. van der Ploeg (1994a), 'Green Policies in a Small Open Economy', *Scandinavian Journal of Economics*, 96(3), 343–63.

(1994b), 'Environmental Policy, Public Finance and the Labour Market in a Second-Best World', *Journal of Public Economics*, 55(3), 349–90.

(1994c), 'Consequences of Environmental Tax Reform for Involuntary Unemployment and Welfare', CentER Discussion Paper, No. 9408, Tilburg University.

(1994d), 'Tax Reform, Structural Unemployment, and the Environment', mimeo, CentER, Tilburg University.

Bovenberg, A.L. and L.H. Goulder (1996), 'Optimal Environmental Taxation in the Presence of Other Taxes: General Equilibrium Analysis', *American Economic Review*, 86, 985–1000.

Bovenberg, A.L. and L.H. Goulder (1997) 'Costs of Environmentally Motivated Taxes in the Presence of other Taxes: General Equilibrium Analysis,' *National Tax Journal*, 50(1), 59–87.

Diamond, P.A. and I.A. Mirrlees (1971), 'Optimal Taxation and Public Production', *American Economic Review*, 61, 8–27, 261–78.

Goulder, L.H. (1994), 'Environmental Taxation and the "Double Dividend": A Readers Guide', paper presented at 50th IIPF Congress on 'Public Finance, the Environment and Natural Resources'.

Hausmann, J.A. (1985), 'Taxes and Labor Supply', in A.J. Auerbach and M.S. Feldstein (eds.), *Handbook of Public Economics*, vol. I, Amsterdam: North-Holland.

Oates, W.E. (1991), 'Pollution Charges as a Source of Public Revenues', Resources for the Future, Discussion Paper QE92-05, November, Resources for the Future, Washington, DC.

Oates, W.E. and R.M. Schwabb (1988), 'Economic Competition Among Jurisdictions. Efficiency Enhancing or Distortion Inducing?', *Journal of Public Economics*, 35, 333–54.

Parry, I.W.H. (1994), 'Pollution Taxes and Revenue Recycling', Working Paper, April, Economic Research Service, US Department of Agriculture.

Pearce, D.W. (1991), 'The Role of Carbon Taxes in Adjusting to Global Warming', *Economic Journal*, 101, 938–48.

Pezzey, J. (1992), 'Some Interactions Between Environmental Policy and Public Finance', Working Paper, University of Bristol.

Repetto, R., R.C. Dower, R. Jenkins, and J. Geoghegan (1992), 'Green Fees: How a Tax Shift can Work for the Environment and the Economy', November, World Resources Institute.

Sandmo, A. (1975), 'Optimal Taxation in the Presence of Externalities', *Swedish Journal of Economics*, 77, 86–98.

Wildasin, D.A. (1984), 'On Public Good Provision with Distortionary Taxation', *Economic Inquiry*, 22, 227–43.

5 International coordination of environmental taxes

Michael Hoel

1 Introduction

Politicians and others often argue that environmental policy, and in particular environmental taxes, ought to be coordinated across countries. Two types of arguments for the desirability of international coordination of environmental taxes are frequently given. The first argument states that uncoordinated tax policy will lead to unequal taxes across countries, with a corresponding distortion of the relative competitiveness of countries. Related to this argument is also the fear that when environmental taxes are set individually at the country level, each country's concern about its own competitiveness may imply that environmental taxes throughout are set too low. The starting point of the second type of argument is that several important environmental problems are characterised by international spillovers, i.e., that the environment in one country depends not only on emissions in this country, but also on emissions in one or more other countries. When the environmental problem is international in this sense, environmental policy must also be coordinated according to this type of argument.

This chapter makes a closer study of the arguments for an international coordination of environmental taxes. Section 2 covers the first type of argument, in the context of an environmental problem with no international spillovers. It is first shown that under 'ideal conditions' there is no need for international coordination of environmental taxes. 'Ideal conditions' include the following assumptions: (a) there are no market failures other than the environmental externality, (b) governments maximise the welfare of a representative household, (c) the environmental externality can be monitored at the micro level, e.g., emission levels from a firm or consumption levels of a good which has a negative impact on the environment.

In practice, the three conditions above will not hold. Section 2 concentrates on (a) and studies the consequences of imperfections in the labour market, market power on the product market, and increasing returns to scale and endogenous plant location. It is shown that under such circumstances, decentralised tax setting may give a suboptimal outcome. Whether non-cooperative taxes are lower or higher than cooperative taxes depends on the situation. Section 2 discusses different effects, some tending to make non-cooperative taxes lower than cooperative taxes, and some tending to make them higher.

The fact that a coordination of environmental taxes might be better than decentralised choices of environmental taxes does *not* mean that environmental taxes should be uniform across countries. Generally, tax rates differ in a social optimum, and there may be quite large differences in the optimal tax rates between countries.

The general case of transboundary environmental problems is treated in section 3. For transboundary environmental problems, a socially optimal outcome requires some kind of coordination between countries, as emissions otherwise will be too high. One possibility is to have an agreement which focuses directly on emission levels of each country. A second type of agreement is one focusing on the environmental policies in each country, such as emission taxes. Also for transboundary environmental problems, the social optimum is in general characterised by optimal tax rates differing between countries.

Sections 4–7 give a more detailed analysis of the climate problem, which has the special feature that it is only the sum of greenhouse gas emissions from all countries which affects the environment in each country. Under certain conditions the social optimum is in this case characterised by carbon tax rates being equalised across countries. A carbon tax is a tax on the use of fossil fuels, with the tax being proportional to the carbon content of the specific fuel.

In sections 5–6 it is shown how the total taxes on fossil fuels should also include fiscally motivated elements as well as elements for correcting other negative externalities of fuel use. Total optimal fuel taxes will therefore generally differ across countries and across fuels (per unit of carbon), and might also depend on where/how the fuels are used. For this reason, as well as for distributional reasons, there may be better types of climate agreements than one which harmonises fuel taxes across countries. Such agreements are discussed in more detail in section 4.

It seems likely that in the foreseeable future only some of the countries in the world will participate in an international climate agreement. Section 7 shows that when this is the case, there may be additional reasons for a carbon tax to differ across fuels (per unit of carbon), and also across sectors within each country.

Finally, some of the most important conclusions are repeated in section 8.

There is a vast literature on most of the issues covered in this study. No attempt has been made to survey this literature. The references given should be considered as examples of some of the work done, and there are for sure a number of important contributions which have not been mentioned.

2 Tax coordination without environmental externalities?

Consider a purely national environmental problem, i.e., there are no transboundary spillovers of the pollutants. According to standard environmental economics, the optimal emission tax in each country should be equal to the marginal environmental cost in the country. Except for the special case in which abatement cost and environmental cost functions are equal across countries, this tax rule will generally imply that environmental taxes will differ across countries.

Environmental externalities may come both from the final consumption of goods and from the production process itself. For the first type of externalities, there does not seem to be any theoretical reasons against letting taxes be set in a decentralised way, with tax differences across countries as a result. In order to tax the consumption of a good, the government must be able to monitor total domestic sales of the good. In some cases this is only possible indirectly, through monitoring domestic production minus exports plus imports. When this is the case, decentralised taxation of the final consumption of a good requires border controls or some other way of monitoring the imported amount of the good. Although border controls exist between most countries, the idea behind for example the single market of the European Community is to abolish such border controls. If the consumption of the good in each country cannot be monitored, one may be forced to tax production instead. If the optimal consumption tax happened to be the same in all countries, a uniform tax on the production of the good in all countries would give the first-best optimum. However, it would be necessary to have some kind of international cooperation to reach such a production tax: for any small country, facing a fixed international price of the polluting good, it is individually optimal to let its own production be untaxed. The reason is that the consumption of the good in this country depends only on the international price, and not on how production is taxed. And since the international price is (practically) independent of the production tax in a small economy (given the taxes in the other countries), the country cannot affect its pollution through taxing its production.

In the more likely case in which the first-best consumption tax differs between countries, a uniform tax on production in all countries will not give the first-best optimum. Nor will any differentiated production tax, as the price facing consumers will be equalised across countries no matter how production is taxed.

Consider next the case in which the environmental externality is related to the production of a good. An emission tax must in this case be paid by the producer of the good. An argument which is sometimes made against environmental taxes differing across countries for this case is that this distorts the competitiveness of countries. However, there is in principle no difference between environmental taxes differing across countries than the price of any (non-traded) input differing across countries: Those who argue against emission tax differences between countries seldom argue for policies to equalise, say, wages or land rents.

A second type of argument against uncoordinated emission taxes has an environmental background. In open economies with mobile capital across countries, the argument goes, governments will compete in giving favourable business conditions in order to attract investment. One form such competition may take is that governments set lower environmental standards, i.e., lower emission taxes, than they would without the international competition. In their attempt to underbid each other with low environmental taxes, all countries end up with emissions which are higher than what is Pareto optimal for the whole group of countries.

The argument above has been studied in more detail by for example Oates and Schwab (1988). An important conclusion is that in a competitive economy without any distortions (except for the environmental externality) there is no need for internationally coordinated tax setting: when the government of each country sets environmental taxes to maximise the utility levels of the country's consumers, we get a Pareto optimal allocation of emissions and capital across countries. To demonstrate this result, and to show that the conclusion might be changed if there are market failures, we shall consider a model similar to the one used by Oates and Schwab (1988).

Consider first a single open economy where aggregate consumption is given by

$$c = x + r(k^* - k) \tag{1}$$

where x is domestic aggregate production, k^* is the total capital stock owned by residents of the country, k is the capital used as an input in domestic production, and r is the international interest rate.

Domestic production is given by

$$x = f(k, \ell, e) \tag{2}$$

where ℓ is employment and e is emissions. The function f is homogeneous of degree one, f_k and f_l and all f_{ij} are assumed to be positive, and $f_e > 0$ for

$e<e^0(k,\ell)$ where e^0 is the emission level for the case of no environmental policy, i.e., e^0 is given by $f_e(k,\ell,e)=0$.

The welfare of the country (i.e., of a representative consumer) is given by

$$u=u(c,e) \tag{3}$$

where $u_c>0$ and $u_e<0$. The ratio $-u_e/u_c$ thus gives the marginal environmental costs in terms of consumption.

Assume that k^* and ℓ are exogenously given. For a small economy, the interest rate r will also be exogenous. The optimal choice of k and e maximises $u(c,e)$ subject to (1) and (2), i.e.

$$f_k(k,\ell,e)=r \tag{4}$$

$$f_e(k,\ell,e)=\frac{-u_e}{u_c} \tag{5}$$

The conditions (4) and (5) have straightforward interpretations. They may be implemented in a competitive economy by using an emission tax t which is equal to the marginal environmental cost $-u_e/u_c$. With such a tax, producers will maximise $f(k,\ell,e)-rk-w\ell-te$ (where w is the wage rate), giving

$$f_k(k,\ell,e)=r \tag{6}$$

$$f_\ell(k,\ell,e)=w \tag{7}$$

$$f_e(k,\ell,e)=t \tag{8}$$

It is thus clear that (6)–(8) give values of k and e which are equivalent to those determined by (4)–(5), provided

$$t=\frac{-u_e}{u_c} \tag{9}$$

(Equations (6)–(8) also determine the equilibrium wage rate w.)

The question raised at the beginning of the section was whether the tax rule (9), which is individually rational for each country, also gives a Pareto optimal outcome when all countries are studied jointly. Using subscript i to identify country i, a Pareto optimal allocation of capital and emissions may be found by solving

$$\max \Sigma_i \alpha_i u_i(c_i,e_i)$$

$$\text{s.t. } \Sigma_i c_i \leq \Sigma_i f_i(k_i,\ell_i,e_i) \tag{10}$$

$$\Sigma_i k_i \leq \Sigma_i k_i^*$$

From this maximisation problem, we find the conditions for Pareto optimality (i.e., the conditions which must hold for all positive values of the parameters α_i):

$$f_{1k}(k_1,\ell_1,e_1)=...=f_{Nk}(k_N,\ell_N,e_N) \tag{11}$$

$$f_{ie}(k_i,\ell_i,e_i)=\frac{-u_{ie}}{u_{ic}}\forall i \tag{12}$$

Comparing this with (4)–(5), it is immediately clear that Pareto optimality will be achieved when each country maximises its own welfare.

The conclusion so far is thus that there is no need to coordinate environmental policy across countries. The fear that competition for mobile capital will lead to a situation where the environment is insufficiently protected thus seems unjustified. One could argue, however, that the model above misses an important point. When for example politicians, union leaders and others argue against a stricter environmental policy in their own country than in other countries, they often point to the possibility of losing jobs. This is often linked to mobile capital: high environmental taxes lead to high costs and thus to a low return on domestic investments. This reduces domestic investments, and also employment.

In the model we have studied, employment in each country is exogenous. In other words, part of the perceived consequences of high environmental taxes are assumed away in our model. One could of course argue that, in the long run, the rate of unemployment is caused by factors other than the cost levels of particular (non-labour) inputs, see for example Layard *et al.* (1991). Nevertheless, since the employment argument seems to play an important role in policy debates about environmental policy, it is of interest to see whether our model can be modified to incorporate endogenous employment. Obviously, it can. The problem is rather that there are many ways of endogenising employment, and it is not obvious that the conclusions from the model are robust with respect to which specification one chooses. A very simple way to endogenise employment is to assume an exogenous wage rate (in each country), and to let employment and the use of capital be determined by equations (6)–(7), which imply that employment and the use of capital depend on emissions and the interest rate[1], i.e.

$$k=k(e,r)$$
$$\ell=\ell(e,r) \tag{13}$$

Consider first a single country, taking r (as well as w and k^*) as exogenous. Maximisation of $u(c,e)$ subject to (1), (2) and (13) gives (using (6) and (7))

$$f_e+w\frac{\partial\ell}{\partial e}=\frac{-u_e}{u_c} \tag{14}$$

The left-hand side of (14) gives the marginal increase in consumption per unit of increased emissions. In addition to the direct effect f_e on consumption, consumption also increases due to the increased employment caused by increased emissions ($\partial \ell / \partial e > 0$ since $f_{le} > 0$). With an emission tax t, firms choose emissions according to (8). It is therefore clear that the optimal emission tax in this case is

$$t = \frac{-u_e}{u_c} - w \frac{\partial \ell}{\partial e} \tag{15}$$

The optimal tax is thus lower than the Pigouvian level $-u_e / u_c$. The reason is that in addition to the negative environmental externality, increased emissions also have a positive effect on consumption via increased employment. This last effect is not taken into consideration in the employment decisions of producers, since they pay a positive wage w, while the social opportunity cost of labour by assumption is zero.

With this simple modelling of employment, uncoordinated environmental policy gives an equilibrium defined by (6)–(8) and (15) for each country. Unlike the equilibrium in the full-employment version of the model, the present equilibrium is not (second-best) Pareto optimal. To see this, consider coordinated emission reductions $de_1, \ldots, de_N$ in all countries (i.e., $de_i < 0 \forall i$). The interest rate r is determined by

$$\Sigma_i k_i(e_i, r) = \Sigma_i k_i^* \tag{16}$$

Since $\partial k_i / \partial e_i > 0$ and $\partial k_i / \partial r < 0$, a reduction in all emission levels will reduce the interest rate. For an arbitrary negative vector $(de_1, \ldots, de_N)$ some k_i will typically increase, while others will decline. Assume however that the vector $(de_1, \ldots, de_N)$ is chosen so that all k_i remain unchanged (i.e., effects of the reduction in e_i and in r on k_i just cancel out). Assume, moreover, that this coordinated emission reduction is accompanied by transfers between countries which offset terms of trade effects via the change in $r(k_i^* - k_i)$ due to the decline in r. From (1), (2) and (13) it follows that consumption in country i is changed according to

$$dc_i = df_i = f_{il} \left[\frac{\partial \ell}{\partial e_i} de_i + \frac{\partial \ell}{\partial r} dr \right] + f_{ie} de_i$$

$$= \left[f_{ie} + w \frac{\partial \ell}{\partial e_i} \right] de_i + w \frac{\partial \ell}{\partial r} dr$$

$$= \frac{-u_{ie}}{u_{ic}} de_i + w \frac{\partial \ell}{\partial r} dr \tag{17}$$

where we have used (7) and (14). Since $du_i = u_{ic} dc_i + u_{ie} de_i$ it follows from (17) that

$$du_i = u_{ic} w \frac{\partial \ell_i}{\partial r} \tag{18}$$

We know that $\partial\ell/\partial r<0$ and that $dr<0$, it therefore follows from (18) that $du_i>0$. In other words, starting with the uncoordinated equilibrium given by (6)–(8) and (15), it is possible to increase the welfare levels of all countries through an appropriate coordinated reduction of emissions (i.e., coordinated increase in emission taxes).

In the model above, all producers were price takers. If this assumption was changed, uncoordinated tax setting could lead to inefficiency even if employment in each country is exogenous. The reason is the same as for the competitive economy with endogenous employment: with monopoly or oligopoly, the social marginal value of capital used domestically may be larger than the private marginal value. Governments may thus attempt to attract capital by choosing a lower emission tax than they would have had capital used domestically been exogenous.

When producers have some market power, uncoordinated emission taxes may give an inefficient outcome even if capital is not internationally mobile. Consider for example the oligopoly case in which there is one producer in each of a group of several countries. Each country in the group is concerned with the negative impact on the environment caused by its production. Finally, all of the output of the oligopoly is sold outside the group of countries under consideration. This situation has been analysed by Barrett (1994a). He shows that with a Cournot oligopoly, each country has an incentive to set its emission tax lower than the marginal environmental cost, while efficiency requires equality between the tax rates and the marginal environmental costs in all countries. This result is closely related to a result in Brander and Spencer's (1985) analysis of export subsidies. They show that with a Cournot oligopoly of the present type, a Nash equilibrium is characterised by each government subsidising its own oligopolist's production. The reason why each country benefits from subsidising its producer (given the subsidies of other countries) is that the cost reduction to its own producer reduces the optimal production quantities of the other oligopolists. Since each country's profit (and therefore welfare in this model) is strictly declining in the quantities of the other oligopolists, it is therefore optimal to subsidise production.[2] In Barrett's analysis, direct production subsidies are ruled out by assumption. Setting an environmental tax below the marginal environmental cost is thus an indirect way of subsidising one's production.

Barrett also shows that if there is more than one producer in each country, it may no longer be optimal for the government in each country to subsidise production through setting the emission tax below the marginal environmental cost. The reason for this is that the profit reduction caused by the domestic output increase in this case is a first-order effect, which must be balanced against the profit increase caused by reduced output in other countries.

David Ulph (1994) has extended Barrett's Cournot oligopoly model to include R&D competition among the oligopolists. With this extension, it is no longer obvious that it is optimal for the government of each country to subsidise production through setting the emission tax below the marginal environmental cost, even for the case of only two producers. Whether non-cooperative taxes are lower or higher than cooperative taxes depends on several factors, one being the form R&D competition takes.

As pointed out by Eaton and Grossman (1986), the result that it may be optimal for governments to subsidise their export industries depends not only on the number of domestic producers, but also on the assumed behaviour of the oligopolist. In the argument above, it was assumed that we had a Cournot oligopoly, i.e., the producers choose the quantities. If producers instead set prices, i.e., we have a Bertrand oligopoly, the results above may be changed. In particular, Barrett shows that, even with one producer in each country, it may be optimal for the government of each country to set its emission tax above its marginal environmental tax. The reason why taxing the export industry in this way may be optimal, is that a domestic cost increase may increase the price charged by producers in other countries. Such price increases have a first-order positive effect on the country's own profit, while the negative effect on the country's profit of its own output reduction is second order when there is only one producer. When there is more than one producer in each country, the reduced domestic production following from the indirect production tax has a positive effect on domestic profits. This strengthens the case for setting an emission tax above the marginal environmental cost.

In the work discussed so far, firms are assumed to have constant or decreasing returns to scale. For such cases, traditional marginal analysis may be used. With fixed costs or other forms of increasing returns, however, important variables may be discontinuous functions of environmental taxes. An important type of discontinuity arises when plant location is endogenous. In this case environmental taxes may affect the location decisions, and a country's welfare as a function of environmental taxes at home and abroad may be discontinuous at some levels of these taxes. These issues have been discussed by for example Markusen *et al.* (1993, 1995), Alistair Ulph (1994), Motta and Thisse (1993) and Hoel (1997). A general result is that there exist coordinated tax policies, combined with transfers between countries, which are Pareto superior to the equilibrium with uncoordinated taxes. It is, however, not obvious whether non-cooperative taxes are lower or higher than cooperative taxes. On the one hand, each country may want to attract industry, giving it an incentive to choose low environmental taxes. This effect tends to make the non-cooperative taxes lower than the cooperative taxes. On the other hand, if disutility from pollution is sufficiently high, each country might prefer that a firm locates only in other countries. This is the 'not in my back yard' (NIMBY) case, which in the extreme case might imply that there is no production of some goods, even if such production is socially desirable. In any case, this NIMBY effect tends to make the non-cooperative taxes higher than the cooperative taxes. In addition to these two effects, relating to plant location, effects of the type discussed above related to the taxation of oligopolistic firms for given locations remain valid also when plant location is endogenous. As explained above, these latter effects may go in either direction, depending on details of the oligopoly situation. It is thus clear that there is no simple answer to the question of whether non-cooperative taxes are lower or higher than cooperative taxes.

In the types of models discussed above, the non-cooperative emission taxes will usually differ from marginal environmental costs. This difference occurs because each individual country is trying to use emission taxes to achieve something in addition to balancing marginal environmental costs with marginal abatement costs. If countries had a sufficiently wide range of other policy instruments, decentralisation of environmental policy would not cause a wedge between marginal abatement costs and marginal environmental costs. Such policy instruments would include taxes/subsidies on outputs and on imports or exports of goods, and taxes/subsidies on the use of or the net import of capital. When there are market imperfections of the types discussed above, a non-cooperative equilibrium will usually not be Pareto optimal. For this reason, there exist international agreements (such as for example the WTO) which restrict the use of tariffs, production subsidies, etc. It is the restrictions on several such policy instruments which may lead countries to use their environmental policies to achieve what they otherwise could have achieved with these other policy instruments. International agreements which restrict the use of tariffs, subsidies, etc., but which do *not* place any restrictions on how environmental taxes are used, may thus lead to an equilibrium which is Pareto inferior to an outcome in which environmental taxes are also coordinated across countries. As a byproduct, the equilibrium with uncoordinated environmental taxes *may* imply that environmental taxes are lower than what is socially optimal. However, it follows from the discussion above that this is not the only possibility. It is also possible that uncoordinated environmental taxes are *higher* than the socially optimal levels.

3 The general case of international externalities

In the model of section 2, all pollution was local in the sense that the environment in each country only depended on its own emissions.

Although several types of environmental problems have this property, there are also many important environmental problems for which the environment in a country depends on the emissions in several countries. Environmental problems of this type, often called 'transboundary' or 'transnational' environmental problems, have received large attention in the literature, see for example OECD (1976), d'Arge (1975), Mäler (1991) and Hoel (1993) for general discussions.

To see the role of emission taxes, consider again the model presented in section 2 (with exogenous employment). To capture the transboundary effect, assume that an environmental variable z_j enters the utility function u_j instead of e_j, i.e., $u_j=u_j(c_j,z_j)$. For each country, the environmental variable z_j may depend on emissions from all countries, i.e.

$$z_j=z_j(e_1,...,e_N) \tag{19}$$

The relationship between the vectors **e** and **z** are assumed to be linear, i.e., $\mathbf{z}=\mathbf{eA}$. The matrix **A** is called a transportation matrix, and the element a_{ij} gives the amount of depositions in country j per unit emission in country i.

The social optimisation model corresponding to (10) for the present case is given by

$$\max \Sigma_i \alpha_i u_i(c_i, \Sigma_h e_h a_{hi})$$

$$\text{s.t. } \Sigma_i c_i \leq \Sigma_i f_i(k_i, \ell_i, e_i) \tag{20}$$

$$\Sigma_i k_i \leq \Sigma_i k_i^*$$

The conditions for Pareto optimality are now

$$f_{1k}(k_1,\ell_1,e_1)=...=f_{Nk}(k_N,\ell_N,e_N) \tag{21}$$

$$f_{ie}(k_i,\ell_i,e_i)=\Sigma_j a_{ij}\left(\frac{-u_{jz}}{u_{jc}}\right) \forall i \tag{22}$$

Equations (21) are the same as for the case with no international spillovers of pollution. The interpretation of (22) is straightforward: the marginal abatement cost in country i should be equal to the sum of marginal environmental costs in all countries per unit of emission in country i.

Since producers choose emission so $f_{ie}=t_i$ when the emission tax is t_i, it is clear from (22) that the emission taxes which give a Pareto optimum are given by

$$t_i=\Sigma_j a_{ij}\left(\frac{-u_{jz}}{u_{jc}}\right) \forall i \tag{23}$$

The optimal taxes will normally differ between counties.

In order to reach a Pareto optimal outcome, there must be some kind of international environmental agreement. In the absence of such an agreement, it is reasonable to expect each country to maximise its utility $u_i(c_i,z_i)$, taking the interest rate as well as emission in other countries as given.[3] The non-cooperative equilibrium is in this case given by (21) and

$$f_{ie}(k_i,\ell_i,e_i)=a_{ii}\left(\frac{-u_{iz}}{u_{ic}}\right)\forall i \tag{24}$$

This equilibrium will typically have higher emissions than the Pareto optimal outcome, since each country now only takes into consideration the harm its emission has on its own environment, and not the harm on the environment in other countries.[4]

If emission taxes are used to implement the non-cooperative equilibrium, they will be given by

$$t_i=a_{ii}\left(\frac{-u_{iz}}{u_{ic}}\right) \tag{25}$$

which will typically be lower than the optimal emission taxes given by (23).

There are two main types of international environmental agreements for transnational environmental problems. The first, and probably most common, focuses directly on emissions in each country. The second type of agreement focuses on environmental policies in each country. An obvious example of the second type would be an agreement which specified the emission tax rates to be used by each country. If these emission taxes satisfy (23) the international agreement will give a Pareto optimal outcome. For an agreement of the first type to be Pareto optimal, the specified emission levels would have to be set in accordance with (22). In principle, both types of agreements can thus give a Pareto optimal outcome. A further discussion of these two types of agreements is given in section 4 for the special case of greenhouse gases.

Although it is in principle possible to design an international environmental agreement in a way which yields Pareto optimality, there are several obstacles to reaching such an agreement. One major obstacle is that there is not only one, but several Pareto optimal outcomes. Even restricting attention to the outcomes which are Pareto preferred to the non-cooperative outcome, there is a continuum of Pareto optimal outcomes. Obviously, countries will generally disagree about which of these outcomes an agreement should attempt to implement. Notice also that an agreement which simply sets emission levels in accordance with (22) or emission taxes in accordance with (23), and does not simultaneously specify any side payments between countries, will give one particular Pareto optimal outcome. A priori, there is no guarantee that such an agreement will be Pareto preferred to the non-cooperative outcome.[5] And, even if it is, some of the countries may well find this agreement 'unfair', in the sense that they would argue that more of the total gains from cooperation ought to go to them.

A second major obstacle to achieving an international environmental agreement is the free-rider problem. Even in a Pareto optimal outcome where all countries are better off than they are in the non-cooperative outcome, it will often be the case that each country is even better off if it behaves non-cooperatively, while all others cooperate (for a further discussion, see for example Barrett (1990) and Mäler (1991)).

The two obstacles mentioned above are relevant even in the hypothetical case in which all countries have complete information about welfare and production functions in all countries. In reality, there will be a large degree of incomplete and asymmetric information about the welfare and production functions. This will make it even more difficult to reach a Pareto optimal agreement.

Given the difficulties above, it seems unlikely that countries will be able to reach a Pareto optimal international environmental agreement. Instead, an agreement of a more simple type seems more likely. Such simple agreements can, in the same way as more sophisticated agreements, be related either to policy instruments or directly to quantities. An example of the first type could be an agreement which specifies an emission tax which is equal for all countries. An example of the second type could be an agreement which requires each country to reduce its emissions by an equal per cent rate relative to some base line. Generally such agreements involve a loss compared to a Pareto optimal agreement. For agreements of the 'uniform reduction' type, Mäler (1989), Bohm and Larsen (1994) have showed that the loss might be quite large. Similar calculations deriving the loss from agreements with equal taxes do not seem to exist. Clearly, such agreements may generally be better or worse than agreements with uniform percentage reductions in emission. For the special case in which all $a_{ij}=1$ (see the next section for a further discussion) it is clear from (23) that all Pareto optimal outcomes have uniform tax rates across countries. This is thus one example where agreements with uniform taxes are better than agreements with uniform percentage emission reductions. However, it is easy to construct examples where the opposite is true.

Emission taxes may play an important role also for agreements which specify emission levels for each country: given the total emissions a country is permitted to have, a domestic emission tax of the appropriate magnitude is a cost-effective way to achieve this target level of total emissions.

4 The climate problem and the role of carbon taxes

The climate problem is a special case of the general transnational environmental problem considered in the previous section. This special case has the property that it is only the sum of emissions from all countries which matters for the climate. i.e., for the environment of each country. Formally, all coefficients of the transportation matrix **A** are equal to 1 for this special case. The efficiency condition (22) for this special case thus becomes

$$f_{ie}(k_i, \ell_i, e_i) = \Sigma_j \left(\frac{-u_{jz}}{u_{jc}} \right) \forall i \tag{26}$$

In other words, efficiency requires that the marginal abatement cost is equal in all countries, and equal to the sum of marginal environmental costs over all countries. Similarly, the emission taxes which may be used to implement this efficient outcome follow from (23). It is clear that in this case the emission tax t should be equalised across countries, and given by

$$t = \Sigma_j \left(\frac{-u_{jz}}{u_{jc}} \right) \tag{27}$$

In the previous section two types of international environmental agreements were discussed. The first of these focused directly on emissions from each country. This type of quantitative agreement will be discussed below. The second type of agreement was one which focused on the environmental policies in each country, with emission taxes as an obvious example. Consider an international agreement which requires that the government of each participating country imposes a specific domestic carbon tax on the CO_2 emissions from its country. In practice, this tax would be a tax on the use of fossil fuels, proportional to the carbon content of the fuel. Assume to begin with that the tax rate is uniform across countries; this issue will be discussed in more detail below. It follows from (27) that, under the assumption of our model, such a system would give an efficient allocation of emissions across countries (and, from the usual argument for emission taxes, among sectors within each country).

There are, however, at least two important difficulties with an agreement which harmonises carbon taxes across countries. The first difficulty is the associated distribution of cost between countries. Even if *marginal* costs are equalised across countries, *total* costs of reducing emissions will generally differ between countries. An analysis by Kverndokk (1993) suggests that the cost as percentage of GDP differs sharply between countries when CO_2 emissions are allocated in a cost efficient manner. Moreover, Kverndokk's analysis suggest that it is richest countries in the world which would have the smallest total costs of reducing emissions (relative to GDP). An international climate agreement with such distributional properties will be unacceptable to a large group of countries, and will therefore in practice be infeasible unless it is supplemented with some kind of side payments between countries.

The second important difficulty associated with harmonising carbon taxes is related to the question of whether an internationally harmonised carbon tax should be an addition to existing taxes on fossil fuels, or should replace such taxes. The answer to this question depends on what the motives are for existing taxes. Since there are many possible motives, a general answer is difficult to give. Two obvious reasons for domestic taxes on fossil fuels are: (a) to raise revenue in the absence of the possibility of lump-sum taxation, and (b) to correct for domestic environmental costs (and other negative domestic externalities, such as traffic congestion). These two motivations for taxing fossil fuels are discussed in more detail in the next two sections. An important conclusion is that, in general, the optimal *total* taxes on fossil fuels will differ between countries. This suggests that a uniform, harmonised, carbon tax should not be a tax which replaces existing taxes on fossil fuels. Ideally, the uniform, harmonised, tax should be added to the existing taxes, while the existing taxes (on fuels as well as on other goods) might at the same time require an appropriate adjustment. The problem is, however, that this optimal tax structure on fossil fuels is difficult to achieve through an international agreement specifying a harmonised carbon tax for all countries. The reason for this difficulty is the free-rider problem mentioned in the previous section. The free-rider incentive implies that it is in each country's interest to have little or no restrictions on its own CO_2 emissions, given the emissions from other countries, or given the policies of other countries. If a country is required to have a specific carbon tax through an international agreement, it is therefore in the interest of that country to try to render this tax as ineffective as possible. One way the government can achieve this is to reduce other domestic taxes on fossil fuels. Even if a government does not directly reduce such domestic taxes, it might raise them less than it would otherwise have done, had it not been for the imposed carbon tax.

In addition to fossil fuel taxes, there are several other prices and policy instruments which have a significant impact on a country's CO_2 emissions. For instance, road pricing and high taxes on automobiles[6] affect CO_2 emissions from the transport sector in a very similar way as taxes on gasoline. A country which makes extensive use of such policy instruments in the absence of a climate agreement may therefore respond to the introduction of an agreement imposing a carbon tax by reducing such prices/taxes. Another way to reduce the effect of the imposed carbon tax is to manipulate the prices of other domestic goods. For instance, governments could tax close substitutes to fossil fuels and subsidise complements. Obvious examples are taxes on other types of energy (e.g., hydroelectric power) and subsidies on automobiles and air conditioning.

The examples above show that there are several ways in which a country can reduce the effect of an imposed carbon tax on the country's consumption and production pattern, and thereby reduce the cost for the country, even though it in a formal sense is adhering to the international agreement to tax CO_2 emissions. To eliminate evasions of this type, the agreement would have to be more complex than simply specifying a uniform carbon tax to be used by all countries. Even if one restricted oneself to existing fossil fuel taxes in the narrow sense, it would be difficult to specify exactly what each country can and can not do with these domestic taxes. Expanding an agreement to include more or less detailed instructions on how each country can use other policy instruments which strongly affect CO_2 emissions would make the agreement very complicated. Moreover, it seems likely that most countries would find detailed specifications and restrictions on their use of various domestic policy instruments over time an unacceptable restriction on their sovereignty.

The discussion above indicates that the only practical alternative seems to be an agreement specifying uniform minimum taxes on fossil fuels for all countries, and let each country decide to what extent this should be added to (or simply replace) existing taxes. Most countries are likely to choose the latter alternative, so that the final outcome will imply uniform carbon taxes across countries. Although this is not in conformity with the optimal tax structure, it is doubtful whether other alternatives would actually be feasible in practice.

As an alternative to harmonising carbon taxes across countries, an international climate agreement could focus directly on the CO_2 emissions from each country. An example of such a type of agreement is an agreement among the cooperating countries to cut back emissions by some uniform percentage rate compared with a specified base year. This type of agreement has two disadvantages. In the first place, equal percentage reductions of emissions from different countries usually give an inefficient outcome, in the sense that the marginal costs of reducing emissions will differ between countries. Whatever the total emissions are, the same environmental goals could therefore have been achieved at lower costs through a different distribution of emission reductions. A second problem with an agreement of equal percentage reductions is that it may give a very uneven distribution of burdens between countries. Without some form of compensating side payments, such an agreement will therefore be unacceptable to many countries, and it will therefore be impossible to achieve sufficiently broad participation.

If one in spite of its weaknesses reaches an agreement of the uniform reduction type, there is nevertheless a role to play for carbon taxes. For any given level of CO_2 emissions a country is allowed to have according to the international agreement, a domestic carbon tax is superior to most other policy instruments for achieving the target level of emissions (at least on efficiency grounds), provided we are considering a country which has reasonably well-functioning markets. The choice of tax rate (or use of other environmental policies) can in this case be left to each country to decide on unilaterally. As long as total emissions from each country are determined through an agreement, there is no need for any further specification of how each country should reach its specified emission level.[7]

Countries may for various reasons not wish to rely solely on a carbon tax to achieve their quantitative emission targets. Although environmental taxes in many cases are superior to most other policy instruments to reduce harmful emissions, it is nevertheless a fact that other policy instruments are more commonly used in most countries to achieve environmental targets of various types. If a carbon tax is to be supplemented with other policy instruments, a climate agreement could specify a minimum carbon tax in addition to the quantitative emission targets for each country. (This minimum rate should not exceed the lowest of the marginal costs of reducing emissions for the different countries, as it otherwise in practice means that it is the tax, and not the quantitative emission target, which is binding for this country.) Each country could then supplement this minimum carbon tax with additional taxes or other policy instruments to obtain the necessary reduction of CO_2 emissions. The efficiency loss due to differences in marginal costs between countries is of course not mitigated by combining a common carbon tax with country-specific use of supplementary policy instruments. The differences in marginal costs between countries will simply be reflected by different countries having to use these supplementary policy instruments more or less extensively. Combining a carbon tax with other instruments will if anything increase each country's costs of achieving its stabilisation target: Tietenberg (1990) has shown that the extra costs following from the use of 'command and control' types of environmental policies instead of using environmental taxes may be very large.

An alternative to an agreement specifying emissions from each country in an inflexible way, is an agreement with tradable emission permits for CO_2. A system of tradable emission permits for CO_2 emissions could work as follows: first the participating countries would have to agree on a total target level of emissions.[8] If the agreement is to be efficient in the sense defined by equation (26), this target level would have to balance marginal costs of emission reductions against marginal costs of a warmer climate.

Once total emissions are agreed upon, one would have to agree on some distribution of initial emission entitlements or emission permits, which would have to sum up to the target level agreed upon.[9] The third part of this scheme is that each country is allowed to buy or sell emission permits from/to other countries.

When there are many countries participating in the CO_2 agreement, and each country is relatively small, a competitive market for CO_2 emission permits is likely to develop.[10] In this case each country will regard the price of CO_2 emission permits as independent of its own CO_2 emissions. Whatever the initial distribution of CO_2 permits is, the marginal cost of CO_2 emissions for each country will be equal to the market price of CO_2 permits: if the country is buying CO_2 permits, it is obvious that the marginal cost of CO_2 emissions is equal to the price of CO_2 permits. The same is true if the country is selling CO_2 permits: the marginal cost of CO_2 emissions is the income forgone from the additional sale of a CO_2 permit, i.e., equal to the market price of a CO_2 permit.

In terms of the model presented in the previous section, country i wants its utility $u_i(c_i,z)$ to be as large as possible. Here z stands for total emissions, which are given through the international agreement, and therefore regarded as exogenous by each country. Country i thus simply wants to maximise its consumption, which is given by

$$c_i = f_i(k_i,\ell_i,e_i) - q(e_i - \beta_i z) \qquad (28)$$

where q is the market price of the emissions permits and β_i is country i's initial share of total emissions. The term $e_i - \beta_i z$ thus represents country i's purchases of additional emission permits (and will of course be positive for some countries and negative for others). The emissions level which maximises c_i is given by

$$f_{ie}(k_i,\ell_i,e_i) = q \qquad (29)$$

Since the market price of emissions q is the same for all countries, we thus get an outcome in which the marginal cost of reducing CO_2 emissions are equal for all countries, which is part of the efficiency condition (26). If total emissions z are appropriately chosen, this common marginal abatement cost will be equal to the sum of the marginal environmental costs, as required for full efficiency, cf. (26).[11]

The most important feature of the scheme above is that whatever the distribution of initial permits is, the end result is a cost-effective allocation of emissions between countries. The initial distribution of emission permits can thus be based entirely on distributional considerations. For a discussion of issues related to the distribution of costs between countries, see for example Bohm and Larsen (1994), Kverndokk (1995) and Welsch (1992).

In an agreement with tradable emission permits, countries are given an incentive, but not a rigid instruction, to reduce their CO_2 emissions. It would be up to each individual country to decide by how much it should reduce its emissions, and to choose appropriate policy instruments to reduce its emissions. A domestic carbon tax is an obvious candidate as a domestic policy response to an international agreement based on tradable emission permits. In terms of the simple model above, it is clear that a domestic emission tax which is equal to the international market price of emission permits will give the outcome described by (29). In this case, the final outcome of the international agreement with tradable emission permits between governments would thus be equal carbon taxes in all participating countries. Compared with an agreement simply imposing a harmonised domestic carbon tax in all countries, there are two important differences. In the first place, under an agreement with tradable emission permits, the participating countries have no free-rider incentive to avoid the effects of its carbon tax. Any policy counteracting the effect of the carbon tax would hurt the country, as its necessary purchase of permits would increase (or sales decline).

The second difference between the two types of agreements is the distribution of costs across countries. With tradable emission permits, any distribution is possible, and determined by the initial allocation of emission permits. With an agreement that directly specifies a carbon tax, we get a particular one of these possible distributions. However, this difference between the two types of agreements vanishes if a common carbon tax is accompanied by suitable side payments. One could for instance agree to distribute the sum of tax revenues in all countries from the domestic carbon taxes in a specified way between countries, instead of simply letting each country keep its own tax revenues.

With various types of market failures and/or more complex objective functions for the governments, a domestic emission tax which is equal to the international market price of emission permits is usually not an optimal response to an international agreement with tradable permits. For instance, the next two sections give examples of cases in which it may optimal for the government of each country to set its domestic tax rate on fuels higher than the market price of emission permits. Moreover, the domestic 'markups' will generally differ between countries.

A close parallel to a system of tradable CO_2 emission permits is an international carbon tax of the following type: Each *country* (through its central government) is taxed by some international agency in proportion to its CO_2 emissions. Except for the administrative costs of the international agency, the tax revenues could be reimbursed to the countries in proportion to a fixed set of reimbursement parameters. Assuming that each country is so small that it considers both total CO_2 emissions, and total tax revenue as (practically) independent of its own CO_2 emissions, it also considers its own reimbursement as given, since this reimbursement is a constant share of the total tax revenue.[12]

As before, country i wants its utility $u_i(c_i,z)$ to be as large as possible. Since z by assumption is regarded as exogenous, country i thus simply wants to maximise its consumption, which in the case of an international tax is given by

$$c_i = f_i(k_i, l_i, e_i) - qe_i + \beta_i qz \tag{30}$$

where q now stands for the international tax rate, qz is total tax revenue, and β_i is country i's share of this revenue. By comparing (30) with (28) we immediately see the equivalence between an international tax of this type and a system of tradable emission permits: in both case each country equates marginal abatement costs with the price of CO_2 emissions, which is equal to the price of emission permits under the system of tradable permits and equal to the carbon tax for the international tax case. In both cases the distribution of costs between countries is determined by the parameters β_i, i.e, by the initial distribution of permits under tradable emission permits and by the distribution of the tax revenue under an international tax.

The main advantage of tradable permits compared with an international tax is that the necessary institutional arrangements are simpler. Also, a system of tradable permits can be introduced into a climate agreement gradually over time: in any agreement with quantitative commitments for emissions for each country, the countries can themselves decide whether and when they want to participate in any kind of trading of emission quotas with other countries. An international tax, on the other hand, is more of an 'all or nothing' option.

A second weakness of a CO_2 tax compared with tradable emission quotas is that it is difficult to know exactly which tax rate corresponds to an agreed-upon level of total CO_2 emissions. However, for the case of CO_2 one is not particularly concerned about the exact emissions in any particular year, but rather about the development over several years. Once one has agreed upon a desirable development of CO_2 emissions, one can decide upon a corresponding initial CO_2 tax rate and a tentative future development of the CO_2 tax. If it turns out that the initial CO_2 tax gives a different level of CO_2 emissions than expected, the CO_2 tax at later dates can be adjusted up or down compared with the original plan for the CO_2 tax development. Through this type of procedure, one should relatively quickly be able to reach a path of CO_2 emissions which is close to the desired path. Nevertheless, a CO_2 tax does make frequent changes in the tax rate necessary, as a consequence of changes in technology, tastes, nominal prices, etc. With tradable permits, the desired path of CO_2 emissions can be obtained accurately and immediately, with the market working out the equilibrium price of quotas. However, in this case the problems are pushed over to each individual country: it is difficult for each country to achieve CO_2 emissions which are exactly equal to its emission quotas. The agreement must therefore in this case specify what the consequence should be for a country which has higher or lower emissions than what corresponds to its emission quotas.

Regarding the appropriate domestic policy response, it makes no difference whether the international agreement is based on tradable emission permits or on an international CO_2 tax of the type described above. In both cases each country faces a price per unit of CO_2 emissions, regarded as exogenous by each individual country.[13] A domestic policy response must be based on this price, but need otherwise not be affected by the institutional details of the international agreement.

It was argued above that the choice of domestic policies could be left to the individual countries. Efficiency at the national level requires that all sectors pay the full costs of the production factors they use. If all relevant markets were perfectly competitive, and governments were 'rational', it follows from the results in section 2 that it would be unnecessary to specify any international rules to prevent countries from subsidising their export industries. In the real world, however, the WTO has had to develop rules to counteract export subsidies. This may partly be due to the incentives for subsidising oligopolistic industries which were discussed in section 2, although this incentive was only present under specific assumptions about the oligopolistic market structure. A second reason why it is necessary to have rules preventing subsidies to export industries could be that export industries in several countries are strong lobbyists. Without any rules against subsidies, we could, therefore, get an inefficient trade pattern, with export industries in many countries being subsidised.

It is likely that export industries in many countries would try to be made exempt from domestic CO_2 taxes which are introduced as a response to an international CO_2 tax (or a system of tradable emission permits). This would lead to inefficiencies at the international (as well as the national) level. To prevent this, the agreement could include a requirement that the same types of policy instruments should be used for the export sectors as for the rest of the economy. If all countries use domestic carbon taxes as their policy responses, and set the rates equal to the international tax rate (or the international price of emission quotas), the agreement would thus imply that the export sectors of all countries would face the same carbon tax.

5 Carbon taxes and fiscally motivated taxes

If lump-sum taxation were feasible, there would be no point in using fuel taxes to raise revenue. In the absence of lump-sum taxation, on the other hand, all taxation involves distortions (except to the extent that taxes correct for negative externalities). In this case, there is an optimal mix of different tax forms, including taxes on fossil fuels. One of the earliest studies of the relationship between environmentally motivated taxes and fiscally motivated taxes is the pioneering work by Sandmo (1975). More recent work, some theoretical and some empirical, include Bovenberg and de Mooij (1993), Bovenberg and van der Ploeg (1994), Goulder (1995), Oates (1991) and Repetto *et al.* (1992).

To understand the relationship between a carbon tax and fiscally motivated taxes, consider the following simple model of an open economy.[14] There is one good produced in the economy (no results would change if we included several goods), and the amount produced (x) depends on the inputs of labour (l) and fossil fuels (z). The production function is

$$x = w\ell + f(z) \tag{31}$$

where $w(>0)$ is a constant technological parameter (equal to the marginal productivity of labour), and $f' > 0$ and $f'' < 0$. All of the production is exported at a price equal to 1, and the export income is used to import fuel input (z) as well as private and public consumption ($c_1 + g_1$) of fossil fuels and private and public consumption ($c_i + g_i$) of $n-1$ other consumer goods. The import prices are exogenously given by the vector $\mathbf{p} = (p_1, \ldots, p_n)$. In other words, the balance of payments constraint is

$$\Sigma_i p_i (c_i + g_i) + p_1 z = x \tag{32}$$

Public consumption of all goods is exogenous, while private consumption is determined by a representative household maximising its utility $u(c_1, \ldots c_n, \ell)$ of all goods (including leisure $-\ell$) given the budget constraint of the household

$$\max u(c_1, \ldots, c_n, \ell) \tag{33}$$

$$\text{s.t.} \Sigma_i q_i c_i = w\ell$$

Here consumer prices are given by the vector $\mathbf{q} = (q_1, \ldots, q_n)$, and $t_i \equiv q_i = p_i$ is the total tax on good i. The wage is w, i.e., equal to the marginal productivity of labour. It is thus assumed that we only have indirect taxation. However, none of the results would change if we also included a tax on wage income. To see this, assume that the budget equation is given by

$$\Sigma_i p_i (1 + \tau_i) c_i = (1 - \tau_w) w\ell \tag{34}$$

where τ_i is the relative tax on good i and τ_w is the relative tax on wages. This can be rewritten as the budget equation in (33), with

$$t_i = q_i - p_i = p_i \left[\frac{1+\tau_i}{1-\tau_w} - 1 \right] = p_i \frac{\tau_i + \tau_w}{1-\tau_w} \qquad (35)$$

The budget equation in (33) implies that the household does not receive any of the profits earned, this corresponds to an assumption that production is run by the government, or more plausibly, that all pure profits are taxed at a rate of 100 per cent.

The government must choose a tax rate t_0 on the fuel input, and tax rates $(t_1,...,t_n)$ on the consumer goods. The tax vector $(t_0,t_1,...,t_n)$ is chosen in order to maximise the utility level of the household, subject to a revenue requirement to cover the public consumption $\Sigma_i p_i g_i$, and a constraint on the total use of fossil fuels (i.e., total carbon emissions).

The optimal tax structure is derived in appendix A. The optimal size of the fuel input tax t_0, which we may call the pure carbon tax, depends on the emission constraint. The less carbon emissions the country is allowed to have, the higher will be t_0. If the country does not face a rigid emission constraint, but may buy carbon emission permits from other countries at a fixed price, the pure carbon tax rate t_0 should be equal to the price of such emission permits.

The optimal taxes on consumer goods are given by

$$t_1 = t_0 + \theta_1 q_1 \qquad (36)$$
$$t_1 = \theta_i q_i \quad \text{for} \quad i=2, 3,...,n$$

For $i>1$, the term θ_i in (36) is the total tax on consumer good i as a percentage of the consumer price. The term θ_1 is the fiscally motivated tax on fuel, i.e., the total fuel tax minus the pure carbon tax, as a percentage of the consumer price of fuel. All the terms θ_i are determined by

$$\Sigma_i \theta_i \epsilon_{ki} = -\delta + \Sigma_i \theta_i q_i \frac{\partial c_i}{\partial a} \quad k=1,...,n \qquad (37)$$

where ϵ_{ki} is the compensated demand elasticity of good k with respect to the price of good i, $\partial c_i / \partial a$ is the income derivative of good i, and δ is the shadow cost of public funds.[15]

Notice that θ_1, and thus $t_1 - t_0$, which is the fiscally motivated tax on fuel, does not depend directly on the size of the pure carbon tax t_0. The pure carbon tax and the fiscally motivated tax on fuel are in this sense additive. It is, of course, true that $t_1 - t_0$, as well as all t_i for $i>1$, will depend on the size of t_0, since the size of t_0 will generally affect the $\theta_i s$ indirectly via the parameter δ and perhaps through the price elasticities and income derivatives.

Even if t_0 is the same for all countries, the total fuel tax t_1 which households pay will normally differ across countries, since revenue requirements, demand elasticities, etc. normally differ across countries.

What if an international agreement specifies a minimum tax rate on all use of fuels, but otherwise places no restrictions on carbon emissions? If the tax is specified as a nominal tax, it follows from (35) that the agreement places no restriction on the choice of taxes for households: From (35) it is clear that any tax vector $(t_1,...,t_n)$ can be achieved for a given value of $p_1\tau_1$, through suitable choices of the other nominal tax rates $(\tau_1,...\tau_n,\tau_w)$.

If the international agreement specifies a minimum real tax rate t_0 on all use of fuels, it follows from the framework above that the optimal response from an individual country is as follows. The tax t_0 will be imposed on the producers. Households will either be faced with the tax t_0 on fuels (and all θ_is determined by (37) and $\theta_1 = t_0/q_1$), or all taxes will be determined by (36) and (37), except that t_0 in (36) will be replaced by 0. In this latter case the requirement $t_1 \geq t_0$ is not a binding constraint. In both cases, the tax structure will differ from the efficient outcome in which the governments take the social costs t_0 of carbon into account when determining their taxes.

6 Energy and carbon taxes in the presence of multidimensional environmental problems

Carbon emissions are only one of several types of externalities (environmental and others) which, at least to some extent, are linked to the use of fossil fuels. Other important emissions from the use of fossil fuels are NO_x, SO_2, VOC. Unlike CO_2, all of these emissions depend on other factors as well as on the total use of fossil fuels. The same is true for externalities associated with road traffic. To see the implications for a carbon tax, we shall consider a simple model with two types of emissions, namely CO_2 and an emission which depends on the use of fossil fuels as well as on other factors.

Let $\mathbf{v}$ be a vector of fossil fuels. The different elements of this vector are distinguished not only by the physical type of fuel, but also by where and how the fuel is used in the economy. Notation is chosen so that each v_j measures fuel in units of CO_2 emitted in the fuel's combustion. Total CO_2 emissions are denoted by x, so that

$$x = \Sigma_i v_i \tag{38}$$

Total emissions of the second pollutant are assumed to depend both on $\mathbf{v}$ and on a vector $\mathbf{z}$ denoting all other factors affecting the y-emissions, i.e.

$$y = f(v,z) \tag{39}$$

The elements of the vector z may include quantities of various inputs, but also parameters describing technology, how equipment is used, etc. If y for example measures emissions of NO_x, the vector z would include elements describing the technology of power plants and other industry using fossil fuels, and of automobiles and other transportation units. If y is a measure of road congestion, it would depend on the amount of gasoline used, as gasoline use is increasing with traffic volume. However, for a given amount of gasoline use, the traffic volume also depends on the fuel efficiency of the car park, which thus must be included in the vector z. In addition to the traffic volume, congestion will depend on when and where the traffic takes place, this type of description must therefore also be included in z in this example.

Total income R is assumed to depend on the vectors v and z, i.e., $R = R(v,z)$. Without any policy of correcting for externalities, producers and households will choose v and z so that R is maximised. Assume that the government has environmental goals given by the constraints

$$x \leq X$$
$$y \leq Y \tag{40}$$

where X and Y are exogenous. (The analysis would not be changed in any fundamental way if we instead of these constraints introduced an environmental cost function.) Maximisation of $R(v,z)$ subject to (38)–(40) gives

$$\frac{\partial R}{\partial v_j} = \lambda + \gamma \cdot \frac{\partial f}{\partial v_j} \tag{41}$$

$$\frac{\partial R}{\partial z_k} = \gamma \cdot \frac{\partial f}{\partial z_k} \tag{42}$$

where λ and γ are the shadow prices of the constraints $x \leq X$ and $y \leq Y$, respectively.

In a first-best world, where both CO_2 emissions x and the emissions y are observable, the optimum conditions (41) and (42) may be implemented by a carbon tax t and an emissions tax s on y-emissions. With these emission taxes, the private sector will maximise $R(v,z) - tx - sy$. Using (38) and (39) this maximisation gives

$$\frac{\partial R}{\partial v_j} = t + s \cdot \frac{\partial f}{\partial v_j} \tag{43}$$

$$\frac{\partial R}{\partial z_k} = s \cdot \frac{\partial f}{\partial z_k} \tag{44}$$

Comparing with (41) and (42), it is thus clear that the social optimum will be reached if the emission taxes are chosen so that $t=\lambda$ and $s=\gamma$.

In practice, CO_2 emissions are not directly observable. However, this is of no consequence, due to the proportionality between fuel use and CO_2 emissions. The carbon tax t is therefore in practice a tax on fossil fuels, proportional to the carbon content of the fuel.

For most environmental externalities linked with the use of fossil fuels, costs of measurement, transactions and administration prevent a comprehensive use of an emission tax. For instance, even though it may be possible to measure and tax emissions of NO_x and SO_2 from some of the largest emitters, it is in practice impossible to monitor for example NO_x emissions from the individual car driver. The same is true for other types of externalities, such as traffic congestion. This externality can at least to some extent be taken care of through appropriate road pricing, with prices depending on place, time and type of vehicle. Although road pricing of this type at least in principle is possible, it is not broadly used in most countries, making it necessary to take congestion externalities into consideration when calculating an optimal tax on gasoline.

If the y-emissions cannot be monitored at the level of the micro unit (i.e., producer and/or household), an alternative is to regulate the use of the z-vector. This can be done either directly or through taxes τ_k on the use of factor k. If taxes on fossil fuel j in this case is t_j, the private sector chooses the v-vector and those elements of the z-vector which are not directly regulated to maximise $R(v,z)-\Sigma_i t_i v_i - \Sigma_i \tau_i z_i$. This gives

$$\frac{\partial R}{\partial v_j}=t_j \tag{45}$$

$$\frac{\partial R}{\partial z_k}=\tau_k \text{ for those } k \text{ which are not directly regulated}$$

In principle, the socially optimal vector z may be achieved through appropriate taxes τ_k and/or direct regulation of elements of the z vector. In practice, it is of course difficult to fine-tune the emission taxes or the directly regulated z_k elements to achieve the full optimum.

Whatever values one ends up with for the vector z, the socially optimal fuel volumes are given by equation (41). Together with (45), it is thus clear that the socially optimal fuel taxes are given by

$$t_j=\lambda+\gamma\cdot\frac{\partial f}{\partial v_j} \tag{46}$$

These fuel taxes consist of two terms. The first term, λ, is a pure carbon tax, and is equal for all types of fuels, and independent of where and how the fuel is used. The second term is fuel specific, and is equal to the marginal impact of the fuel on the other emission type which is of concern. From the definition of the vector v given above, it is clear that total fuel taxes should not only differ between different physical types of fuels (per unit of carbon) but also depend on where and how the fuels are used. It is important to realise that this conclusion is valid even if the government uses specific policy instruments (taxes or other) directed towards the z-vector. Examples of such policy instruments are technological specifications aimed at limiting for example emissions of NO_x and SO_2 (such as catalytic converters on automobiles) or high taxes on cars to limit total road traffic. As long as the concern for the y-externality is not completely accounted for through policies aimed directly at the quantity y, total fuel taxes will have to include terms of the type given by the second term in equation (46).

We conclude this section by considering a recent analysis of Newbery (1992). He studies the relationship between a carbon tax, on the one hand, and, on the other hand, a gasoline tax designed to internalise various externalities associated with road traffic. He shows that the carbon tax and the specific gasoline tax are additive, corresponding to our equation (46). With Newbery's assumptions, the marginal cost of traffic externalities, corresponding to our shadow price γ, is constant. Newbery argues that in this case the long-run value of the specific gasoline tax, corresponding to the second term in our equation (46), will be higher the stricter the CO_2 goal is, i.e., the higher the shadow price λ is. The reason is that as λ increases, the total gasoline tax and thus the consumer price of gasoline increases. In the long run, this price increase will induce increased fuel efficiency, thus giving a larger volume of traffic per unit of gasoline. In equation (46), this corresponds to an increase in $\partial f / \partial v_j$ (when j is gasoline for road transport), thus increasing the second term in (46).

7 Should carbon taxes be equalised across countries, types of fossil fuels and sectors?

In a first-best world, carbon taxes should be equalised across countries, across sectors within each country, and across types of fossil fuels. As mentioned previously, a carbon tax is in practice a tax on the use of fossil fuels. In sections 5 and 6, we argued that there are several reasons why the *total* taxes on fossil fuels ought to differ between countries, and that the total taxes on fossil fuels (per unit of carbon) within each country ought to differ between types of fuels and between different sectors of the economy.

In this section we consider a pure carbon tax, i.e., we ignore taxes on fossil fuels for fiscal purposes or for correcting other externalities. In this case a first-best optimum would imply equal carbon taxes for all countries. If, however, side payments between countries for some reason are ruled out (or at least restricted), a situation with different carbon taxes for different countries may be Pareto optimal. To see this, consider the following thought experiment: Starting with equal carbon taxes in all countries, taxes are reduced in some countries and increased in others, in such a way that total emissions from all countries remain unchanged. Obviously, welfare will increase for the countries which reduce their tax, since they get lower domestic distortions, without any deterioration of their environment. Countries which increase their carbon tax must for the same reason get a reduction in their welfare. If side payments are ruled out, neither of the two situations (uniform versus differentiated carbon taxes) is Pareto inferior to the other. Thus, both situations are (constrained) Pareto optimal.[16]

Although one can give a theoretical justification for a differentiation of carbon taxes across countries, it is difficult to defend the crucial assumption of ruling out side payments. In section 4 it was argued that side payments are a built in feature of a scheme of tradable emission permits. In such a scheme, a rational response of each country would be to set the pure carbon tax equal to the market price of emission permits, thus making the pure carbon tax equal across countries.

Consider next the issue of whether or not carbon taxes should be equalised across sectors within a country. According to standard welfare theory, all users of carbon should face the same carbon tax, as the environmental (i.e., climate) externality of using carbon is independent of where it is used. This argument for equal carbon taxes across sectors is certainly valid in a situation where there are no other distortions in the economy. If other distortions are present, however, it is no longer obvious that it is (second-best) optimal to equalize carbon taxes across sectors. One important possible distortion is that an international climate agreement may be incomplete: as was argued above, in a situation where side payments were feasible, a Pareto optimum would imply that the marginal abatement costs of CO_2 emissions was the same in all countries. However, this is only possible to achieve if one could succeed in getting all countries to participate in an international climate agreement. Limited participation in a climate agreement seems to be quite likely during the next decade or so. There is a strong incentive for each country to be a free rider, i.e., not to participate in the agreement. By not participating, a country can enjoy (almost) the same benefits of reduced emissions as if it participates in the agreement, while it does not bear any of the costs of reducing emissions.

The issue of free riding has been studied in more detail by for example Barrett (1990, 1992), Bauer (1992), Carraro and Siniscalco (1993) and Hoel (1992). These studies demonstrate that, in spite of the free-rider incentive, a stable coalition of cooperating countries may exist, in the sense that it is not in the self-interest of any country to break out of the coalition. It is beyond the scope of this study to give a detailed discussion of how large such a coalition might be, and of what mechanisms might exist giving countries incentives to cooperate in spite of the free-rider incentive. In the subsequent discussion, we shall simply assume that cooperation to reduce CO_2 emissions is limited to a fixed coalition of countries. In such a case, one could make the following argument: a high carbon tax for carbon-intensive tradable sectors in the cooperating countries will reduce the production of goods from these sectors, and therefore CO_2 emissions, in the cooperating countries. However, this will to a large extent be counteracted by increased production of such goods in the countries which have no climate policy. And, since it is only *total* CO_2 emissions from *all* countries which are relevant for the climate, there is no point in a policy which simply relocates CO_2 emissions from the cooperating countries to the countries which have no climate policy. According to this line of reasoning, carbon-intensive tradable sectors should thus face a lower carbon tax than other sectors of the economy.

This issue has been treated in detail in Hoel (1996a).[17] The starting point of this paper is a situation in which a group of countries, for example the EU or the OECD countries, have committed themselves to cooperate. These countries, which we call the signatories, are assumed to coordinate their policies in a way which maximises the sum of welfare for the signatories. This level of welfare depends on the signatories' consumption of all goods as well as total CO_2 emissions. Since the environmental (=climate) effect of CO_2 emissions depends on the sum of emissions from *all* countries, it is *total* CO_2 emissions which affect the welfare of the signatories. Emissions from the non-signatories will generally depend on international prices of several goods, in particular of the prices of fossil fuels and of energy-intensive traded goods. As international prices generally depend on the net import vector of the signatories, foreign emissions will also depend on the net import vector of the signatories. This relationship must be taken into consideration in the optimisation problem of the signatories.

The optimal climate policy for the signatories is derived in appendix B and in Hoel (1996a).[18] An important conclusion is that the social optimum may be implemented by a carbon tax which is the same for all users of fossil fuels, i.e., both for consumers and for all sectors using fossil fuels as an input in production (among the signatories). The possible effect of the consumption and production of traded goods among the signatories on emissions from the non-signatories (through international prices) may be taken care of via tariffs on the traded goods, i.e., as a tax or subsidy on net imports or net exports.

This result is not surprising. There are two types of externalities within the cooperating countries, which may be internalised through appropriate taxes (or subsidies). First, there is the environmental externality of the emissions from the signatories, which may be internalised through a uniform tax on the use of carbon. Second, there are externalities via the net imports of various goods, which affect the environment via the effect of the net imports on the behaviour of other countries. Obviously, it is not the signatories' production or consumption of a good which affects the behaviour of the non-signatories, but only the net import of the good. This externality may thus be internalised through appropriate taxes (positive or negative) on the net imports of traded goods.

In addition to affecting the environment through the effect on the behaviour of non-signatories, changing the net import of a good will generally have a terms of trade effect. This effect is not internalised by the individual firms in a competitive economy. The optimal tariffs should thus reflect both these terms of trade effects as well as the environmental effects, see appendix B and Hoel (1996a) for details.

It also follows from the analysis in appendix B that the carbon tax should be equalised across fuels (per unit of carbon). However, the optimal tariffs will generally differ between fuels. If the optimal tariff of a fuel i is negative, but smaller in absolute value than the carbon tax (when both are measured per unit of carbon), the combination of the carbon tax and the tariff is a method of discouraging both the use and the production of the fuel in the countries who are participating in the climate agreement. To see this, denote the international price of fuel i by p_i, its optimal tariff by τ_i, and the optimal carbon tax by t (everything measured per unit of carbon of the fuel). Then the price to consumers is $p_i + \tau_i + t$, while the producers (in the cooperating countries) get $p_i + \tau_i$. The same prices for users and producers of the fuel could alternatively have been achieved with taxes θ_i^c and θ_i^p on use and production, respectively. This would give consumers and producers the prices $p_i + \theta_i^c$ and $p_i - \theta_i^p$, respectively, which are equal to the prices $p_i + \tau_i + t$ and $p_i + \tau_i$ if $\theta_i^p = -\tau_i$ and $\theta_i^c = \tau_i + t$. Clearly, θ_i^c and θ_i^p are both positive if $t > -\tau_i > 0$, so that in this case both consumption and production of fossil fuels are discouraged by an optimal climate policy (see Golombek *et al.* (1994, 1995) and Hoel (1994) for a further discussion).

What if one for some reason rules out the use of tariffs (i.e., taxes/subsidies on net imports), and also production taxes/subsidies and other policy instruments affecting the production of goods? Not surprisingly, the constrained social optimum in this case requires a differentiation of carbon taxes across sectors. However, it is shown in Hoel (1996a) that the exact calculation of the optimal tax structure in this case is quite complex. In particular, more detailed numerical information of the economy is required for this calculation than for the calculation of the optimal tariffs. There is no simple relationship between for example fossil fuel intensity or the effect on foreign emissions, on the one hand, and the optimal carbon tax, on the other hand.

If one rules out the use of tariffs, it may thus be optimal to differentiate carbon taxes across sectors. It is, however, difficult to find good reasons for why one should rule out the use of tariffs. Trade policy arguments could be made against import and export taxes/subsidies. However, similar arguments could also be made against differentiating taxes (in this case carbon taxes) across sectors. Moreover, the non-signatories are not in a very strong position to argue against tariffs which might hurt them. The justification for the tariffs is after all an attempt to avoid excessive carbon emissions from the non-signatories. Any non-signatory which claims to be adversely affected by the tariffs can avoid the tariffs by participating in the climate agreement instead of being a free rider.

The constrained optimum in which both tariffs on the net imports of fuels and taxes/subsidies on the production of fuels (as well as other policy instruments affecting production) are ruled out has been treated in detail by Golombek *et al.* (1994, 1995). In this case it will generally be optimal to differentiate the carbon tax across fuels (per unit of carbon). In a numerical illustration given in Golombek *et al.* (1995), it is assumed that the signatories consist of all the OECD countries, and that all non-OECD countries are non-signatories. In this numerical illustration the carbon tax is higher for oil than for coal and natural gas.

8 Conclusions

Several issues have been touched upon in this chapter. Although the treatment of most of the issues has been rather brief, a number of conclusions have been drawn. Some of these conclusions have important policy implications. This section therefore gives a brief repetition of the most important points which follow from the analyses of the previous sections.

1 For national environmental problems (i.e., no international externalities), no coordination of environmental taxes between countries is necessary under 'ideal conditions'. 'Ideal conditions' include the following assumptions: (a) there are no market failures other than the environmental externality, (b) governments maximise the welfare of a representative household, (c) the environmental externality can be monitored at the micro level, for example emission levels from a firm or consumption levels of a good which has a negative impact on the environment.

2 In practice, the three conditions mentioned under conclusion 1 will not hold. In this case an appropriate coordination of environmental taxes will be Pareto superior to the non-cooperative outcome in which taxes are determined at the country level.

3 The fact that a coordination of environmental taxes might be better than a decentralised determination of environmental taxes does *not*

mean that environmental taxes should be uniform across countries. Generally, tax rates differ in a social optimum, and there may be quite large differences in the optimal tax rates between countries. If tax coordination for practical reasons means a harmonisation of taxes across countries (i.e., equal environmental taxes in all countries), it need no longer be true that a cooperative outcome is better than the non-cooperative outcome in which taxes are determined at the country level.

4 For transnational environmental problems, one will usually need some kind of international environmental agreement. There are two main types of international environmental agreements: those that focus directly on emissions in each country, and those that focus on environmental policies in each country. An example of the second type is an agreement which specifies the emission tax rates to be used in each country. In this case the optimal taxes will normally differ between counties.

5 Emission taxes may play an important role also for international environmental agreements which directly specify emission levels for each country: Given the total emissions a country is permitted to have, an appropriately chosen domestic emission tax is a cost-effective way to achieve this target level of total emissions.

6 The climate problem is a special case of a transnational environmental problem. For this special case international cost effectiveness requires that the marginal costs of reducing CO_2 emissions should be equal across countries. This could be achieved through an agreement specifying an equal carbon tax in all countries.

7 Even if a (pure) carbon tax should be equalised across countries, total taxes on fossil fuels should also take into consideration other externalities as well as fiscal effects (in the absence of lump-sum taxation). Total fuel taxes will therefore normally differ across countries in a social optimum.

8 It may be difficult to design a good climate agreement which is based on a coordination of fuel taxes across countries. One difficulty is that total fuel taxes ought to differ between countries, cf. conclusion 7. A second (and related) difficulty is the free-rider incentive each country will have, implying that it is in its interest to have little or no restriction on its own CO_2 emissions, given the emissions from other countries, or given the policies of other countries. If a government is required to have a specific carbon tax through an international agreement, it is therefore in the interest of that government to try to reduce the effect of this tax, for instance by reducing other domestic taxes on fossil fuels. A third difficulty is the distribution of cost between countries associated with an agreement specifying an equal carbon tax for all countries. Even if *mar-*

ginal costs of reducing CO_2 emissions are equalised across countries, *total* costs of reducing emissions will generally differ between countries.

9 An international climate agreement could specify a reduction of emissions in all countries by some uniform percentage rate compared with a specified base year. However, equal percentage reductions of emissions from different countries usually give an inefficient outcome, in the sense that the marginal costs of reducing emissions will differ between countries. Whatever the total emissions are, the same environmental goals could therefore be achieved at lower costs through a different distribution of emission reductions. Moreover, an agreement specifying uniform percentage reductions of emissions may give a very uneven distribution of burdens between countries.

10 For the climate problem, an international agreement based on tradable emission permits for CO_2 has several advantages compared both with an agreement specifying a particular carbon tax to be used by all countries, and with a uniform percentage reduction type of agreement of the type described in conclusion 9.

11 In an agreement with tradable emission permits, countries are given an incentive, but not a rigid instruction, to reduce their CO_2 emissions. It would be up to the government of each individual country to decide by how much it should reduce its emissions, and to choose appropriate policy instruments to reduce them. A domestic carbon tax is a possible domestic policy response to an international agreement based on tradable emission permits.

12 The optimal rate of a domestic carbon tax as a response to an international agreement with tradable emission permits depends on the international market price of emission permits. Under specific simplifying assumptions about the functioning of the economy, an optimal response is to set the domestic carbon tax equal to this market price of emission permits. However, with various types of market failures and/or more complex objective functions for the governments than assumed in the simplest models, the optimal rate of the domestic carbon tax may differ from the international market price of emission permits. Sections 5 and 6 give examples of cases in which it may be optimal for the government of each country to set its domestic tax rate on fuels higher than the market price of emission permits, with the domestic 'markups' generally differing between countries.

13 In a climate agreement where some, but not all countries participate, the participating countries should take the response of the non-participating countries into account when they determine their climate policy. In section 7, it is shown that this may be done through appropriate tariffs on imports and exports of goods to and from the group of cooperating

countries. If such tariffs for some reason are ruled out, it may be optimal for the cooperating countries to let their carbon taxes differ across sectors and across fuels (per unit of carbon).

Appendix A Derivation of optimal taxes on fuel and other goods in the absence of lump-sum taxation

The maximisation problem defined by (33) gives the demand and supply functions $c_i(\mathbf{q})$ and $\lambda(\mathbf{q})$. The indirect utility function is defined by

$$v(\mathbf{q}) \equiv u(c_1(q), \dots, c_n(q), \ell(q)) \tag{A1}$$

and has the property

$$\frac{\partial v}{\partial q_k} = -\lambda c_k \tag{A2}$$

where λ is the household's marginal utility of a hypothetical lump-sum transfer of 1 dollar. Equations (31)–(33) give us the government's budget constraint

$$\Sigma_i t_i c_i(\mathbf{q}) + [f(z) - p_1 z] = \Sigma_i p_i g_i \equiv T \tag{A3}$$

In other words, total tax revenue is equal to the tax revenue from the indirect taxation plus profits from production $(= x - w\ell - p_1 z = f(z) - p_1 z)$.

The government's optimisation problem may now be formulated as (where $\mathbf{t} = (t_1, \dots, t_n)$)

$$\max_{z, t_1, \dots, t_a} \quad v(\mathbf{p} + \mathbf{t})$$

$$\text{s.t.} \quad \Sigma_i t_i c_i(\mathbf{p} + \mathbf{t}) + [f(z) - p_1 z] = T$$

$$c_1(\mathbf{p} + \mathbf{t}) + z \leq E \tag{A4}$$

The inequality $c_1(\cdot) + z \leq E$ represents a constraint stating that total carbon emissions (=total use of fossil fuels) must not exceed E. For now, we may think of E as imposed through a rigid form of international agreement. We shall return to the case in which E is chosen by the government within the framework of an international agreement with tradable emission permits.

The Lagrangian corresponding to (A4) is

$$L = v(\mathbf{p} + \mathbf{t}) + \mu[\Sigma_i t_i c_i(\mathbf{p} + \mathbf{t}) + f(z) - p_1 z - T] + \gamma[E - z - c_1(\mathbf{p} + \mathbf{t})] \tag{A5}$$

Straightforward derivations, using (A2), give the following first-order conditions

$$f'(z) = p_1 + \frac{\gamma}{\mu} \tag{A6}$$

$$(\mu - \lambda)c_k + \mu \Sigma_i t_i \frac{\partial c_i}{\partial q_k} - \gamma \frac{\partial c_1}{\partial q_k} = 0 \tag{A7}$$

The interpretation of (A6) is that producers should pay a carbon tax $\tau = \gamma/\mu$. Equation (A7) may be rewritten as

$$\left(1 - \frac{\lambda}{\mu}\right)c_k + \left(t_1 - \frac{\gamma}{\mu}\right)\frac{\partial c_1}{\partial q_k} + \Sigma_{i>1} t_i \frac{\partial c_i}{\partial q_k} = 0 \tag{A8}$$

According to the Slutsky equations

$$S_{ki} = S_{ik} = \frac{\partial c_i}{\partial q_k} + c_k \frac{\partial c_i}{\partial a} \tag{A9}$$

where S_{ik} are the compensated price derivatives and $\partial c_i/\partial a$ is the income derivative for good i (a is a hypothetical lump-sum transfer to the household). Inserting (36) and (A9) into (A8) and using the definition $\epsilon_{ki} = S_{ki}q_i/c_k$ of the compensated price elasticities we find

$$\Sigma_i \theta_i \epsilon_{ki} = -\left(1 - \frac{\lambda}{\mu}\right) + \Sigma_i \theta_i q_i \frac{\partial c_i}{\partial a} \quad k = 1,\ldots,n \tag{A10}$$

which is equivalent to (37) when the parameter δ is defined as $(\mu - \lambda)/\mu$.

In the optimisation problem defined by (A4), E was a rigid ceiling on the country's total carbon emissions, imposed through an international agreement. As discussed in section 4, a more flexible form of international agreement would allow the government to buy additional emission permits (or sell excess permits) at a market price Q. In this case E would be the initial allocation of emission permits to the country, and the revenue requirement of the government would be $T + Q \cdot [c_1(\mathbf{p}+\mathbf{t}) + z - E]$. The optimisation problem would thus be changed from (A4) to

$$\max_{z, t_1, \ldots, t_a} v(\mathbf{p}+\mathbf{t})$$

$$\text{s.t.} \quad \Sigma_i t_i c_i(\mathbf{p}+\mathbf{t}) + [f(z) - p_1 z] = T + Q \cdot [c_1(\mathbf{p}+\mathbf{t}) + z - E] \tag{A11}$$

and the corresponding Lagrangian is

$$L = v(\mathbf{p}+\mathbf{t}) + \mu[\Sigma_i t_i c_i(\mathbf{p}+\mathbf{t}) + f(z) - p_1 z - T - Q \cdot (z + c_1(\mathbf{p}+\mathbf{t}) - E)] \tag{A12}$$

Comparing this equation with (A5), we see that the only change from our original optimisation problem is that γ is now replaced by μQ. This means that γ/μ in (A6) must be replaced by Q. In other words, the optimal pure carbon tax rate is in this case equal to the market price of emission permits (i.e., $t_0 = Q$).

Appendix B Fuel taxes and import/export tariffs in an incomplete climate agreement

Consider an economy consisting of a group of cooperating countries, with a consumption vector $\mathbf{c}=(c_1,\ldots,c_n)$, where the first m goods are fossil fuels. The corresponding production vector is $\mathbf{x}=(x_1,\ldots,x_n)$, and international prices are given by the vector $\mathbf{p}=(p_1,\ldots,p_n)$.[19] The production function of sector j is given by

$$x_j = F_j(\ell_j, v_{1j}, \ldots, v_{mj}) \tag{B1}$$

where ℓ_j is labour used in sector j and v_{ij} is fuel i used as an input in sector j. Total labour input is exogenously given, equal to L, so that

$$\Sigma_i \ell_i = L \tag{B2}$$

Each international price may in general depend on the vector $\mathbf{c}+\mathbf{v}-\mathbf{x}$ of net imports, where $\mathbf{v}=(\Sigma_j v_{1j},\ldots,\Sigma_j v_{mj})$, so that the balance of payments constraint may be written as

$$\sum_i p_i(\mathbf{c}+\mathbf{v}-\mathbf{x})\cdot(c_i+v_i-x_i)=0 \tag{B3}$$

The environmental costs of carbon emissions depends on emissions from *all* countries, i.e., also on emissions from the countries not participating in the climate agreement. These latter emissions, which henceforth are called foreign emissions, will in general depend on all international prices. Since these prices may depend on the net imports of the cooperating countries, foreign emissions will in general depend on the net import vector $\mathbf{c}+\mathbf{v}-\mathbf{x}$. Denoting this relationship by the function $h(\mathbf{c}+\mathbf{v}-\mathbf{x})$, total emissions are thus given by

$$e = \Sigma_i a_i(c_i + \Sigma_j v_{ij}) + h(\mathbf{c}+\mathbf{v}-\mathbf{x}) \tag{B4}$$

where a_i is the carbon content of fuel i (so that $a_i=0$ for all non-fuel goods, i.e., for $i>m$).

The welfare of the cooperating countries (V) is equal to the utility of the consumption vector minus the environmental costs of total emissions, i.e.

$$V = U(\mathbf{c}) - D(e) \tag{B5}$$

The cooperating countries thus want to maximise V subject to (B1)–(B4). The Lagrangian corresponding to this maximisation problem is

$$\begin{aligned}
H = & U(\mathbf{c}) - D(e) + \Sigma_j \delta_j [F_j(\ell_j, v_{1j}, \ldots, v_{mj}) - x_j] \\
& + \gamma[e - \Sigma_i a_i(c_i + \Sigma_j v_{ij}) - h(\mathbf{c}+\mathbf{v}-\mathbf{x})] \\
& - \lambda[\Sigma_i p_i(\mathbf{c}+\mathbf{v}-\mathbf{x})\cdot(c_i + \Sigma_j v_{ij} - x_i)] \\
& + \mu[L - \Sigma_j \ell_j]
\end{aligned} \tag{B6}$$

Define

$$h_i = \frac{\partial h}{\partial(c_i + \Sigma_j v_{ij} - x_i)}$$

and

$$T_i = \Sigma_k (c_k + \Sigma_j v_{kj} - x_k) \frac{\partial p_k}{\partial(c_i + \Sigma_j v_{ij} - x_i)}$$

The term h_i measures the change in foreign emissions as a consequence of a marginal increase of imports of good i. This term may be negative or positive, depending on the characteristics of the good. If for example good i is relatively energy intensive, we would expect h_i to be positive, as increased net import of such a good increases its international price, thus increasing foreign production and therefore foreign emissions. The opposite is true for a good which uses little or no fossil fuels: an increased international price caused by increased net imports will increase foreign production of this good, and thus reduce foreign production of other goods, which are more energy intensive. In this latter case we therefore have h_i negative.

The term T_i measures the terms of trade effect of an increase of the import of good i. If cross-price effects are small, we would expect T_i to be negative or positive depending on whether good i is an export or an import good.

After some manipulation, the first-order conditions of this maximisation problem may be written as

$$\frac{\partial u}{\partial c_j} = \lambda \left[p_j + T_j + \frac{\gamma}{\lambda}(a_j + h_j) \right]$$

$$\left[p_j + T_j + \frac{\gamma}{\lambda} h_j \right] \frac{\partial F_j}{\partial v_{ij}} = p_i + T_i + \frac{\gamma}{\lambda}(a_i + h_i)] \qquad \text{(B7)}$$

$$\left[p_j + T_j + \frac{\gamma}{\lambda} h_j \right] \frac{\partial F_j}{\partial \ell_j} = \frac{\mu}{\lambda}$$

$$D'(e) = \gamma$$

Consider next a competitive economy, with a fuel tax t per unit of carbon and taxes τ_j on the net import of good j (i.e. a subsidy τ_j on the net export of good j). With such taxes the domestic proces are as follows:

consumers pay $p_j + \tau_j + a_j t$ for good j
producers get $p_j + \tau_j$ for good j
producers pay $p_i + \tau_i + a_i t$ for fuel i
producers pay w for labour

With these prices, households' utility maximisation and producers' profit maximisation gives

$$\frac{\partial u}{\partial c_j} = \xi[p_j + \theta_j + a_j t]$$

$$[p_j + \tau_j]\frac{\partial F_j}{\partial v_{ij}} = p_i + \tau_i + a_i t \tag{B8}$$

$$[p_j + \tau_j]\frac{\partial F_j}{\partial \ell_j} = w$$

Comparing (B7) with (B8), we immediately see that these two equations are equivalent if the carbon tax and the tariffs are chosen as follows

$$t = \frac{\gamma}{\lambda}$$

$$\tau_j = T_j + th_j \tag{B9}$$

With these taxes, $\xi = \lambda$ is the marginal utility of income, and the equilibrium wage rate is given by $w = \mu/\lambda$. The interpretation of (B9) is that the carbon tax is equal to the marginal environmental cost of carbon emissions measured in money: $\gamma = D'$ is the marginal environmental cost measured in utility, while λ is the marginal utility of income. D'/λ is thus a monetary measure of the marginal environmental cost of carbon emissions. The tariff τ_j consists of two terms. The first term (T_j) measures the terms of trade effect of an increase of imports of good j. The second term (th_j) measures the value of the change in foreign emissions as a consequence of a marginal increase of imports of good j. Since neither T_j nor h_j is unambiguously signed, the sign of τ_j is also indetermined. Typically, the vector $(\tau_1,...,\tau_n)$ will have some negative and some positive elements.

We can thus conclude that a social optimum may be implemented by a common carbon tax on all users, combined with appropriately chosen taxes/subsidies on exports and imports of the tradable goods.

As an alternative to a carbon tax combined with import/export tariffs, one could implement the social optimum with an equivalent scheme of consumer and producer taxes/subsidies on all goods: the domestic prices given after (B7) could be achieved with consumer taxes given by $\tau_j + a_j t$ on all goods (applying also to fuels used as inputs by producers) and output taxes equal to $-\tau_j$ on the domestic production of all goods. These 'taxes' will generally consist of some negative and some positive elements, i.e., for some goods one will either subsidise consumption or production in a social optimum. In particular, it can never be optimal to have a positive tax both on consumption and on production of non-fuel goods, since $-\tau_j$ has the opposite sign of $\tau_j + a_j t$ when $a_j = 0$.

Notes

Significant parts of this chapter draw heavily on research done at the Foundation for Research in Economics and Business Administration in Oslo, and financed by the Research Council of Norway, the Nordic Council of Ministers, and the European Communities' Environment programme. Financial support from the Fondazione Eni Enrico Mattei is gratefully acknowledged. I also thank Elin Halvorsen for useful assistance.

1 k and l of course also depend on w. However, as w is kept constant in the analysis, we omit it from the functions $k(\cdot)$ and $l(\cdot)$.
2 There is also a distortionary cost of subsidising one's own production. However, at the initial point of zero subsidies, this is a second-order effect, while the benefit of reduced output by other oligopolists is a first-order effect.
3 See Hoel (1990) for a discussion of what happens if some, but not all, countries act in a more altruistic way.
4 One cannot rule out the possibility that a non-cooperative outcome may have lower emissions for *some* (but not all) countries than a Pareto optimal outcome, see, e.g., Hoel (1996b).
5 It is not difficult to construct realistic examples for which some countries prefer the non-cooperative outcome to the Pareto optimal outcome without side payments. This will for example be the case for country j in an 'upstream-downstream' environmental issue, where country j is the most upstream country. For this case $a_{ij} = 0$ for $i \neq j$, so that any change in the emission level of country j away from the non-cooperative emission level will reduce this country's welfare.
6 Possibly also differentiated between different cars, depending on fuel efficiency.
7 As will be shown below, this might need to be slightly qualified, due to international trade considerations.
8 In practice, one would have to agree upon a *time path* of emissions, and allocate emission permits for each period (which could be a year, or a period of say five years) within the total time span covered by the agreement.
9 Notice that an agreement of uniform percentage reductions is a special case of these two first steps: one agrees upon some target level of total emissions, and distributes entitlements in proportion to each country's emissions in a specified base year. If the target level for total emissions is equal to say 80 per cent of total emissions in this base year, this is equivalent to an agreement of all countries reducing their emissions by 20 per cent from their base year emissions.
10 There is of course no guarantee that a competitive market in emission permits, in which all countries are price takers, will develop. For discussions of cases in which some or all countries are not price takers, see for example Hahn (1984), Misiolek and Elder (1989) and Hoel (1996b).
11 In Hoel (1991) it is shown that this efficiency property of a system of tradable emission permits is valid under quite general assumptions about the objective

functions of the countries' governments, the constraints on policies and the functioning of the economies.

12 See Hoel (1996b) for a discussion of the complications which arise if some countries are 'large', in the sense that they do not ignore their own influence on total emissions.

13 This must be qualified somewhat for 'large' countries, cf. Hoel (1996b).

14 Unlike most of the work mentioned above, the presentation in this chapter considers taxation both of producers, using fuel as an input, and households. Moreover, the concern for the environment is in this presentation modelled as an obligation to adhere to an international climate agreement.

15 A 1 dollar reduction of the government's revenue requirement increases the utility level of the household just as much as a lump-sum transfer of $1 + \delta$ dollars.

16 Cf. also Chichilnisky and Heal (1994), who show that marginal emission costs in general will differ across countries in a constrained Pareto optimum (i.e., in a Pareto optimum where side payments are ruled out).

17 Some of the results of this study were first derived by Markusen (1975).

18 Hoel (1994b) uses a more general description of the production technology than the analysis in appendix B, and also explicitly includes non-traded goods in the analysis. On the other hand, different types of fuels are explicitly included in the analysis in appendix B, while there is only one aggregate fuel in the analysis of Hoel (1994a).

19 To simplify notation, all goods are assumed to be tradable. As shown in Hoel (1996a), the results remain valid also when non-tradable goods are included in the analysis.

References

d'Arge, R.C. (1975), 'On the Economics of Transnational Environmental Externalities', in E. Mills (ed.), *Economic Analysis of Environmental Problems*, New York: Columbia University Press, pp. 397–434.

Barrett, S. (1990), 'The Problem of Global Environmental Protection', *Oxford Review of Economic Policy*, 6 (1), 68–79.

    (1994a), 'Self-Enforcing International Environmental Agreements', *Oxford Economic Papers*, 46, 878–894.

    (1994), 'Strategic Environmental Policy and International Trade', 54(3), 325–38.

Bauer, A. (1992), 'International Cooperation over Environmental Goods', mimeo, Seminar fuer empirische Wirtschaftsforschung, Universität München.

Baumol, W.J. and W.E., Oates (1988), *The Theory of Environmental Policy*, 2nd edn., Cambridge University Press.

Bohm, P. and B. Larsen (1994), 'Fairness in a Tradeable-Permit Treaty for Carbon Emissions Reductions in Europe and the former Soviet Union', *Environmental and Resource Economics*, 4(3), 219–39.

Bovenberg, A.L. and de R.A. Mooij (1993), 'Do Environmental Taxes Yield a Double Dividend?', Research Memorandum 9302, Research Centre for Economic Policy, Erasmus University, Rotterdam.

Bovenberg, A.L. and F. van der Ploeg (1994), 'Environmental Policy, Public Finance and the Labour Market in a Second-Best World', *Journal of Public Economics*, 55, 349–90.

Brander, J.A. and B.J. Spencer (1985), 'Export Subsidies and International Market Share Rivalry', *Journal of International Economics*, 18, 83–100.

Carraro, C. and D. Siniscalco (1993), 'Strategies for the International Protection of the Environment', *Journal of Public Economics*, 52, 309–28.

Chichilnisky, G. and G. Heal (1993), 'Who Should Abate Carbon Emissions? An International Viewpoint', *Economics Letters*, 44(4), 443–9.

Eaton, J. and G.M. Grossman (1986), 'Optimal Trade and Industrial Policy under Oligopoly', *Quarterly Journal of Economics*, 101, 383–406.

Golombek, R., C. Hagem and M. Hoel (1995), 'Efficient Incomplete International Climate Agreements', *Resource and Energy Economics*, 17, 25–46.

— (1994), 'The Design of a Carbon Tax in an Incomplete International Climate Agreement', in C. Carraro (ed.), *Trade, Innovation, Environment*, Kluwer.

Goulder, L.H. (1995), 'Effects of Carbon Taxes in an Economy with Prior Tax Distortions: An Intertemporal General Equilibrium Analysis', *Journal Environmental Economics and Management*, 29(3), 271–97.

Hahn, R.W. (1984), 'Market Power and Transferable Property Rights', *Quarterly Journal of Economics*, 99, 753–65.

Hoel, M. (1990), 'Global Environmental Problems: The Effects of Unilateral Actions Taken by One Country', *Journal of Environmental Economics and Management*, 20, 55–70.

— (1991), 'Principles for International Climate Cooperation', in T. Hanisch (ed.), *A Comprehensive Approach to Climate Change*, Oslo: CICERO.

— (1992), 'International Environment Conventions: The Case of Uniform Reductions of Emissions', *Environmental and Resource Economics*, 2, 141–59.

— (1993), 'Cost-Effective and Efficient International Environmental Agreements', *International Challenges*, 13 (2), 36–46.

— (1994), 'Efficient Climate Policy in the Presence of Free Riders', *Journal of Environmental Economics and Management* (forthcoming).

— (1996a), 'Should a Carbon Tax be Differentiated Across Sectors?', *Journal of Public Economics*, 59, 17–32.

— (1996b), 'How Should International Greenhouse Gas Agreements be Designed?, in P. Dasgupta, K.-G. Mäler and A. Vercelli (eds.), *The Economics of Transnational Commons*, Oxford University Press.

— (1997), 'Environmental Policy as with Eulogenous Plant Locations', *Scandinavian Journal of Economics*, forthcoming.

Kverndokk, S. (1995), 'Tradeable CO_2 Emission Permits: Initials Distribution as a Justice Problem', *Environmental Values*, 4, 129–48.

— (1993), 'Global CO_2 Agreements: A Cost-Effective Approach', *The Energy Journal* 14 (2), 91–112.

Layard, R., Nickell, S. and R. Jackman (1991), *Unemployment. Macroeconomic Performance and the Labour Market.* Oxford University Press.

Mäler, K.G. (1989), 'The Acid Rain Game', in H. Folmer and E. van Ierland (eds.),

Valuation Methods and Policy Making in Environmental Economics, Amsterdam: Elsevier.

(1991), 'Incentives in International Environmental Problems', in H. Siebert (ed.), *Environmental Scarcity: The International Dimension*, Tubingen: J.C.B. Mohr (Paul Siebreck).

Markusen, J.R. (1975), 'International Externalities and Optimal Tax Structures', *Journal of International Economics*, 5, 15–29.

Markusen, J.R., E.R. Morey and N. Olewiler (1993), 'Environmental Policy when Market Structure and Plant Locations are Endogenous', *Journal of Environmental Economics and Management*, 24, 69–86.

(1995), 'Competition in Regional Environmental Policies when Plant Locations are Endogenous', *Journal of Public Economics* 56(1), 55–77.

Misiolek, W.S. and H.W. Elder (1989), 'Exclusionary Manipulation of Markets for Pollution Rights', *Journal of Environmental Economics and Management*, 16, 156–66.

Motta, M. and J.-F. Thisse (1994), 'Does Environmental Dumping Lead to Delocation?', *European Economic Review*, 38 (3–4), 563–76.

Newbery, D. (1992), 'Should Carbon Taxes be Additional to Other Transport Fuel Taxes?', *The Energy Journal*, 13 (2), 49–60.

Oates, W.E. (1991), 'Pollution Charges as a Source of Public Revenue', Working Paper QE92–05, Resources for the Future, Washington, DC.

Oates, W.O. and R.M. Schwab (1988), 'Economic Competition among Jurisdictions: Efficiency Enhancing or Distortion Inducing', *Journal of Public Economics*, 35, 333–54.

OECD (1976), *Economics of Transfrontier Pollution*, Paris.

Repetto, R., R.C. Dower, R. Jenkins and J. Geoghegan (1992), *Green Fees: How a Tax Shift Can Work for the Environment and the Economy*, World Resources Institute.

Sandmo, A. (1975), 'Optimal Taxation in the Presence of Externalities', *Swedish Journal of Economics*, 77, 86–98.

Tietenberg, T. (1990), 'Economic Instruments for Environmental Regulation', *Oxford Review of Economic Policy*, 6 (1), 17–33.

Ulph, A. (1994), 'Environmental Policy, Plant Location and Government Protection', in C. Carraro (ed.), *Trade, Innovation, Environment*, Kluwer.

Ulph, D. (1994), 'Strategic Innovation and Strategic Environmental Policy', in C. Carraro (ed.), *Trade, Innovation, Environment*, Kluwer.

Welsch, H. (1992), 'Equity and Efficiency in International CO_2 Agreements', in E. Hope and S. Strøm (eds.), *Energy Markets and Environmental Issues*, Scandinavian University Press.

6 Environmental policy and international trade

Alistair Ulph

1 Introduction – the issues

There are three main factors linking environmental policies and international trade. First, to the extent that international trade affects both the extent and the pattern of production and consumption of goods in different countries, if these production and consumption activities have external, detrimental, effects on the environment of the countries where consumption and production take place then trade will affect the environment; policies which affect trade will affect the environment and policies which affect the environment will affect trade. Second, production and consumption activities in one country could have international spillover effects on the environment of other countries – as in the acid rain problems of Europe and North America, the problems of pollution of rivers such as the Rhine or global commons problems such as climate change. While such transboundary pollution problems could arise in the absence of any trade between countries, if there is trade between the affected countries, then, in the absence of any direct agreement between the countries to deal with transboundary environmental problems countries may use trade policies to affect the pattern of production or consumption in other countries, and hence the amount of transboundary pollution to which they are exposed. This is related to the third factor: international trade policies may be used to enforce international environmental agreements, not necessarily with a view to directly affecting the pollution generated by that country but simply as part of package of sanctions for failing to join or comply with an international environmental agreement. In this chapter I will be concerned mainly with the first factor, and will deal briefly with the second factor, but will not discuss the third factor (see Cesar (1993) and Folmer et al. (1993) for analysis of 'issue linkage' as this factor has come to be called).

The interaction between environmental policy and trade policy has been the focus of considerable debate in recent years sparked by the moves towards further trade liberalisation in the Single European Market, the

147

Uruguay Round of GATT, and, particularly, NAFTA (see, for example, the debate between Bhagwati and Daly in the Scientific American (1993), and, the contributions in Low (1992)). In this debate, a number of environmentalists argued that any gains from trade liberalisation would be substantially outweighed by the damage trade liberalisation would do to the environment. There were a number of strands to this argument. To the extent that trade liberalisation led to an increase in consumption and production this would lead to an increase in associated damage to the environment through pollution and loss of natural resources; a particular aspect of this concern is the energy-intensive nature of transportation of goods between countries (see, for example, Hudson (1992)). A more substantial concern was that in the absence of traditional trade policy instruments governments might seek to distort their environmental policies as a surrogate for trade policy. In particular, in the case of environmental damage related to 'production and process methods' (PPM) in the language of GATT, governments might be concerned that imposing tough environmental policies could damage their domestic industries, either through loss of market share or by 'flight of capital' to 'pollution havens' abroad. In the case of transboundary pollution, or more particularly global commons problems such as global warming, this international relocation of capital would not only be economically damaging, but could also damage the environment of the countries that lost capital if the relocation of capital did little to reduce aggregate world pollution (the 'carbon leakage' problem in the context of global warming). These concerns could lead governments to 'harmonise standards' downwards in a process of legislative competition. To counter such a process it was argued that governments should be allowed to intervene in trade in order to 'harmonise upwards' environmental standards, for example by imposing countervailing import tariffs on products coming from countries with lower environmental standards – where the lower standards were seen as a form of 'ecological dumping' and the countervailing tariffs as anti-dumping devices (see, for example, Arden-Clarke (1991)). Such policies were incorporated in the International Pollution Deterrence Act introduced into the US Congress in 1991 and received support from Vice-President Al Gore. The rejection by GATT of such measures in the famous tuna–dolphin case between the US and Mexico reinforced the view of some environmentalists that free trade and environmental policy were incompatible. Behind these specific proposals lies a general view that trade should be discouraged, with countries, and indeed smaller communities, becoming more self-sufficient, in part as a means of forcing a greater internalisation of the environmental costs of economic activities.

Most economists have rejected this analysis and the policy proposals that stem from it. The conventional argument can be summarised as follows. When there are externalities present then obviously *laissez-faire* is not desirable, and it can certainly be the case that, for example, an expansion of exports due to trade liberalisation could cause an uncontrolled increase in environmental damage that outweighs the gains from expanded trade (see Pethig (1976), for example). But the theory of policy targeting (for example, Bhagwati (1971)) tells us that since the environmental damage is due to an uncontrolled externality, not to trade, then the first-best policy is to correct that externality through appropriate environmental policies. Provided something close to optimal environmental policies are imposed, then the usual welfare gains from trade (allowing properly for environmental damage) will apply (see Dean (1992), Anderson (1992) amongst others). Whether a free-trade equilibrium with optimal environmental policies would have higher or lower environmental damage than an autarkic equilibrium is an empirical question, but with strong enough environmental preferences the welfare gains from trade liberalisation can be taken in part in improvements to the environment in all countries (Rauscher (1992a), Pearce (1992)). Assuming for the moment that environmental damage is purely domestic, because of differences in resource endowments or preferences there are no reasons to suppose that optimal environmental policies will be the same in each country, and attempts to harmonise environmental standards would deny some countries the ability to exploit their comparative advantage in being well endowed with environmental resources, and can result not just in an inefficient economic outcome but in greater environmental damage (see Dean (1992), Robertson (1992)). Obviously with transboundary pollution, policies which are optimal from an individual country's perspective will not be optimal from a global perspective, so there will need to be international *coordination* of environmental policy, but this need not imply harmonisation.

Of course it may be difficult for countries, particularly LDCs, to implement something close to first-best environmental policies, perhaps because of transactions costs, badly defined property rights, or the fact that the political process does not properly reflect environmental preferences, and in the absence of such environmental policies some second-best policies may be required; but these need not be trade policies as such, for example they could be production taxes or consumption taxes rather than just trade taxes. Trade policies are likely to be third-best policies, and in addition to any economic efficiency losses they may fail even to protect the environment (see Barbier and Rauscher (1992), Braga (1992)). But the above reasons for not imposing environmental policies are not the same as the claim that governments have incentives for 'ecological dumping'. In the 'small-country' case, governments have no incentive to distort their environmental policies from the first-best rule (equating marginal damage costs and marginal abatement costs) (Markusen (1975b), Long and Siebert (1991) amongst many). Of course this calculation will need to take account of the fact that the country is open to trade, so the *levels* of environmental policy instruments will differ from the levels in autarky, but the *rules* for setting the instruments are the same.

Allowing countries to have market power will give governments an incentive to manipulate terms of trade in their favour, but the first-best policies will again involve trade taxes to manipulate the terms of trade and environmental policies to address the environmental distortion (Markusen (1975a,b), Panagariya *et al.* (1993) amongst many). In the absence of trade instruments governments may well use environmental policies to address both sets of distortions, in which case environmental policies will not be set using the simple first-best rule outlined above. But there can be no presumption that this will involve *relaxing* environmental policies by all governments; if an exported good causes pollution in production then the government will wish to set too tough environmental policies, essentially as a proxy for the optimal export tax.

So the conventional economic analysis, where producers and consumers act competitively but governments may or may not be able to influence world prices, provides no support for the concerns about general relaxation of environmental policies in a liberalised trade regime. But there remains the question of what happens when producers themselves exploit market power, due to significant increasing returns to scale, and governments engage in 'strategic behaviour' to try to shift rents towards their domestic producers. There have been a number of studies recently which have taken the framework of strategic trade theory (see Helpman and Krugman (1989) for a useful summary) and applied it to the analysis of environmental policy. As I shall show, this can produce an argument supporting 'ecological dumping', though as I shall also show this argument is by no means robust. The introduction of strategic behaviour by governments will also allow me to address another claim that emerged in the debate over recent moves towards trade liberalisation, a claim that is sometimes associated with the name of Michael Porter (the 'Porter hypothesis', (Porter (1991)), namely that far from setting environmental policies which are too lax, governments acting strategically would set policies which are too tough (relative to the first-best rule) as a way of inducing their producers to innovate new 'green technologies' ahead of their rivals and thus gain a long-term competitive advantage, even if this meant a short-term competitive disadvantage. The literature on strategic behaviour by governments in trade and environmental policies provides a framework for assessing this claim too.

In the next section of this chapter I will give a more technical account of the traditional arguments sketched above, and then in the rest of the chapter I will survey the more recent literature which has addressed these questions in the framework of strategic trade theory. Since this is both more recent and less familiar, this will comprise the bulk of this survey. Despite its recent nature, this literature is now quite substantial, and I will not go into equal detail on all aspects. In particular, I shall not say much about international capital movements (relocation of plants to other countries) since this is covered by an excellent survey by Rauscher (1993b); nor shall I cover all aspects of the impact of environmental policy on incentives to innovate green technologies since this is also the subject of a recent survey by Ecchia and Mariotti (1994).

2 Survey of traditional analysis

In this section I shall provide a more technical review of some of the results of the traditional analysis of the interactions between environmental policy and international trade which I mentioned in the previous section. By traditional analysis I mean that households and firms are all assumed to act competitively, and if there is any market power to be exploited that is done by the government. I shall use the dual approach to international trade theory (see, for example, Dixit and Norman (1980), and the exposition will draw on the very useful papers by Copeland (1994) and Panagariya *et al.* (1993). There are a number of factors which need to be taken into account: (a) whether a country is small or large; (b) whether environmental damage is purely domestic or there are transboundary spillovers; (c) whether factors of production are internationally mobile or not; and (d) whether the government is able to use a full set of policy instruments and whether it is setting its policy instruments at the optimal level or whether it is carrying out a partial policy reform. In this section I will be almost wholly concerned with the case where factors of production are immobile internationally. I will set out the notation and then consider various combinations of the remaining assumptions.

I will refer to a typical country, and assume that there are n goods and m pollutants; world prices are denoted by the n-vector p and domestic prices by $q=p+t$ where t is a vector of trade taxes; good 1 will be the numeraire with $q_1=p_1=1$; $t_1=0$. Pollution emissions are related solely to the activities of production, and I denote by z the m-vector of emissions associated with domestic production of the n-vector of outputs y; the production feasibility of (y,z) is given by requiring that $(y,z) \in T(v)$ where $T(v)$ is the production possibility set given the endowment vector of factors, v. Letting s denote a vector of emission taxes on the pollutants, z, I shall represent the production side of the economy by the revenue function:

$$R(q,s,v) \equiv \max_{y,z}\{(q.y - s.z) \text{ s.t. } (y,z) \in T(v)\}$$

By the usual duality relationships we have:

$$y = R_q; \; z = -R_s$$

Governments may not use emission taxes as a policy instrument, and may use some form of quantity constraint such as emission standards or tradable emission permits. I shall refer to this approach in shorthand as the use of emission standards, but I shall assume that these are allocated efficiently across individual producers; I model this approach by simply assuming that the authorities set an upper limit on aggregate emissions, say $\bar{z}$, and that producer behaviour can be captured by the *restricted revenue function*:

$$\bar{R}(q,\bar{z},v) \equiv \max_y\{q.y \text{ s.t. } (y,z) \in T(v), \; z \le \bar{z}\}$$

Again, $y = \bar{R}_q$; while $\bar{R}_z$ now stands for the marginal cost of reducing emissions, i.e., the *marginal abatement costs*.

I assume that the consumption side of the economy can be represented by a single household; I shall suppose that environmental damage is purely of the 'eyesore' type – i.e., it damages household utility but not production; to allow for the possibility of spillovers from other countries I shall represent the environmental damage suffered by the household in this economy by $d = D(z,Z)$, where Z is the flow of emissions generated by the rest of the world and I assume that $D_z > 0$; $D_Z \ge 0$; with $D_Z = 0$ when there are no transboundary spillovers. I represent the household side of the economy by its dual representation in the form of the expenditure function:

$$E(q,d,u) = \min_c\{q.c \text{ s.t. } u(c,d) \ge u\}$$

where c is the n-vector of consumption, and $u(c,d)$ is the household's utility function, with $u_c > 0$; $u_d < 0$. Again there is the usual duality relationship that $c = E_q$; while E_d represents the household's willingness to pay for reductions in environmental damage (i.e., the marginal damage cost). To complete the description of the economy, I let M denote the vector of net imports to the economy (positive if imports, negative if exports), where $M = E_q - R_q$; then assuming that the revenues from trade taxes and emission taxes are redistributed to the household as a lump-sum subsidy we can summarise the equilibrium for the economy given any vector of trade taxes t and emission taxes s by

$$E(q,d,u) = R(q,s,v) + t.M + s.z \tag{1}$$

$$M = E_q(q,d,u) - R_q(q,s,v) \tag{2}$$

$$z = -R_s(q,s,v) \tag{3}$$

In the case where the government uses emission standards, (1) will contain no emission tax revenues, and the revenue function is replaced by the restricted revenue function. This completes the notation. I now turn to the results.

2.1 The small country case

2.1.1 No transboundary pollution.

First-best policy Total differentiation of (1) yields:

$$E_u.du = -[E_d D_z - s]dz + t.dM \tag{4}$$

This tells us that for an optimum the first-best policy involves setting emission taxes equal to marginal damage costs, i.e., $s = E_d.D_z$, which I will refer to as the *first-best* policy rule for setting emission taxes, and setting trade taxes equal to zero ($t=0$) i.e., the country should pursue free trade. In the case of the use of emissions standards, (4) becomes

$$E_u.du = -[E_d D_z - R_z]dz + t.dM \tag{4'}$$

This has the same interpretation: first-best policy involves setting emission standards so that marginal costs of abatement equal marginal damage costs (the *first-best* rule for emission standards), and no trade taxes (i.e., free trade). Thus with first-best policy emission taxes and emission standards are equivalent. This is a standard result and can be found in Markusen (1975a,b), Long and Siebert (1991), Anderson (1992), Copeland (1994), among others. Thus, provided countries adopt the appropriate (first-best) environmental policies there is no case for interfering with free trade. Under the assumptions made so far, if all countries follow these policies the resulting resource allocation will be Pareto optimal.

Second-best policy. To derive these policies totally differentiate (2) and (3) to obtain

$$dz = -[R_{sq}.dt + R_{ss}.ds] \tag{5}$$

$$dM = [E_{qq} - R_{qq}]dt + E_{qd}.D_z dz + E_{qu}.du - R_{qs}.ds \tag{6}$$

Define $\Sigma_{qq} \equiv R_{qq} - E_{qq}$, a positive-definite matrix of substitution effects, $m \equiv E_{qu}/E_u$, a vector of marginal propensities to consume, and $\delta \equiv E_d D_z - t.E_{qd}.D_z - s$ a vector which represents a vector of *environmental distortions*, i.e., the difference between emission taxes and the full social costs of additional emissions, which includes not just the direct damage costs to consumers but also the tariff distortion of any additional consumption triggered by additional environmental distortions – e.g., if extra pollution in a country causes households to take more foreign holidays, and these have trade taxes on them, then this will be part of the social costs of pollution. Inserting (5) and (6) in (4) yields a general expression for the welfare effects of a change in trade and emission taxes (see Copeland (1994))

$$E_u.du(1-t.m)=(\delta R_{sq}-t.\Sigma_{qq})dt+(\delta R_{ss}-t.R_{qs})ds \qquad (7)$$

Assuming that the equilibrium is stable, the term $(1-t.m)$ is positive. The terms in brackets on the RHS of (7) shows that the welfare effects of a change in either trade taxes or emission taxes must take account of the existing distortions in both trade taxes and emission taxes. It is easily seen that first-best again requires the imposition of the first-best Pigovian taxes and free trade.

Now suppose that the government uses emission standards for its environmental policy, but trade taxes for its trade policies, then a similar set of calculations to those above yields an equivalent expression to (7) for the welfare effects of a change in trade taxes and emission standards

$$E_u.du(1-t.m)=-(\overline{\delta}+t.R_{qz})dz-t\Sigma_{qq}dt \qquad (7')$$

where

$$\overline{\delta}\equiv E_d.D_z-t.E_{qd}D_z-R_z$$

is again a measure of the distortion of emission standards, taking account of the full social costs of a change in emission standards when there are trade distortions in the economy. While (7') has a similar form to (7) there is one important difference, namely that the effect of a change in trade taxes has no term for the impact on the environmental distortion; the reason is simple – if environmental policy is implemented through quantity constraints which bite, then a change in trade taxes cannot change the extent of environmental distortion.

Now suppose that the government is not able to set the first-best policies, and in particular that there are fixed, non-zero, environmental distortions. Then we can calculate the second-best trade policies. Thus in (7) set $ds=0$, then to obtain $du=0$ we require:

$$t^*\equiv\delta.R_{sq}(\Sigma_{qq})^{-1} \qquad (8)$$

assuming that the matrix of substitution terms is of full rank. Equation (8) tells us that in the absence of the first-best environmental policy there may be a case for deviating from free trade as a surrogate for not being able to modify environmental policy. Note though that this simple model just assumes that the only other policy instruments are trade taxes; in general the government will have available to it a range of production, consumption and trade taxes, and will want to optimise over whatever instruments are assumed to be available, and it is not obvious that this will require the use of trade taxes. To interpret (8) note first that R_{sq} is itself a function of t. Suppose that there is only good, other than the numeraire good, which is subject to both a fixed (perhaps zero) environmental tax and a trade tax; suppose that initially $t=0$ and $s=0$, so that $\delta>0$, i.e., marginal damage cost is above the current emission tax (zero); clearly $R_{sq}<0$ while the last term in (8) is >0, so for this case what (8) tells us is that the optimal policy is for a *subsidy* to imports, for the obvious reason that this will reduce domestic production which is already excessive because the pollution externality has not been internalised (Panagariya *et al.* (1993)).

If emission standards are being used, then the policy prescription is very simple. Set $dz=0$ in $(7')$; then the optimal trade policy is free trade ($t=0$), again for the obvious reason that since the pollution externalities are being controlled by the quantity restrictions then there is no interaction between trade and environmental policy, so even if environmental policy is not first best there is no reason for interfering with free trade.

So far I have considered optimal trade policy given restrictions on environmental policy. I now briefly consider optimal environmental policy in the face of fixed, but non-zero, trade taxes. In both (7) and $(7')$ set $dt=0$. Optimality of environmental policy requires that the terms multiplying ds in (7) and dz in $(7')$ be zero; the deviations from first-best environmental policies in the cases of emission taxes and emission standards are given by

$$E_d D_z - s = t.[E_{qd}.D_z + R_{qs}.(R_{ss})^{-1}] \qquad (9a)$$

$$E_d D_z - R_z = t.[E_{qd}.D_z - R_{qz}] \qquad (9b)$$

The first term in brackets on the RHS of (9a) and (9b), as already noted, reflects the effect of changes in environmental damage on consumption decisions, while the second term reflects the impact of environmental policy on firms' output decisions; since these are both distorted by the trade taxes t this has to be reflected in the setting of environmental policy. The interpretation of (9) is straightforward. It will pay to relax environmental policy (have taxes (equal to marginal abatement costs) below marginal damage costs) if that encourages the net imports of goods which have a positive trade tax, since that trade tax means that, in the absence of environmental policy, imports would be too low. Of course if relaxing environmental policy discourages such imports, then (9) tells us that governments should set environmental policy to be tougher than first best.

Policy reforms The formulae in (7) and (7′) allow a more general analysis of policy reforms, but space limitations prevent me pursuing this. For an excellent discussion see Copeland (1994).

2.1.2 Transboundary pollution

To date the analysis has presumed that environmental damage is purely domestic. I now allow for transboundary pollution, and for brevity I will just discuss the case of first-best policies. As I noted above, with no transboundary pollution the first-best policies of Pigovian taxes and free trade, or optimal emission standards and free trade, will yield a Pareto efficient world allocation of resources. If transboundary pollution is introduced, but the small-country assumption is retained, then individual countries have no impact on world prices and so obviously cannot affect the environmental policies of other countries, so the policies which were optimal in the case of no transboundary pollution remain optimal from the individual counties' perspective when they take the other countries' environmental policies as given. But the outcome will no longer be Pareto optimal, for the obvious reason that each country is just taking account of the effect of its policies on its own domestic damages, and not on the spill-over effects on damage to other countries. Thus (4) and (4′) now characterise a Nash equilibrium in either pollution taxes or pollution standards (see Markusen (1975a) for the analysis of taxes and Panagariya *et al.* (1993) for an analysis of pollution standards). To achieve a Pareto efficient allocation would require a cooperative equilibrium in which each country pursues free trade but sets emission taxes equal to the *global* marginal damage cost of their emissions (or emission standards which equate marginal abatement cost to global marginal damage cost); if this is to be individually rational, taking the Nash equilibrium as the starting point, then these policies may need to be accompanied by income transfers (see Markusen (1975a)) in order to induce all countries to cooperate. However I do not wish to pursue this question of inducing cooperation in an environmental agreement.

2.2 The large country case

2.2.1 No transboundary pollution

The key difference between this and the small country case is that world prices are now endogenous. I capture this very simply by assuming that the demand for net imports is given by $M = E_q - R_q = \phi(p)$. I therefore write the budget constraint in the cases of emission taxes and emission standards as, respectively

$$E(q,d,u) = R(q,s,v) + t\phi(p) + sz \tag{10a}$$

$$E(q,d,u)=\overline{R}(q,z,v)+t\phi(p) \tag{10b}$$

First-best policy Total differentiation of (10a) and (10b) yield, respectively

$$E_u.du,=[t\phi_p(p)-\phi(p)]dp+[s-E_d.D_z]dz \tag{11a}$$

$$E_u.du,=[t\phi_p(p)-\phi(p)]dp+[\overline{R}_z-E_d.D_z]dz \tag{11b}$$

First-best policy then requires that governments impose first-best environmental policies (Pigovian emission taxes equal to marginal damage costs, emission standards set where marginal damage costs equal marginal abatement costs) plus optimal tariffs defined by

$$t=\phi(p).[\phi_p(p)]^{-1} \tag{12}$$

The case where import demand depends only on the own-price of each good (12) is just the familiar optimal tariff-rule

$$\frac{t}{p}=\frac{\phi(p)}{p.\phi'(p)} \tag{13}$$

i.e, the *ad valorem* tariff rate is inversely proportional to the elasticity of net import demand.

Second-best policy In the case of emission taxes, a complete analysis of second-best policy at the same level of generality as I presented for the small-country case becomes rather messy, and would go beyond the scope of this chapter so I shall make two simplifying assumptions: I ignore income effects (i.e., $E_{qu}=0$) and I assume separability between the externality and consumption demand (i.e., $E_{qd}=0$). Furthermore, I consider only the case where the government takes its trade taxes as fixed (i.e., $dt=0$). Then totally differentiating (3) and the import demand function yields:

$$\phi_p.dp=-\Sigma_{qq}.dp-R_{qs}.ds$$

$$dz=-R_{sq}.dp-R_{ss}.ds$$

Substituting in (11a) and rearranging yields

$$E_u.du=(s-E_d.D_z)B.ds-(t\phi_p-\phi).A.R_{qs}ds$$

where $A\equiv[\phi_p+\Sigma_{qq}]^{-1}$ and $B\equiv-[R_{sq}.A.R_{qs}+R_{ss}]$
Then the optimal set of environmental taxes are given by

$$s-E_d.D_z=(t\phi_p-\phi).C=(t-\hat{\imath}(p)).\phi_p.C \tag{14}$$

where $C\equiv A.R_{qs}.B^{-1}$ and $\hat{\imath}(p)\equiv\phi.(\phi_p)^{-1}$ where $\hat{\imath}(p)$ is the formula for the optimal tariff. Thus (14) says that in this second-best, environmental taxes should differ from marginal damage costs in a way that reflects the deviations of tariffs from their optimal value. To get a bit more intuition for what is implied, suppose that $t=0$ and consider the case of a single good with a single pollutant; then C in (14) is a positive scalar, and (14) says that the government should set its environmental tax above marginal damage cost if the good is a net export and below marginal damage if it is a net import. The rationale is obvious: if the country exports the good then the government wants to exert market power by raising the price its producers set, and it does this by driving up their environmental costs; on the other hand, if the good is an import, then the government wants to expand domestic production of the good in order to drive down import demand and hence import prices, and it does this by relaxing the environmental policy it imposes on its domestic producers (see Markusen (1975b), Krutilla (1991), Rauscher (1993a), Long and Siebert (1991)).

In the case of emission standards, analysis is somewhat more straightforward. I define $\theta \equiv (t\phi_p - \phi).A = (t - \hat{t}(p))\phi_p.A$ as a measure of the distortion of trade taxes away from the optimal tariff. Then (11b) can be written as

$$E_u.du(1 - \theta.m) = -(\hat{\delta} + \theta.\overline{R}_{qz})dz - \theta\Sigma_{qq}.dt \qquad (15)$$

where $\hat{\delta} = E_d.D_z - \theta E_{qz} - \overline{R}_z$

(15) is a direct analogue of (7′) in the small-country case, except that θ replaces t as the measure of trade tax distortion the measure of environmental policy distortion is modified accordingly. Thus much of the discussion of second-best policy in the small-country case carries over to the large-country case, with the difference that the trade taxes from which distortions are measured are the optimal tariffs, not zero. In particular, it follows that if emission standards are set at a level different from their first-best value, then the optimal trade policy still consists of just setting the optimal tariffs, for the same reason as before, that trade policy does not spillover on to environmental policy as long as environmental emissions are constrained by the emission standards. In the case of fixed trade taxes, the optimal second-best environmental policy is given by

$$E_d.D_z - \overline{R}_z = \theta.(E_{qz} - \overline{R}_{qz}) \qquad (16)$$

(16) is again a straightforward analogue of (9b) in the small-country case, with θ replacing t. To see the relationship with the emission tax case, I impose the same simplifying assumptions as in the emission tax case (no income effects and separability), then (16) becomes

$$\overline{R}_z - E_d.D_z = (t\phi_p - \phi).\overline{C} = (t - \hat{t}(p)).\phi_p.\overline{C} \qquad (17)$$

where $\quad \overline{C} \equiv A\overline{R}_{qz}$

(17) is the analogue of (14) and has the same interpretation I gave there.

2.2.2 Transboundary pollution

To complete this section I introduce transboundary pollution into the model of the large-country case; as in the small-country case I shall consider only the case where countries use a full set of instruments. I shall also consider only two possible sets of policy instruments: the case where both countries use emission taxes and the case where both use emission standards; mixed regimes could be considered, but space precludes that. Household utility is now affected by foreign emissions, Z, of pollution, and this has two implications for the model I have constructed so far. First, I need to say how foreign emissions are determined. In the case of emission standards, foreign emissions are just equal to foreign emission standards, and I assume that these are taken as given by the country I am concerned with (i.e., again I am considering a non-cooperative Nash equilibrium). In the case of emission taxes, foreign emissions are determined by the condition that marginal abatement costs equal foreign emission taxes, i.e., a condition analogous to (3). But this means that foreign emission can now be affected by world prices, so in the case of emission taxes I write $Z = \psi(p)$. But, in the same way that I assume that the level of domestic environmental damage can affect household demand, so the level of foreign demand can be affected by foreign damages, which in turn are affected by the level of emissions from the country under consideration. I represent this generally by writing, in the cases of emission taxes and standards

$$M = \phi(p,s,S) \tag{18a}$$

$$M = \phi(p,z,Z) \tag{18b}$$

where S is the level of foreign emission taxes. In the case of emission taxes, for simplicity I shall again assume separability between emission damages and household demand in both countries, so that in (18a) I suppress both the emission tax arguments and simply use the form of import demand function I have been using earlier.

Then for emission taxes, the model can be summarised by

$$E(q,D(z,Z),u) = R(q,s,v) + s.z + t.M \tag{19a}$$

$$M = \phi(p) \tag{19b}$$

$$Z = \psi(p) \tag{19c}$$

while for emission standards it is written as

$$E(q,D(z,Z),u)=\bar{R}(q,z,v)+t.M \tag{20a}$$

$$M=\phi(p,z,Z) \tag{20b}$$

Z exogenous.

In the case of emission taxes, total differentiation of (19a), using (19b) and (19c) yields

$$E_u.du=-(E_d.D_z-s)dz+(t\phi_p-\phi-E_d.D_z.\psi_p)dp$$

Thus first-best policy requires the imposition of standard first-best Pigovian taxes, but trade taxes can be written as

$$t=\hat{t}(p)+E_d.D_z.\psi_p(\phi_p)^{-1} \tag{21}$$

This shows that trade taxes should differ from the optimal tariff by a term which reflects the impact of trade taxes on world prices and hence on the level of emissions generated by foreign producers. The implication is broadly that if higher world prices increase foreign emissions of pollution, then for an imported good it may pay to set tariffs higher than the optimal tariff in order to drive down world prices and hence drive down foreign pollution. In this case, then, environmental policy is unaffected by trans-boundary pollution but trade policy needs to take account of its impact on foreign emissions. Of course in the more general case where foreign damage affects foreign demand, and hence import demand, environmental policy will need to take account of its impact on trade, so environmental policy would no longer be the simple Pigovian policy.

In the case of emission standards, total differentiation of (20a) yields

$$E_u.du=-(E_d.D_z-\bar{R}_z-t.\phi_z)dz+(t.\phi_p-\phi)dp \tag{22}$$

This tells us that trade policy should now just be to set tariffs equal to the optimal tariff, since trade policy cannot influence foreign emissions, while environmental policy should differ from the first-best Pigovian tax by the need to take account of how domestic environmental policy affects foreign damages and hence foreign demand for goods and thus import demand.

As with the small-country case, what has been demonstrated has been the optimal policy for a single country taking as given the policies of other governments, so, as I have said, what this characterises is a non-coopera-tive Nash equilibrium in policies. For the same reasons as discussed in the small-country case, this will not be Pareto optimal, not just because of the failure to take account of the damage caused by domestic emissions on foreign countries (except to the extent that this influences foreign demand for goods), but also because countries are distorting trade. A Pareto optimum would be the same as in the small-country case.

2.3 Mobile factors of production

The analysis so far has assumed that all factors of production are immobile. It is possible to introduce mobile factors of production (see, for example, Copeland (1994) in the small-country case). This leaves many of the results unaltered. Thus consider the large-country case where there is market power in the capital market. Then a capital exporting country will have incentives to relax its environmental policy in order to raise the return on domestic capital, reduce the export of capital and hence drive up the return it earns on its foreign investment (see Long and Siebert (1991), Rauscher (1993a, b)). This is consistent with the results derived above in that a country which is capital rich is likely to be environmentally poor, and so will be a net importer of pollution-intensive goods and, as I have shown above, a net importer of polluting goods. This country has incentives to relax environmental policy while a net exporter has incentives to set excessively tough environmental policy.

2.4 Summary of traditional analysis

To summarise the main findings of this section, in the small-country case there is no reason for interfering with free trade, provided governments have optimal environmental policies in place; indeed in the case where governments use emission standards, even if environmental policy is not first best, there is no case for deviating from free trade. In the large country case, there will be standard reasons why individual countries may seek to move away from free trade, but this has nothing to do with environmental factors, and again as long as environmental policy is first best, trade policy is given by conventional optimal tariffs; this remains the optimal policy in the case of emission standards even if these are not first best. If policy is second best, then in the absence of optimal first-best emission taxes there is a case for distorting trade taxes as a surrogate for first-best emission taxes, but this is driven by domestic considerations rather than by what is happening in other countries. Conversely, if trade policy is not first best, environmental policy will need to take this into account. But this does not suggest that governments have universal incentives for weakening environmental policies; thus in the large-country case a country which sets its export tariff below the optimum could set environmental policy which is tougher than first best as a means of capturing some additional monopoly profits. Introducing transboundary pollution gives standard reasons why in a non-cooperative equilibrium environmental policies in all countries will be too lax, but the correct solution is to get countries to agree to toughen their domestic environmental policies while agreeing to abolish trade restrictions. Finally, I have noted that with first-best policies there is no difference between policy instruments, provided they are efficiently imposed domestically, but when second-best policies are considered there are important differences, particularly for trade policy.

One caveat should be noted about the discussion of traditional analysis. I have asumed that the only two sets of distortions to the economy arise from either trade policies or environmental policies. Of course in practice there will be many other distortions in economies, and in such a second-best world these distortions will have implications for environmental policies. For example, it is sometimes argued that an important reason for governments to relax environmental policies is concern about the employment consequences, implying distortions in labour markets. I have not pursued such questions in this survey as I wish to focus on trade-related reasons for distorting environmental policies. To the extent that concern with employment is related to concern to maintain a country's share of output in particular markets, then the models in the next two sections will shed some light on employment concerns, though again there will be no explicit modelling of imperfections in the labour market.

3 Imperfect competition and strategic environmental policy – some simple models

In the last section I summarised some of the results from the traditional analysis where it is assumed that producers and consumers act competitively and it is governments that exploit market power through their trade or environmental policies. I showed that this analysis did not support many of the concerns expressed by environmentalists summarised in the introduction. In particular, if trade liberalisation prohibits governments from using trade policies directly to influence their terms of trade, so they may resort to distortions to their environmental policies as a surrogate way of influencing their terms of trade, then there is no general presumption that governments would want to set too lax environmental policies. Thus governments of countries which are net exporters of pollution intensive goods will set pollution policies which are tougher than first best as a means of restricting supply of such goods and driving up the price paid by foreign countries.

While perfect competition may be a plausible description of some markets, for many markets for manufactured goods, for which there may be significant scale economies in production, imperfect competition may be a better characterisation of the market structure; as is well known the phenomenon of intra-industry trade, which is also characteristic of such markets, is consistent with an assumption of imperfect competition. In the 1980s a substantial literature emerged exploring the implications for trade policy of imperfectly competitive international markets (see Helpman and Krugman (1989)) and more recently this literature has been adapted to explore the implications for environmental policy, especially in regimes where trade policy is outlawed. There are two reasons why the introduction of imperfect competition might be thought to provide more rationale for governments to set too lax environmental policies. First, the fact that producers are able to exploit market power directly, may reduce the need for governments to exploit market power through their trade or environmental policies, so in the case of exporters of pollution-intensive products there is less need or incentive for the government to drive up prices if their producers are doing that. Second, the introduction of imperfect competition allows producers to earn rents and provides incentives for governments to try to shift those rents in favour of their domestic producers, by manipulating the market game in their favour. It seems plausible that in order to help their domestic producers governments will seek to relax their environmental policies, so this approach may be capable of demonstrating why governments of all producing countries may have incentives to relax environmental policies. However, it may be asked, in light of the first point, why governments need to distort their policies at all if their producers are already taking steps to earn some rents. The reason is that governments are presumed to be able to commit themselves to policies prior to the decisions by producers to set output or prices, and it is this ability to *precommit* which allows governments the scope to manipulate markets in a way which is not available to producers themselves. This prior manipulation of markets is referred to as *strategic behaviour.*

In the rest of this chapter I will review this recent literature to assess how far the intuitions sketched above can be supported by economic analysis. I begin in this section by outlining the simplest class of models, and in subsequent sections I shall introduce extensions. The simplification I make in this section is that producers confine themselves to setting output or prices; in subsequent sections I also allow producers to engage in strategic behaviour. As the discussion above of strategic behaviour makes clear, strategic behaviour depends crucially on the structure of moves by different agents. Thus all the models in this literature consist of multi-stage games, and it is important to specify the structure of these moves. The models I review in this section have, in general, a three-stage game structure. In stage 1, governments choose the *form* of environmental policy they will employ. In the second stage governments choose the *level* at which they set their policy instruments. Finally in stage 3, producers choose their market variables – either output or price. What I shall do in this section is to go through a particular example of such a model to illustrate how such models work, and then discuss how the results of this model are modified by changing the basic assumptions. The basic model is similar to that developed by Barrett (1994), Conrad (1993a, b), Kennedy (1994) and Ulph (1996b), and is a variant of the original Brander and Spencer (1985) model.

I suppose that there are two firms which produce a particular product, each firm located in a separate country. There are no consumers of the product located in these countries, so their output is sold in a third group of countries. I shall assume that the two firms and countries are identical, so need only set out the structure for one country. Demand for the product is summarised by the total revenue function of a firm $R(x,y)$ where x is own output and y is the rival firm's output. I assume $R_x > 0$, $R_{xx} < 0$, $R_y < 0$, $R_{xy} < 0$. The firm has total cost function $C(x)$, which has either constant or diminishing returns to scale (there might also be some fixed cost present to help explain why there are only two firms in the market, but I do not model entry explicitly). In the third-stage market game firms set output levels, i.e., I model Cournot competition. I assume that units of measurement are chosen so that each unit of output produces one unit of pollution, but the firm is able to abate pollution; letting a denote the amount of pollution abated, $A(a)$ is a (convex) total abatement cost curve. Net emissions to the environment by the firm are therefore $e = x - a$. I assume that pollution is entirely domestic, and pollution damage can be represented by a total damage cost function $D(e)$ which is strictly convex. The government can choose two forms of environmental policy – an emission tax, t, or an emission standard, e, an upper limit on the units of emissions by the firm. Note that with the assumption of a single firm, in the absence of any trade considerations, these two forms of environmental policy would be equivalent; note also that the policy choices are rather wider than suggested – for example an emissions trading scheme in which the domestic firm was only a small part of the total market, and hence is a price taker, would be equivalent to the emission tax, while a similar scheme with a bubble covering the firm would be equivalent to the emission standard. Governments act to maximise welfare which is total revenue minus total social costs (production costs plus abatement costs plus damage costs). I shall use τ and ϵ to refer to the policy instruments of the rival government. I now calculate a (subgame perfect) Nash equilibrium of the three-stage game, beginning by solving the stage 3 and stage 2 games when the government uses emission taxes and standards respectively.

3.1 Emission taxes

3.1.1 Stage 3 – market game

The firm takes as given the emission tax, t, and the output of the rival firm, y, and chooses output, x, and abatement, a, to maximise $\pi \equiv R(x,y) - C(x) - A(a) - t.(x-a)$ for which first-order conditions are

$$R_x - C' - t = 0 \qquad\qquad (23a)$$

$$A'(a) - t = 0 \qquad\qquad (23b)$$

(23a) is just the condition that marginal revenue equals marginal cost plus the emission tax, while (23b) is the condition that the firm abates pollution to the point where marginal abatement cost equals the emission tax. (23b) can be inverted to yield $a = B(t)$ where $B \equiv (A')^{-1}$ and $B' = (A'')^{-1}$ while (23a) can be rewritten as the firm's reaction function

$$x = r(y, t)$$

where

$$r_1 = \frac{-R_{xy}}{R_{xx} - C''}, \quad -1 < r_1 < 0 \qquad\qquad (24)$$

and

$$r_2 = \frac{1}{R_{xx} - C''} < 0$$

Thus reaction functions are downward sloping and stable, and an increase in the emission tax will reduce the domestic firm's output for any given output by the rival, i.e., it shifts downwards the domestic firm's reaction function.

Nash (Cournot) equilibrium is given by solving the reaction functions to yield the *equilibrium* output level

$$x = r[r(x, \tau), t] \equiv \rho(t, \tau)$$

where

$$\rho_1 = \frac{r_2}{(1 - r_1^2)} < 0 \qquad\qquad (25a)$$

and

$$\rho_2 = \frac{r_1 . r_2}{(1 - r_1^2)} > 0 \qquad\qquad (25b)$$

(25) tells us that an increase in the emission tax will reduce the equilibrium output of the domestic firm and expand the equilibrium output of the rival firm, with the absolute impact on the domestic firm being greater than that of the rival firm.

3.1.2 Stage 2 – Choice of emission tax level

The government takes as given the emission tax set by the rival government, τ, and chooses its own emission tax rate, t, to maximise welfare

$$W \equiv R(x, y) - C(x) - A(a) - D(x - a)$$

where $x=\rho(t,\tau)$, $y=\rho(\tau,t)$ and $a=B(t)$:
The first-order condition is

$$W_t=[R_x-C'-D'].\rho_1+R_y.\rho_2-[A'-D'].B'=0$$

i.e.

$$t-D'=A'-D'=\frac{R_y.\rho_2}{B'-\rho_1}<0 \tag{26}$$

(26) thus says that each government of the producing countries has an incentive to relax environmental policy (set emission tax below marginal damage cost). The reason is obvious: by doing that it effectively shifts out the domestic firm's reaction function, thereby hoping to reduce the rival firm's output level. Note that the incentive for strategic behaviour, as (26) makes clear, arises solely because the government thinks it can manipulate the output of the *rival* producer; the domestic producer is correctly choosing its output level to maximise profits net of emission tax, but the domestic firm takes as given the output of the rival firm while the government is able to manipulate the output of the rival. This arises solely because it is assumed that governments are able to commit themselves to emission taxes prior to the firm's choice of output.

Equation (26) implicitly defines the reaction function for the government, since ρ depends on both t and τ. By symmetry, the Nash equilibrium for the stage 2 game is given by setting $t=\tau$ in (26), so both governments (in general all governments of producing firms) will relax their environmental policies in attempt to increase the market shares of their domestic producers. Note that these attempts to increase the market shares of their domestic producers are doomed, since both governments act in the same way, and, by symmetry, in equilibrium each firm must have an equal share of the market; the net effect is rather to expand industry output, driving down profits of both firms and increasing pollution in both countries, making both governments worse off than if they had followed the first-best policy of setting emission tax equal to marginal damage cost.

3.2 Emission standards

I now carry out a similar analysis for the case where both governments use emission standards as their policy instruments.

3.2.1. Stage 3 – market game

The firm takes as given the emission standard, e, and the output of the rival firm, y, and chooses output, x, to maximise

$$\overline{\pi}=R(x,y)-C(x)-A(x-e)$$

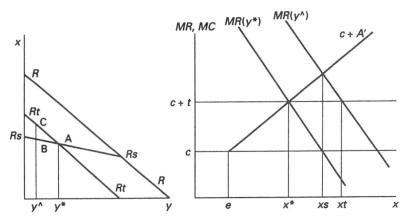

Figure 6.1a,b

for which the first-order condition is

$$R_x - C' - A' = 0 \qquad (27)$$

i.e., marginal revenue equals marginal production cost plus marginal abatement cost.

(27) can be rewritten as the firm's reaction function

$$x = \bar{r}(y,e)$$

where

$$\bar{r}_1 = \frac{-R_{xy}}{R_{xx} - C'' - A''} - 1 < \bar{r}_1 < 0 \qquad (28)$$

and

$$\bar{r}_2 = \frac{-A''}{R_{xx} - C'' - A''} 1 \geq \bar{r}_2 \geq 0$$

Again the reaction functions are downward sloping and stable, and an increase in the emission standard by one unit increases the domestic firm's output, though, in general, by less than one unit (the extra unit of emissions will be used partly to expand output and partly to reduce abatement so as to ensure that condition (27) is maintained). Comparison with (24) shows immediately that $|\bar{r}_1| \leq |r_1|$; i.e., the reaction function with emission standards is shallower than with emission taxes (the domestic producer will increase output more in response to a decrease in the rival's output if the government uses standards rather than taxes). The reason is clear from Figure 6.1.

In Figure 6.1(a) $R-R$ is the reaction function for the firm in the absence of any environmental policy, i.e. corresponding to the firm being faced with marginal cost c (assumed for simplicity constant) in figure 6.1(b). If the government uses emission taxes, then the firm's effective marginal cost curve becomes $c+t$ in figure 6.1(b), and this gives reaction function $Rt-Rt$. If the government uses emission standards, then as long as output is less than e there is no need to abate pollution, but when output exceeds e each extra unit of output requires an extra unit of abatement, and so production costs are now effectively $c+A'$; this results in reaction function $Rs-Rs$. Given that the rival firm produces output y^*, the emission tax and emission standard have been set so that the firm produces the same output, x^*, i.e., the two reaction functions intersect at point A in figure 6.1(a). Now consider the effect of reducing rival firms' output to $\hat{y}$; this shifts out the marginal revenue curve in figure 6.1(b), and equilibrium output rises to xs in the case of standards but to xt in the case of taxes. Thus the response is greater in the case of taxes than standards, for the obvious reason that the firm pays a constant tax for each extra unit of pollution produced under taxes, but a rising marginal cost of abatement under emission standards. As (27) shows, the difference between taxes and standards depends crucially on the shape of the marginal abatement cost curve; if $A''=0$, i.e., there are constant unit costs of abatement then there is no difference between the slopes; on the other hand, if $A''\to\infty$ the slope of the reaction function tends to 0, i.e., if abatement becomes effectively prohibitively expensive, then output becomes constrained to be $x=e$.

On the other hand, comparison of (27) and (24) shows that the relative magnitudes of the absolute values of the effects of the emission tax and emission standard on the domestic firm's reaction function can go either way depending on parameter values, in particular the size of A''.

As in the case of emission taxes, equilibrium values of output are obtained by solving the pair of reaction functions

$$x=\bar{r}[\bar{r}(x,\epsilon),e]\equiv\bar{\rho}(e,\epsilon)$$

with

$$\bar{\rho}_1=\frac{\bar{r}_2}{(1-\bar{r}_1{}^2)}>0 \tag{29}$$

and

$$\bar{\rho}_2=\frac{\bar{r}_1\cdot\bar{r}_2}{(1-\bar{r}_1{}^2)}<0$$

Thus an increase in emission standards shifts out the domestic firm's reaction function increasing its output but reducing the output of the rival firm, with an overall increase in output.

3.2.2 Stage 2 game – choice of emission standards

The government takes as given the emission standard of the rival government, ϵ, and chooses e to maximise welfare

$$\overline{W} \equiv R(x,y) - C(x) - A(x-e) - D(e)$$

where

$$x = \overline{p}(e,\epsilon), \quad y = \overline{p}(\epsilon,e).$$

for which the first-order condition is

$$\overline{W}_e = [R_x - C' - A'].\overline{p}_1 + R_y.\overline{p}_2 + A' - D' = 0$$

or

$$A' - D' = -R_y.\overline{p}_2 < 0 \tag{30}$$

Thus as with emission taxes, the use of emission standards induces the government to relax its environmental policy, by setting emission standards at a level where marginal abatement cost is below marginal damage cost. The reason again is the desire to reduce the output of the rival producer.

Equation (30) gives the reaction function for the government, and, using symmetry, the Nash equilibrium of this second-stage game would involve setting $e = \epsilon$. As with emission taxes, the equilibrium leaves both governments worse off than if they had not relaxed their environmental policies.

3.3 Stage 1 game – choice of policy instruments

Much of the literature (Barrett (1994), Kennedy (1994), Conrad (1993a, b)) has only considered the first two stages assuming either that both governments use emission taxes (Kennedy and Conrad) or both use emission standards (Barrett), but Ulph (1992, 1996a, b) has considered the question of the choice of policy instruments. As results are more ambiguous here, I shall be brief and only sketch the arguments. I begin by comparing the outcomes when both governments choose to use taxes with that where both use standards. From (26) and (30) we get a comparison of the size of the distortion under taxes and standards. In general this is ambiguous. To see why, recall that the incentive for strategic behaviour is determined by the reduction in rival's output resulting from a shift in the domestic firm's reaction function. There are two aspects to this, as shown in figure 6.2. $R^* - R^*$ is the rival firm's reaction function; $Rs - Rs$ is the firm's reaction function under standards, $Rt - Rt$ the firm's reaction function under taxes, chosen so that both give the same initial equilibrium, point A. Now suppose that as a result of relaxing environmental policy, the firm's reaction functions shift out *by the same amount for the original output level of the rival*, i.e., both

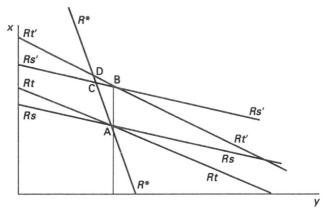

Figure 6.2

shift upwards by the distance AB. Then it is clear that with standards the equilibrium will shift from A to C while with taxes it will shift from A to D, and so there is a greater gain in market share when the government uses taxes than standards. However there is no reason to believe that the shift in reaction functions will be the same for the two policy regimes; in particular, as (28) shows a unit increase in emission standards can cause an outward shift in the reaction function by anything between 0 and 1 depending on the degree of convexity of the marginal abatement cost curve. Thus while for some class of models (see Ulph (1996b)) distortions are larger with taxes than with standards, this is not a general result.

To evaluate what policy regime will be chosen, we need to compare not just the payoffs to the governments when both use taxes and both use standards, but also the payoffs when one uses taxes and the other standards, and I have not presented the analysis for that case. But the same factors leading to ambiguity in comparing the distortions in the symmetric case apply here too. To see the range of outcomes that can occur, consider the extreme case where abatement is not available, so the use of emission standards allows governments to precommit the output of their firm. In this case it is clear that if one government uses standards then there is no incentive for the rival government to engage in strategic behaviour, since it cannot shift the rival's output; in particular, if both governments use standards then there will be no strategic behaviour, while if both use taxes both will act strategically, so both are better off using standards than taxes. Moreover it is clear that the use of standards will be a dominant strategy, since if one government uses taxes and the other standards, the one using taxes engages in no strategic behaviour, while the one using standards will engage in strategic behaviour, and in fact will set standards consistent with its firm becoming a Stackelberg leader, making the government with standards better off than the government using taxes. This was the case analysed in Ulph (1992).

However it is possible to construct other examples, e.g., where marginal abatement costs are linear, where, for a wide range of parameter values the use of taxes gives a greater market share to the domestic firm than the use of standards, so that the use of taxes becomes a dominant strategy (see Ulph (1996a, b). In this case the choice of policy instruments is a Prisoner's Dilemma since the use of taxes results in greater strategic behaviour by producers, resulting in greater output and pollution than would be the case if both governments selected emission standards. In this case there is a double set of Prisoner's Dilemmas: governments would be better off if they could commit to using standards rather than taxes; but they would be even better off to commit to not distorting their environmental policies at all (in which case the choice between taxes and standards would be irrelevant).

3.4 Extensions

The model outlined above suggests that the introduction of imperfect competition and strategic behaviour by governments substantially change the conclusions about the interactions between environmental policy and trade that were derived from traditional analysis. For in this model the governments of all countries producing and exporting a pollution-intensive good have incentives to relax their environmental policies with respect to this good, whereas the traditional analysis suggested that governments of countries exporting pollution-intensive goods would have incentives to set environmental policy which was too tough. The rationale for this difference in conclusion is the one given at the outset of this section – because firm's themselves exploit market power there is less need for governments to try to get firms to restrict their output and there is now an incentive for governments to try to shift rents in favour of their domestic producers by relaxing their environmental policies. This is much more in line with the kind of arguments advanced by environmentalists which I summarised in the introduction.

But, even within the broad structure of the three-stage game used in this section, it is clear that the model I have used is very simple – deliberately so since I wanted to highlight the nature of the purely strategic incentives for distorting environmental policy. The question I want to address in the rest of this section is just how robust are the conclusions reached so far to relaxation of some of the simplifying assumptions. I deal with six variants of the simple model.

Other instruments It has to be emphasised that the results above arise solely because it is assumed that governments are operating second-best policies in the sense that they are having to use a single policy instrument to achieve both environmental and trade targets. As Barrett (1994) has shown, as soon as governments can also use trade policy instruments (e.g., a production subsidy) then there is no longer any need to distort environmental policy; indeed even if the government has two environmental policy instruments (say an emission tax and a subsidy to pollution abatement) Conrad (1993a) has shown that this will restore the efficiency of environmental policy. This is very much in line with the conclusion of the traditional analysis where distortions to environmental policy arose solely from inability to set appropriate trade policy.

Other kinds of environmental policies I have considered a rather limited range of environmental policies, which, in a non-strategic context would be equivalent (Ulph (1992, 1996a, b)). Verdier (1993) considers the choice between emission standards (which again would be equivalent to emission taxes) and the use of 'design standards' where firms are required to invest in particular technologies for pollution abatement or carry out prescribed minimum amounts of emission reduction (the BATNEEC policies in the UK could be of this type). Unlike the policies I have discussed, there is an inherent inefficiency in the use of design standards (since they prevent firms making the cost-minimising choice between abating pollution and cutting output). But he shows that there can be incentives for governments to use design standards as a strategic device to try to help their domestic producers to gain a larger market share. The results are consistent with the broad findings set out above, although Verdier does not address the question of the *level* of policy instruments since he assumes prespecified targets for emissions.

Number of firms I have assumed a single producer in each country; given the output of other producers, this firm produces the profit-maximising level of output. But now suppose there is more than one firm in each country. Because they compete with each other, as well as with foreign producers, for any given output by foreign rivals, the domestic firms now produce too much output – they would be better off colluding and acting like a single firm. This means the government now has two conflicting incentives; it still has the rent-shifting incentive for relaxing policy, but, as with the traditional analysis it also has an incentive for toughening environmental policy to get domestic firms to cut their output. Again, if environmental policy is the only instrument it can use to achieve these goals it is not obvious which way environmental policy will be distorted; as Barrett

(1994) shows the larger the number of firms the greater is the incentive to toughen environmental policy (in the limit as the number of firms gets very large we just get back to the competitive model of section 2). Thus this factor could act to offset the conclusion of governments setting too lax environmental policies.

Form of competition In the model outlined above it was assumed that the third-stage game involved Cournot competition in which firms set output levels. An alternative assumption is that firms set prices (Bertrand competition). As Barrett (1994) and Ulph (1996d) have shown this makes a substantial difference to the results derived above. First, governments now have an incentive to set environmental policy that is tougher than the first best. The reason is straightforward. When firms set their prices they assume that other producers keep their prices fixed, and so are reluctant to raise their prices. However, as is well known, reaction functions are upward sloping in Bertrand competition – so if one firm raises its price other firms will also raise theirs, though not necessarily by the same amount. Governments recognise this when setting their environmental policies so their interest is in getting their domestic firms to raise their prices and hence the prices of rival producers. They do this by forcing up the domestic firms' costs by setting tougher than first-best environmental policies. Ulph (1996d) also shows that in a model which, under Cournot competition, would have the use of emission taxes resulting in greater distortion than the use of emission standards the reverse is true under Bertrand competition. This is for the same reason as in figure 6.1 – when the rival firm cuts its output (raises its price) the domestic firm will respond by a greater increase in price (lower increase in output) when the government sets standards rather than taxes; since the government's strategic interest is in raising domestic prices it has more incentive to distort policy when it is using standards rather than taxes. Thus the form of market competition is crucial for the direction of distortion of environmental policy. This should come as no surprise to those familiar with the literature on strategic competition.

Domestic consumers I have assumed that the countries producing the good did not also consume the good. How does introducing domestic consumers affect the argument? Governments now have to take account of the fact that with imperfect competition while raising prices and restricting output is, up to a point, beneficial to producers, it is damaging to consumers. As is well known, even in a closed economy, if the government only has one instrument to deal with both environmental pollution and imperfect competition, then this may lead to the government setting environmental taxes below the level suggested by first-best Pigovian rules in order to reflect the fact that output under imperfect competition is set below the desirable level. The same argument applies here. Introducing consumers into producing economies can only reinforce the incentive for relaxing environmental policy in the case of Cournot competition, though it could mitigate the argument for toughening environmental policy under Bertrand competition (see Conrad (1993b) for a discussion in the case of Cournot competition).

Transboundary pollution I now introduce the fact that there may be transboundary pollution. As in the traditional analysis this means that policies which are first best from a single country's perspective when it is acting non-cooperatively will not be first best from an international perspective. Thus any relaxation of environmental policy from a purely domestic first best is an even greater distortion from the global first best. I shall stick to the case of non-cooperative behaviour. As Kennedy (1994) shows, in a model of Cournot competition, the presence of transboundary pollution *increases* the incentive for rent-shifting behaviour. The argument is straightforward. As Barrett (1994) notes, the incentive for rent-shifting through environmental policy is less than it would be with, say, a production subsidy financed by a lump-sum tax, for the simple reason that increasing domestic production at the expense of rival producers increases domestic pollution and that has a cost. But with transboundary pollution, there will be an additional incentive for switching production to domestic firms – namely that it reduces foreign production and hence any associated transboundary pollution.

3.5 Summary

To summarise this section then, I have shown that it is possible to build a simple model of imperfectly competitive trade with strategic behaviour by governments which produces radically different conclusions from those of traditional analysis, namely that governments of countries exporting pollution-intensive goods have incentives for relaxing environmental policy where traditional analysis suggested they would set too tough policy. Such a model can rationalise the concept of 'ecological dumping'. However the conclusions are by no means robust. While the introduction of domestic consumers and transboundary pollution reinforce the arguments for governments setting lax environmental policies, allowing for a large number of domestic firms could reverse the conclusion, and allowing for Bertrand competition certainly reverses the conclusion and suggests that governments will set too tough environmental policy. The analysis also shows that in addition to concern about the stringency of environmental policy, the choice of environmental policy instruments also takes on a strategic dimension, although results here are less sharp. In the next section of this chapter I explore the implications of going beyond the simple three-stage game format discussed here by allowing a further stage where producers can act strategically.

4 Imperfect competition, innovation and strategic environmental policy

In the last section I introduced some models of imperfect competition in which the government has incentives for acting strategically; if the government is limited to using only one environmental policy instrument, whether a tax or a standard then, as with the traditional analysis it will want to distort its environmental policy to try to achieve both trade and environmental objectives. However, in stark contrast to the traditional analysis it is possible to construct models where governments of countries exporting pollution-intensive goods will wish to relax their environmental policies – i.e., to engage in 'ecological dumping', though this result is by no means robust. However, an important feature of all the models surveyed in the last section was that they assumed that producers were limited to just setting either prices or output, and all the strategic behaviour was done by governments. In this section I will review some models where producers also take strategic action.

There are two reasons why this extension of the models presented in section 3 is of interest. First, the rationale for governments using their environmental policies for strategic purposes was that it was assumed that only governments could precommit to certain courses of action (setting environmental policy) so governments were able to exploit opportunities not available to producers. But in practice, producers can also make precommitments which can be used for strategic purposes – such as investing in capital equipment or R&D investment designed to influence their costs in the market game, or sinking investments in goodwill or advertising to influence the demand for their products, and there is a large literature in industrial economics devoted to analysing such behaviour (see Tirole (1989)). The question then arises whether this kind of strategic behaviour by producers eliminates, or at least reduces, the need for governments to act strategically. As I shall show the answer to this question is mixed, in part because while there may be some substitution between strategic behaviour by governments and producers, the fact that producers are acting strategically gives another avenue by which governments can use environmental policy to influence the market – by affecting the strategic behaviour of producers. This leads to the second reason for introducing strategic behaviour by producers. I shall interpret strategic behaviour by producers solely in terms of R&D investments (though as indicated the scope is much wider than this), since that allows me to address directly the hypothesis raised by Porter, among others – that governments may have an incentive to set too tough environmental policy in order to encourage their producers to engage in more 'green' R&D and hence gain a long-term competitive advantage even if there was a short-term loss by using an overly tough environmental policy. These are the two issues I wish to address in this section.

To introduce strategic behaviour by producers requires that an extra stage be added to the three-stage games considered in the last section. Thus the general structure of the game I will consider in this section is as follows: stage 1 – governments choose environmental policy instruments; stage 2 – governments choose levels of environmental policy instruments; stage 3 – producers choose investments in R&D; stage 4 – producers choose either prices or outputs. Note that this structure of moves has an important implication: it implies that when producers choose their R&D decisions they are able to take as given the environmental policies of governments. While this may have been a natural assumption in section 3 when firms only chose output or price, it is much less obvious that governments can commit themselves to environmental policies for the duration of an R&D project. An alternative ordering of moves would be to interchange stages 2 and 3, so that producers would choose R&D prior to governments choosing levels of environmental policies. In this case, what will matter will be producers' *expectations* of future R&D policies, rather than the current R&D policies, and this can have important implications for how one might test the impact of environmental policy on decisions such as choice of R&D (or more generally other strategic variables such as location, choice of products, investment in plant, etc.).

While the extra stage makes the models considerably more complex than those I considerd in section 3, the broad logical structure of the models is very similar so I will not go through the models in as much detail as I did in the last section. The models surveyed in this section are those developed by myself and David Ulph, either jointly or separately. What I shall do is to sketch the results of the most general model we have developed (Ulph and Ulph (1996)) and then say how these relate to other results we have obtained. (In fact the model I shall outline is slightly simpler than the one we develop in that I shall assume pollution is entirely domestic whereas our model allows for transboundary pollution; however nothing new is added by introducing transboundary pollution relative to what I said in the previous section.)

4.1 The model

The model is very similar to that outlined in section 3 – two firms located in different countries selling to a third set of countries, with quantity-setting (Cournot) behaviour in the market game. I shall set out the version where governments both use emission taxes.

Stage 4 game At this stage the model is somewhat simpler than in section 3 in that I assume there is no abatement technology available, and producers have constant unit costs of production. It is sufficient therefore to summarise the outcome of the stage 4 game in terms of a maximum profit function for firm 1 (again I assume symmetry) denoted: $\pi(c_1,c_2)$ where c_i is the unit cost of firm i. This profit function has the usual properties – it is decreasing in own costs, increasing in rival's costs and, importantly, is strictly convex in own costs. The implication of the latter is that the higher are the costs of the firm the *smaller* is the gain in profits to the firm from reducing its costs by one unit.

Stage 3 game This is the new stage of the game. I assume that firm 1's unit costs in stage 4 are given by:

$$c_1 = k(g_1) + t.e(h_1)$$

where $k(g)$ is the production cost which depends on the level of *process R&D*, g, and $e(h)$ is the level of emissions per unit of output, which depends on the level of *environmental R&D*, h. Both $k(.)$ and $e(.)$ are decreasing convex functions of their R&D levels, so that R&D has diminishing returns. In general it is assumed that the firm can invest in both forms of R&D, but special cases are where the firm can invest only in process R&D (A. Ulph (1996b, 1996d)) or only in environmental R&D (D. Ulph (1994)). In this stage 3 game firm 1 takes as given the R&D of the rival firm and chooses its own levels of R&D to maximise:

$$\pi(c_1,c_2) - g_1 - h_1$$

This can be divided into two stages: (a) the allocation of any given total of R&D expenditure, denoted η_1, between the two forms of R&D so as to minimise costs of production; this will be done efficiently; (b) the determination of the total level of R&D – the first-order condition for this is

$$1 = -\frac{dc_1}{d\eta_1}\left[x - R_y \cdot \frac{\partial y}{\partial c_1}\right] \tag{31}$$

The left-hand side is the marginal cost of R&D, the RHS is the marginal benefit. The term outside the bracket is positive, as are the terms inside the brackets. If R&D was being determined *efficiently* then the term in brackets in (31) would only contain x. The second term is the *strategic* element in the firm's R&D decision, and represents the fact that if firm 1 reduces its costs of production through R&D that will reduce rival's output in equilibrium and hence benefit firm 1. Thus firm's will *overinvest* in R&D as a means of driving down their costs and increasing their market share.

Now (31) is effectively firm 1's *R&D reaction function* which can be shown to be downward sloping. Thus we can solve for equilibrium levels of R&D. These will depend on the level of environmental taxes set by the two governments in stage 2. Rather than dealing explicitly with the equilibrium levels of R&D what is actually of interest is the equilibrium level of costs that emerge from this stage. I write this as

$$c = \gamma(t, \tau)$$

What we are interested in is the effect of a change in emission tax by domestic and foreign governments on firm 1's costs. It turns out that these signs are ambiguous. To see why, consider the effect of an increase in t. This will have two effects. First, holding constant the R&D level this will raise costs. But second, it will affect the amount of R&D the firm does. There are two aspects to this. First the convexity of costs means that a higher t reduces the effect of a unit reduction in costs on profits; so this means that higher emission taxes discourage domestic R&D, which will raise costs reinforcing the first effect. But the higher tax also means that a given amount of environmental R&D will have a larger impact in lowering the firm's costs, so the *effectiveness* of environmental R&D goes up. This will increase the incentives to do R&D and hence will lower costs. So the net effect of these three factors is ambiguous. Similarly for the cross effect: to the extent that a higher emission tax by the foreign government raised foreign costs, that would increase the benefits of firm 1 doing R&D; but since, as I have shown, the impact of emission taxes on own costs is ambiguous so must be the cross effect.

However it should be clear from the above argument that in the case where there is no environmental R&D only the first two effects are present, and so a higher tax by one government unambiguously raises its domestic firm's costs and lowers its process R&D while it increases the rival firm's process R&D, lowering its costs (A. Ulph (1996b, 1996d)). In the case where there is also environmental R&D then it turns out that the net effect of an emission tax on costs depends crucially on the shape of the function $e(.)$; in the case where it is negatively exponential then it turns out that emission taxes have *no effect* on costs, i.e., additional environmental R&D is just sufficient to offset the effect of the higher emission tax (D. Ulph (1994), Ulph and Ulph (1996)). This is the assumption made by Bradford and Simpson (1993), and it is clearly a very special case.

Stage 2 game In this stage each government takes as given the emission tax of the rival firm and chooses its own emission tax to maximise welfare, which is defined as in section 3. The outcome can be summarised as follows. In general, emission taxes will diverge from marginal damage costs; there are several ways in which this divergence can be decomposed. I follow that in A. Ulph (1996b, 1996d). Here there are two effects: the *direct rent-shifting* effect which is the same as before, and unambiguously leads governments to relax environmental policy; and the *indirect strategic investment effect* where governments try to manipulate the R&D decisions of the producers. This latter effect is in general ambiguous, because, as we have seen, the effects of a tax on R&D are ambiguous. Where a higher emission tax discourages domestic R&D and encourages foreign R&D (e.g., in the case of only process R&D) this effect will go in the direction of giving governments incentives for relaxing environmental policy; if higher taxes encourage domestic R&D and discourage foreign R&D then governments will want to raise environmental taxes. The net effect is thus ambiguous.

I make three comments.

(a) In the case of pure process R&D, where both the direct and indirect effects go in the direction of governments relaxing environmental policy, it would appear that introducing strategic behaviour by producers has *increased* the distortion in R&D, going against the presumption that producer R&D might substitute for government R&D. This is not quite right, for, as shown in Ulph (1996b), the direct effect is *smaller* when producers act strategically than when they do not, so whether there is more or less distortion to government policy when producers act strategically is ambiguous. For a particular class of models, Ulph (1996b) shows that the reduction in the direct effect outweighs the indirect incentive to manipulate R&D decisions, so that the distortion to government environmental policy is indeed smaller when producers act strategically. When environmental R&D is involved, then we have seen that the indirect effect of environmental policy on R&D can go in the opposite direction to the direct effect, so the presumption would be that the net distortion when producers act strategically would be smaller than when they do not act strategically, though this has not been directly tested.

(b) In relation to the Porter hypothesis it is clear that there is no general presumption that governments will want to set environmental policies tougher than first best. This is for two reasons. First, raising environmental taxes may well discourage domestic R&D and encourage foreign R&D – the opposite of what was presumed by Porter. Second, even if the effects of emission taxes on R&D go in the direction presumed by Porter, while that gives *one* factor which goes in the direction of wanting to raise environmental taxes there is still the other direct factor which acts to lower emission taxes, so there is still ambiguity about the overall sign of the distortion to environmental policy.

(c) The model set out here assumed Cournot competition. In Ulph (1996d) Bertrand competition was assumed, though, as in Ulph (1996b), only process R&D was considered. The use of Bertrand competition changes the results discussed so far in two ways. First, I noted that when only governments acted strategically Bertrand competition changed the strategic incentive from that of relaxing environmental policy to that of toughening environmental policy, so it changes the strategic incentive for producers from underinvestment in R&D to overinvestment. Second, the strategic incentive for the government to manipulate the R&D game is the *same* as in Cournot competition, so the *indirect* strategic incentive is for governments to relax environmental policy, so now the direct and indirect effects go in the *opposite* direction with Bertrand competition. The rationale is straightforward. In the market game firms take the price of their rival as fixed, whereas in fact reaction functions slope upwards so that if one firm raises its price the rival will follow; so firms are being too cautious in their pricing policies and can afford to raise them; the strategic behaviour of both firms and governments is designed to exploit this by trying to raise production costs as a way of committing firms to set higher prices. On the other hand in the R&D game, firms take as given their rival's R&D level, whereas, under both Bertrand and Cournot competition, R&D reaction functions slope downwards, so that the incentive for governments is to induce firms to expand their R&D, recognising that the rival will be induced to cut its R&D; in the case of pure process R&D, I have shown that the government needs to lower environmental taxes to induce more R&D by the domestic firm. Introducing environmental R&D means that R&D reaction functions still slope downwards, but now it is ambiguous what the effect of a tax increase will be on the domestic firm's R&D. In Ulph (1996d) it was shown that, for a particular class of models, the indirect incentive to manipulate R&D was actually larger than the direct incentive to raise costs, so that the net effect was that, even with Bertrand competition, governments would want to relax environmental policy. However in the numerical simulations this net effect was tiny, so that the introduction of producer strategic behaviour virtually eliminated any incentive for governments to distort their environmental policies.

Stage 1 game In this stage governments choose their environmental policy instruments. This game has not been fully analysed in the literature. In Ulph and Ulph (1996) and A. Ulph (199b, d) all that is done is to compare the cases where both governments use the same policy instrument, either taxes or standards. Since a full analysis is not available I just make a few remarks. The first general point to make is that there are now two sets of distortions in these models – distortions to environmental policy and distortions to R&D, so one cannot assess the welfare implications just by looking at the distortion to government environmental policy.

In Ulph (1996b) where there is Cournot competition and only process R&D, for the particular class of models studied there, the use of standards led to lower distortions to both environmental policy and R&D investment than did the use of emission taxes, and welfare was higher when both governments used standards; although, as I have shown, the introduction of strategic behaviour by producers lowers the distortion to environmental policy, compared with the case where there is no strategic behaviour by producers, welfare is lower, for the simple reason that there are now two distortions.

In Ulph (1996d) where there is Bertrand competition, but only process R&D, I said that with emission taxes the indirect incentive to distort R&D goes in the opposite direction to the direct effect, and indeed exceeds the direct effect, though only just. With emission standards the two effects again go in the opposite direction but the indirect effect is not as strong as the direct effect, so environmental policy remains tougher than first best, though not as tough as when there was no strategic behaviour by producers. However note that with Bertrand competition strategic behaviour by governments and producers is no longer self-defeating in two ways: first it is in the mutual interest of both firms that prices get raised towards the monopoly level so this raises welfare; since it also means cutting output and setting excessively tough environmental policy that raises welfare; and finally while the attempts to boost one firm's R&D at the expense of the other fails, so that both levels of R&D get increased, this is from a situation of *underinvestment* in R&D. So welfare is higher when either governments or producers act strategically and highest when both act strategically. Welfare is higher when governments use standards rather than taxes.

Finally Ulph and Ulph (1996) consider Cournot competition but both process and environmental R&D. I said that with emission taxes it was ambiguous whether environmental policy would be too tough or too lax because of the ambiguity about the effect of emissions taxes on R&D. In the case where emission standards are used, the model is much simpler because there is no direct abatement of emissions; so once firms have chosen their environmental R&D, and hence their emissions per unit of output, the imposition of an emission standard puts an upper limit on output, and assuming that bites this means that output of the rival firm cannot be manipulated. So there is no direct strategic effect in this model, and the R&D decisions of firms will be efficient. So the only strategic role left for government is to try to manipulate the R&D decision of the rival producer. For similar reasons to that of emission taxes the effect of relaxing emission standards on rival R&D is ambiguous, so it is also ambiguous whether environmental policy will be too lax or too tough when emission standards are used; but as shown in Ulph and Ulph (1996) it would be rather unusual for environmental policy to be too tough with emission standards.

4.2 Conclusions

I said there were two reasons for wanting to introduce the possibility of strategic behaviour by producers into the model of section 3 – to see whether this reduced the need for governments to distort their environmental policies and to address the Porter hypothesis that governments might set tough environmental policies to manipulate the R&D decisions of their producers. On the first point we have seen that introducing strategic producer behaviour gives an additional route by which governments can use environmental policy to affect market outcomes – by manipulating the R&D decisions of producers. While on the face of it this might be thought to increase the distortion to environmental policy, I have shown that this is not so, for two reasons. First, even when the incentive to distort environmental reasons for both direct and indirect reasons go in the same direction, the fact that producers act strategically can reduce the direct incentive for distorting environmental policy, and, in the studies available to date, that effect outweighs the indirect effect. Second, the indirect (R&D) incentive for distorting can go in the opposite direction to the direct effect, either because of the nature of competition in the final stage game, or because, when there is environmental R&D and emission taxes, the effect of emission taxes on R&D can be ambiguous.

As far as the Porter hypothesis is concerned the studies surveyed in this section do not provide universal support for this hypothesis again for two reasons. First, as I have just noted, the effect of environmental policy, especially taxes, on R&D is ambiguous; toughening R&D policy reduces the profit incentive for doing R&D, though it may increase the effectiveness of R&D. Second, even if, as the Porter hypothesis presumes, tougher environmental policy was to induce higher R&D by domestic producers and lower R&D by rivals, that does not imply that governments will want to set tougher environmental policies, for there may still be a direct rent-switching incentive for relaxing environmental policy which could outweigh the indirect incentive for toughening environmental policy. I shall say a bit more about the Porter hypothesis in the next section.

5 Further aspects of strategic environmental policy

In the two previous sections I outlined, in some detail, a number of models which moved away from the traditional discussion of trade and environmental policy by introducing imperfect competition, and showed that this could make a significant difference to the implications for environmental policy when the government is restricted in its available policy instruments and so uses environmental policy to achieve both environmental objectives and as a tool of strategic trade policy. I went into those models in some detail to illustrate the logical structure behind such models. However there are a number of aspects in the general literature on strategic environmental policy and trade which I have not covered so far, and in this section I shall very briefly cover five such aspects. The first three are extensions or variants of the models I have surveyed in sections 3 and 4, and the last two are further implications of the models.

5.1 Pollution related to consumption

In all the models I have considered so far, I have been concerned with problems of pollution related to production activities. But a number of pollution problems are related to consumption activities, such as exhausts from private motor cars, disposal of household waste, etc. This case has been well covered in the traditional analysis where many of the results presented in section 2 go through, with the obvious modification that, in trade terms, pollution is now related to the importing of goods rather than to the exporting of goods (see Anderson (1992), Dean (1992) for further discussion). Thus a country which is an *importer* of a pollution-intensive good will impose excessively tough environmental policy.

There has been much less analysis of consumption-related pollution in the strategic context. An exception of which I am aware is that by Motta and Thisse (1993a). They begin with a closed economy and consider the incentives for producers to design products with lower emissions of pollution when faced with a population with different preferences for environmental damage. Although there exist private incentives for introducing environmentally friendly goods, there is no reason to suppose that these are socially correct, and Motta and Thisse go on to examine the effects of the government imposing a minimum standard on environmental quality, and calculate the optimal minimum environmental standard (MES). In an open economy they note that the unilateral imposition of an MES will not only raise that country's welfare by improving the environment but will also protect that country against imports from other unregulated countries. However, they assume that when a country imposes an MES it is the same as the one they would have imposed in autarky, so they are not able to explore the question of whether countries would impose excessively tough MES as a trade device, although their analysis is suggestive that this would be the case. However this would not be out of line with what the traditional analysis suggests.

5.2 Innovation

The discussion of the Porter hypothesis in the last section can be criticised on the grounds that the model of R&D competition used there is a rather special model – it is what is called a non-tournament model in the R&D literature in the sense that both firms are able to benefit from the R&D they carry out. It might be thought that a more compelling framework for discussing the Porter hypothesis might be a tournament model where, say, because of patents, the first firm to innovate gains a long-term technological advantage over other firms. So the focus is on being the first to innovate. D. Ulph (1994) explores such a model. General results are more difficult to obtain for this case but for a particular class of model it is shown that again governments will set environmental policies which are too lax relative to first best. So the Porter hypothesis does not gain any strength by changing the nature of the R&D game. The conclusion remains that it is difficult to find compelling economic foundations for the Porter hypothesis (for a similar conclusion drawn from a rather broader discussion see Oates, Palmer and Portney (1994), and for a more extensive survey of the modelling of strategic environmental policy, trade and R&D the survey by Ecchia and Mariotti (1994)).

5.3 Location of firms

In the models in sections 3 and 4 there were a fixed number of firms whose location was also fixed. While this captured one strategic reason why governments may be tempted to relax environmental policies – to try to win a larger market share for their domestic firm – it does not capture one feature that underlies some of the popular debate: the possibility that tough environmental policy may drive firms out of the domestic market to relocate elsewhere. This 'delocation of capital' was referred to briefly at the end of section 2 where I noted that the traditional analysis could be extended to allow for mobile factors. It has also been included in some models of imperfect competition (Markusen, Morey and Olewiler (1993a, b), Ulph (1994), Motta and Thisse (1993b), Hoel (1994)). I will not go into any detail on these (see Rauscher (1993b) for a survey of the issue in general, including these papers) but just make a couple of points. First the broad structure of these models is very similar to those in section 4, except that in place of the stage 3 decision by firms as to investment in R&D there is a stage 3 decision about how many plants to build and where to locate them. Second, an interesting new feature of these models is that if different geographical markets are considered to be segregated (i.e., no resales between them, though trade takes place between them), then the degree of competitiveness of different markets becomes endogenous in the sense that if many plants locate in a market then the market becomes quite competitive, while if only a few firms are located in a market, perhaps faced by competition from imports, then that market can be quite uncompetitive. One interesting implication of this (see Ulph (1994)) is that countries can impose quite high environmental taxes without necessarily imposing high prices on their consumers, if the market is quite competitive.

Third, actions taken by governments to try to protect domestic firms or prevent their flight can be counterproductive. Thus Motta and Thisse (1993b) show that erecting trade barriers (e.g., increasing transport costs) may be harmful to an economy, because instead of a domestic firm being able to set up foreign plants and serve the domestic market from there it may force the domestic firm to close altogether and be served solely by foreign firms. In a similar vein Ulph (1994) showed that having firms which were not very 'footloose', i.e., faced high costs of locating plants in foreign countries, could be a significant handicap to a country, because it may prevent the domestic firm from being able to serve foreign markets if its domestic costs are raised by environmental policies, and so cause the domestic firm to lose a substantial share of world markets. Finally, the only paper which fully addresses the question of how non-cooperative governments may set their environmental policies is that by Markusen et al. (1993b) who consider the case of a single firm deciding whether to locate in one of two countries, from which it will serve both markets. They show that if environmental damage costs are low, both governments will set too lax environmental policies, essentially as a means of attracting the firm to locate in their country; but if damage costs are high both governments set too tough environmental policy, because they are trying to get the other country to incur the environmental damage ('nimbyism'). Thus, yet again we have no clear cut presumption that governments will set either too tough or too lax environmental policies.

5.4 Empirical studies

So far I have surveyed only theoretical arguments about the links between environment and trade, but there has also been an empirical literature trying to assess the impact of environmental policy on the patterns of international trade and factor (especially capital) mobility and the reverse question of whether environmental quality is adversely affected by the openness of an economy to trade. Obviously a major difficulty in such studies is constructing appropriate indices of the degree of rigour of environmental policy in different countries or the degree of environmental damage in different countries. Again I do not propose to survey all this literature – Dean (1992) and Rauscher (1993b) contain very good surveys of the results to date. The general thrust of the literature is that the empirical evidence for some of the theoretically predicted links between environmental damage and trade is mixed, but that the effects all appear to be rather small; this has led Cropper and Oates (1992), for example, to argue that environmental economists need not be too concerned about the impact of environmental policy on trade. The only caveat I would wish to make to this view is that much of the empirical work is based on the traditional view of international markets as being competitive. In particular, one strand of the empirical literature uses models of international trade, either econometrically estimated models, or, more usually, calibrated computable general equilibrium models and then simulates the effects of imposing environmental policies. Even quite large environmental taxes, such as carbon taxes, seem to have little impact on trade (see Boero, Clarke and Winters (1991), Hoeller, Dean and Nicolaisen (1991) for surveys). However there has been much less empirical work based on the strategic analysis of sections 3 and 4. One exception is the work of Ulph (1994, 1996a) which uses calibrated models of the fertiliser industry to simulate the effects of environmental policy. This work suggests that environmental policy can have much larger impacts than is suggested by the empirical work based on competitive markets. However these studies used very simple models, with quite restrictive functional forms and other assumptions so it is not clear that they are a particularly good representation of the fertiliser industry. Moreover they are subject to the usual criticism of calibrated models that because they are based very closely on the underlying economic theory they do not provide any independent test of that theory (e.g., Rauscher (1993b)). What this suggests is that there is a need for more empirical research that takes account of the recent developments in the theory of environment/trade linkages before dismissing these linkages as being of little quantitative importance.

5.5 Policy implications

I return briefly to some of the issues of international policy I touched on in the Introduction (for more detailed discussions see Pearce (1992), Tudini (1993), Ulph (1996c) among others). The kind of questions to be addressed are the following. (a) In the European Union the subsidiarity principle implies that responsibility for dealing with a particular issue should be delegated to the lowest level of jurisdiction unless a case can be made for passing it to a higher level; what does this imply for environmental policy? (b) Under GATT rules countries are allowed to impose regulations on the imports of *products* which might damage the environment of the importing country (i.e., pollution is related to consumption of the product) provided this is done in a non-discriminatory way (as between domestic and foreign sources, or between different foreign sources). Should this be extended to *production and process methods* (*PPM*), i.e., to allow countries to regulate or tax imports whose production has taken place under less stringent environmental controls than in the importing country?

As I noted in the introduction the answers given to such questions based on traditional analysis would be that (a) subsidiarity should mean that member states should be allowed to deal with their own purely domestic pollution problems and any role for the Commission should come in dealing with transboundary pollution or in representing the EU in international environmental agreements (see, for example, Siebert (1991)); *prima facie* this would suggest that, for example, the European Drinking Water Directive violated the subsidiarity principle (CEPR, 1993). (b) There is no case for extending GATT rules on products to PPM since this would deny countries the opportunity to exploit comparative advantage in environmental resources. Does the analysis of sections 3 and 4 require that such views be modified?

The obvious rationale for challenging the above traditional conclusions is that, again, countries may seek to exploit purely domestic environmental policy related to PPM for strategic trade reasons (such a justification appears to underlie the European Drinking Water Directive – see CEPR (1993)). So to the extent that the studies in sections 3 and 4 gave some support for believing that governments could seek to use environmental policy for strategic reasons this might provide support for overriding member states' environmental policies even for purely domestic environmental issues and allowing GATT to scrutinise PPM as a potential source of environmental trade barriers. Moreover, the analysis in those sections suggested that not only the rigour of environmental policy might be a matter of concern, but also the choice of environmental policy instruments.

The difficulty, though, is that it is not at all obvious from the analysis what form of intervention might be required. For a start, what has been shown in sections 3 and 4 is that we cannot even be confident about the *direction* in which environmental policy might be distorted, let alone the *extent* to which it might be distorted. It is also clear that the analysis provides no support for some of the proposals being made. Thus there is absolutely no case for *harmonisation* of environmental policies; harmonisation is neither necessary nor sufficient to ensure the absence of distortions to policy; it is not sufficient because, as shown in section 3, if all countries were identical they could all impose the same environmental tax or standard but that could still be distorted, and it is not necessary because if countries differ in marginal damage costs or marginal abatement costs then first-best environmental policies should differ between countries. This also means that policies of imposing countervailing tariffs on imports to compensate for the difference in compliance costs between countries have no justification. A policy of imposing a *minimum* standard, but allowing countries to impose tougher regulations if they wanted would be difficult to justify. First it presumes that distortion takes the form of excessively lax regulation, not excessively tough, and in principle we should be equally concerned about distortions in both directions, while, as I have said, no such presumption emerges from the literature. Second, even if that was the correct direction of distortion all it would ensure would be that the country with the weakest first-best environmental policies would be deterred from relaxing its policy – but countries who had tougher first-best environmental policies could still relax theirs, and would have incentives to do so.

The only real check as to whether countries are exploiting environmental policy for purely trade reasons is to compare the marginal abatement and marginal damage costs of their policies (even this could be problematic if there were other, purely domestic, reasons why environmental policy was having to address several distortions), but of course this raises formidable questions of asymmetries of information.

In conclusion, while the recent economic analysis gives some support for thinking governments may seek to set their environmental policies for strategic trade reasons, the research has yet to properly address the policy implications of this line of work.

6 Conclusions

In this chapter I have surveyed a number of recent studies examining the link between environmental policy and international trade. The literature has been timely in that the issue has been one of considerable public debate, and the literature has been well placed to address some of the issues raised by that debate, since the literature has focused on imperfect competition and the potential scope for governments to manipulate environmental policy for strategic reasons. I have shown that this recent literature is capable of providing starkly different predictions about environmental policy under liberalised trade regimes from those derived from the traditional trade and environmental literature, but that there is a severe problem of non-robustness of results. This is especially problematic when it comes to trying to draw policy conclusions from this new literature, although the analysis does not support some of the policy prescriptions discussed in popular debates.

For future research I think the main priorities are to establish better empirical results, so that a judgement can be reached whether any of these strategic trade effects on environmental policy are likely to be quantitatively very significant. If these turn out to be significant, then more work needs to be done on appropriate policy design.

Note

Paper presented to Workshop on 'Designing Economic Policy for the Management of Natural Resources and the Environment', Crete, 7–9 September 1994. I am grateful to Frank Stahler, Carlo Carraro, Michael Hoel and other participants in the Workshop for comments on an earlier version. Remaining errors are my own. The financial support of Fondezione ENI E. Mattei is gratefully acknowledged.

References

Anderson, K. (1992), 'The Standard Welfare Economics of Policies Affecting Trade and the Environment', in Anderson and Blackhusrt (eds.).

Anderson, K. and R. Blackhurst (eds.) (1992), *The Greening of World Trade*, Hemel Hempstead: Harvester Wheatsheaf.

Arden-Clarke, C. (1991), *The General Agreement on Tariffs and Trade, Environmental Protection and Sustainable Development*, Gland, Switzerland: World Wildlife Fund for Nature.

Barrett, S. (1994), 'Strategic Environmental Policy and International Trade', *Journal of Public Economics*, 54 (3), 325–38..

Bhagwati, J. (1971), 'The Generalised Theory of Distortions and Welfare', in J. Bhagwati *et al.* (eds.), *Trade, Balance of Payments and Growth*, Amsterdam: North-Holland.

―― (1994), 'Free Trade: Old and New Challenges', *Economic Journal*, 104, 231–46.

Bhagwati, J. and H. Daly (1993), 'Debate: Does Free Trade Harm the Environment?', *Scientific American*, November, 17–29.

Boero, G., R. Clarke and A. Winters (1991), *The Macroeconomic Consequences of Controlling Greenhouse Gases: A Survey*, Department of Environment Environmental Economics Research Series, London: HMSO.

Brander, J. and B. Spencer (1985), 'Export Subsidies and International Market Share Rivalry', *Journal of International Economics*, 18, 83–100.

Carraro, C. and D. Siniscalco (1993), 'Strategies for the International Protection of the Environment', *Journal of Public Economics*, 52, 309–28.

Cesar, H. (1993), 'The Comedy and Tragedy of the Commons', Ph.D. Thesis, EUI, Florence.

CEPR (1993), 'Making Sense of Subsidiarity', CEPR Annual Report, Moitoring European Integration 4.

Conrad, K. (1993a), 'Taxes and Subsidies for Pollution-Intensive Industries as Trade Policy', *Journal of Environmental Economics and Management*, 25, 121–35.

(1993b), 'Optimal Environmental Policy for Oligopolistic Industries in an Open Economy', Department of Economics Discussion Paper 476–93, University of Mannheim.

Copeland, B. R. (1994), 'International Trade and the Environment: Policy Reform in a Polluted Small Open Economy', *Journal of Environmental Economics and Management*, 26, 44–65.

Cropper, M. and W. Oates (1992), 'Environmental Economics: A Survey', *Journal of Economic Literature*, 30, 675–740.

Dean, J. (1992), 'Trade and Environment: A Survey of the Literature', chapter 2 in Low (ed.).

Ecchia, G. and M. Mariotti (1994), 'A Survey on Environmental Policy: Technological Innovation and Strategic Issues', *Nota di Lavoro* 44.94, FEEM, Milan.

Folmer, H., P. V. Mouche and S. Ragland (1993), 'Interconnected Games and International Environmental Problems', *Environmental and Resource Economics*, 3, 313–36.

Helpman, E. and P. Krugman (1989), *Trade Policy and Market Structure*, Cambridge, MA: MIT Press.

Hoel, M. (1994), 'Environmental Policy as a Game Between Governments When Plant Locations Are Endogenous', paper presented to 21st Annual EARIE Conference, Crete, 4–6 September 1994.

Hoeller, P., A. Dean and J. Nicolaisen (1991), 'Macroeconomic Implications of Reducing Greenhouse Gas Emissions: a Survey of Empirical Studies', *OECD Economic Studies*, 16, 45–78.

Hudson, S. (1992), 'Trade, Environment and the Pursuit of Sustainable Development', chapter 4 in Low (ed.).

Kennedy, P. W. (1994), 'Equilibrium Pollution Taxes in Open Economies with Imperfect Competition', *Journal of Environmental Economics and Management*, 27, 49–63.

Krutilla, K. (1991), 'Environmental Regulation in an Open Economy', *Journal of Environmental Economics and Management*, 20, 127–42.

Long, N. V., and H. Siebert (1991), 'Institutional Competition versus Ex-ante Harmonisation – the Case of Environmental Policy', *Journal of Institutional and Theoretical Economics*, 147, 296–312.

Low, P. (ed.) (1992), *International Trade and the Environment*, Washington, DC: World Bank.

Markusen, J. (1975a), 'Cooperative Control of International Pollution and Common Property Resources', *Quarterly Journal of Economics*, 89, 618–32.

(1975b), 'International Externalities and Optimal Tax Structures', *Journal of International Economics*, 5, 15–29.

Markusen, J., E. Morey and N. Olewiler (1992), 'Noncooperative Equilibria in Regional Environmental Policies When Plant Locations Are Endogenous', NBER Working Paper 4051.

(1993), 'Environmental Policy When Market Structure and Plant Location Are Endogenous', *Journal of Environmental Economics and Management*, 24, 69–86.

Motta, M. and J.-F. Thisse (1993a) 'Minimum Quality Standard as an Environmental Policy: Domestic and International Effects', *Nota di Lavora* 20.93, FEEM, Milan.

(1993b) 'Does Environmental Dumping Lead to Delocation?' *Nota di Lavoro* 77.93 FEEM, Milan.

Merrifield, J. D. (1988), 'The Impact of Selected Abatement Strategies on Transnational Pollution, the Terms of Trade, and Factor Rewards: A General Equilibrium Approach', *Journal of Environmental Economics and Management*, 15, 259–84.

Oates, W., K. Palmer and P.R. Portney (1994), 'Environmental Regulation and International Competitiveness: Thinking About the Porter Hypothesis', Discussion Paper 94–02, Resources for the Future, Washington, DC.

Oates, W. and R. M. Schwab (1988), 'Economic Competition Among Jurisdictions: Efficiency Enhancing or Distortion Inducing?', *Journal of Public Economics*, 35, 333–54.

Panagariya, A., K. Palmer, W. Oates and A. Krupnick (1993), 'Toward an Integrated Theory of Open Economy Environmental and Trade Policy', Working Paper No 93–8, Department of Economics, University of Maryland.

Pearce, D. (1992), 'Should the GATT be Reformed for Environmental Reasons?', CSERGE Working Paper GEC 92–06.

Pethig, R. (1976), 'Pollution, Welfare and Environmental Policy in the Theory of Comparative Advantage', *Journal of Environmental Economics and Management*, 2, 160–9.

(1996), 'Noncooperative National Environmental Policies and Capital Mobility', in J. Braden, H. Folmer and T. Ulen (eds.), *Environmental Policy with Economic and Political Integration: The European Community and the United States*, Edward Elgar, pp. 175–206.

Porter, M.C. (1991), 'America's Green Strategy', *Scientific American*, 264(4), 96.

Rauscher, M. (1992), 'Economic Integration and the Environment: Effect on Members and Non-Members', *Environmental and Resource Economics*, 2, 221–36.

(1993a), 'On Ecological Dumping', in C. Carraro (ed.) *Trade, Innovation and the Environment*, Dordrecht: Kluwer.

(1993b), 'Environmental Regulation and International Capital Allocation', *Nota di Lavoro 79.93*, FEEM, Milan.

Robertson, D. (1992), 'Trade and the Environment: Harmonisation and Technical Standards', in Low (ed.), chapter 17.

Runge, C. F. (1996), 'Economic Trade and Environmental Protection', in J. Braden, H. Folmer and T. Ulen (eds.), *Environmental Policy with Economic and Political Integration: The European Community and the United States*, Edward Elgar, pp. 209–34.

Siebert, H. (1991), 'Europe '92. Decentralising Environmental Policy in the Single Market', *Environmental and Resource Economics*, 1, 271–88.

Simpson, D. and R. Bradford (1993), 'Taxing Variable Costs: Environmental Regulation As Industrial Policy', Discussion Paper ENR 93–12, Resources for the Future, Washington DC.

Tirole, J. (1989), *The Theory of Industrial Organisation*, Cambridge, MA: MIT Press.

Tudini, A. (1993), 'Trade and Environment: the Issue of Process and Production Methods', *Nota di Lavoro* 7.93, FEEM, Milan.

Ulph, A. (1992), 'The Choice of Environmental Policy Instruments and Strategic International Trade', in R. Pethig (ed.), *Conflicts and Cooperation in Managing Environmental Resources*, Berlin: Springer-Verlag.

(1994), 'Environmental Policy, Plant Location and Government Protection', in C. Carraro (ed.), *Trade, Innovation Environment*, Dordrecht: Kluwer, pp. 123–66.

(1996a), 'Environmental Policy Instruments and Imperfectly Competitive International Trade'. *Environmental Resource Economics*, 7(4), 335–55.

(1996b), 'Environmental Policy and International Trade When Governments and Producers Act Strategically', *Journal of Environmental Economics and Management*, 30(3), 265–81.

(1996c), 'Strategic Environmental Policy, International Trade and the Single European Market', in J. Braden, H. Folmer and T. Ulen (eds.), *Environmental Policy with Economic and Political Integration: The European Community and the United States*, Edward Elgar 235–56.

(1996d), 'Strategic Environmental Policy and International Trade – The Role of Market Conduct', in C. Carraro, Y. Katsoulacos and A. Xepapadeas (eds.), *Environmental Policy and Market Structure*, Dordecht: Kluwer, pp. 99–130.

Ulph, D. (1994), 'Strategic Innovation and Strategic Environmental Policy' in C. Carraro (ed.) '*Trade Innovation Environment* 'Dordrecht: Kluwer, pp. 205–228.

Ulph, A. and D. Ulph (1996), 'Trade, Strategic Innovation and Strategic Environmental Policy – A General Analysis' in C. Carraro, Y. Katsoulacos and A. Xepapadeas (eds.), *Environmental Policy and Market Structure*, Dordecht: Kluwer, pp. 181–208.

Verdier, T. (1993), 'Strategic Trade and the Regulation of Pollution by Performance or Design Standard', *Nota di Lavoro* 58.93, FEEM, Milan.

7 Environmental regulation and international capital allocation

Michael Rauscher

1 What are the issues?

In economic theory, free international trade in goods and factors is seen as a source of wealth and welfare gains. Restrictions on trade and factor movements prevent the factors of production from moving to the locations of their most efficient utilisation and are, therefore, in general undesirable. The exceptions to this rule are based either on second-best arguments (the infant industry argument) or on strategic considerations that lead to Prisoner's Dilemma situations (the optimum tariff and strategic trade policy). Moreover, the stylised facts of post-war economic history suggest that outward-oriented development strategies employed, e.g., by East Asian countries have been much more successful than import substitution and the striving for self-reliance that were the philosophies of development in many Latin American countries and the Council of Mutual Economic Aid. On the background of this historical experience and of the theoretical work of the last decades, most economists now accept the general validity of the free-trade principle, at least as a good rule of thumb (Krugman (1987)). This view has come under attack again, now by environmentalists.[1]

There are several reasons for environmentalists to be sceptical about free trade and unrestricted factor movements. Free trade has specialisation effects and inevitably some countries will specialise in the production of pollution-intensive goods. This will increase environmental disruption in these countries and, if there is transfrontier pollution, also elsewhere. The second problem is that of capital mobility and foreign direct investment. Owners of capital are looking for the most profitable investment opportunities. Since high levels of environmental regulation raise production costs, capital will, *ceteris paribus*, move to the country with the lowest pollution abatement requirements. If all countries strive to attract capital, they will adjust their environmental regulations accordingly. These downward adjustments, so the argument goes, will ultimately result in undesirably low

193

levels of environmental regulation and disastrous environmental disruption on a world-wide scale. Thirdly there is the problem of increased output and consumption, being the result of the more efficient factor allocation under a regime of free trade and factor movements. The fourth argument against free trade is the increase in transport which damages the environment. Finally, there is the issue of the effectiveness of unilateral emission reductions in the case of global environmental problems. If a country unilaterally imposes a substantial tax on greenhouse gases, the industries affected by the tax will reduce their emissions – however not necessarily by employing cleaner technologies, but simply by moving abroad where taxes are lower or non-existent. Thus, each unit of emissions avoided at home is accompanied by an increase in foreign emissions and the effectiveness of unilateral greenhouse policies is reduced. This phenomenon has been addressed in the literature under the heading 'carbon leakage'.

The question is whether these arguments are substantial enough to provide a serious challenge to the dogma of free trade. This is not only an empirical but also a theoretical question. Are the arguments logically correct and consistent? This chapter is an attempt to provide an answer. It will concentrate on the relationship between environmental policy and the allocation of capital in an integrated world. If capital is mobile, either internationally or intersectorally inside a country, its allocation will be affected by the environmental regulation of production processes. But not only do emission taxes and standards affect international capital movements, there is also a feedback impact of capital movements on emissions and environmental quality. This leads us to ask the question whether free trade and unrestricted factor movements are beneficial from an economic welfare point of view or whether there exist serious 'green' motives for trade interventions.

There will be some aspects of the trade and environment debate which will not be addressed in this chapter, in particular the issues of consumption and transportation externalities. The external effects caused by consumption and transportation can be easily internalised by setting appropriate taxes or standards.[2] In the context of the more interesting questions like those of disastrous competition among environmental regulations and of carbon leakage they are of minor importance.

There are in principle two approaches to the subject. On the one hand, one can assume that capital is mobile across sectors within an economy. This corresponds to the standard model of international trade. Environmental disruption has been introduced into this model by Markusen (1975), Pethig (1976), Asako (1979), Krutilla (1991) and Rauscher (1991a). Environmental regulation then affects the allocation of factors within an economy and therefore the patterns of trade and specialisation. On the other hand, one can look at international factor movements. In these models, capital is not intersectorally mobile but internationally. See Rauscher (1991b, 1992, 1994, 1997). Moreover, one can synthesise the two approaches and look at the combination of both kinds of factor movements in a unified model framework, see McGuire (1982) and Merrifield (1988). The approach to be chosen here is the second one: capital moves across national borders. The model has the advantage that its simplest version allows to restrict the analysis to a one-good economy. This simplifies the notation and the derivation of results tremendously. Moreover, the insights to be gained into the basic issues by considering more complicated models is only marginal. This will become obvious when the results derived from the standard two-goods trade model are reviewed towards the end of the chapter. The model used in the remainder of the chapter is based on the standard approach to international factor mobility developed by Jasay (1960), MacDougall (1960) and Kemp (1964, chapter 13).[3] This model has been extended by the introduction of environmental variables by Rauscher (1997, chapter 3, 1994) and a variation of this model will be used here.

Two kinds of environmental externalities will be considered. Both of them are due to production activities. On the one hand, there are negative externalities affecting environmental quality as a public consumption good, i.e., a kind of eye-sore pollutant is considered. This is the way we are used to thinking about environmental externalities. However, there are also external effects on production. Industries that rely on clean air and water, e.g., agriculture and tourism, are negatively affected by environmental damage. This will be taken into account by modelling the public-input aspect of environmental quality as well.

The chapter is organised as follows. The model will be introduced in the next section. Section 3 tries to identify determinants of international capital mobility. What is the impact of environmental regulation on the international allocation of capital? Afterwards, we will deal with the welfare effects of international capital movements. Is the environmentalists' view correct that free factor mobility enhances environmental disruption and leads to welfare losses? The impact of environmental regulation on the economy of a country that is integrated in international factor markets is addressed in section 5. Some counterintuitive results will be derived, e.g., a stricter environmental policy may lead to increased pollution. Section 6 addresses the issue of optimal environmental policies under conditions of free factor mobility. It will be seen that in open economies environmental regulation can be used to achieve non-environmental economic policy objectives. Section 7 is devoted to the international dimension of optimal environmental policies. Under which circumstances does optimisation by individual governments lead to unacceptably high levels of emissions and what are the gains from cooperation? In section 8, capital market interventions will be introduced as a second policy instrument and the question will be addressed whether these instruments can be used for 'green' objectives. In sections 9 and 10, the model will be extended by looking at the political economy of environmental policy making and at non-competitive market structures. Section 11 will give a brief overview of results that can be derived in an international trade framework where capital is assumed to be mobile across sectors inside an economy rather than internationally across borders. The empirical evidence will be reviewed in section 12. Finally, section 13 will summarise the results.

2 The model of international capital movements

Consider a world consisting of two countries, the home country and the foreign country. All variables concerning the home country will be represented by lower-case letters and the variables of the foreign country by the corresponding upper-case letters. We look at aggregated economies, i.e. there is a single commodity which is produced and consumed. There is no trade in this commodity.[4] In the following paragraphs, the model will be introduced for the case of the home country. Most of the equations for the foreign country follow by analogy. The rest will be presented explicitly.

Technology There are two private factors of production, capital, k, and an environmental resource, e. The resource input is defined as the share of the resource which is used up during the production process, e.g., the quantity of clean air or water contaminated due to production. e will also be referred to as emissions.[5] $f(.,.)$ is a neoclassical production function combining capital and emissions. It is assumed to exhibit non-increasing returns to scale. Decreasing returns may be justified by the existence of other factors like labour and land that do not occur explicitly in the model. However, for some of the graphical representations, constant returns to scale are very useful – as will be seen below. The substitutability of emissions and capital implies that there is a capital-intensive pollution abatement technology, which, however, is not modelled explicitly. The public input is environmental quality, measured by the negative magnitude of pollution, p. It is assumed that a high level of environmental quality enhances the productivity of the other factors. This is modelled by introducing an efficiency factor $g(.)$, which is an increasing concave function of environmental quality. Thus, output, q, is

$$q = g(-p) f(k,e)$$ (1)

with

$$f_k>0, f_e>0, f_{kk}<0, f_{ee}<0, f_{ke}>0, f_{kk}f_{ee}-f_{ke}^2\geq 0;^6 \ g'>0, g''<0$$

where primes denote derivatives of univariate functions and subscripts represent partial derivatives of multivariate functions with respect to the variable in question. The condition that $f_{ke}>0$ is of major importance for the following results. This condition is satisfied for constant returns to scale production functions that have the usual properties. In the case of decreasing returns to scale, it is an additional assumption, which is, however, satisfied by conventional specifications of production functions like Cobb–Douglas. The magnitude of the cross derivative f_{ke} is closely related to the technological substitution possibilities between capital and environmental resources. In the case of constant returns to scale, the elasticity of substitution[7] is given by

$$\sigma=\frac{f_k f_e}{ff_{ke}}$$

Thus, if f_{ke} is large, the substitution possibilities are limited. It will be seen that the size of f_{ke} is positively related to the strength of the capital-relocation effects after environmental policy changes. This has to be interpreted such that limited substitution possibilities raise the necessity of adjusting the capital stock.

Capital mobility The initial endowment of the home country with capital, k^0, is given and constant. Foreigners can move a part of their capital stock, I, to the home country such that the capital employed in the home country is

$$k=k^0+I \tag{2}$$

and, correspondingly,

$$K=K^0-I \tag{2'}$$

in the foreign country. A negative value of I means that a part of the domestic capital stock is employed in the foreign country. I will sometimes be referred to as 'foreign direct investment' in the following sections, although it is a stock and not a flow variable.

Pollution Pollution is caused by domestic and foreign emissions. Let a and A (both in the interval $(0,1)$) be the shares of emissions that remain within the borders of the polluting country. $(1-a)$ and $(1-A)$ are the transfrontier pollution coefficients. Assume that domestic and foreign emissions have the same characteristics such that they can be added up. Thus the level of pollution, p, is

$$p=ae+(1-A)E \qquad (3)$$

Consumption and welfare Income is domestic output plus the return on capital invested abroad or minus interest payment made to the owners of foreign capital. Let r be the international rate of interest. Since all income is consumed, the consumption possibilities are

$$c=g(-p)f(k^0+I,e)-r\,I \qquad (4)$$

Pollution causes welfare losses. These will be modelled here in a very simple fashion by assuming that welfare, w, is a linear function of consumption and pollution. Moreover, a parameter b is introduced which measures the impact of pollution. This parameter may also be interpreted as a measure of environmental consciousness. Thus, by inserting equation (3), welfare turns out to be

$$w=g(-ae-(1-A)E)f(k^0+I,e)-r\,I-b\,(ae+(1-A)E) \qquad (5)$$

Policy instruments Two policy instruments will be considered: an emission tax and a tax on repatriated profits. The latter tax may be negative, i.e., a subsidy. The redistribution of tax revenue is assumed to take place in the shape of lump-sum payments and, therefore, does not distort the allocation of factors.[8] Moreover, perfect competition is assumed, i.e., factors are paid their marginal products.

If there is an emission tax, the allocation in a perfectly competitive economy is characterised by

$$g(-p)f_e(k,e)=t \qquad (6)$$

where t is the emission tax rate.

The barrier to international factor mobility may take the shape of a quantitative restriction on foreign direct investment or of a tax on repatriated profits. In a perfectly competitive world, these instruments are equivalent. If there is a quantitative restriction, one can always derive the tax equivalent as the wedge between the marginal productivity of capital and the world market rate of interest, r. Let us assume that I is positive. Then the tax equivalents, ϑ and $\varTheta$, are given by

$$g(-p)f_k(k,e)=r+\vartheta \qquad (7)$$

$$G(-P)F_K(K,E)=r-\varTheta \qquad (7')$$

If foreign investors have to pay a tax on repatriated profits in the home country, they will only invest there if the marginal productivity of capital exceeds the international interest rate by the tax rate. If they are taxed in their own country, they will invest abroad only if the international rate of return exceeds the capital productivity at home.

The major difference between this and other models of international factor mobility is the occurrence of external effects on production. This will cause a number of ambiguities in the results and it will sometimes be useful to also present the results of the simplified version of the model in which there are no such externalities.

3 Patterns of factor mobility and their explanation

Capital will move from the country where its marginal productivity is low to the country where its marginal productivity is high. Thus, taking account of capital income taxation, it moves from the foreign to the home country if

$$g(-p)f_k(k^0,e)-\vartheta>r>G(-P)\,F_K(K^0,E)+\Theta \tag{8}$$

How can this result be produced by differences in environmental regulation between two countries? In principle, two approaches can be taken. The first one is to look at existing levels of environmental regulation, i.e., at given emission standards or emission taxes. They define the actual scarcity of environmental resources. The second approach is based on preferences. How does the degree of environmental consciousness or concern affect the allocation of capital? In this case we need to model a benevolent government which takes account of the preferences of the citizens it represents. The government's policy would then reflect the true scarcity of environmental resources. We start with given environmental policies that are not necessarily optimal. The method of the analysis is to look at the domestic economy, vary one parameter, and determine the effect on the marginal productivity of capital.

Let us first consider the case of a small economy. A change in emissions implies

$$\frac{d(gf_k)}{de}=gf_{ke}-ag'f_k \tag{9}$$

The sign is ambiguous. On the one hand, increased emissions enhance the productivity of capital but they also cause pollution which negatively affects the productivity of capital. If there is an emission tax, equation (6) has to be taken into account and

$$\frac{d(gf_k)}{dt}=\frac{gf_{ke}-ag'f_k}{gf_{ee}-ag'f_e} \tag{10}$$

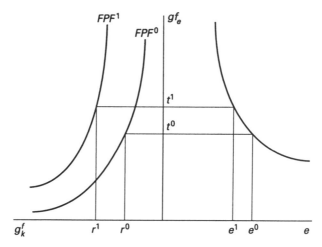

Figure 7.1 Changes in emissions and the marginal productivity of capital

Since the denominator is negative, the right-hand side of equation (10) has just the opposite sign of that of equation (9). The following proposition can be derived:

Proposition 1: A country is capital poor, i.e., it attracts foreign direct investments, if it has a restrictive environmental regulation and the external effect of pollution on production is substantial or if it has a lax regulation and the external effect on production is small.

This is depicted in figure 7.1. If $f(.,.)$ exhibits constant returns to scale, the interest rate r is a declining convex function of the emission tax rate, t, for a given level of pollution. This is the factor-price frontier, denoted FPF and depicted in the left-hand part of the figure. The right-hand side depicts the marginal productivity of emissions (which equals the emission tax rate under perfect competition) as a declining function of emissions. A more restrictive environmental policy leads to an increase in the tax rate from t^0 to t^1 and to a reduction of emissions from e^0 to e^1. This implies that environmental quality is improved and the factor-price frontier is shifted upwards. The direction of change of the interest rate is in general ambiguous. In the special case depicted here, the remuneration of capital is increased. The direct effect of reducing emissions (corresponding to the shift along the factor-price frontier) is dominated by the external effect (represented by the shift of the factor-price frontier itself).

This result that restrictive environmental policies may help to attract foreign capital is quite remarkable, albeit not particularly surprising or counterintuitive. In reality, this may in particular apply if there is a high degree of capital–labour complementarity and mobile labour is not willing to move to hot-spot areas.

If the environmental policy takes account of the preferences of the inhabitants of a country, the scarcity of environmental resources (and that of capital) can be traced back to variables like environmental consciousness. Thus, consider a benevolent government which maximises social welfare. The first-order condition of optimality is

$$gf_e = ag'f + ab \qquad (11)$$

where gf_e is the optimal emission tax rate in the competitive economy. It equals the marginal damage due to emissions which is composed of the productivity effect and on the reduction of environmental quality as a consumption good. Total differentiation of equation (11) gives a relationship between the environmental consciousness parameter, b, and the optimal level of emissions. This can be used to determine the impact of b on the marginal productivity of capital

$$\frac{d(gf_k)}{db} = \frac{gf_{ke} - ag'f_k}{gf_{ee} - 2ag'f_e + a^2g''f} \qquad (12)$$

Proposition 2: Let the environmental policy be welfare maximising. Then a country attracts foreign direct investment either if its citizens are environmentally concerned compared to those of the other country and the external effect of environmental disruption on production is substantial or if its citizens care less about environmental quality and the external effect on production is relatively unimportant.

Matters are slightly more complicated if the country under consideration is large. In this case, its emissions have a substantial impact on the foreign level of environmental quality. Due to the pollution spill-over, increased emissions have a negative effect on foreign capital productivity. If this effect is substantial, the home country can use a lax environmental policy to reduce the competitiveness of the foreign industry and attract more mobile capital. The probability of winning a beauty contest is increased if one manages to make the other competitors more ugly.

4 Welfare effects of international capital mobility

One of the concerns expressed by environmentalists is that trade and international capital mobility cause welfare losses due to their impact on the allocation of factors of production. For instance, emissions may be increased as a consequence of international economic integration. The following analysis will begin by looking at the small-country case. The country under consideration is not able to affect the world market interest rate. Increased openness is modelled by the removal of a quantitative restriction on foreign direct investments. If the level of emissions remains constant, matters are simple. Environmental quality will not be changed and there is an increase in the consumption possibilities due to the more efficient allocation of capital. This is rather obvious and may be shown graphically by the conventional *Harberger* triangle techniques.

Now consider the case of an emission tax. Totally differentiating equation (5) yields

$$\frac{de}{dI}=\frac{gf_{ke}}{ag'f_e-gf_{ee}}>0 \tag{13}$$

An increase in the capital stock leads to an increase in emissions. With the larger capital stock, emissions become more productive and, at a given tax rate, producers will discharge more pollutants. In the other country, there is the opposite effect. It increases its foreign direct investment and, therefore, loses a part of its capital stock. The emissions will be reduced. Thus, emissions 'move' from the capital-rich to the capital-poor country – a phenomenon which may be characterised as 'polluting thy neighbour via foreign direct investment'.[9] This does, however, not mean that the capital-exporting country exploits the capital-importing country. The change in emissions is a result of voluntary exchange and may be welfare increasing. The welfare effect can be determined via equation (5):

$$\frac{dw}{dI}=gf_k-r+(gf_e-ag'f-ab)\frac{de}{dI} \tag{14}$$

gf_k-r is positive since the marginal productivity of capital exceeds the interest rate in the capital-poor country if factor mobility is restricted. This is the efficiency gain that is known from the standard models. The other terms represent the effect of changes in environmental quality. The sign of the term in brackets is ambiguous. If the environmental policy is optimal, i.e., if equation (11) holds, then it is zero. It is positive if the emission tax rate is too high and negative if the tax rate is too low. Thus, in the case of a suboptimal environmental policy there will be welfare losses that may dominate the traditional efficiency gains. The capital-rich country, however, will experience additional welfare gains in such a situation since the level of emissions that has been too high initially is now reduced. Loosely speaking, unrestricted factor mobility can be a substitute for a good environmental policy. The following theorem summarises the results.

Proposition 3: Let the environmental policy instrument be an emission tax. Increased openness will lead to an increase in pollution if the country is capital poor and to a reduction in emissions if the country is capital rich. The impacts on the other variables and the welfare effects are ambiguous. If the environmental policy is optimal, the welfare effects are always positive.

Before the large-country case is considered, one may wish to address the question of how a country opening its borders to international capital movements should adjust its environmental policy. The optimality condition, (11), has to be differentiated totally with respect to e and I. This yields

$$\frac{de^*}{dI}=\frac{-(gf_{ke}-ag'f_k)}{gf_{ee}-2ag'f_e+a^2g''f} \tag{15}$$

where the asterisk denotes the optimal value. The sign of the numerator on the right-hand side is ambiguous. If the external effect on production is small, the home country should raise its emissions. If this effect is substantial, it should reduce its emissions. The opposite result is obtained for the capital-rich country. If the foreign direct investment is induced by differences in environmental regulation, the following conclusion may be drawn

Proposition 4: If the externalities that affect production are small, the environmental policies tend to diverge as a result of integration. If these externalities are substantial, they tend to converge.

In the large-country case, the effects of integration on the world market rate of interest and transfrontier pollution have to be considered. It will be seen that welfare losses are possible even if the countries employ optimal environmental policies initially. Let us assume that emission taxes are given in the two countries. The welfare effects of increased capital mobility on the home and the foreign country are

$$\frac{dw}{dI}=gf_k-r-I\frac{dr}{dI}+(gf_e-ag'f-ab)\frac{de}{dI}+(1-A)b\frac{dE}{dI} \tag{16}$$

$$\frac{dW}{dI}=-(GF_k-r)+I\frac{dr}{dI}+(GF_E-AG'F-AB)\frac{dE}{dI}+(1-a)B\frac{de}{dI} \tag{16'}$$

There are four effects. The first one is the efficiency gain. This effect is always positive since $gf_k>r>GF_k$. The second term is the interest rate effect. It vanishes if the initial situation is one of pure autarky, i.e., $I=0$. Otherwise, the sign of this effect is ambiguous. One of the countries will gain, the other will lose. The third effect is the impact of the change in own emissions, which is zero in the case of an optimal environmental policy. The fourth effect is the transboundary pollution effect. Its sign is positive in the capital-poor home country since the capital-rich country reduces its emissions and negative in the foreign country since domestic emissions rise. Thus one may conclude:[10]

Proposition 5: In the large-country case, the welfare effects of integration are ambiguous. Even in the case of optimal environmental policies is it possible that both countries lose as a consequence of increased capital mobility.

This result is in accordance with the fears expressed by environmentalists. Nevertheless the mechanics are not necessarily those that environmentalists have in mind, e.g., negative effects from integration may arise from changes in the rate of interest. The other potentially negative effects of increased factor mobility arise from insufficient environmental policies, that do not internalise domestic and/or international externalities. Thus, it is neither correct nor useful to blame economic integration for these negative welfare effects. The best of all worlds would be one with perfect environmental policy and unrestricted factor movements. If there is policy failure in the field of environmental affairs, the first-best solution is to improve environmental policies. Intervening into international capital markets can provide only second-best results.

5 Effects of changes in environmental policy

Having investigated the impact of changes in factor mobility on pollution and environmental quality, we will now turn to the question of how environmental policy can be used to influence the allocation of capital. This has already been the subject of section 3 where the impact of environmental policy on capital productivity has been considered for the autarchic economy. We will now investigate the large open economy case.

A large open economy influences the world market interest rate by changing its environmental policy. Two cases will be distinguished. In the first scenario, the emissions of the foreign country are given. In the second, scenario, they are variable and we assume that there is a constant emission tax rate. It will be seen that this has a substantial impact on the results.

In the case of constant foreign emissions, equations (7) and (7') can be used to eliminate the interest rate

$$g(-p)f_k(k^0+I,e) - \vartheta = G(-P)F_K(K^0-I,E) + \Theta \qquad (17)$$

It follows that

$$\frac{dI}{de} = \frac{-gf_{ke} + ag'f_k - (1-a)G'F_k}{gf_{kk} + GF_{KK}} \tag{18}$$

$$\frac{dI}{de} = \frac{GF_{KE} - AG'F_K + (1-A)gf_k}{gf_{kk} + GF_{KK}} \tag{18'}$$

Three effects can be distinguished. They correspond to the three terms occurring in the numerators of equations (18) and (18'). The direct productivity effect is positive: high emissions make the country more attractive for mobile capital. The second effect is the domestic externality on production: capital will be repelled. The third effect is the external effect on production in the other country. Since increased emissions lead to reduced factor productivities there, the other country will lose mobile capital. This corresponds to the results derived in section 3. If the external effects are relatively small, i.e., if g' and G' are close to zero, then

$$\frac{dI}{de} = \frac{-gf_{ke}}{gf_{kk} + GF_{KK}} > 0$$

$$\frac{dI}{dE} = \frac{GF_{ke}}{gf_{kk} + GF_{KK}} < 0 \tag{19}$$

Let us now consider the case in which the policy instrument in the other country is an emission tax. In addition to equation (17), the emission tax equation (6) of the home country and the corresponding equation of the foreign country,

$$GF_E = T \tag{5'}$$

have to be considered. The results of the model with external effects on production turn out to be very complicated and are hardly interpretable. Thus, the analysis will be restricted to the simplified model in which $g' = G' = 0$. Total differentiation then yields

$$\begin{pmatrix} gf_{kk} + GF_{KK} & gf_{ke} & -GF_{KE} \\ gf_{ke} & gf_{ee} & 0 \\ -GF_{KE} & 0 & GF_{EE} \end{pmatrix} \begin{pmatrix} dI \\ de \\ dE \end{pmatrix} = \begin{pmatrix} 0 \\ dt \\ dT \end{pmatrix} \tag{20}$$

The comparative static results are

$$\frac{dI}{dt} = \frac{-GF_{EE}gf_{ke}}{GF_{EE}(gf_{kk}gf_{ee} - gf_{ke}^2) + gf_{ee}(GF_{KK}GF_{EE} - GF_{KE}^2)} \tag{20a}$$

$$\frac{de}{dt} = \frac{GF_{EE}(gf_{kk} + GF_{KK}) - GF_{KG}^2}{GF_{EE}(gf_{kk}gf_{ee} - gf_{ke}^2) + gf_{ee}(GF_{KK}GF_{EE} - GF_{KE}^2)} \qquad (20b)$$

$$\frac{dE}{dt} = \frac{-GF_{KE}gf_{ke}}{GF_{EE}(gf_{kk}gf_{ee} - gf_{ke}^2) + gf_{ee}(GF_{KK}GF_{EE} - GF_{KE}^2)} \qquad (20c)$$

and similar results are obtained for the effects of emission tax changes in the foreign country. The denominators in equations (20a,b,c) are zero if the production function exhibits constant returns to scale. This results from the constancy of the factor price frontier in this special case. A given emission tax rate implies a particular level of the marginal productivity of capital. If the capital productivities are the same in the two countries, the allocation of capital is indeterminate. Otherwise, the whole capital stock is moved to the country which offers the higher rate of interest, i.e., in which, *ceteris paribus*, the level of environmental regulation is lower. If there are decreasing returns to scale, interior solutions are possible over a wider range of parameters and the following results can be established. Lower emission taxes make the country more attractive for investors (20a), its emissions will be increased (20b) and the emissions of the foreign country will be reduced (20c).

Proposition 6: Let there be an emission tax in the other country. If there are no externalities affecting production, an increase in emission taxes reduces foreign direct investment and leads to an increase in the emissions in the other country.

The negative impact of domestic regulation on foreign emissions has the following intuitive explanation. The direct effect of a domestic tax increase is a reduction in domestic emissions and in foreign direct investment. Since the capital stock employed in the foreign country is now larger than before, the marginal productivity of emissions is raised and exceeds the emission tax rate. Thus, foreign producers will increase their emissions until the productivity equals the tax rate again.

Turning the argument around, the following counterintuitive implication can be deducted:

Proposition 7: A country may reduce its environmental quality by adopting a more restrictive environmental policy.

The country adopting stringent environmental policy measures repels mobile capital. This capital is invested abroad and the marginal productivity of emissions is raised. At a given and constant emission tax rate, this creates incentives to increase emissions. Since a part of the pollutants spill over to the home country, environmental quality tends to be reduced.

This result is not of mere academic interest. It implies that unilateral approaches to address international environmental problems can be rather ineffective. In addition to the free-rider problems associated with unilateral environmental policies, they may create wrong incentives for the producers. Emissions are reduced not by developing cleaner technologies but, instead, by moving the capital to less regulated regions. The reduction of emissions at home is accompanied by the increase in emissions abroad. In the recent literature on the economics of the greenhouse effect, this problem has been addressed under the heading 'carbon leakage'. CO_2 taxes, imposed unilaterally by single countries, may lead to an international relocation of energy-intensive production processes such that the effect of the tax is reduced or even reversed.

6 Optimal environmental policies

Having analysed the effects of changes in environmental policies on consumption and environmental quality, we may now ask how the various effects of changes in environmental policy on income and environmental quality are translated into welfare gains and losses. The benevolent policy maker's objective is to trade off these gains and losses and find an environmental policy that maximises social welfare. In a first step, it is assumed that emission control is the only environmental policy instrument. Later on, a tax on repatriated profits will be introduced into the model.

The home country's welfare function is differentiated with respect to emissions. Rearranging terms then yields the following condition for the optimal level of emissions[11]

$$gf_e = ab + ag'f + \frac{I[gf_{ke}GF_{KK} - ag'f_k GF_{KK} - (1-a)G'F_K g f_{kk}]}{gf_{kk} + GF_{KK}} \quad (21)$$

A similar result is obtained for the foreign country. The term on the right-hand side is the optimal emission tax rate.[12] This tax rate consists of three components. The first term is the marginal cost of reducing environmental quality as a consumption good. The second term is the cost of reducing environmental quality as a factor of production. These two terms take account of the pure environmental externalities. The third term is the impact on the remuneration of the mobile factor of production. It itself consists of the three components that are represented by the terms in the numerator. The first term denotes direct the impact of increased emissions, which is positive. The second and third terms denote the external effects, which negatively affect the interest rate. These effects are multiplied by I.

Thus, given that the home country is capital poor (i.e., $I>0$), it has to pay foreigners for providing capital and it will, therefore, benefit from a low interest rate. This can be achieved by means of a high emission tax rate if the direct effect of emissions on capital productivity dominates, or by means of a low emission tax rate if the external effects are stronger. The opposite results are obtained for the capital-rich foreign economy.

Let us now consider the case of a given emission tax in the other country. Moreover, assume again that the external productivity effects are relatively small, i.e., $g'=G'=0$. The optimal tax rate is

$$
gf_e = ab + \frac{G^2(F_{KK}F_{EE}-F_{KE}^2)gf_{ke}}{G^2(F_{KK}F_{EE}-F_{KE}^2)+GF_{EE}gf_{kk}}I
$$
$$
- \frac{(1-A)gf_{ke}GF_{KE}}{G^2(F_{KK}F_{EE}-F_{KE}^2)+GF_{EE}gf_{kk}}b \tag{22}
$$

The first term is the domestic externality of increased emissions. The second term is the rate-of-return effect. If the country is capital poor, there is an incentive to reduce the interest rate by means of a restrictive environmental policy. The foreign country, which is capital rich, should choose a less restrictive environmental policy since it benefits from high interest rates. The third term is due to the increase in foreign emissions. If the government knows that by employing strict environmental policy measures, capital will be driven out of the country and the foreign economy will increase its emissions, then it should refrain from using too restrictive environmental regulations if the transboundary pollution spillover is substantial.

The results derived in this section can now be summarised as follows:

Proposition 8: The optimal emission tax serves three purposes. It internalises the domestic external effects of production. It is used to affect the world market rate of interest. Finally, it deals with the transfrontier pollution problems that are induced by international factor mobility.

As the comparison of equations (21) and (22) shows, it makes a difference for the determination of the optimal environmental policy whether the other country chooses an emission tax or an emission level.[13] In order to get an impression concerning the economic intuition behind these differences, rewrite equation (22) such that

$$
gf_e = ab + \frac{GF_{KK}gf_{ke}I}{GF_{KK}+gf_{kk}} + \frac{GF_{KE}gf_{kk}I}{GF_{KK}+gf_{kk}}\frac{dE}{de} + (1-A)b\frac{dE}{de} \tag{23}
$$

dE/de has been derived by eliminating dt from equations (20b) and (20c). dE/de is negative for the case of constant emission taxes in the other country and zero for the case of constant emission levels. If we move from a scenario with given emission levels to a scenario with given emission taxes, two effects can be observed. Firstly, the rate-of-return effect is diminished. If additional emissions at home reduce the emissions abroad, then the pressure on capital to move to the home country is increased. Therefore, the necessity to adjust the emission tax in order to influence the rate of return is reduced. The second effect is due to the fact that a change in domestic environmental policy affects the emissions in the other country as well. Taking this into account, the government should move to laxer environmental standards.

Proposition 9: For a given level of emissions in the foreign country, the domestic emissions are larger if the foreign country chooses a tax than if it chooses a constant emission level. The foreign country also chooses a less restrictive environmental policy if the transfrontier externality is large compared to the rate-of-return effect. If the latter effect dominates, the optimal emissions are higher in the tax scenario than in the constant-emissions case.

It is desirable to identify the impact of the assumption made on the policy instrument used in the other country, not only on the decision of a single country but also on the resulting Nash equilibrium. Rauscher (1997) shows that all kinds of results are possible. Depending on the parameters of the model, scenarios are feasible in which both countries raise or reduce their emissions or one of them increases its emissions whereas the other reduces emissions.

7 Nash equilibria and the gains from cooperation

As in all international policy games in which governments act strategically in the national interest and, thereby, accept that disadvantages accrue to the inhabitants of other countries, there will be gains from cooperation. Before dealing with cooperation, it will be useful to identify the external effects the countries impose on each other in the case of uncoordinated policies. These externalities are given by

$$\frac{dW}{de} = -(1-a)(G'F+B)$$

$$+\frac{gf_{ke}GF_{KK}-ag'f_kGF_{KK}-(1-a)G'F_Kgf_{kk}}{gf_{kk}+GF_{KK}}I \tag{24}$$

$$\frac{dw}{dE} = -(1-A)(g'f+b)$$

$$-\frac{GF_{KE}gf_{kk} - AG'F_K gf_{kk} - (1-A)g'f_k GF_{KK}}{gf_{kk} + GF_{KK}}I \qquad (24')$$

The first term is the transfrontier pollution spillover, which is always negative. The second effect is the interest-rate effect. Its sign is indeterminate. The gains from cooperation can be determined by looking at a Nash equilibrium of environmental policies in which each country has chosen its optimum response to the other country's policy and then identifying the potential of Pareto improvements. Thus, assume that there exists a unique Nash equilibrium. The iso-welfare curves for the home country and the foreign country can be inferred from the external effects. The Nash equilibrium, N, and the iso-welfare contours, w and W, are depicted in figure 7.2. Four cases can be distinguished:[14]

The first diagram depicts a situation in which both countries would benefit from a mutual reduction in emissions. This case is a possible result of transfrontier pollution spillovers. Since governments do not care about damages that occur on the other side of the border, emissions will be too high. A Pareto superior solution could be established if both countries reduced their emissions.

In the second diagram, the home country imposes a negative externality on the foreign country, but itself is positively affected by foreign emissions. This is possible if the external effects on production are negligible ($g' = G' = 0$) and the problem of transfrontier pollution is of minor relevance. The home country chooses a strict environmental policy in order to keep the interest rate low. The foreign country, in contrast, chooses a lax policy since it prefers a high interest rate. Both countries would be better off if the home country increased its emissions and the foreign country used stricter environmental standards.

Diagram (c) shows the opposite external effects. They are possible if, for instance, the external effects on production are substantial and the transfrontier pollution spill-overs are negligible. In this case, the rate of return on capital is reduced by lax environmental policies and increased by strict standards. Thus, the capital-poor home country would benefit from higher emissions in the foreign country. The foreign country would be better off if the home economy chose a more restrictive environmental policy.

The final diagram depicts a situation in which emissions are too low in both countries. This is possible if transfrontier pollution is not a major problem. If the external effect on production is small in the home

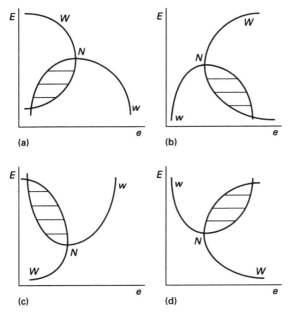

Figure 7.2 National environmental policies and gains from cooperation

country and large in the foreign country, both countries try to influence the rate of return in their own favour by restricting emissions. Less
restrictive policies yield welfare gains for both countries.

Proposition 10: Non-cooperative equilibria are not Pareto optimal.
Whether the countries should increase or reduce their emissions to achieve
Pareto improvements, depends on the parameters of the model.

From the point of view of an environmentalist, the most interesting scenario is the one in which environmental regulations are too lax in both
countries. In the interpretation of the diagram, this has been motivated by
transfrontier pollution. However, if there is transfrontier pollution, a
welfare-maximising government will never have the incentive to internalise
all social costs of environmental disruption – independently of whether
there are international capital movements or not. The destructive potential
of capital movements would become obvious, if scenario (a) could be the
result of the policy game with purely domestic social costs. To show that
this is indeed possible, set $a=A=1$ in equations (24) and (24'):

$$\frac{dW}{de}=\frac{gf_{ke}-ag'f_{k}}{gf_{kk}+GF_{KK}}IGF_{KK}$$

$$\frac{dw}{dE} = -\frac{GF_{KE} - AG'F_K}{gf_{kk} + GF_{KK}} Igf_{kk}$$

dW/de is negative if g' is large. dw/dE is negative if G' is small. In this case both countries try to influence the rate of return on capital in their own favour by using lax environmental policies and thereby negatively affect the other country's national income.

Proposition 11: Even without international pollution spillovers, it is possible that the objective to influence international capital movements leads to undesirably low levels of environmental regulation in both countries.

The cooperative solution can be obtained by maximising the sum of the welfare functions of the two countries:[14]

$$w = g(-ae - (1-A)E)f(k^0 + I, e) - rI - b(ae - (1-A)E)$$
$$+ G(-AE - (1-a)e)F(K^0 - I, E) + rI - B(AE - (1-a)e) \qquad (25)$$

The optimal environmental policies are characterised by

$$gf_e = ab + ag'f + (1-a)B + (1-a)G'F \qquad (26)$$

$$GF_E = AB + AG'F + (1-A)b + (1-A)g'f \qquad (26')$$

The four effects on the right-hand sides of these equations are the damages due to the reduction in domestic consumption possibilities, to the reduction of domestic environmental quality, to the reduction of foreign consumption, and to the reduction of foreign environmental quality. All interest rate effects cancel out.

The welfare gains of cooperation are twofold. Firstly, there is a perfect internalisation of external effects including transboundary pollution. Secondly, environmental policy is not influenced by considerations concerning the remuneration of the mobile factor.

8 Barriers to capital mobility as an instrument of environmental policy

Up to now, the analysis has concentrated on the policy instrument of environmental regulation. An optimising government may find it useful to consider additional policy instruments. From an economic theory point of view, they can be justified on the basis of second-best considerations. Usually one policy instrument is required for each policy objective. In this model, the emission tax serves up to three purposes. It internalises the domestic social cost, it internalises a part of the transboundary externality and it improves the country's position in the world capital market. Such a policy is usually not first best. Thus, it may be better to use additional instruments such as capital market interventions. From a more policy-oriented point of view, capital market interventions can be useful to address the problem of carbon leakage. If high environmental standards induce capital movements to other countries with lower levels of environmental regulation, one may wish to restrict these capital movements in order to enhance the efficiency of unilateral environmental policies.

The optimal policy can be determined by differentiating the welfare function with respect to e and ϑ. Let us first consider the case where the other country has chosen the emission level as its policy instrument. The optimality conditions turn out to be

$$\vartheta^* = -GF_{KK}I \tag{27}$$

and

$$t^* = ab + ag'f - (1-a)G'F_K I \tag{28}$$

The condition for the optimal tax rate on repatriated profits is well known from the literature on capital taxation (see Sinn (1989, chapter 7).[15] The home country should impose a tax on repatriated profits. This drives capital to the foreign country, and due to the decreasing marginal productivity of capital the interest rate tends to be reduced. This is good for the capital-poor country. The foreign country is interested in a high remuneration of capital. This can be achieved by reducing its direct investment in the home economy. The appropriate strategy is a positive tax on repatriated profits. The optimal emission tax rate consists of three components. The first one is the marginal cost of loss of environmental quality as a consumption good. The second one is the marginal cost of loss of environmental quality as a factor of production. The third component is a rate-of-return effect which is caused by environmental disruption. The emissions spill over to the foreign country and cause a decline of capital productivity there. The international interest rate is reduced. If the country under consideration is capital poor, it benefits from this effect. Therefore, this component of the tax rate is negative in this case. In the capital-rich country, this effect has the opposite sign.

The more interesting case, particularly from the policy maker's point of view, is the scenario in which the other country's emission tax rate is given. Can carbon leakage be avoided by intervening into international capital movements? For the sake of simplicity, we will again assume that the externalities affecting production can be neglected. The optimal tax rates are

$$\vartheta^* = -\frac{G(F_{EE}F_{KK} - F_{KE}^2)I}{F_{EE}} + (1-A)b\frac{F_{KE}}{F_{EE}} \tag{29}$$

and

$$t^* = ab \tag{30}$$

The optimal emission tax simply internalises the domestic external effects. The tax on repatriated profits consists of two components. The first one is the interest-rate effect. A tax on foreign capital leads to a relocation of this factor of production. The capital stock employed in the foreign country is now larger. If there are decreasing returns to scale in the foreign industry (i.e., $F_{KK}F_{EE} - F_{KE}^2 > 0$), then the world interest rate is reduced and the home country is better off. In the case of constant returns to scale, the interest-rate effect is zero.[16] The second component of the tax on capital is a transfrontier pollution effect. It is negative; the domestic government subsidises foreign investors. This leads to an increased capital stock in the home country. The transfrontier pollution spillover is reduced and the government can subject the foreign capital employed in the home country to its environmental regulation. Similar considerations can be applied for the foreign country. As well as the home country, the foreign country is interested in keeping capital inside its own borders to avoid additional transfrontier pollution coming from the other country. The second component of the optimal capital tax is increasing in the parameter b, which measures environmental consciousness or assimilative capacities. The more severe the environmental problem, the more important this component of the tax. Thus, this may be interpreted as a 'green' capital market intervention.

Summarising the results yields:

Proposition 12: The optimal tax on repatriated profits is used to take account of changes in the world interest rate and of the effects of capital movements on transfrontier pollution. The optimal emission tax internalises merely the domestic social cost of environmental disruption.

Thus, intervening into international capital movements may be an optimal strategy to solve transfrontier pollution problems. Nevertheless, taxes and subsidies instruments are unlikely to be efficient. They are distortive and lead to suboptimal factor allocation. Usually, lump-sum transfers are better since they do not involve efficiency losses. The present model is no exception from the rule. This can be shown by the following graphical representation which is based on Rauscher (1997, chapter 3). Assume that the foreign technology exhibits constant returns to scale. This implies that, according to equation (29), the interest-rate effect of capital taxation vanishes and we can concentrate on transfrontier pollution. Figure 7.3 consists of two parts. The right-hand part of the diagram depicts the foreign country's factor-price frontier, which is fixed due to constant returns to

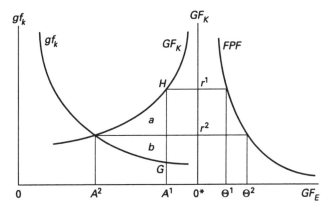

Figure 7.3 Factor market interventions versus side payments

scale. The foreign emission tax rate (equalling the marginal productivity of emissions, GF_E) determines the foreign country's marginal productivity of capital. This equals the world interest rate, r. The left-hand side of figure 7.3 depicts the marginal productivities of capital depending on the size of the capital stocks employed in the home and the foreign country. Assume that the foreign government has chosen the emission tax rate Θ^1. We start from a situation in which the domestic government uses a subsidy to attract foreign capital and to reduce transfrontier pollution. $0A^1$ and $0*A^1$ represent the capital stocks employed in the home and in the foreign country, respectively. The subsidy is GH. Now consider a situation in which the domestic government is able to persuade the foreign government to change its environmental policy such that the foreign emissions remain unchanged but the subsidy can be removed. If foreign emissions are unchanged, the GF_K curve in the left-hand part of the diagram remains unchanged as well. Thus the equilibrium has to be shifted along the GF_K curve until the point of intersection with the gf_k curve is reached. The allocation of the capital stock is now determined by A^2, where the foreign country has reduced its direct investment by A^1A^2. The interest rate is reduced from r^1 to r^2 and the foreign country's emission tax rate rises from Θ^1 to Θ^2. What are the impacts on income and the welfare effects? The home country gains since it does not subsidise any more. The foreign country, however, loses since its capital earns only the lower rate of interest, r^2.[17] The net income gain is $a+b$. Since the foreign country loses, it has no incentive to change its policy by itself. However, the domestic government can use a part of its income gains to 'bribe' the foreign policy makers. A transfer scheme which makes both countries better off is possible. This shows that intervening in international factor markets is only a second-best approach of dealing with transfrontier pollution problems. Cooperative solutions involving side payments yield the same level of environmental quality at a lower cost.

9 Political factors determining environmental policies in open economies

The results presented up to here are based on the premise that a benevolent government maximises social welfare. In reality, benevolent governments are a rare species. But even in situations where it is not the government but the people who decide (i.e., in a direct democracy), it is not guaranteed that the policy outcome is optimal.

A direct democracy model of an open economy has been presented by Mayer (1984). His considerations can be applied to the model that has been investigated here as well. In a direct democracy, the median voter decides on the policy to be made. The median voter, however, is not always the representative individual. Consider for instance a situation in which capital is unevenly distributed amongst individuals. Given the normal skewness properties of income and wealth distributions, the median capital endowment is smaller than the average endowment. Thus, the median voter owns less than the economy's per-capita capital stock and her concern about capital income will be correspondingly low. On the other hand, the welfare effects of a clean environment tend to be more equally distributed, in particular if the effect of pollution on capital income is small. Thus, the median voter tends to be biased towards environmentalism and there will be a tendency to overinternalise the social cost of environmental disruption. In an international context, this may help to internalise transfrontier pollution externalities.

Not only environmentalists argue that environmental concerns tend to be under- instead of overrepresented in the political decision-making process. This observation is compatible with the median-voter model only if some *ad-hoc* assumptions, e.g., concerning participation in elections, are introduced. The more appropriate approach is the representative democracy model. In a representative democracy, the policy maker is not so controlled by the electorate. This gives him some discretion and allows him to follow his own selfish objectives, which now are not necessarily compatible with those of the voters. Knowing that, groups of agents with idiosyncratic interests will try to affect the policy-making process. This can be achieved by bribery, campaign contributions to political parties and by influencing the public opinion via the media. If these lobbies are successful, the policy decisions will be biased and will represent neither the will of the community as a whole nor that of the median voter.

In situations of mass unemployment and declining profits, industries are viewed to be particularly vulnerable to foreign competition. If there is a concern that keystone industries will be moved to other countries, there tend to be strong pressures towards subsidisation. However, the donation of open subsidies is in many cases not in agreement with international treaties and laws. Thus the policy maker may be asked to give indirect subsidies that are less observable, e.g., by means of lax environmental regulation. This is then sometimes advertised as a measure to increase the competitiveness of the economy as a whole. A formalised model of the influence of 'pro-competitive' lobbies on environmental policy has been presented by Rauscher (1994, 1997). Usually, the extension of the model in this respect yields less restrictive levels of environmental regulation. In the international policy game, the welfare effect of lobbying is ambiguous. On the one hand, it tends to aggravate the transfrontier pollution problems; on the other hand, lobbies may unintentionally internalise negative interest-rate effects and may therefore improve social welfare.

These models are very simple and partially based on *ad-hoc* arguments, but a coherent theory of environmental lobbying in open economies is still lacking.[19]

10 Non-competitive market structures and environmental regulation

Besides the inadequacy of the benevolent government model for positive economic analyses, there is a second shortcoming which limits its applicability to real-world situations. Up to now, we have assumed perfectly competitive factor markets. Notwithstanding that this is seldom a correct description of reality, it is in many cases not even a useful approximation. Many investment decisions that have major environmental implications are made by large multinational enterprises with substantial market power. If the agents on the other side of the market are small, e.g., small developing countries, regions or local communities, there may be increased pressure on environmental standards and governments may be played off against each other by the investor. Models considering this situation have been developed by Markusen, Morey and Olewiler (1993, 1994), Motta and Thisse (1993) and Ulph (1993). Nonetheless, a different approach will be chosen here and monopoly power will be introduced into the capital mobility model that has been discussed in the preceding sections. Afterwards, the results of the other models will be presented and discussed.

The model is changed by introducing a monopolist on the supply side of the capital market. The monopolist intends to undertake an investment in a country which offers a high return on capital. On the demand side, there is a large number of capital-poor countries that compete for investments. These may be thought of as developing countries but also as small entities inside a country like counties or communities. Let us assume that the small countries have only limited access to the international capital market and therefore rely on the capital supplied by the monopolist. The interest rate is r. This is the opportunity cost of investment to the monopolist. Due to her market position, she can use a mark-up m and charge a higher rate of interest.

Let the demand side be represented by a country of the type assumed in the previous sections of the chapter. Its optimal environmental policy is determined by equation (11) and its demand for capital is given by

$$gf_k=r+m \tag{31}$$

Totally differentiating equations (11) and (31) yields

$$\begin{pmatrix} gf_{ee}-2ag'f_e+a^2g''f & gf_{ke}-ag'f_k \\ gf_{ke}-ag'f_k & gf_{kk} \end{pmatrix}\begin{pmatrix} de \\ dI \end{pmatrix}=\begin{pmatrix} 0 \\ dm \end{pmatrix}$$

The matrix on the left-hand side is a Hessian with negative diagonal elements and a positive determinant, Δ. It follows that

$$\frac{dI}{dm}=\frac{1}{\Delta}(gf_{ee}-2ag'f_e+a^2g''f)<0 \tag{32}$$

$$\frac{de}{dm}=-\frac{1}{\Delta}(gf_{ke}-ag'f_k) \tag{33}$$

The demand for foreign capital is a declining function of its remuneration. The impact of the mark-up on emissions is ambiguous. If the external effect of environmental quality on production is small, then the impact is negative. If the mark-up is large, the demand for capital is small, and the smaller capital stock results in a smaller productivity of emissions. Since the marginal costs of emissions are constant, it is optimal to reduce emissions. The opposite result is obtained if the external effect on production is large.

The quantity of emissions should not be mistaken for an index of the level of environmental regulation. Even if emissions are a declining function of the interest rate, this is not necessarily the result of strict environmental policies; it may also be caused by the limited availability of capital and the smaller output. The appropriate measure of the strictness of the environmental regulation is the emission tax rate. In a competitive economy, this tax rate equals the marginal productivity of emissions, gf_e. Differentiating this with respect to m and taking account of equations (32) and (33) yields

$$\frac{d(gf_e)}{dm}=\frac{1}{\Delta}[a^2gf_{ke}g''f+ag'f_k(gf_{ee}-ag'f_e)]<0 \tag{34}$$

Proposition 13: Monopolistic supply of foreign capital leads to lower emission taxes.

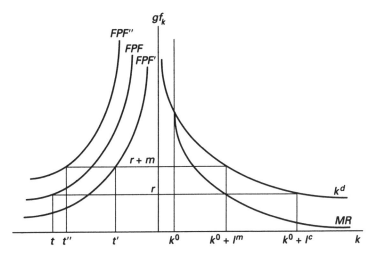

Figure 7.4 Monopoly on the capital market and environmental regulation

Figure 7.4 provides a graphical interpretation of this result. The right-hand part of this figure shows the demand for capital, k^d, which is a declining function of the remuneration of capital, $r+m$. It should be noted that this is not the usual marginal-productivity curve, derived for fixed inputs of the other factors. Instead, environmental concerns are taken into account and emissions vary along this curve. Nonetheless, this is a normal demand curve. Therefore, the usual textbook analysis of monopolistic behaviour is applied and the monopolist's mark-up over the interest rate is determined by equalising the marginal revenue, MR, and the marginal opportunity cost, i.e., the competitive interest rate. Of course, the mark-up is positive and the foreign direct investment I^m is smaller than the one which would have occurred under perfect competition, I^c. The left-hand side depicts the factor-price frontier (FPF). For the sake of a simpler graphical representation assume that the production function exhibits constant returns to scale. Then, the location of the factor-price frontier is fixed for any constant level of environmental quality. If environmental quality is improved (deteriorated), the curve is shifted upwards (downwards). This is denoted by primes (double primes). The emission tax rate, t, can now be derived from the factor-price frontier. Two scenarios may be considered since the factor price frontier is shifted by changes in emissions (see equation (33)). Both scenarios are shown in the diagram. According to the algebraic result, equation (34), the resulting emission tax rate in the monopoly case will always be below that of the competitive scenario.

Models of imperfect competition that are more complex have been discussed by Markusen, Morey and Olewiler (1992,1993), Ulph (1993) and Motta and Thisse (1993). In all these models, the impact of environmental policies on firm location is modelled by multistage games. In the first stage, the government chooses its environmental policy. In the second stage, the firms choose their locations. In the third stage, finally, the firms determine their optimal outputs. Due to the fact that only two countries and a small number of firms are involved in the game, the models produce discontinuities in the solutions and are, therefore, illustrated by numerical examples by their authors.

Markusen, Morey and Olewiler (1993) look at a model with two countries and two firms. The major ingredients of the model are plant-specific fixed costs (that limit the number of plants), trade costs (that limit the ability of a firm to open a foreign branch and re-import final goods to its home country) and variable costs that are affected by environmental regulation (limiting the profitability of investing in a country with 'green' environmental laws). The authors show that depending on the cost parameters different market structures are possible. Higher emission taxes tend to expel the firms out of the country. Due to discrete changes in market structure, smooth changes in environmental policy may produce discontinuous welfare changes.

A similar model has been used by Ulph (1993) to analyse carbon-leakage effects. Ulph generalises the model by allowing for additional countries and firms. He shows that the effects of environmental policies on locational choices may be rather strong such that the carbon-leakage effects are much more significant than those that have been computed in perfect-competition models.

Motta and Thisse (1993) modify the original model by introducing sunk costs. This implies that the incentives for an incumbent firm to relocate are much smaller than in the other models. An additional result that they are able to establish is that barriers to trade are not always good instruments to accompany strict environmental policies. Strict environmental policies may drive a firm out of the country. In the case of low tariffs, the firm will open a subsidiary plant abroad and re-import final goods. If, however, barriers to trade are introduced that raise trade costs, the foreign plant may turn out to be not profitable and the domestic firm chooses to leave the market totally. Only the foreign firm remains in the market and the home country will experience welfare losses in terms of consumer surplus and profits.

Markusen, Morey and Olewiler (1992) look at a model with only one firm but analyse the strategic interaction of governments that use their environmental policies to play a non-cooperative game against each other. The reference scenario is a situation in which the countries cooperate and the investor builds a plant in only one location. Side payments stabilise the agreement. Then a non-cooperative situation is considered. It is shown that two scenarios are possible. Depending on the parameters of the model, it may happen that the firm invests in both countries or in neither of them. In the first case, there is too much pollution and it corresponds to the situation depicted in figure 7.4. The second scenario is the case of 'not in my backyard' in which neither of the countries wishes to bear the cost of the investment in terms of environmental disruption while sharing the fruit, i.e., the availability of consumption goods, with the other country. This model has the advantage that it provides a large variety of results, albeit at the cost that it can be solved only for numerical examples.

11 Foreign trade, environmental regulation and the allocation of capital

International capital movements are not the only way in which producers react to changes in environmental legislation. Environmental regulation may (and does) also induce structural change inside an economy. Industries that are particularly affected by environmental regulation face rising costs and can, therefore, lose their competitiveness if other countries implement laxer policies. Factors will move from these industries to the sectors that have comparative advantages. Environmental legislation thus affects a country's patterns of specialisation, the allocation of its factors of production and, if it is large, also its terms of trade. Emission taxes and standards can, therefore, be used to achieve trade-related policy goals. Moreover, the trade regime has an impact on environmental quality and pollution. Thus, trade restrictions may under certain circumstances be used for environmental purposes. The literature on trade and the environment has its origin in the economy and ecology debate of the early seventies. Major contributions are Baumol (1971), Markusen (1975), Pethig (1976), Siebert (1977,1979), Asako (1979), Siebert, Eichberger, Gronych and Pethig (1980), Krutilla (1991), Rauscher (1991a) and Snape (1992). This section will survey this literature and show the link with the capital mobility model discussed in the previous sections. It will be seen that the results are very similar and in some cases even the same. However, the underlying mechanics that produce the results are rather different.

The literature on international trade and the environment has not considered external effects on production, i.e., the fact that factor productivities and, therefore, comparative advantages may be affected by the state of the environment.[19] For this reason, this issue will be neglected here.

According to the standard theorems of international trade, a country will specialise in the production of the commodities that are relatively intensive in the use of the abundant factor of production. Thus, countries that are well endowed with environmental resources tend to export resource-intensive goods. The endowment of a country with environmental resources is determined by the strictness of environmental policy, which may be measured by the level of (explicit or implicit) emission taxes. In the case of benevolent governments, the environmental policy reflects the assimilative capacity of the country and the preferences of the people. Differences in environmental regulation across countries can, therefore, be justified on grounds of different natural conditions and different attitudes. There is no need to harmonise environmental regulations. On the contrary, harmonisation would artificially eliminate the comparative advantages that are the basis of mutually advantageous exchange of commodities and of the gains from trade.

What are the effects of foreign trade? A country that starts to trade experiences a change in relative prices and the Stolper–Samuelson theorem can be applied. Additional effects can be observed if the country uses a kind of environmental regulation that allows for variable emissions. The country well-endowed with environmental resources is subject to an increase in the price of environmentally intensive goods. Thus the marginal-value product of emissions will be increased in this sector. At given emission tax rates, there is an incentive to increase the emissions. One can show that this increase in emissions exceeds the emission reduction due to the decline in the other industries. The net effect is an increase in emissions. The other country experiences the opposite pattern of specialisation and will reduce its emissions. Thus, emissions 'move' from the capital-rich country to the country which is better endowed with environmental resources. Siebert (1992, p. 168) has coined the term 'pollute thy neighbour via trade' for this phenomenon. Although international trade is a device for shifting pollution from one country to the other, this is not a problem that demands a solution in the shape of state intervention. It is just a reflex of changes in patterns of specialisation.

The welfare effects of economic integration are positive if the country under consideration employs an environmental policy that keeps emissions fixed, e.g., a tradable-permits scheme. In the case of variable emissions, there may be additional welfare gains or welfare losses. Consider a situation in which the environmental policy is not strict enough, i.e., emissions are higher than socially desirable. The resource-rich country tends to increase its emissions, that have already been too high. This produces welfare losses. The underlying cause of these welfare losses, however, is not foreign trade but the insufficiency of environmental policy. The correct solution to the problem would, therefore, be to adjust environmental legislation rather than to restrict international trade. The opposite conclusions can be drawn for the capital-rich economy. It moves to a position closer to the social optimum by reducing its emissions. For this country, trade is, so to speak, a substitute for a good environmental policy. Additional welfare effects have to be considered if there is transboundary pollution. If the capital-rich country is the downstream country, it may suffer from increased pollution since the other country increases its emissions. If this has negative welfare effects, the country may be tempted to intervene in foreign trade in order to achieve environmental objectives.[20]

As in the case of international factor mobility, environmental regulation should be adjusted in response to increased openness. The resource-rich countries should use stricter standards whereas the capital-rich country should relax its standards. As in the capital mobility model, there tends to be a convergence of environmental policies.

What is the impact of changes in environmental regulation on the economy? If the country under consideration is small, the Rybczinsky theorem can be applied. By increasing the strictness of environmental regulation, the output of the commodity which uses environmental resources intensively is diminished, the output of less pollution-intensive goods is raised. Matters are more complicated if the country under consideration is large. The change in the supply of the final goods results in a change in world market prices. In general, this terms-of-trade effect is ambiguous. Under normal parameter conditions, however, it has the expected sign.[21] Thus, the price of environmentally intensive goods will be increased as a consequence of stricter environmental standards. This is good for the country which is well endowed with environmental resources and bad for the capital-rich country. This terms-of-trade effect corresponds to the interest-rate effect discussed earlier in the chapter.

Moreover, the change in the terms of trade produces a feedback effect on factor allocation and on pollution. If the prices of environmentally intensive goods rise, then this is an incentive for producers to raise the output of these goods. If the environmental-policy regime is one with emission taxes, this will lead to an increase in emissions. Thus, by making its environmental standards stricter, a country induces additional emissions in the rest of the world. If there is transfrontier pollution, this negatively affects the country that has changed its environmental policy. This is again the carbon-leakage effect that has already been discussed in the capital mobility model.

Given the direction of the terms-of-trade effects, the capital-rich country should not completely internalise the domestic environmental externalities in order to avoid the decline in its terms of trade. The other country benefits from overinternalising pollution externalities. The Nash equilibrium in which each country chooses its environmental policy for given policies in the other country is not Pareto optimal. Welfare improvements can be achieved if the capital-rich country increases its emissions and the capital-poor country reduces its emissions. Additionally, one may wish to consider transfrontier pollution spillovers. If transboundary pollution is substantial, there tends to be incomplete internalisation. This compensates for the over-internalisation strategy chosen on the basis of terms-of-trade considerations by the capital-poor country, but it aggravates the problem of underinternalisation by the capital-rich country.

Transfrontier pollution problems and particularly the carbon-leakage effect may induce policy makers to take trade interventions into consideration as instruments of environmental policy. As in the case of international capital movements the objective is to reduce emissions abroad and attract pollution-intensive industries to have them under the control of domestic environmental regulation. If the country is an importer of pollution-intensive goods, this can be achieved by a tariff. The tariff reduces world market demand and, therefore, the world market price of this good. With a lower world market price, foreign production will be shifted to the 'clean' sectors of the economy and transboundary pollution is reduced. If the country exports the pollution-intensive goods, it should subsidise its exports. This raises world market supply and reduces the world market price. As in the case of interventions into capital markets, this approach is rarely efficient. An instrument which affects only a part of the foreign production (namely the exports) directly is used to solve a problem which is caused by foreign production as a whole. In general, this causes inefficiencies in the allocation of factors of production that can be avoided by cooperative behaviour involving side payments.[22]

The impact of non-competitive market structures on environmental policies in open economies has been analysed in a strategic trade policy framework by Barrett (1992a, b) and Conrad (1993a, b). The strategic trade policy model is due to Brander and Spencer (1985). They look at an international duopoly: two firms located in two different countries play Nash–Cournot on a third country's market. By providing export subsidies, the domestic government can encourage its firm to increase its production at the expense of foreign output and sales. If the rate of subsidisation is chosen correctly, the increase in profit exceeds the cost of subsidisation and the net welfare effect is positive. The new position of the firm is that of a Stackelberg leader. Since in a simultaneous one-shot game the firm cannot credibly commit itself to produce more than the Nash equilibrium output, it needs the support of its government. It has been argued that direct subsidisation can be detected by foreign competitors rather easily and that, therefore, more subtle types of subsidisation are desirable. One of the candidates is environmental legislation. By using industry-specific regulations that do not fully internalise external effects, the government gives hidden subsidies to domestic producers. It is shown by Barrett (1992a) and Conrad (1993a, b) that there are indeed incentives for underregulation. The disadvantage compared to direct subsidies is that now one instrument is used to address two policy objectives, i.e., to deal with environmental problems and to increase the market power of domestic firms. If the other country retaliates, then the levels of environmental regulation in both countries tend to be too low. The problem is aggravated by transfrontier pollution. If the foreign firm does not only steal the domestic firm's market share but also pollutes the domestic environment, this provides additional reasons to help the domestic firm by relaxing environmental standards.

In what respect does the model of international trade differ from the model of international capital mobility? The channels through which changes in environmental regulation affect capital allocation and other economic variables are rather different. In trade models, capital moves from one industry to the other and these movements are induced by changes in world market prices that cause temporary differentials in sector-specific factor prices. In the capital-movement model, capital reacts more directly to interest-rate differentials and moves across national borders. Nevertheless, the results derived from the two models are basically the same. One model can be translated into the other by substituting terms-of-trade effects for interest-rate effects or vice versa. Thus, the simple capital mobility model provides a good intuition of what may happen in more complex models that deal with other aspects of the interaction of environmental policy and international markets.

12 The empirical evidence

The considerations of the preceding sections have shown that there is a strong link between environmental regulation and the international allocation of capital – at least in theory. But how relevant is this in practice? Is there considerable evidence that environmental regulation indeed has an impact on capital movements and foreign trade? And is environmental quality significantly affected by factor relocation? The empirical literature has been surveyed by Ugelow (1982) and Dean (1992). These surveys will be updated and special emphasis will be placed on the issue of international capital movements.

The largest problem of any empirical assessment of the relationship between international factor allocation and the environment is the measurement of the environmental variables. Basically, two variables are of major interest. Since one of the hypotheses is that environmental regulation affects the allocation of capital, we need to quantify environmental regulation. The other hypothesis is that international factor mobility and international trade affect environmental quality. But how can environmental quality be measured? These measurement problems are the more difficult, the more aggregated the model is. And the models discussed here are highly aggregated. Two ways out of this dilemma are possible. On the one hand, people have indeed tried to construct measures of the strictness of environmental regulation or a pollution index for an economy as a whole. All these measures can only be proxies and it is to be hoped that they are unbiased. The other possibility is to look at case studies that involve particular sectors, regions and/or pollutants. The results are, however, often not generalisable. These conceptual shortcomings should be kept in mind during the review of the empirical results.

A major part of the empirical studies deals with the impact of environmental regulation on the allocation of factors of production and on the patterns of trade and foreign direct investment. The first of the studies have been devoted to testing trade models. Only more recently have international capital movements been the subject of empirical analyses.

Walter (1973) was one of the first to look at the impact of environmental regulation on international trade. Basically his approach is the one first employed by Leontief (1954) in his famous study. Walter uses proxies for the costs of pollution abatement for all sectors of the US economy. He then employs input–output techniques to determine so-called 'overall environmental-control loadings', i.e., the ratio of environmental-control costs, including those of the intermediate inputs, to the final price of the output. This is then multiplied by the value of US exports and imports to obtain the environmental-cost component of US trade. The result is that the abatement-cost content of US exports is slightly higher than that of US imports. If the Heckscher–Ohlin theory of international trade is correct, this implies that the USA is relatively well endowed with environmental resources compared to the rest of the world. Although Walter's study provides some insight into the relationship between environmental regulation and international trade, it is by no means a test of the Heckscher–Ohlin model. The Heckscher–Ohlin theorem is a proposition which derives the pattern of trade from observations of the factor intensities of production and of the endowment of a country with factors. Like Leontief (1954), Walter (1973) and other authors in the seventies (see Ugelow (1982) for a survey) did not incorporate endowment data in their studies.

Robison (1988) uses a similar model. Changes in environmental regulation – and, therefore, in the endowment of the USA with environmental resources – are taken into account by looking at different years for the period 1973–1982. During these years, US environmental regulation has become increasingly restrictive. It is shown that the abatement-cost contents of output, exports and imports have risen over this period. The strongest increase is observed for imports. This indicates a shift in US imports from goods with low abatement requirements towards goods subject to stricter regulation. At a first glance, this result seems to be in accordance with the Heckscher–Ohlin model. Nonetheless, it is not a test of this model since the environmental regulation of the USA's trading partners is not taken into account. Endowment differences between countries matter; absolute endowment measures are irrelevant for international trade theory.

More recent studies have used international data sets on environmental regulation. Tobey (1989, 1990), for instance, uses a set of factor endowment variables that includes an index measuring the stringency of pollution control policies in an UNCTAD survey that involves a large group of countries. The dependent variable is the net exports of pollution-intensive commodities per country. In all of the five industries under consideration, the environmental-policy variable turns out to be significant. An omitted-variables test (the omitted variable being environmental regulation) reveals the same result. This lack of empirical evidence, however, does not necessarily mean that there is no impact of environmental regulation on international trade. Murrell and Ryterman (1991) also use an omitted-variables test in a similar model framework. Using 1975 data, they find no evidence of an influence of environmental policies on international trade. These studies, therefore, cast some doubt on the empirical relevance of the Heckscher–Ohlin theory of environmental regulation and international trade. The theory may be saved by the argument that the Heckscher–Ohlin model represents a long-run view of international trade. Factor relocation across sectors takes time, sometimes decades. Thus, one may be led to argue that the changes in environmental regulation that took place in the mid seventies have their repercussions in the patterns of trade only with a lag of several years.[23]

The other way in which trade influences the international allocation of capital is through foreign direct investment. If the theory is correct, pollution-intensive production processes should move to countries with lax environmental standards, where abatement costs are relatively low. Several studies have tested this hypothesis. Walter (1982) Leonard (1988) and Bartik (1988) test the hypothesis itself and do not find substantial support for it in the data. Other studies that use indirect methods to identify the impact of environmental regulation on international capital movements come to different conclusions. Hettige, Lucas and Wheeler (1992) and Lucas, Hettige and Wheeler (1992), for instance, find that low-income countries have experienced higher growth rates of pollution intensity per unit of output than high-income countries. This can be interpreted as a result of the relocation of pollution-intensive industries to less-regulated developing countries. Moreover, they observe cross-country differences in the development of pollution intensities over time. In the seventies and eighties, i.e., during the period in which industrialised countries tightened their environmental standards, pollution intensities grew more rapidly in low-income countries than in high-income countries. This evidence is supported by results obtained by Low and Yeats (1992), who show that during the period 1965–1988 the share of 'dirty' industries in exports has increased for some developing countries whereas it has declined for the industrial countries.

Besides the impact of environmental regulation on factor allocation and trade, the other great issue is the impact of free trade and international factor movements on environmental quality. Environmentalists fear that there is a negative relationship and economic theory says that it depends on the parameters. Two approaches have been chosen in the literature to address this question. One is to test the impact of the trade regime on environmental quality directly. The other method is to do policy simulations with a computable general equilibrium model whose parameters have been empirically determined.

Hettige, Lucas and Wheeler (1992) and Lucas, Hettige and Wheeler (1992) use the first approach. They find that the pollution intensity of production has increased much more for high-growth inward-oriented economies than for high-growth outward-oriented developing countries. They explain this by differences in the investment behaviour between industrialising countries. The open economies react to world market prices and tend to expand labour-intensive production. Closed economies, in contrast, expand their capital-intensive industries, that are more pollution intensive. This supports the hypothesis that free trade is good for the environment – at least in the industrialising countries. In the rest of the world, one should observe the opposite pattern of specialisation and, therefore, the opposite effect on the environment. Unfortunately this question has not been addressed in this study.

Van Bergeijk (1991) uses a data set of OECD countries. The emissions of three air pollutants are regressed on a set of explanatory variables that include a variable measuring trade distortions. For two of the pollutants, van Bergeijk finds a significant negative impact (albeit only at the 90 per cent confidence level). The third parameter has the same sign but is insignificant. Openness tends to be good for the environment. One may explain this result by specialisation effects. Alternatively one may argue that gains from trade raises the income and, if environmental quality is a superior good, this leads to a tougher environmental policy.[24]

Another study is that by Birdsall and Wheeler (1992) who examine Latin American countries to find out whether increased openness has led to increased environmental damages. They find a negative impact of openness on the toxicity of production. This is supported by results of a case study for the Chilean economy. The authors explain this observation by the fact that open economies have better access to new technologies which are generally less pollution-intensive. This hypothesis is supported by Wheeler and Martin (1992) who look at the international diffusion of clean technologies in the pulp industry. Their result is that adaptation lags for the introduction of new, clean technologies are significantly higher in inward-oriented than in open economies.

Burniaux, Martin and Oliveira-Martins (1992) use an indirect approach to address the impact of trade on the environment. They carry out policy simulations with the OECD general equilibrium model. According to their study, the removal of existing distortions in energy markets, whose purpose is predominantly protectionist, would result in a drastic reduction of CO_2 emissions on a global scale. Thus free trade in energy resources tends to mitigate the greenhouse effect.

Another indirect test of the relationship of free trade on the environment is performed by Anderson (1992a,b). He takes the world market for agricultural products as the subject of the investigation. This market is highly distorted by subsidies and trade barriers. Anderson shows that there is a high correlation between domestic prices of agricultural products and the utilisation of fertiliser and pesticides. Potential importers of agricultural products use more fertiliser and pesticides than potential exporters. If barriers to trade are removed, agricultural production will shift from highly protected industrialised countries with intensive use of chemicals to less-developed countries that produce with a lower input of chemicals. The expected net effect of trade liberalisation would be a reduction in the use of pesticides and fertiliser.

It may be true that the global effect of trade liberalisation on environmental quality is positive for some markets like energy resources and agricultural products. There are, however, also counter examples. Consider for instance tropical deforestation and the trade in endangered species. In both cases, trade contributes to the problem. Nonetheless, empirical studies confirm the theoretical result that trade restrictions are rarely the first-best instruments to deal with the problem. See Amelung and Diehl (1992) for the case of tropical deforestation and Barbier (1991) for a case study dealing with the ebony trade.

The final set of empirical studies is devoted to the carbon-leakage effect. Will unilateral greenhouse policies by one country or a group of countries cause substantial increases in emissions in the rest of the world? This question has been addressed by doing policy simulations with calibrated models. Burniaux and Oliveira-Martins (1992) use the OECD computable general-equilibrium model and find carbon-leakage effects of up to 16 per cent.[25] Their model is based on the assumption of perfect competition and international factor immobility. Ulph (1993) relaxes both these assumptions and, depending on the parameter constellations, he finds carbon-leakage effects of much larger magnitude, in some cases even more than 100 per cent.

Summarising the results of the empirical studies, one may conclude that the evidence concerning the relationship between trade and international capital movements on the one hand and environmental regulation and environmental quality on the other is rather mixed. Direct methods of testing the hypothesis that environmental regulation affects trade and international capital movements tend to reject such a relationship. Indirect methods produce some evidence in favour of the hypothesis. These should, however, be interpreted with care since they are often based on exploratory data analysis rather than on consistent economic models. The tests of the reverse relationship, that of trade on the environment, receive more support. However, some of the studies are based on policy simulations with calibrated models. Since the models have been constructed by using elements of economic theories, it is not amazing that the results confirm these theories. Similar arguments can be applied to the carbon-leakage models. The general conclusion, therefore, seems to be that we still lack a true proof of the theoretical models that have been discussed in the preceding sections. Further research is necessary to fill this gap.

13 Summary and conclusions

This chapter has looked at various variants of a two-country model of international factor movements in a world in which environmental pollution matters. An obvious limitation of this model is its restriction to the two-country case. The world consists of more than two countries and it would be worthwhile to extend the model in this respect. As far as allocational issues are concerned, however, no pathbreaking results should be expected. The literature on higher-dimensional models of foreign trade has shown that the results derived from the standard two-country model also hold for more complicated models, at least 'on average', see Ethier (1984) for a survey. Nonetheless, there are other issues where a generalised model could provide insights that are really new. Recently, models have been developed that look at cooperative solutions to international environmental problems, see Barrett (1992b) and Black, Levi and de Meza (1993). One of the central issues in this literature is to analyse the incentives to join coalitions that cooperate in their environmental policies versus the incentives to stay in the non-cooperative fringe. A related model has been developed by Kowalczyk and Sjöström (1993) for the analysis of international trade agreements. It would be interesting to combine these approaches. The close interdependencies of trade and environmental policies may have an important impact on the processes of bargaining and coalition building. Since coalitions can sensibly be discussed only in models with more than two countries, an extension of the model in this respect is desirable and should be on the agenda for future research.

One of the central results of the chapter (and of the literature on environmental regulation in open economies in general) is a normative one and it concerns the shape of the best of all worlds. If a welfare economist were allowed to design a regime of environmental and trade regulations, she would opt for free trade in commodities and factors plus a system of emission standards and taxes that internalise the full social cost of environmental disruption including transfrontier externalities. However, the world is far from perfect and it may be naive take such a scenario as a serious policy recommendation. Nevertheless, it is important to keep it in mind as a point of reference.

The picture of the real world is less rosy. It is characterised by insufficient environmental policies and lacking in international policy coordination. This has consequences for economic welfare and a number of implications for economic policy. Firstly, the gains from trade and free factor mobility are not necessarily positive. If the environmental regulation is not sufficiently tough, a country that attracts foreign capital may experience welfare losses since the effects of environmental disruption may offset the positive income effects. Secondly, on the international scale, there is the carbon-leakage effect. By using stricter environmental standards, a government drives capital out of the country. The domestic emissions reduction is accompanied by an increase in foreign emissions. If the capital moves to a pollution haven, the net effect may actually be an increase in emissions and, thus, the unilateral policy addressing the international environmental problem may even be counterproductive. One of the solutions to the problem is to combine the environmental policy measure with intervention into capital markets that stops the outflow of capital. Thirdly, the investigation of Nash equilibria has shown that the lack of international policy coordination may lead to suboptimal environmental policies. Even without transfrontier pollution, is it possible that welfare-maximising governments choose too lax environmental standards. The probability of too lax environmental standards is increased by the impact of lobbying activities and non-competitive market structures.

Many of the undesirable results are caused by the utilisation of environmental policies for non-environmental objectives, such as influencing the rate of remuneration of mobile capital and the terms of trade or satisfying the needs of trade lobbies. The main policy conclusion, therefore, is that the objectives of environmental policies should be restricted to the internalisation of external effects. However, in an increasingly integrated world where trade policy measures are often not available this claim may remain unheeded.

As far as the empirical evidence is concerned, it is at best mixed. Many studies did not find any significant links between environmental regulation and factor movements or international trade. Cropper and Oates (1992), in their survey of environmental economics, argue that for this reason environmental economists need not care too much about international competitiveness. This view may be mistaken, however. On the one hand, there have been enormous measurement problems and the variables chosen as proxies for the tightness of environmental regulation may not have been good enough. On the other hand, environmental regulation indeed had only a minor impact on production costs in the past, possibly with the exception of a couple of particular industries. Therefore, it has rarely been among the major criteria on which investors have based their locational decisions. This may, however, change in the future. If environmental problems like ozone depletion, climatic change, and general air and water pollution continue to become increasingly pressing and if, moreover, existing regulatory deficits are eliminated, the internalised environmental costs of production will be considerably higher in the future than they are today. This will have consequences for international capital movements and foreign trade that are relevant not only for the inhabitants of ivory towers but also for the 'real' people.

Notes

The Author gratefully acknowledges the financial support of Fondezione ENI E. Mattei. The paper has benefitted from helpful comments and suggestions by Carlo Carraro, Sebastian Killinger and Angelica Tudini. The usual disclaimer applies.

1 Morris's (1991) article in *The Ecologist* entitled 'Free Trade: the Great Distroyer' is a good example. Other references include Cobb/Daly (1989), Ekins (1989), Shrybman (1991, 1991/2) and Arden-Clarke (1992), for instance.
2 They are discussed comprehensively in Rauscher (1997).
3 For a survey including this and other approaches, see Ruffin (1984).
4 The implicit assumption is that factor mobility is a substitute for international trade in final commodities. This may not always be the case as has been shown by Markusen (1983) and Wong (1986).
5 Modelling emissions as an input into the production process rather than a joint output is a quite common approach in the literature. See McGuire (1982), Rauscher (1991a,b,1992, 1994). Rauscher (1997, chapter 2) shows that the two approaches are equivalent and can be translated into each other.
6 Equality holds if and only if $f(...)$ exhibits constant returns.
7 See for instance Burmeister and Dobell (1970, p. 11).
8 If the tax on capital income turns out to be negative, i.e., if a subsidy is given,

the tax revenue necessary to finance the subsidisation is assumed to be generated by lump-sum taxes.

9 Siebert (1992, p. 168) has coined the term of 'polluting thy neighbour via trade' in the context of an international trade model.

10 For a more detailed analysis of the effects of economic integration see Rauscher (1991b, 1992).

11 The first-order condition is sufficient for an optimum if the welfare functions are strictly concave in emissions. This is, however, hard to prove here. The objective function contains terms which are derivatives of a function, i.e., the marginal productivities of capital. Thus second derivatives of the production function occur in the first-order condition and the second-order condition contains third derivatives. Thus, instead of proving strict concavity, we will simply assume that the second-order condition is satisfied.

12 In the case of perfect competition, the tax rate equals the marginal productivity of emissions.

13 A similar result has been established by Wildasin (1988) in a model in which the mobile factor of production is taxed.

14 Usually a cooperative solution involves side payments. The introduction of side payments is not necessary here since welfare is expressed in terms of the output. The marginal utility of consumption is 1 in both countries and no improvements can be achieved by means of side payments.

15 Note that the restriction does not have to take the shape of a tax. A quantitative restriction can also be used. Equation (27) then represents the tax equivalent of the barrier to factor movements.

16 Since constant returns to scale imply a fixed factor-price frontier, the remuneration of capital is determined by the foreign emission tax rate via a technological relationship and cannot be influenced by domestic policies.

17 The magnitudes of these effects depends on the initial capital endowments of the two economies, that are not depicted in this figure.

18 A model which deals with the opposite kind of question, namely the impact of green interests on trade policy, has been developed by Hillman and Ursprung (1992, 1993). Additional considerations have been made by Hoekman and Leidy (1992).

19 These external effects are contained in the model analysed by Herberg, Kemp and Tawada (1982).

20 These trade interventions are the more effective the larger the share of foreign production which is exported to the home country.

21 The normality condition is a 'manna' condition. If manna falls from heaven, one may expect that its price will decline unless manna is a Giffen good. In the case of an integrated world economy, however, this is not always true. The manna condition specifies the range of parameter values for which the intuition is correct even in the case of an international-trade general equilibrium.

22 There is one exception from this rule. If the home country imports the whole foreign output, then a tariff has the properties of a production tax and, therefore, is an efficient means to address transfrontier pollution problems;

234   **Michael Rauscher**

see Snape (1992). However, this scenario is probably of mere academic interest.

23 This possibity is considered by Tobey (1989, 1990), who also regresses changes in net exports on the stringency of environmental policy. Nonetheless, this method does not provide evidence in favour of the hypothesis either.

24 This argument is used as well by Grossman and Krueger (1991) in their attempt to assess the environmental effects of the North-American Free Trade Associaton. They find a strong negative correlation of pollution and income in medium-income industrialising countries. From this they conclude that Mexico is likely to employ a stricter environmental regulation as a consequence of the gains from trade liberalisation. Similar results are reported by Holtz-Eakin and Selden (1992), who show that the CO_2 intensity of production declines in growing economies.

25 Higher carbon-leakage rates are possible only for unrealistic parameter values.

References

Amelung, T. and M. Diehl (1992), *Deforestation of Tropical Rain Forests: Economic Causes and Impact on Development*, Tübingen: Mohr.
Anderson, K. (1992a), 'Effects on the Environment and Welfare of Liberalizing World Trade: The Cases of Coal and Food', in K. Anderson and R. Blackhurst, *The Greening of World Trade Issues*, New York: Harvester Wheatsheaf, pp. 145–72.
(1992b), 'Agricultural Trade Liberalisation and the Environment: A Global Perspective', *The World Economy*, 15, 153–71.
Arden-Clarke, C. (1992), 'South–North Terms of Trade – Environmental Protection and Sustainable Development', *International Environmental Affairs*, 4, 122–38.
Asako, K. (1979), 'Environmental Pollution in an Open Economy', *Economic Record*, 55, 359–66.
Barbier, E.B. (1991), 'Managing Trade and the Environment: The Demand for Raw Ivory in Japan and Hong Kong', *World Economy*, 14, 407–30.
Barrett, S. (1992a), 'Strategic Environmental Policy and International Trade', Norwich: CSERGE Working Paper GEC 92-19.
(1992b), 'Self-Enforcing International Environmental Agreements', Norwich: CSERGE Working Paper GEC 92-34.
Bartik, T.J. (1988), 'The Effects of Environmental Regulation on Business Location in the United States', *Growth and Change*, 19, 22–44.
Baumol, W.J. (1971), *Environmental Protection, International Spillovers, and Trade*, Stockholm: Almkvist and Wicksell.
Baumol, W.J. and W.E. Oates (1988), *The Theory of Environmental Policy*, 2nd edn, Cambridge University Press.
Birdsall, N. and D. Wheeler (1992), 'Trade Policy and Industrial Pollution in Latin America: Where Are the Pollution Havens?', in P. Low (ed.), *International Trade and the Environment*, New York: World Bank, pp. 159–67.

Black, J., M.D. Levi and D. de Meza (1993), 'Creating a Good Atmosphere: Minimum Participation for Tackling the Greenhouse Effect', *Economica*, 60, 281–93.

Brander, J. and B. Spencer (1985), 'Export Subsidies and International Market Share Rivalry', *Journal of International Economics*, 18, 83–100.

Burmeister, E. and A.R. Dobell (1970), *Mathematical Theories of Economic Growth*, New York: Macmillan.

Burniaux, J.M., J.P. Martin and J. Oliveira-Martins (1992), 'The Effect of Existing Distorsions in the Energy Markets on the Cost of Policies to Reduce CO_2 Emissions', *OECD Economic Studies*, 19, 141–65.

Conrad, K. (1993a), 'Trade Policy under Taxes and Subsidies for Pollution Intensive Industries', *Journal of Environmental Economics and Management*, 25, 121–35.

(1993b), 'Optimal Environmental Policy for Oligopolistic Industries in an Open Economy', Mannheim: Department of Economics Discussion Paper 476–93.

Cropper, M. and W. Oates (1992), 'Environmental Economics: A Survey', *Journal of Economic Literature*, 30, 675–740.

Dean, J.M. (1992), 'Trade and the Environment: A Survey of the Literature', in P. Low (ed.), *International Trade and the Environment*, New York: World Bank, pp. 15–28

Ekins, P. (1989), 'Trade and Self-Reliance', *The Ecologist*, 19, 186–90.

Ethier, W.J. (1984), 'Higher Dimensional Issues in Trade Theory', in R.W. Jones and P.B. Kenen (eds.), *Handbook of International Economics*, vol. I, Amsterdam: North-Holland, pp. 131–84.

Grossman, G.M. and A.B. Krueger (1991), 'Environmental Impacts of a North American Free Trade Agreement', NBER Working Paper No. 3914.

Herberg, H., M.C. Kemp and M. Tawada (1982), 'More on Variable Returns to Scale', *Journal of International Economics*, 13, 65–84.

Hettige, H., R.E.B. Lucas and D. Wheeler (1992), 'The Toxic Intensity of Industrial Production: Global Patterns, Trends, and Trade Policy', *American Economic Review (Papers and Proceedings)*, 82, 478–81.

Hillman, A.L and H.W. Ursprung (1992), 'The Influence of Environmental Concerns on the Political Determination of International Trade Policy', in K. Anderson, R. Blackhurst et al. (eds.), *The Greening of World Trade Issues*, New York: Harvester Wheatsheaf, pp. 195–20.

(1993), 'Greens, Supergreens and International Trade Policy: Environmental Concerns and Protectionism', in C. Carraro (ed.), *Trade, Innovation, Environment*, Amsterdam: Kluwer.

Hoekman, B. and M. Leidy (1992), 'Environmental Policy Formation in a Trading Economy: A Public Choice Perspective', in K. Anderson and R. Blackhurst (eds.), *The Greening of World Trade Issues*, New York: Harvester Wheatsheaf, pp. 221–46.

Holtz-Eakin, D. and T. Selden (1993), 'Stoking the Fires? CO_2 Emissions and Economic Growth', NBER Discussion Paper 4248.

Jasay, A.E. (1960), 'The Social Choice between Home and Overseas Investments', *Economic Journal*, 70, 105–13.

Kemp, M.C. (1964), *The Pure Theory of International Trade*, Englewood Cliffs: Prentice Hall.

Kemp, M.C. and R.W. Jones (1962), 'Variable Labor Supply and the Theory of International Trade', *Journal of Political Economy*, 70, 30–6.

Kowalczyk, C. and T. Sjöström (1994), 'Bringing GATT into the Core', NBER Discussion Paper 4343.

Krugman, P.R. (1987), 'Is Free Trade Passé?', *Journal of Economic Perspectives*, 1, 131–44.

Krutilla, K. (1991), 'Environmental Regulation in an Open Economy', *Journal of Environmental Economics and Management*, 10, 127–42.

Leonard, H.J. (1988), *Pollution and the Struggle for the World Product: Multinational Corporations, Environment and International Comparative Advantage*, Cambridge University Press.

Leontief, W. (1954), 'Domestic Production and Foreign Trade: The American Capital Position Re-examined', *Economia Internazionale*, 7, 9–45.

Low, P. and A. Yeats (1992), 'Do "Dirty" Industries Migrate?', in P. Low (ed.), *International Trade and the Environment*, New York: World Bank.

Lucas, R.E.B., D. Wheeler and H. Hettige (1992), 'Economic Development, Environmental Regulation, and the International Migration of Toxic Industrial Pollution: 1960–1988', in P. Low (ed.), *International Trade and the Environment*, New York: World Bank.

MacDougall, G.D.A. (1960), 'The Benefits and Costs of Investment from Abroad. A Theoretical Approach', *Economic Record*, 36, 13–35.

Markusen, J.R. (1975), 'International Externalities and Optimal Tax Structures', *Journal of International Economics*, 5, 15–29.

——— (1983), 'Factor Movements and Commodity Trade as Complements', *Journal of International Economics*, 14, 341–56.

Markusen, J.R., E.R. Morey and N. Olewiler (1992), 'Noncooperative Equilibria in Regional Environmental Policies when Plant Locations Are Endogenous', NBER Working Paper No. 4051.

——— (1993), 'Environmental Policy when Market Structure and Plant Locations Are Endogenous', *Journal of Environmental Economics and Management*, 24, 68–86.

Mayer, W. (1984), 'Endogenous Tariff Formation', *American Economic Review*, 74, 970–85.

McGuire, M.C. (1982), 'Environmental Regulation Factor Rewards and International Trade', *Journal of Public Economics*, 17, 335–54.

Merrifield (1988), 'The Impact of Abatement Strategies on Transnational Pollution, the Terms of Trade, and Factor Rewards: A General Equilibrium Approach', *Journal of Environmental Economics and Management*, 15, 259–84.

Morris, D. (1991), 'Free Trade: The Great Destroyer', *The Ecologist*, 20, 190–5.

Motta, M. and J.-F. Thisse (1993), 'Does Environmental Dumping Lead to Delocation?', *European Economic Review*, 38, 563–76.

Murrell, P. and R. Ryterman (1991), 'A Methodology for Testing Comparative Economic Theories: Theory and Application to East-West Environmental Problems', *Journal of Comparative Economics*, 15, 582–601.

Oliveira-Martins, J., J.-M. Burniaux and J.P. Martin (1992), 'Trade and the Effectiveness of Unilateral CO_2 Abatement Policies: Evidence from GREEN', *OECD Economic Studies*, 19, 123–40.

Pethig, R. (1976), 'Pollution Welfare and Environmental Policy in the Theory of Comparative Advantage', *Journal of Environmental Economics and Management*, 2, 160–9.

Rauscher, M. (1991a), 'Foreign Trade and the Environment', in H. Siebert, *Environmental Scarcity: The International Dimension*, Tübingen: Mohr, pp. 17–31.

—— (1991b), 'National Environmental Policies and the Effects of Economic Integration', *European Journal of Political Economy*, 7, 313–29.

—— (1992), 'Economic Integration and the Environment: Effects on Members and Non-members', *Environmental and Resource Economics*, 2, 221–9.

—— (1994), 'Environmental Policy and International Capital Movements', in K.-G. Mäler, *International Environmental Problems: An Economic Perspective*, Amsterdam: Kluwer.

—— (1997), *International Trade, Capital Movements and the Environment*, Oxford University Press.

Robison, H.D. (1988), 'Industrial Pollution Abatement: The Impact on the Balance of Trade', *Canadian Journal of Economics*, 30, 187–99.

Ruffin, R.J. (1984), 'International Factor Movements', in R.W. Jones and P.B. Kenen (eds.), *Handbook of International Economics*, vol. I, Amsterdam: North-Holland, pp. 237–88.

Shrybman, S. (1991), 'International Trade and the Environment: An Environmental Assessment of the General Agreement on Tarriffs and Trade', *The Ecologist*, 20, 30–4.

—— (1991/92), 'Trading Away the Evironment', *World Policy Journal*, 93–110.

Siebert, H. (1977), 'Environmental Quality and the Gains from Trade', *Kyklos*, 30, 657–73.

—— (1979), 'Environmental Policy in the Two-Country Case', *Zeitschrift für Nationalökonomie*, 39, 259–74.

—— (1985), 'Spatial Aspects of Environmental Economics', in: A.V. Kneese and J.L. Sweeney (eds.), *Handbook of Natural Resource and Energy Economics*, vol. I, Amsterdam: North-Holland, pp. 125–64.

—— (1992), *Economics of the Environment*, 3rd edn., Berlin: Springer.

Siebert, H., J. Eichberger, R. Gronych and R. Pethig (1980), *Trade and the Environment: A Theoretical Inquiry*, Amsterdam, North-Holland.

Sinn, H.-W. (1987), *Capital Income Taxation*, Amsterdam: North-Holland.

Snape, R.H. (1992), 'The Environment, International Trade and Competitiveness', in K. Anderson and R. Blackhurst (eds.), *The Greening of World Trade Issues*, New York: Harvester Wheatsheaf, pp. 73–92.

Tobey, J.A. (1989), 'The Impact of Domestic Environmental Policies on International Trade'. Ph.D. Dissertation, Dept of Economics, University of Maryland.

—— (1990), 'The Effects of Domestic Environmental Policies on Patterns of World Trade: An Empirical Test', *Kyklos*, 43, 191–209.

Ugelow, J.L. (1982), 'A Survey on Recent Studies on Costs of Pollution Control and the Effects on Trade', in S.J. Rubin and T.R. Graham (eds.), *Environment and Trade: The Relation of International Trade and Environmental Policy*, Totowa, NJ: Allanheld and Osmun, pp. 167–90.

Ulph, A. (1993), 'Environmental Policy, Plant Location and Government Protection', in C. Carraro (ed.), *Trade, Innovation, Environment*, Rotterdam: Kluwer.

van Bergeijk, P.A.G. (1991), 'International Trade and the Environmental Challenge', *Journal of World Trade*, 25(6), 105–15.

Walter, I. (1973), 'The Pollution Content of American Trade', *Western Economic Journal*, 11, 61–70.

(1982), 'Environmentally Induced Industrial Relocation to Developing Countries', in S.J. Rubin and T.R. Graham (eds.), *Environment an Trade: The Relation of International Trade and Environmental Policy*, Totowa, NJ: Allanheld and Osmun, pp. 67–101.

Walter, I. and J.L. Ugelow (1979), 'Environmental Policies in Developing Countries', *Ambio*, 8(2–3), 102–9.

Wheeler, D. and P. Martin (1992), 'Prices, Policies, and the International Diffusion of Clean Technology: The Case of Wood Pulp Production', in P. Low (ed.), *International Trade and the Environment,* New York: World Bank.

Wildasin, D.A. (1988), 'Nash Equilibria in Fiscal Competition', *Journal of Public Economics*, 35, 229–40.

Wong, K.-Y. (1986), 'Are International Trade and Factor Movements Substitutes?', *Journal of International Economics*, 21, 25–43.

8 Towards a theory of international environmental cooperation

Scott Barrett

1 Introduction

Twenty-five years ago, in an introductory article to research in environmental economics, Kneese (1971) distinguished between two types of environmental problem: 'global' problems which affect the entire planet and 'regional' problems which include 'all those other than global'. In justifying this last classification, Kneese reasoned:

> One must use a word like regional rather than terms pertaining to political jurisdictions such as nations, states, or cities because the scale of pollution resulting from the emissions of materials and energy follows the patterns, pulses, and rhythms of meterological and hydrological systems rather than the boundaries of political systems – and therein lies one of the main problems.

The conclusion to this sentence hints at a possibly important research agenda: international management of environmental resources. Yet, it is only fairly recently that this topic has been the subject of serious examination by economists.[1] The purpose of this chapter is to explain why the transboundary aspect of environmental protection should be 'one of the main problems' of environmental management, and to develop elements of a theory which explain the extent to which institutions may be capable of correcting such problems.

2 The dilemma of international pollution control

The essence of international environmental relations is that countries interact. When any one country chooses its transboundary pollution policy, it will consider what policies other countries will choose, or how others will respond to its own choice. It is in this sense that international pollution control is a 'game'.

Reciprocal externalities are often portrayed using the game shown in figure 8.1. There are two players, countries A and B, and each must choose

239

an action. This choice is binary; the countries may Abate or Pollute. Within each cell, the number on the left is A's payoff, and the number on the right is B's. One can think of these payoffs as being measured in monetary terms, although in this particular example this interpretation is not necessary; all that matters for this game is that each player be able to discern whether one outcome is preferred to another, and not whether one outcome yields a payoff precisely twice or three times the size of another. We shall assume that each country would prefer a larger payoff to a smaller one, but does not care about the payoff received by the other country. The figure shows that if country A chooses to abate its pollution, it receives a payoff of 5 if B also chooses Abate, and a payoff of 2 if B chooses Pollute. B receives payoffs of 5 and 6, respectively, in these two outcomes. The interdependence between A and B is reflected in the fact that each country's payoff depends not only on its own action but also on what the other country does. What policies will the countries choose?

Consider player A's problem. Because of the interdependence that exists, player A, in deciding whether or not to abate its pollution, will wish to consider how the payoff it receives depends on player B's choice. Suppose B chooses to abate its pollution. Then A receives a payoff of 5 if it chooses Abate and 6 if it pollutes. Given that B abates its pollution, A's best response is to choose Pollute. If B chooses Pollute, A receives 2 if it abates and 3 if it pollutes. Hence, given that B pollutes, A's best response is to pollute, too. In other words, A's best strategy is to pollute, whatever B does. It is easy to confirm that the situation is entirely symmetric for B; B's best strategy is also to pollute, whatever A does. Hence, there exists a unique equilibrium to this game, and it is that both players pollute. The outcome (Pollute, Pollute) is an equilibrium (formally, a Nash equilibrium) because neither player would improve its payoff by deviating unilaterally from this outcome. The equilibrium is unique because both players would choose to deviate unilaterally, starting from any of the other three possible outcomes.

The game depicted in figure 8.1 is known as the 'Prisoner's Dilemma'. The dilemma, in the context of the international pollution game, is that both countries choose to pollute even though both would be better off if they abated their emissions instead. The outcome is inefficient.

The example demonstrates how countries could find themselves in an outcome which is mutually less desirable than a feasible alternative outcome. But it does not quite demonstrate why we should be surprised that countries can, sometimes, achieve the mutually preferred outcome. To demonstrate this requires some knowledge of the norms which govern relations between states.

Country B
Abate   Pollute

		Abate	Pollute
Country A	Abate	5, 5	2, 6
	Pollute	6, 2	3, 3

Figure 8.1

Country B
Abate   Pollute

		Abate	Pollute
Country A	Abate	5, 5	4, 4
	Pollute	4, 4	3, 3

Figure 8.2

3 Sovereignty and self-enforcement

Upon a little reflection, we might propose that the countries formally negotiate an agreement which specifies how each country should behave and a
penalty for failing to behave in the prescribed manner. Let us suppose that
the agreement specifies that, if either party choses to pollute, it would have
to pay the other party a fine equal to 2. This agreement changes the payoffs
(which must now be measured in money terms), and the revised game is
shown in figure 8.2. If B abates its pollution and A doesn't, A receives a
payoff of 6 minus a fine of 2, or 4, and B receives a payoff of 2 plus a fine of
2, or 4. The payoffs are the same if A abates and B pollutes. If both parties
pollute or both abate, the payoffs are unchanged compared with figure 8.1.
The equilibrium to this adjusted game is quite different from the earlier
one; now A will choose to abate its pollution, whatever B does, and B will
choose to abate its pollution, whatever A does. The agreement would thus
seem to have removed the dilemma.

However, the agreement will only succeed if it is *binding* on both countries. That is, a third party must be able to enforce the agreement. This is not
a problem for domestic conflicts; a party which violates a contract can be
taken to court. However, there does not exist a 'supernational' authority, or
a World Government, which can enforce an agreement between countries.

The priority accorded to sovereignty in international relations means that agreements between nations must be *self-enforcing* (Barrett (1990)). The agreement to impose a fine as a means of removing the dilemma is not self-enforcing. Knowing that it could not be compelled to pay the fine, A's best strategy is to pollute. So is B's. The only self-enforcing outcome in the game described in figure 8.1 is (Pollute, Pollute). Enforcement of an agreement which produces a mutually more satisfying outcome, without third party intervention, is not possible in this game, however much the two parties may desire such an outcome.

4 The *N*-country pollution dilemma game

Many environmental problems involve more than two countries; some, such as global climate change, involve all countries. How would the number of countries involved affect the above analysis?

Consider a problem involving *N* countries in total. From the perspective of any single country, there are $N-1$ other countries. All countries are assumed to have the same payoff function, and all face a binary choice of either polluting or abating. If a country pollutes, its payoff is Π_P; if it abates, its payoff is Π_A. Let k be the number of countries which choose to abate. The payoffs are

$$\Pi_P = a + bk, \ \Pi_A = c + dk \qquad (1)$$

where a, b, c and d are parameters. For the problem given in figure 8.1, $a=3$, $b=3$, $c=-1$, and $d=3$ when $N=2$. Using these parameter values and assuming $N=10$, the problem may be described by figure 8.3.[2]

The payoff to polluting is always greater than the payoff to abating for any given country, irrespective of the number of other countries which choose to abate. Aggregate net benefits are $\Pi = k\Pi_A + (N-k)\Pi_P$. For specification (1), and using the above parameter values, the average aggregate payoff is $\Pi/N = 3 + 2.6k$. Aggregate payoffs are maximised when *all* countries abate their pollution. However, it is not rational for any to do so.

5 International environmental agreements

While the games considered so far tell us that cooperative agreements are not sustainable when they must be self-enforcing, a large number of such agreements do in fact exist. This suggests that the games we have considered thus far are deficient in some respects.[3]

The United Nations Environment Programme lists 132 multilateral agreements adopted before 1991, and several others have been adopted since then. A number of the better known, or more interesting, multilateral agreements are summarised in table 8.1.

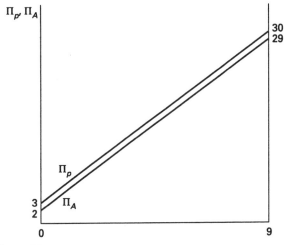

Figure 8.3

An important element in the analysis of IEAs is the number of countries which share a resource and the number which cooperate in the collective management regime. The former number can range from two to the total number of countries that exist – a surprisingly imprecise figure, but one which is close to 200. Typically, fewer countries are parties to an IEA than the number which have an interest in the outcome; IEAs are typically incomplete. As well, most IEAs do not become 'binding' (in the legal, and not the game-theoretic, sense) on parties until ratified by a minimum number of countries. These characteristics of IEAs should be explained by the theory of international environmental cooperation.

6 Two alternative games

While the Prisoner's Dilemma game is typically used to describe collective management problems, not all games are of this type. Let us suppose that the payoff functions are exactly as specified in equation (1), but now change the parameter values for the abating country, letting $c=4$ and $d=2$. Then the game is described by figure 8.4. The equilibrium to this game has four countries abating and six polluting. This game is like the Prisoner's Dilemma insofar as the equilibrium is inefficient and the efficient outcome is one where all countries choose Abate. But in this game, it is better (or at least not worse) to abate if three or fewer other countries are abating, and to pollute if more than three other countries are abating. The outcome where four countries abate and six pollute is self-enforcing. In fact, it is the only self-enforcing outcome.[4]

Table 8.1. *Selected international environmental agreements*

Agreement	Objectives	Date of adoption	Date of entry of entry	Number of signatories[1] Potential	Actual	Minimum
Framework Convention on Climate Change	To stabilise concentrations of greenhouse gases at a level that would prevent dangerous interference with the climate system	1992	1994	All	158	50
Convention on Biological Diversity	The conservation of biological diversity, the sustainable use of it components and the fair and equitable sharing of the benefits arising out of the utilisation of genetic resources	1992	1993	All	157	30
Montreal Protocol on Substances that Deplete the Ozone Layer	To protect the ozone layer by reducing the emissions of substances that can significantly deplete the ozone layer	1987	1989	All[2]	150	11*
Protocol on the Reduction of Sulphur Emissions or their Transboundary fluxes by at least 30 per cent	To provide for a 30 per cent reduction in sulphur emissions or their transboundary fluxes by 1993	1985	1987	30	19	16
Convention on International Trade in Endangered Species of Wild Fauna and Flora	To protect certain endangered species from overexploitation via a system of import/ export permits	1973	1975	All	112	10
International Convention for the Regulation of Whaling	To ensure proper conservation and development of whale stocks	1946	1948	All	36	6**
Convention on Conservation of North Pacific Fur Seals	To achieve maximum sustainable productivity from the fur seal resources of the North Pacific	1911	1911	4	4	4

Notes:
[1] The number of countries that ratify a treaty is more relevant than the number which sign a treaty. The number of signatories is approximate.
[2] Technically, membership is restricted to countries that are members of the Vienna Convention for the Protection of the Ozone Layer, but membership of this convention is open.
* Representing at least two-thirds of global consumption of listed substances.   ** Including five mentioned by name.

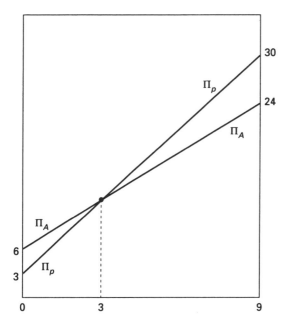

Figure 8.4

This game is consistent with the observation that some, but not all, countries are parties to an IEA. What is more, the countries which pollute (the non-signatories) are better off than those which abate (the signatories). Hence, the polluters can be identified as free-riders.

Further, one can vary the parameter values to obtain different outcomes, including full participation. Consider a special case where full participation is an equilibrium, but not the only equilibrium. Let $a=6$, $b=3$, $c=-1$ and $d=4$. Then we obtain the interactions shown in figure 8.5. In this case, there are two equilibria. In one, all countries pollute. In the other, all abate. The intersection between the two curves indicates a threshold level of participation. If less than three countries are signatories to the agreement, none wishes to accede. If three or more are signatories, all wish to accede. The full cooperative outcome can be sustained by an agreement which specifies that the obligations are only 'binding' (in the legal, rather than the game-theoretic, sense) on all countries if the number of ratifying parties is three or more. For then, if two or fewer countries ratify the agreement, the agreement would not come into force, and those countries which did sign the agreement therefore lose nothing. If, however, the number of signatories is three or more, then all countries will participate in the agreement. In fact, if three or more countries do sign the agreement, then all will sign. The

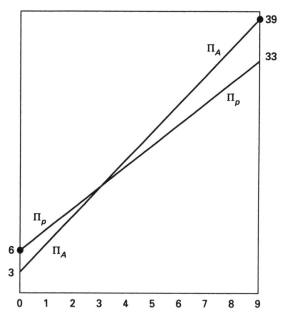

Figure 8.5

outcome where all countries choose Abate is not only the outcome which maximises joint payoffs, but it is also the outcome which is most preferred by every country. Simple coordination, therefore, should allow countries to sustain this outcome.

These results follow from our choice of parameter values, and these were given exogenously. But our real interest lies in showing how countries can effect such a change in parameter values through the institution of an international agreement. That is, starting from a problem like that depicted in figure 8.3, what kind of mechanisms might countries employ in such an agreement in order to sustain full, or at least partial, participation in an IEA? How can institutions transform a problem like that depicted in figure 8.3 into ones like those depicted in figures 8.4 and 8.5?

In developing such a theory, it would also be desirable to allow for a continuum of actions. Binary choices are relevant for some game situations, such as whether one should bother to vote or get vaccinated. But choices that have an effect on the environment are typically continuous: how much to abate (or pollute), how many fish to catch, and how much tropical rain forest to preserve are just three examples. The binary choice that is relevant to international cooperation is accession to an IEA.

Below I offer games which allow for both a continuum of actions (here, choice of abatement levels) and the binary choice of whether a country should accede to, or withdraw from, an IEA. The underlying game is compatible with the essence of the Prisoner's Dilemma, but the IEA shall employ explicit devices which effectively change the nature of the game into one resembling either figure 8.4 or figure 8.5.

7 The payoff functions

As above, let N be the number of countries with an interest in an environmental problem and let Π_i denote country i's payoff. Π_i is the difference between i's benefit of abatement (the environmental damage avoided by abatement), B_i, and i's cost of abatement, C_i. Interdependence will typically mean that B_i depends not only on q_i but also on the abatement undertaken by the other $N-1$ countries. By our assumption of symmetry, only the aggregate of abatement undertaken by these $N-1$ countries affects i; the distribution of this abatement is of no interest to i. Let us make a slightly stronger assumption: that B_i depends on the entire aggregate of abatement Q, where $Q = \Sigma^N_{i=1} q_i$. This assumption is appropriate for environmental problems like stratospheric ozone depletion and global climate change. Depletion of stratospheric ozone over any country i depends on global emissions of ozone-depleting substances, and not in any special way on local emissions. Similarly, the local damages from global climate change depend on atmospheric concentrations of greenhouse gases, which in turn depend on global emissions of greenhouse gases.[5] Finally, let us assume that C_i depends only on q_i; that is, $C_i = C(q_i)$. We then have

$$\Pi_i = B(Q) - C(q_i) \text{ for } i = 1, \ldots, N \qquad (2)$$

B and C will typically be increasing functions. Hence, increased abatement by countries other than i will typically make i better off. However, increased abatement by i will not always make i better off, for the increased abatement by i will typically increase C_i as well as B_i.

8 The equilibrium in unilateral policies

If each country i chooses its own abatement q_i without regard to the consequences for other countries but only so as to maximise its own payoff Π_i, if this choice is made independently of the choices made by the other $N-1$ countries, and if the functions Π_i are continuous and differentiable, then i's choice will be the solution to

$$\frac{dB(Q)}{dQ}\frac{\partial Q}{\partial q_i} = \frac{dC(q_i)}{dq_i} \text{ for } i = 1, \ldots, N \qquad (3)$$

where of course $\partial Q/\partial q_i = 1$. Equations (3) form N equations in $N+1$ unknowns $(q_1, ..., q_N, Q)$. However, recalling that $Q = \Sigma^N_{i=1} q_i$, we may solve (3) for q_i. By symmetry, all countries will choose the same abatement level in equilibrium. Hence, the equilibrium in unilateral policies (denoted by the superscript u) may be rewritten as

$$\frac{dB(Q^u)}{dQ} = \frac{dC(q^u)}{dq} \text{ where } Q^u = Nq^u \tag{3'}$$

The solution requires that each country choose an abatement level q^u at which its *own* marginal benefit of abatement (the increase in B_i associated with a one unit increase in q_i, taking the abatement levels of all other countries to be fixed) equals its *own* marginal cost of abatement (the increase in C_i associated with a one unit increase in q_i). If we further assume that $\partial^2 \Pi_i/\partial q^2_i < 0$ for all i over the relevant range of abatement levels, then (3') will be sufficient for a maximum. What is more, since any country i could not do better by deviating from q^u, given that all other countries play q^u, equation (3') will also be sufficient for a Nash equilibrium.

9 The full cooperative outcome

If countries cooperate fully, they could do no better than to choose q_i jointly so as to maximise their aggregate payoff $\Pi = \Sigma^N_{i=1} \Pi_i$,

$$\Pi = NB(Q) - \sum_{i=1}^{N} C(q_i) \tag{4}$$

The necessary conditions for a maximum are

$$\frac{NdB(Q)}{dQ} \frac{\partial Q}{\partial q_i} = \frac{dC(q_i)}{dq_i} \text{ for all } i \tag{5}$$

By symmetry, (5) may be rewritten (denoting the full cooperative outcome by the superscript c) as

$$\frac{NdB(Q^c)}{dQ} = \frac{dC(q^c)}{dq} \text{ where } Q^c = Nq^c \tag{5'}$$

Equation (5') is the usual condition for the optimal provision of a public good (see Samuelson (1954)): each country undertakes abatement up to the level at which the *aggregate* marginal benefit equals the country's *own* marginal cost. The aggregate marginal benefit is larger (in fact, N times larger) than each country's own marginal benefit, and so our assumptions about B and C imply $q^c > q^u$ and $\Pi_i(q^c) > \Pi_i(q^u)$. When countries choose unilateral policies, none can do better than to play q^u. However, all countries would be better off if every country played q^c instead. The equilibrium in unilateral policies is inefficient.[6]

10 Example

Suppose $B(Q)=\omega Q$ and $C(q_i)=cq^2_i/2$. Then $dB(Q)/dQ=\omega$ and $dC(q_i)/dq_i=cq_i$. Upon substituting these expressions in $(3')$ and $(5')$ we obtain $q^u=\omega/c$ and $q^c=N\omega/c$. Notice that, because $dB(Q)/dQ$ is a constant, each country's optimal abatement level is independent of the abatement undertaken by other countries; play q^u is thus a dominant strategy for each country. The strategy play q^u is thus analogous to the strategy play Pollute in the Prisoner's Dilemma game. Similarly, since q^c maximises the aggregate of payoffs, the strategy play q^c is analogous to the strategy play Abate in the dilemma game.

11 The self-enforcing IEA

In the dilemma game, play Abate is the only alternative to play Pollute. But in the game above, q^c is not the only alternative to q^u; countries are free to choose from the continuum of feasible abatement levels (for the above example, country i is free to choose any $q_i \geq 0$). What distinguishes q^c from the other feasible abatement levels is that q^c is Pareto efficient; when *all* countries play q^c a deviation by any country makes at least one country worse off. Hence, there is some rationale in having i play q^c when all the other $N-1$ countries play q^c; q^c is collectively rational, although of course it is not individually rational. But there is little logic in requiring that i choose q^c when the other $N-1$ countries do not play q^c. A more compelling alternative is to have i select an abatement level which maximises the aggregate of the payoffs of all countries which cooperate with i (including i's own payoff). This way, i plays q^c only if all other countries play q^c (and i plays q^u only if all other countries play q^u).

Suppose, then, that a subset k of the N countries cooperate by choosing an abatement level which is rational for this group of countries, while the remaining $N-k$ countries pursue unilateral policies.[7] Given that the k countries cooperate, it would seem that they should have an opportunity to meet, to discuss their problem, and to agree on what it is they intend to do. Let this intention be specified in an *agreement*. The k countries which cooperate are thus *signatories* (or parties) to the agreement while the remaining $N-k$ countries are *non-signatories* (non-parties). Denote the former type of country by the subscript s and the latter by the subscript n.

Non-signatories choose q_n by solving (3). The solution requires

$$\frac{dB(Q)}{dQ}=\frac{dC(q_n)}{dq}\tag{6}$$

where $Q=Q_n+Q_s$, $Q_n=(N-k)q_n$, and $Q_s=kq_s$. Equation (6) is thus a single equation in three unknowns (q_n, q_s and k). Only if $dB(Q)/dQ$ were a constant would (6) solve uniquely for q^*_n. Notice that $q^*_n = q^u$ if $k=0$; if an agreement is not sustained, all countries are nonsignatories and all play q^u.[8]

Collectively, signatories can do no better than to choose abatement levels for each signatory which maximise the aggregate payoff of all signatories, Π^s, where

$$\Pi^s = kB(Q) - \sum_{j=1}^{k} C(q_j) \tag{7}$$

The solution requires

$$\frac{kdB(Q)}{dQ}\left[\frac{\partial Q}{\partial Q_s} \cdot \frac{\partial Q_s}{\partial Q_j} + \frac{\partial Q}{\partial Q_n} \cdot \frac{\partial Q_n}{\partial Q_s} \cdot \frac{\partial Q_s}{\partial Q_j}\right] = \frac{dC(q_j)}{dq_j} \tag{8}$$

for all $j=1$, ...,k. Obviously, $\partial Q/\partial Q_s = \partial Q_s/\partial q_j = \partial Q/\partial Q_n = 1$. If $k=N$, then $Q_n = 0$ and $\partial Q_n/\partial Q_s = 0$. In this case, (8) is equivalent to (5′); $q_s = q^c$. This is just as we should expect.

What determines $\partial Q_n/\partial Q_s$? If this term were taken to be a reaction, then we would have to insist on $\partial Q_n/\partial Q_s = 0$. Since the game is not repeated, there is no opportunity for one type of country to react to another's choice. Hence, to assume anything other than $\partial Q_n/\partial Q_s = 0$ would not be rational. However, $\partial Q_n/\partial Q_s$ can be interpreted differently; it can be taken to be a specification of the agreement rather than a reaction. In allowing $\partial Q_n/\partial Q_s \neq 0$, we are essentially allowing the agreement to specify that $q_s(k)$ vary other than in direct proportion to k. The term $\partial Q_n/\partial Q_s$ can take any number of forms. Suppose $\partial Q_n/\partial Q_s = -(k-1)/k$. Then the agreement specifies that signatories behave in the same way as non-signatories (that is, (8) becomes equation (6)). Alternatively, suppose $\partial Q_n/\partial Q_s = (N-k)/k$. Then signatories play q^c, irrespective of the number of signatories. As noted above, such an agreement would not be group rational.

Plainly, choice of $\partial Q_n/\partial Q_s$ cannot be arbitrary. Here I shall assume that $\partial Q_n/\partial Q_s$ is chosen by signatories such that they would not wish to revise their choice after observing the abatement decisions actually made by non-signatories. These decisions are governed by (6). Upon totally differentiating (6), and noting that $dQ = dQ_n + dQ_s$ and $dq_n = dQ_n/(N-k)$, we obtain

$$\frac{\partial Q_n}{\partial Q_s} = -\frac{\dfrac{d^2B(Q)}{dQ^2} \cdot (N-k)}{\left[\dfrac{d^2C(q)}{dq^2} - \dfrac{d^2B(Q)}{dQ^2} \cdot (N-k)\right]} \tag{9}$$

If $d^2B(Q)/dQ^2=0$ (the marginal benefit of abatement is constant) and $d^2C(q)/dq^2<0$, we can use (6) to solve directly for q^*_n, which is a dominant strategy. Choice of Q_s does not affect Q_n, and there is no way that the agreement can be specified to modify the behaviour of non-signatories to the advantage of signatories. If $d^2B(Q)/dQ^2<0$ and $d^2C(q)/dq^2=0$, then $\partial Q_n/\partial Q_s=-1$. In this case, every increase in Q_s is offset by a decrease in Q_n of an equivalent magnitude. The effective marginal benefit to signatories of their own abatement is zero. I shall consider both of these cases later in the chapter.[9]

Write $f(q_n,q_s,k)=\partial Q_n/\partial Q_s$. Then, upon substituting (9) into (8), and adding (6) we obtain

$$\frac{dB(k^*q_s^*+(N-k^*)q_n^*)}{dQ}=\frac{dC(q_n^*)}{dq} \tag{6'}$$

$$k^*[1+f(q_n^*,q_s^*,k^*)]\frac{dB(k^*q_s^*+(N-k^*)q_n^*)}{dQ}=\frac{dC(q_s^*)}{dq} \tag{8'}$$

Equations (6') and (8') are in three unknowns, q^*_n, q^*_s and k^*. Unlike q_n and q_s, k is not a choice variable. However, the agreement must satisfy one further condition: if the agreement is self-enforcing then it must be the case that no signatory can gain by withdrawing unilaterally from the agreement, taking the status (signatory versus non-signatory) of other countries as given, and it must further be the case that no non-signatory can gain by unilaterally acceding to the agreement, again taking the status of other countries as given. Formally, the self-enforcing IEA must satisfy[10]

$$\Pi_s(k^*)\geq\Pi_n(k^*-1) \text{ and } \Pi_n(k^*)\geq\Pi_s(k^*+1) \tag{10}$$

As we shall see, this condition, in combination with (6') and (8'), allows us to solve for q^*_n, q^*_s, and k^*.

12 Example continued

Let us now solve for the self-enforcing IEA for the example given in section 10. From equation (6') we know $q^*_n=q^u=\omega/c$. Since q^u is a dominant strategy when no countries cooperate it must also be a dominant strategy for non-signatories when $k<N$ countries cooperate. Since q^*_n is a constant, $\partial Q_n/\partial Q_s=0$ for k given. Equation (8') then yields $q^*_s=k\omega/c$; abatement by signatories is proportional to the number of signatories to the agreement. Substituting q^*_n and q^*_s into (2) yields

$$\Pi_n(k)=\omega^2[2k^2+2(N-k)-1]/2c \tag{11a}$$

$$\Pi_s(k) = \omega^2[k^2 + 2(N-k)]/2c \tag{11b}$$

$$\Pi_n(k-1) = \omega^2[2(k-1)^2 + 2(N-k) + 1]/2c \tag{11c}$$

$$\Pi_s(k+1) = \omega^2[(k+1)^2 + 2(N-k-1)]/2c \tag{11d}$$

Substituting (11b) and (11c) into (10), we find that $1 \leq k^* \leq 3$. Substituting (11a) and (11d) into the second part of (10), we find that $k^* \leq 2$. The self-enforcing IEA thus consists of $2 \leq k^* \leq 3$ countries. Clearly, if $N=2$, then both countries will sign the IEA, and $q^*_s = q^c$. It is easy to show that $\Pi_s(3) = \Pi_n(2)$. Hence, if $N \geq 3$, a third country neither gains nor loses by acceding to the IEA. Assuming that under such circumstances the third country will accede, we find that $k^* = 3$ for $N \geq 3$.

The solution is illustrated in figure 8.6 for the case where $N=5$ and $\omega = c = 1$. If all countries pursue unilateral policies, each receives a payoff $\Pi_n(0) = \Pi^u$. If all countries cooperate fully, each receives $\Pi_s(N) = \Pi^c$. The two payoff curves cross where $\Pi_s(3) = \Pi_n(2)$, a result obtained algebraically above. The important point to notice in the figure is that, while signatories receive a higher payoff than they would in the absence of the agreement, non-signatories do better than signatories at k^*. Non-signatories do better because they 'free ride' on the abatement undertaken by signatories. As the agreement is specified, the game reflects both the Prisoner's Dilemma and the Game of Chicken. The game of whether or not to be a signatory is a Game of Chicken (see Carraro and Siniscalco (1993)). But the observation that both signatories and non-signatories would be better off in the full cooperative outcome than with the self-enforcing IEA is reminiscent of the Prisoner's Dilemma.

13 Compliance

If signatories obey equation (8′), then they are behaving in their collective interests. However, they are not necessarily behaving in their self-interests, for what is to prevent a signatory from deviating, not by withdrawing from the agreement (that incentive is already accounted for in condition (10)), but by reducing its abatement slightly below q^*_s? The agreement cannot be enforced by a third party, and there is no internal mechanism in the agreement which punishes such a deviation (only withdrawals are punished by the agreement). Hence, the above notion of a 'self-enforcing IEA' assumes that compliance is full. Is it reasonable to assume that signatories will comply with such an agreement?

In practice, states do comply with international agreements.[11] Chayes and Chayes (1991, p. 311) introduce their analysis of compliance by noting that 'International lawyers and others familiar with the operations of inter-

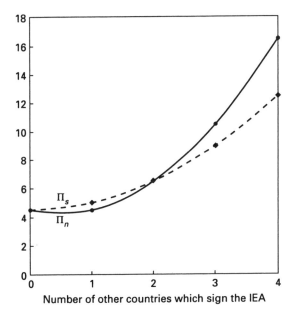

Figure 8.6

national treaties take for granted that most states comply with most of their treaty obligations most of the time'. Where states do not comply with an agreement, the reason is often that states do not have the means to comply rather than that they do not have the desire to comply.[12] According to Chayes and Chayes (1991, p. 311): 'Although there are some obvious exceptions where states have signed treaties without a serious intention to comply, ordinarily the decision is made in good faith, presumably after a process, however imperfect, that weighs the costs and benefits of compliance.' What this implies is that states decide whether or not to accede to a treaty by comparing the payoffs they receive as signatories and nonsignatories, with the understanding that if they do accede then they will comply with the agreement. This reasoning is entirely consistent with the model developed above.

But more is needed to justify the assumption of full compliance. First, suppose that $\partial Q_n/\partial Q_s = -(k-1)/k$. Then the agreement specifies that signatories play q^u. Such an agreement obviously poses no problem for compliance. However, in most cases the above model requires that signatories do *more* than they would in the absence of the agreement. If countries were observed to comply with agreements which only required that signatories do what they would have done in the absence of the agreement, then the observation that compliance tends to be full would not justify the assumption of full compliance for agreements which require that states do much more than they would have done in the absence of the agreement. On this, Chayes and Chayes (1991, p. 311) find that there is no convincing empirical evidence to support the view that widespread compliance merely reflects the fact that treaties require that signatories take actions that they were prepared to take in the absence of the agreement: 'states' behavior in entering into treaties suggests that they believe they are accepting significant constraints on future freedom of action to which they expect to adhere over a broad range of circumstances'.

Second, as the agreement specified by equation (8) does not include a mechanism which penalises non-compliance and rewards compliance, the assumption of full compliance could only be justified if the observed compliance were not attributable to such a mechanism. Here again, Chayes and Chayes (1991, p. 313) are clear in supporting the assumption: 'not only are formal enforcement mechanisms seldom used to secure compliance with treaties, but they are rarely even embodied in the treaty text'. Hence, from a practical point of view, the assumption of full compliance appears reasonable.

14 Compliance, reciprocity, and linkage

But the above discussion begs the question: Why do signatories comply with international agreements? Chayes and Chayes (1991, p. 320) conclude that reciprocity and linkages in other relations are the main reasons for compliance:

The unwillingness and even inability of international regimes to mobilize formal sanctions and incentives does not mean that there are no penalties for non-compliance or benefits from compliance. As in other relatively small communities of actors in continuing and thickly-textured relationships, members of a treaty regime have available a wide range of informal pressures and inducements to secure compliance with community norms. States have dealings and continuing relationships with each other over a range of issues. Questions of treaty compliance arise in an environment of diffuse reciprocity, with manifold opportunities for subtle expressions of displeasure, suspicion and reluctance to deal with treaty-violators in other contexts. A reputation for unreliability cannot be confined to the area of activity in which it is earned. It is inevitable that a state's defection from treaty rules will generate repercussions and linkages throughout the network of its relationships with others in the community.

The model we are working with here is not sophisticated enough to accommodate these reasons for compliance. To incorporate reciprocity will require a fully dynamic model. To allow for linkage requires that the strategies available to players be expanded. We shall consider these problems later in the chapter.

15 Group rationality

With full compliance, the only aspect of the game examined above which limits cooperation is the assumption of *group rationality* – that q_s is chosen by each signatory, taking k as given, to maximise the joint payoffs of all signatories. If this assumption is relaxed, it is easy to show that any number of agreements is possible, including the full cooperative outcome. Consider the following primitive agreement: play $q_s = q^u$ for $k < N$ and $q_s = q^c$ for $k = N$. Then, with all countries in the agreement, none can gain by deviating unilaterally. However, this agreement is not group rational for $1 < k < N$. Once the assumption of group rationality is abandoned, given the assumption of full compliance, virtually any feasible outcome can be sustained by an IEA.

To appreciate the logic in the assumption of group rationality, consider the above primitive agreement. The agreement is group rational for $k = N$. But suppose one signatory defects from the complete agreement. Then the remaining signatories (as well as the defector) play q^u. This punishes the defector severely. However, the reduction in abatement also harms the remaining $N-1$ signatories. If all N players sought to cooperate initially, it cannot be credible for the remaining $N-1$ countries not to rewrite the agreement and try to cooperate among themselves or to re-establish cooperation among all N countries; given the defection, the remaining $N-1$ countries would not wish to play q^u because they could do better playing q^*_s. In fact, the original defector could have foreseen that the remaining $N-1$ signatories would renegotiate their agreement in this way, and it is for this reason that the defection may have been rational. A self-enforcing agreement must plainly be immune to renegotiation. Hence the primitive agreement specified above cannot be self-enforcing. The self-enforcing IEA must be group rational.[13]

16 Decreasing marginal benefits

The results presented above, which indicate that a self-enforcing IEA can sustain only a small number of signatories, are for a particular functional specification (see Barrett (1994b), Carraro and Siniscalco (1994a) and Hoel (1992b) for a similar result). However, the results are sensitive to the functional specification, and the assumption that the marginal benefits of abatement are constant will not be appropriate for many if not most environmental problems. In most cases the marginal benefit of abatement will fall as abatement increases. Let us therefore consider this more plausible functional specification. In particular, suppose

$$B_i = B(Q) = \frac{b(aQ - Q^2/2)}{N} \text{ and } C_i = C(q_i) = cq_i^2/2 \qquad (12)$$

where $-b$ is the slope of the aggregate marginal benefit curve, $2b/N$ is the slope of i's marginal benefit curve, and c is the slope of i's marginal abatement cost curve. Because the marginal benefit of abatement equals zero when $Q = a$, the parameter a can be interpreted as the aggregate level of emissions that would result if there were no abatement. Alternatively, the parameter a may denote a threshold where marginal damage is zero for emission levels less than a.[14]

Using (3′) and (5′), we can derive the equilibrium in unilateral policies and the full cooperative outcome. These solutions are

$$q^u = \frac{a}{N(\gamma+1)}, \; q^c = \frac{a}{(N+\gamma)} \qquad (13)$$

where $\gamma \equiv c/b$. It is easy to show algebraically that $q^c = q^u$ for $N = 1$ and $q^c > q^u$ for $N > 1$. When countries pursue unilateral policies, each chooses an abatement level which equates its own marginal cost and its own marginal benefit of abatement: q^u. If countries were to cooperate fully, each would select an abatement level which equates its own marginal cost and the aggregate marginal benefit of abatement: q^c.

Let us now derive the self-enforcing IEA. Solving for (6) we obtain

$$q_n = \frac{(a - kq_s)}{[N(\gamma+1) - k]} \qquad (14)$$

From (14) we see that $\partial Q_n / \partial Q_s = -(N-k)/[N(\gamma+1)-k]$. Solving for (8′) yields

$$q_s = \frac{ak\gamma N}{[N(\gamma+1)-k]^2 + \gamma k^2 N} \qquad (15)$$

Finally, substituting (15) into (14) gives

$$q_n = \frac{a[N(\gamma+1)-k]}{[N(\gamma+1)-k]^2 + \gamma k^2 N} \qquad (16)$$

Equations (15) and (16) form two equations in three unknowns. However (10) must also be satisfied. In the earlier example we were able to solve analytically for k^*. Here I am unable to do so. However, this turns out not to be a great problem. What we can do is conduct a number of simulations using various values for γ (that is, for c and b) holding N (and a) fixed, and solve for k^* in each case. It turns out that k^* is always unique and can be approximated by an analytical expression.

Table 8.2 shows k^* for a number of simulations assuming $N = 100$, for

Table 8.2

k^* for various values of c and b,
assuming $N=100$

		c				
		.01	.1	1	10	100
	.01	3	3	2	2	2
	.1	11	3	3	2	2
b	1	51	11	3	3	2
	10	92	51	11	3	3
	100	100	92	51	11	3

various values of b and c (see Barrett, 1994b).[15] Notice that, unlike the case where the marginal benefit of abatement is constant, here k^* depends on the parameter values, and the self-enforcing IEA may even sustain the full cooperative outcome when $N=100$. Notice, too, that k^* does not vary along the diagonals. This implies that k^* depends on γ rather than on c and b.

As k increases, the term in brackets in (8′) (that is, $1+f$) increases. This means that q_s increases in k. Define k^+ to be the value of k at which signatories abate q^u. That is, $q_s(k^+)=q^u$. It is easy to show that $k^+=N(\gamma+1)/(\gamma N+1)$. Furthermore, one can show that $k^* \approx k^+ +1$. For all the simulations I have run (see Barrett (1994b)), $k^+<k^*<k^+ +2$. We now see that, contrary to first appearances, the results for specification (12) do not differ markedly from the results for the case where the marginal benefit of abatement is constant. In the latter case, $k^+=1$ and $k^*=3$ for all $N\geq 3$, irrespective of parameter values (assuming that a country accedes when the payoff it gets by being a signatory equals the payoff it gets by being a non-signatory, holding the labels of all other countries fixed).[16] This implies that a self-enforcing IEA can only depart marginally from the equilibrium in unilateral policies.

The observation that the self-enforcing IEA can only depart marginally from the equilibrium in unilateral policies suggests that IEAs cannot achieve very much, even when signed by a large number of countries, and simulations in Barrett (1994b) confirm this in the case where $N=100$. However, here again the results are sensitive to functional specification, as demonstrated below.

17 Constant marginal costs

Let us consider one more functional form. Suppose that B_i is as in (12) but that $C_i=\sigma q_i$; that is, marginal abatement costs are constant and equal to

$\sigma > 0$. Using (3') and (5'), but also recognizing that abatement must be non-negative, we find

$$q^u = \frac{(ab - \sigma N)}{bN} \text{ if } ab - \sigma N \geq 0; \ q^u = 0 \text{ otherwise,}$$ (17a)

$$q^c = \frac{(ab - \sigma)}{bN} \text{ if } ab - \sigma \geq 0; \ q^c = 0 \text{ otherwise.}$$ (17b)

As in the previous examples, $q^c = q^u$ for $N = 1$ and $q^c > q^u$ for $N > 1$ if the solutions are 'interior'. Notice that if $ab - \sigma N < 0$ while $ab - \sigma < 0$, then the equilibrium in unilateral policies involves all countries undertaking *zero* abatement even while all would be better off if all undertook *positive* abatement (of the amount q^c).

The solution to the self-enforcing IEA proceeds as in the earlier examples with the exception that we must now allow for possible 'corner' solutions. Non-signatories choose q_n to maximise Π_n, taking the abatement of the other $N-1$ countries as given, subject to $q_n \geq 0$.[17] The solution requires

$$q_n = 0 \text{ if either } ab - \sigma N \leq 0 \text{ or } ab - \sigma N > 0 \text{ and } Q_s \geq \frac{(ab - \sigma N)}{bN} \quad (18a)$$

$$q_n = \frac{1}{(N-k)} \left[\frac{ab - \sigma N}{b} - Q_s \right] \text{if } ab - \sigma N > 0$$

$$\text{and } Q_s < \frac{(ab - \sigma N)}{bN} \quad (18b)$$

Signatories will play

$$q_s = 0 \text{ if } \frac{bk}{N}(a - Q_n - Q_s)\left(1 + \frac{\partial Q_n}{\partial Q_s}\right) < \sigma \quad (19a)$$

$$q_s = \frac{abk - \sigma N}{bk^2} \text{ if } q_n = 0 \text{ and } k > \frac{\sigma N}{ab} \quad (19b)$$

What is interesting and different about this functional form is that the equilibrium involves at least one type of country undertaking zero abatement and no more than one type undertaking positive abatement. To see this, notice that if $q_n > 0$ then (18b) holds, implying $\partial Q_n / \partial Q_s = -1$. But from (19a) we see that this implies $q_s = 0$. In all, there are three possible outcomes:

$$q_n = q_s = 0 \text{ if } ab \leq \sigma N \text{ and } k \leq \sigma N / ab \quad (20a)$$

$$q_n = \frac{ab - \sigma N}{b(N-k)} \text{ and } q_s = 0 \text{ if } ab > \sigma N \quad (20b)$$

$$q_n = 0, \; q_s = \frac{abk - \sigma N}{bk^2} \text{ if } k > \sigma N / ab \qquad (20c)$$

If $ab > \sigma N$ and $k > \sigma N/ab$ we cannot tell whether (20b) or (20c) will hold. To determine this one must know the conditions under which signatories will play $q_s = 0$ as opposed to $q_s > 0$; given this behaviour the actions of non-signatories are specified by (20b) and (20c). It is easy to show that signatories receive a higher payoff under (20b) for $k^- < k < k^+$ where $k^- = \{ab - [(ab - \sigma N)(ab + \sigma N)]^{1/2}\}/\sigma N$ and $k^+ = \{ab + [(ab + N) \; (ab + \sigma N)]^{1/2}\}$ $/\sigma N$. However, one can show that $0 < k^- < 1$. Hence the full solution is as follows

$$q_n = 0, \; q_s = 0 \text{ if } ab \leq \sigma N \text{ and } k \leq \sigma N/ab \qquad (21a)$$

$$q_n = \frac{ab - \sigma N}{b(N - k)}, \; q_s = 0 \text{ if } ab > \sigma N \text{ and } 0 < k < k^* \qquad (21b)$$

$$q_n = 0, \; q_s = \frac{abk - \sigma N}{bk^2} \text{ if } ab \leq \sigma N \text{ and } k > \sigma N/ab \text{ or} \qquad (21c)$$

$$\text{if } ab > \sigma N \text{ and } k \geq k^* \qquad (21d)$$

For this functional specification there is a sharp change in the payoff functions at k^*. This is because the behaviour of signatories and non-signatories switches at k^*. These discontinuities mean that agreements can improve substantially on the non-cooperative outcome, even when the number of signatories sustained by the self-enforcing IEA is small, as the simulations in table 8.3 illustrate. For example, row 1 shows that $Q^u = 1$ and $Q^c = 99$ while $Q^*_n = 0$ and $Q^*_s = 50.5$. Hence, just two signatories out of 100 are able to narrow the gap in abatement between the non-cooperative and full cooperative outcomes very substantially. Indeed, if the parameter values allow, the self-enforcing IEA can even sustain the full cooperative outcome. The last row of table 8.3 gives such an example. Here, the agreement specifies that, if there are 99 or fewer signatories, each must carry out zero abatement but that if there are 100 signatories, each must abate $q^c = 0.99$ units. This last example is identical to the one considered in section 15, with the exception that the agreement noted above *is* group rational.

18 Some alternative concepts

This last example is helpful in illustrating two other concepts discussed in the literature. Heal (1993) considers a 'minimum critical coalition' in the context of a binary choice problem. He considers an example where it is not rational for any country to undertake positive abatement unilaterally but

Table 8.3. *Simulations for various parameter values assuming ab>σN and N=100*

a	b	σ	k⁺	k⁺	qᵘ	qᶜ	Πᵘ	Πᶜ	qₙ	qₛ	Πᵤ	Πₛ
100	1	0.99	1.15	2	0.01	0.99	0.99	49.01	0	25.25	37.75	12.75
100	1	0.75	2.22	3	0.25	0.99	21.69	49.25	0	25.00	46.88	28.13
100	1	0.65	2.71	3	0.35	0.99	28.65	49.35	0	26.11	47.65	30.68
100	2	1.98	1.15	2	0.01	0.99	1.97	98.03	0	25.25	75.50	25.50
100	2	1.5	2.22	3	0.25	0.99	43.38	98.51	0	25.00	93.75	56.25
100	2	1.3	2.71	3	0.35	0.99	57.30	98.70	0	26.11	95.31	61.36
1,000	1	9.9	1.15	2	0.10	9.90	98.51	4901.49	0	252.50	3774.88	1275.13
1,000	1	7.5	2.22	3	2.50	9.93	2168.75	4925.28	0	250.00	4687.50	2812.50
1,000	1	6.5	2.71	3	3.50	9.94	2864.75	4935.21	0	261.11	4765.28	3068.06
1,000	2	19.8	1.15	2	0.10	9.90	197.02	9802.98	0	252.50	7549.75	2550.25
1,000	2	15.0	2.22	3	2.50	9.93	4337.50	9850.56	0	250.00	9375.00	5625.00
1,000	2	13.0	2.71	3	3.50	9.94	5729.50	9870.42	0	261.11	9530.56	6136.11

Simulations for various parameter values assuming ab<σN and N=100

a	b	σ	σN/ab	k*	qᵘ	qᶜ	Πᵘ	Πᶜ	qₙ	qₛ	Πᵤ	Πₛ
100	1	2	2	3	0	0.99	0	98.51	0	25.00	93.75	56.25
100	1	10	10	11	0	0.99	0	98.51	0	8.47	99.54	86.83
100	1	99	99	100	0	0.99	0	98.51	0	0.99	—	98.51

where it is rational for a group of countries to do so. This is not quite the problem described above because I allow for continuous choices above. However, the cases are sufficiently similar that I believe the concept can still be applied. Heal essentially considers the case where $ab < \sigma N$ and $ab > \sigma$. If the members of the coalition choose group-rational abatement levels, then they will play q_s. The minimum critical coalition is thus k', where $k' = \sigma N / ab$. As Heal notes, the concept is a necessary but not a sufficient condition for a self-enforcing agreement, and as table 8.3 shows, the model developed above identifies a slightly higher value as the number of signatories to a self-enforcing IEA. Heal suggests that in a model where there exists a minimum critical coalition of at least two countries, then there is 'a form of increasing returns to size in the process of coalition formation'. It is precisely this which accounts for the relative success of an IEA based on the assumption of constant marginal costs. However, this is of course only a special case.

Chander and Tulkens (1994, 1995) consider an alternative approach to that employed above, based on the concept of the *core* of a cooperative game. They identify an agreement comprising all countries which has the property that, if a coalition of countries (consisting of at least one country) withdraws, the remaining 'signatories' (in the sense of the term used above) effectively disband the agreement and do not attempt to form another one; instead, they each obey equation (3') and thus behave as 'non-signatories'. This behaviour on the part of signatories ensures that, under certain conditions, it is not optimal for any such coalition of 'defectors' to form. Hence, full cooperation can be sustained. This approach imposes a very harsh punishment on defection and that is why it can sustain full cooperation. However, would it really be credible for signatories to behave in this way? It can be, but only in very special cases. The example given in the last row of table 8.3 is one such case. In this case, if one country defects from the agreement, the remaining 99 countries can do no better than to play q^u $(=q_s(99))=0$. However, in general countries will want to renegotiate an agreement specified as above. Such an agreement, therefore, cannot be self-enforcing.

19 Transfers to encourage accession

Starting from any self-enforcing IEA which is incomplete in the sense that there exists at least one non-signatory, if an additional country does accede, the original signatories will increase their abatement, and in doing so reward the country for acceding. Given that the original IEA was self-enforcing, however, it must be the case that this reward is smaller than the cost to the country of accession. It is this imbalance which limits participation in the IEA.

However, notice that those countries which are parties to the IEA would also receive higher payoffs if an additional country were to accede; while their additional abatement rewards the acceding country, this additional abatement, combined with the increase in abatement by the acceding country, also increases the payoff to the original signatories. This suggests that the original signatories might offer non-signatories a transfer to induce the latter to accede to the IEA. Carraro and Siniscalco (1993) demonstrate that such a transfer would result in expanded membership of the IEA, but that the resulting agreement would not be self-enforcing; any of the original signatories offering the transfer would do better still by withdrawing from the agreement. Hence, to facilitate transfers, and thereby to expand membership to the IEA, requires *commitment*. If countries are committed to being signatories, then the self-enforcement constraint can be ignored, and transfers can be sustained which increase the size of the IEA. Carraro and Siniscalco (1993) consider a number of forms of commitment and types of transfer, and demonstrate that it is even possible for the full cooperative outcome to be sustained in certain cases.

Now, as we saw in section 3, if commitment is possible, then contracts can be made binding, and cooperation can be easily sustained. Indeed, with commitment, full cooperation can be easily sustained.[18] Admittedly, Carraro and Siniscalco (1993) introduce only a limited form of commitment, such as commitment only by the original signatories; but this only begs the question of why some countries can commit and others cannot. Of course, IEAs sometimes do employ transfers as a means of increasing participation (Mäler, 1990). But such transfers are employed to take account of asymmetries between countries, and in Carraro and Siniscalco's (1993) paper countries are symmetric. When countries are asymmetric, transfers may expand participation even under the constraint of self-enforcement.

20 Minimum participation in IEAs

Black *et al.* (1993) have examined a different approach to sustaining (partial) cooperation. They assume that an agreement becomes binding on parties provided the number of countries acceding to the agreement exceeds a specified minimum level of participation. In assuming that the agreement becomes binding, Black *et al.* (1993) are assuming that commitment is feasible. In this sense, this approach is similar to that adopted by Carraro and Siniscalco (1993).

Now, if the game is one of complete information, then we know that commitment can sustain the full cooperative outcome trivially. In this case, the commitment mechanism would work as follows. All countries are better off in the full cooperative outcome than in any other feasible outcome.

Countries must choose simultaneously whether they wish to accede to the agreement, knowing that if all countries accede, then the full cooperative outcome is sustained, but that if even one country does not, only the non-cooperative outcome is sustained (in this sense the model is reminiscent of Chander and Tulkens, 1994 and 1995). Given this choice, and knowing that the offer will not be repeated, there exists a unique equilibrium, and it is that all countries choose to accede to the IEA.

In fact, Black *et al.* (1993) examine a non-trivial problem. They assume that there is incomplete information; each country does not know the benefits of global abatement to each of the other countries. The choice facing each country is binary; each country either accedes to the agreement or it does not. If the country accedes, then it abates and incurs a cost c. The benefit to one country of abatement undertaken by any country is also constant, but this benefit is not known with certainty. Calling this benefit b, Black *et al.* (1993) assume that $c>b$. In other words, if a country fails to accede, then it will choose not to abate. (This framework is thus similar to that employed in Heal, 1993.)

Assuming a distribution for b, Black *et al.* (1993) then carry out a number of simulations showing how the expected aggregate payoff varies with the specified minimum participation level. They show that, for these simulations, the optimal minimum participation level is about 70 per cent of the total number of countries. Depending on parameter values, this minimum participation level may result in expected aggregate payoffs improving substantially on the non-cooperative outcome, or it may have very little effect.

This approach is interesting, not least because IEAs typically do specify a minimum participation level. However, the analysis suffers from a number of problems. One is that the choice of a minimum participation level is not made endogenously by the negotiating parties, although Black *et al.* (1993, p. 290) argue that it 'seems reasonable that countries might agree *ex ante* to establishing a bureau that impartially computes [the minimum participation level] and incorporates it into the treaty'. A second problem is that the analysis assumes that the decision to accede is not repeated. In fact, the agreement would be extremely vulnerable to renegotiation. If the minimum participation level were not realised, then the parties would have an incentive to recalculate this level and choose again whether to accede. If the minimum participation level were exceeded, then parties would have an incentive to withdraw from the agreement. And, of course, all parties would know this when choosing their strategies in the first instance. It is in this sense that the assumption of commitment clashes with the notion of self-enforcement. Later in this chapter we shall examine a model in which minimum participation is specified endogenously, and where the resulting agreement is self-enforcing.

21 Heterogeneous IEAs

One problem with applying the above analysis to real international relations is that countries are not symmetric; some countries have higher marginal abatement benefits than others, and some have higher marginal abatement costs than others. It is conceivable that such differences may have a profound influence on the ability to sustain an IEA which substantially improves global well being. In particular, the United States, the European Union (EU) and the former USSR account for about one-half of global carbon dioxide emissions. If these countries alone could sustain an IEA which reduced their emissions substantially, then perhaps global well being really could be improved, despite the incentives which the large number of other countries might have to free ride.

Unfortunately, the analysis of heterogeneous IEAs is far more complicated than the homogeneous case. The reason is that heterogeneous countries have *two* substantive problems to solve: first, they must reach agreement on the obligations which signatories to the IEA must bear; and, second, they must devise credible punishments/rewards that can sustain this negotiated outcome despite free-rider incentives. When countries are identical, the first problem is trivial (identical countries must bear identical obligations), and so negotiators have only to solve the second problem. When countries are different, the first problem can be immensely complicated. Indeed, cooperative game theory offers numerous solution concepts for this first problem.

Three papers have explored the problem of negotiating a self-enforcing IEA when countries are heterogeneous. Hoel (1992a) assumes that marginal abatement benefits are constant but different for all countries, and fixes the distribution of the marginal benefit parameter across all countries. He also assumes that the marginal abatement cost function is linear and *identical* for all countries. Finally, he assumes that the countries that cooperate agree to adopt the *uniform* emission level which is the most preferred emission level of the median country among the cooperating countries. Bauer's (1992) model differs from Hoel's by allowing the abatement cost parameter to vary among countries, but she fixes the difference between the marginal abatement benefit and cost parameters for all countries. Further, Bauer assumes that the cooperating countries choose abatement levels so as to maximise their collective payoffs (so that abatement need not be uniform across all cooperating countries). Under these different assumptions, Hoel finds that the self-enforcing IEA consists of at most three countries, while Bauer finds that it consists of no more than two countries.[19]

Barrett (1994c) employs the same basic functional form as the above two papers but, unlike these papers, I allow both cost and benefit parameters to vary without restriction. Following Bauer, I assume that signatories choose abatement levels so as to maximise their collective net benefits. However, unlike Bauer, I allow negotiators to make side payments. As is well known, side payments can be essential to reaching an agreement among heterogeneous negotiators (see, for example, Mäler, 1989). In Barrett (1994c), side payments are determined by allocating to each signatory its Shapley value. The advantage of the Shapley value is that it yields a *unique* outcome that satisfies both individual and group rationality. However, alternative solution concepts from cooperative game theory have their own appealing features. This analysis demonstrates that the self-enforcing IEA consists of at least two, but never more than three, signatories.

These results are hardly shocking. After all, as shown in section 12 above, if *identical* countries have constant marginal benefits and linear marginal costs, then the number of signatories to the self-enforcing IEA is three, irrespective of parameter values. Hence, we should not be surprised to find that the self-enforcing IEA can support no more than three different countries when marginal benefits are constant, marginal costs are linear and countries are heterogeneous. More interesting is the case examined in section 16 above where parameter values do affect participation in the self-enforcing IEA, and this is also examined in Barrett (1994c). Here, I find that heterogeneity does not so much affect participation in the IEA as the gains from cooperation. Consider the case where $N=100$. Suppose that 97 of these countries are 'small' and three are 'large'. The large countries have substantially higher marginal benefits from abatement and substantially smaller marginal costs.[20] This means that these countries will undertake substantial abatement even in the absence of cooperation. I find that cooperation results more in a redistribution of abatement than in an overall increase in abatement. The observation that the gains to cooperation will be smaller, for any given N, when countries are heterogeneous was recognised long ago by Olson (1965). He reasoned (pp. 28–9) that 'A group composed of members of unequal ['size'] . . . will show less of a tendency toward suboptimality (and be more likely to provide itself with some amount of a collective good) than an otherwise identical group composed of members of equal size.'

22 IEAs as repeated games

The model developed in section 11 is essentially one-shot. Cooperation is only supported by the assumption of full compliance. Though, as section 13 argued, compliance is not normally a problem for international agreements, it would be far preferable to work with a model in which full compliance is not assumed. However, once the assumption of full compliance is dropped, cooperation can only be sustained if further alterations are made to the model. One of these is that the game is repeated.

It is well known that the full cooperative outcome of the one-shot game can be sustained as a subgame perfect equilibrium of the infinitely repeated game if the rate of discount is sufficiently small. This can be shown very easily for the specification given by equation (1). Denote the (common) discount factor by δ, net benefits to country i under the full cooperative outcome by Π_i^c, net benefits to country i under the non-cooperative outcome by Π_i^u, and net benefits to i if i, and i alone, defects from the full cooperative outcome by Π_i^d. If all players play the 'grim' strategy of cooperating on the first move and cooperating on every successive move provided all other players cooperated on every previous move, but choosing their non-cooperative abatement levels if any player did cheat on a previous move, then no single player would want to deviate if the following condition is satisfied (see Shapiro, 1989)

$$\delta \geq (\Pi_i^d - \Pi_i^c)/(\Pi_i^d - \Pi_i^u), \text{ for all } i \tag{22}$$

For the specification given by equation (1), condition (22) reduces to $\delta \geq \frac{1}{2}$, irrespective of N. In other words, provided the common rate of discount does not exceed 100 per cent, the full cooperative outcome can be sustained by *any* number of countries.

Since environmental games like climate change and biodiversity conservation are played repeatedly, this result – and the folk theorem, more generally – would seem to suggest, in contrast to the IEA model discussed previously, that IEAs could well reflect the full cooperative outcome.[21] However, it turns out that the above infinitely repeated game may not be self-enforcing; as shown below, such games may be vulnerable to renegotiation.

Consider the above repeated game. As we have seen, cooperation can be sustained as a subgame perfect equilibrium if players adopt the strategy of indefinite Cournot reversion after any player cheats. However, if one player did cheat, and the others threatened indefinite punishment, all players would have an incentive to renegotiate and begin cooperating again. Since all players would be aware of this incentive to renegotiate, the above grim strategy cannot characterise a self-enforcing IEA; to be self-enforcing, IEAs must be *renegotiation proof*. As will be shown below, renegotiation-proof IEAs may not be able to sustain the full cooperative outcome, even for arbitrarily small discount rates.[22]

Let Π_i now denote country i's *average* payoff in the infinitely repeated game, and consider the functional specification where marginal abatement costs are constant. Adjusting payoffs by a constant we have

$$\Pi_i = b(aQ - Q^2/2)/N - \sigma q_i - (ab - \sigma N)^2/2bN \tag{23}$$

The constant term ensures that each country is guaranteed a payoff of at least zero. The full cooperative outcome yields a global payoff of $\sigma(N-1)(2ab - \sigma(N+1))/2b$. Hence, the set of feasible, individually rational payoffs is

$$V^* = \{v \mid v_i \ge 0, \ \Sigma v_i \le \sigma(N-1)([2ab - \sigma(N+1)]/2b\}$$

Following Farrell and Maskin (1989), a payoff vector v is (weakly) renegotiation proof (for discount rates near zero) if abatement levels q_j^j, q_k^j can be chosen to punish j for cheating, such that

$$\max_{q_j}\{(b/N)[a(q_j + (N-1)q_k^j) - (q_j + (N-1)q_k^j)^2/2]$$
$$- \sigma q_j - (ab - \sigma N)^2/2bN\} \le v_j q_j \tag{24}$$

$$(b/N)[a(q_j^j + (N-1)q_k^j) - (q_j^j + (N-1)q_k^j)^2/2]$$
$$- \sigma q_k^j - (ab - \sigma N)^2/2bN \ge v_k \tag{25}$$

Condition (24) ensures that any one country cannot gain by cheating on the agreement. Condition (25) ensures that countries have no incentive to renegotiate.[23] For this problem, it also makes sense to require that the payoff vector v be Pareto efficient in the punishment phase.

Inequalities (24) and (25) can now be rewritten as

$$\sigma(N-1)q_k^j \le v_j \tag{26}$$

$$\sigma[2abN - \sigma(N^2+1)]/2bN - \sigma q_k^j \ge v_k \tag{27}$$

If j chooses for q_j^j its minimax abatement level, $q_j^j = (ab - \sigma N)/b$, then $q_k^j = \sigma/b$. Substituting, we require for every country i

$$\sigma[2abN - \sigma(N+1)^2]/2bN \ge v_i \ge \sigma^2(N-1)/b \tag{28}$$

Under the full cooperative outcome, every country receives a payoff of $\sigma(N-1)(2ab - \sigma(N+1))/2bN$. Substituting this value into (28), we find that the full cooperative outcome can be sustained as a self-enforcing agreement if the number of countries N does not exceed

$$\overline{N} = \min(ab/\sigma - 1, \ 2ab/3\sigma - 1/3) \tag{29}$$

It is easy to see that $\overline{N}$ is increasing in b, and decreasing in σ. However, the potential gain to cooperation ($\Pi_c - \Pi_u = \sigma^2(N-1)^2/2b$) is decreasing in b and increasing in σ. Hence, as we showed above, an IEA can sustain a large number of signatories, but only when the gains to cooperation are relatively small; when these gains are large, a self-enforcing IEA can sustain only a smaller number of signatories. Clearly, then, even infinite repetition of the game may not sustain the full cooperative outcome provided IEAs must be self-enforcing.[24]

Before concluding this section, we should reflect that supergames, like the one considered above, assume that players face the same set of feasible actions and per-period payoffs in each of infinitely many periods. But if emissions persist in the environment for some time, then the payoffs attainable in period t will depend on the actions undertaken in previous periods; the game is history dependent. History dependence will be relevant for most environmental problems of interest, and so we should ask how important history dependence can be to the analysis. Unfortunately, while some work has explored the non-cooperative and full cooperative outcomes in differential games (see, for example, van der Ploeg and de Zeeuw (1992)), no analysis has yet been done on self-enforcing IEAs as differential games.

23 Linkage

As noted in section 14, compliance with IEAs is achieved partly through repetition of an interaction (discussed above) and partly through issue linkage. In both cases, deviant countries can be punished and cooperating countries can be rewarded, whereas such punishments and rewards are not feasible in a one-shot game.

Cesar and de Zeeuw (1994) consider the problems of repetition and issue linkage jointly. They consider an asymmetric Prisoner's Dilemma game[25] in which the unique Nash equilibrium is (Defect, Defect). In the absence of side payments, this outcome is Pareto optimal. However, both parties would be jointly better off if the outcome (Cooperate, Cooperate) were sustained instead, and it is in this sense that Cesar and de Zeeuw take this game to be a Prisoner's Dilemma. The paper shows that the full cooperative outcome of the one-shot game cannot be sustained as a subgame perfect equilibrium of the infinitely repeated game, a result which follows from the fact that the full cooperative outcome is not Pareto optimal. However, when this game is linked to its mirror image game, the authors find that the full cooperative outcome can be sustained as a subgame perfect, renegotiation-proof equilibrium. The rationale behind this result is quite straightforward. In linking the asymmetric Prisoner's Dilemma game with its mirror image, the combined game is a symmetric Prisoner's Dilemma. Van Damme (1989) has shown how the full cooperative outcome of the symmetric Prisoner's Dilemma can be sustained as a subgame perfect, renegotiation-proof equilibrium of the infinitely repeated game. Hence, Cesar and de Zeeuw need only invoke van Damme's theorem to prove their result.

Carraro and Siniscalco (1994b) also examine the issue of linkage, but in the context of the model developed in section 11 and the example considered in section 12 (constant marginal abatement benefits and symmetric countries). They suppose that, in addition to the agreement on abatement, countries may also negotiate an agreement which increases the spillovers from R&D only among cooperating countries. The game is in three stages. In stage I, countries decide whether or not to be signatories to the linked agreement on pollution abatement and R&D spillover. In stage II, signatories and non-signatories choose their abatement levels.[26] In stage 3, firms choose production and R&D levels. Using simulation analysis, Carraro and Siniscalco find that the full cooperative outcome can be sustained as a self-enforcing agreement (assuming, implicitly, full compliance) for certain parameter values (and $N=100$). This is in contrast to the model presented in section 12 in which an agreement consisting of only three countries can be sustained as a self-enforcing IEA.

There has been one further attempt to model linkage in international negotiations. However, since this paper (Barrett, 1994d) considers interactions in international trade, it would be appropriate to precede the description of this model with a discussion of international environmental cooperation in the context of international trade.

24 'Leakage' and incomplete agreements

In general, international trade exacerbates the free-riding problem. Abatement by cooperating countries increases the costs to industry in these countries, and therefore shifts comparative advantage in pollution-intensive production towards non-cooperating countries. Output of pollution-intensive goods should therefore rise in non-cooperating countries, as should emissions. In the case of climate change and stratospheric ozone depletion, abatement by cooperating countries would also lower world demand for carbon-intensive fossil fuels and ozone-depleting substances, and hence lower the prices of such products traded in international markets. But, as these prices fell, the quantity demanded by non-cooperating countries would increase; and so, too, would emissions. It should be emphasised that these two responses by non-cooperating countries do not result from any deliberate policy to increase emissions, but rather result from the absence of a policy to reduce emissions. Hence this effect is quite different from that considered thus far in this chapter.

The magnitude of such 'leakage' is normally reported as a 'leakage rate', which may be defined as the increase in emissions by non-cooperating countries divided by the reduction in emissions by cooperating countries. A number of studies have attempted to estimate this leakage for unilateral carbon dioxide abatement programmes, but different studies come to different conclusions. Pezzey (1992) estimates that a 20 per cent reduction in carbon emissions within the European Union (EU) alone (relative to a baseline trend in emissions) would be associated with a leakage rate of 80 per cent. In other words, for every 10 tons of carbon abated by the EU, global emissions would fall by only 2 tons. Pezzey also calculates that a 20 per cent reduction in OECD emissions would be associated with a leakage rate of 70 per cent. These leakage rates suggest that unilateral policy would be largely ineffective. By contrast, Oliveira-Martins, Burniaux and Martin (1992), using the OECD's GREEN model, estimate much lower leakage rates for policies aimed at stabilising carbon emissions at their 1990 levels. They estimate leakage rates for a unilateral EU policy of 11.9 per cent in 1995 and 2.2 per cent in 2050, and for a unilateral OECD policy of 3.5 per cent in 1995 and 1.4 per cent in 2050. These leakage rates suggest that leakage does not render unilateral policy ineffective. Given the different results from these analyses, all that can now be said is that leakage is a potentially serious problem for unilateral policies.

Hoel (1993a,b) considers policies for reducing leakage.[27] To reduce the shift in comparative advantage resulting from a unilateral policy, Hoel (1993b) demonstrates that signatories should impose a tariff against non-signatories. To reduce leakage as transmitted through the product markets (the markets for ozone-depleting substances or fossil fuels), Hoel (1993a) shows that a policy of taxing both consumption and production is required. However, while these policies may reduce leakage, they are not directed at reducing free riding.

Both leakage and free riding can be reduced if more countries can be encouraged to cooperate. Indeed, both problems can be eliminated if cooperation can be made full. Below I consider a mechanism which serves this purpose.

25 Trade sanctions in IEAs

The Montreal Protocol on Substances that Deplete the Ozone Layer bans trade in certain products between cooperating and non-cooperating countries, so as to reduce leakage and enforce the agreement by deterring free riding. To understand the implications of trade restrictions for both membership in an IEA and welfare, I have developed a theoretical model which captures a number of the important features of the Montreal Protocol (Barrett (1994d)). While the model is highly specialised, and hence its results may not hold generally, I believe that it does reveal some striking insights about trade and IEAs.

Intuitively, trade restrictions are good insofar as they succeed in increasing cooperation, but bad insofar as they deprive both signatories and non-

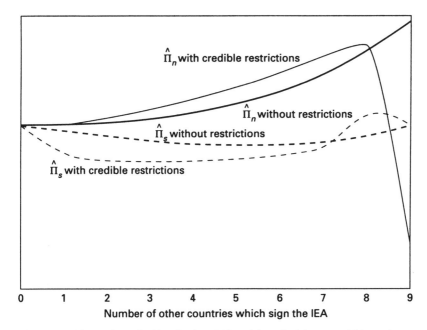

Figure 8.7 Illustration of self-enforcing IEAs with and without credible trade restrictions

signatories of some of the gains from trade. A trade restriction that would be hard to argue against would be one which succeeded in securing universal participation, for such a restriction would achieve full cooperation in pollution abatement without diminishing the gains from trade. The Montreal Protocol has effectively succeeded in this, as participation in this agreement is virtually full.

The model is similar in design to the one described in section 12 (constant marginal benefits and symmetric countries). However, emissions arise from production by a single firm in each country. The firms (like the countries) are symmetric and they produce a homogeneous good. The countries trade in this good because each firm is assumed to choose a level of output to be shipped to each of the N markets. In stage I, governments choose to be signatories or non-signatories. In stage II, firms make their output/shipment decisions. Simultaneous with this choice, governments choose their emission standards. In addition, signatory governments may choose possible limits on trade with non-signatories.

A simulation of the model is shown in figure 8.7 for a case with ten countries. The solid and broken curves in bold show the payoffs to signatories and non-signatories when trade restrictions by signatories cannot be chosen. Unlike the case shown in figure 8.6, a self-enforcing IEA consisting of two or more countries does not exist (the Π_n and Π_s curves never cross). This is because cooperation in this model implies leakage; emissions by non-signatories rise as a consequence of greater abatement by signatories, not because marginal benefits change (marginal benefits are constant in this model) but because output rises in non-signatory countries. The pattern with trade restrictions is similar until nine countries accede to the agreement. When eight or fewer countries are parties to the agreement, an import ban is not credible. However, when nine countries are parties to the IEA, an import ban is credible. There are thus two equilibria in this model with trade restrictions. One is where a self-enforcing IEA consisting of two or more countries does not exist. The other is where the IEA is complete and sustains the full cooperative outcome. Importantly, it is not the restriction in trade that sustains cooperation but the credible *threat* to impose trade restrictions.

However, such a credible threat is not sufficient to sustain full cooperation. It must also be the case that this equilibrium is chosen over the alternative equilibrium of no cooperation. To sustain the Pareto efficient outcome, a device is needed to *coordinate* the actions of different countries. When the full cooperative outcome can be sustained by a trade ban, one can identify a threshold number of countries, where, once the threshold has been crossed, it is not attractive for any country to remain a non-signatory, but where, when the threshold is not met, it is not attractive for any country to become a signatory. To ensure that the threshold is exceeded, the agreement must simply specify a minimum number of countries which must accede to the agreement before the agreement comes into force (that is, becomes 'legally' binding). Then, no country loses by acceding if the threshold is not met, and once the threshold is met, all other countries will accede. In figure 8.7, the threshold consists of nine countries. To sustain the full cooperative outcome in this case, one requires an agreement which: (i) specifies that each signatory must play q^c, (ii) would not come into force until signed by at least nine countries and (iii) restricts trade between signatories and non-signatories. This is very similar to the design of the Montreal Protocol. This agreement specifies that stringent emission ceilings for signatories would not come into force until ratified by at least 11 countries, accounting for at least two-thirds of global consumption of the controlled substances, and requires that trade between signatories and non-signatories be restricted.

As indicated earlier, this analysis is based on a highly specialised model, and it would be hazardous to generalise. However, the analysis is useful insofar as it encourages us to consider the magnitude of credible trade restrictions and the effects that these have on participation in an IEA. If trade restrictions are never in fact practiced, but the (credible) threat of using them is sufficient to command full participation in an agreement, then there would seem to be no reason why such restrictions should be prohibited. However, the above analysis assumes that all countries are identical. In a more realistic setting, trade restrictions imposed on 'non-cooperating' countries might be unfair, just as tariffs imposed on such countries might be unfair. To justify trade restrictions, the agreement that is made available for accession must be fair.[28]

26 Fair agreements

The Montreal Protocol offers an example of a fair agreement. The protocol distinguishes between developed and developing countries, and imposes much harsher requirements on the former. Further, the 1990 revision to the Montreal Protocol established a Multilateral Fund, which compensates developing countries for the costs of complying with the agreement. Hence, accession to the Montreal Protocol should not harm developing countries. If one believes that the developing countries would not benefit from the abatement of ozone-depleting substances, or that they should not be required to pay for the abatement (perhaps because one believes that developed countries are responsible for ozone depletion), then it seems one could not countenance the application of trade restrictions against developing countries which do not accede to an agreement which imposes the same obligations on both developed and developing countries. However, given that the Montreal Protocol essentially guarantees that developing countries are no worse off as signatories than they would be as non-signatories, it is hard to object to the use of trade restrictions in this agreement.

Although the Montreal Protocol is unusual in a number of respects, in general IEAs are fair.[29] Other fair agreements include the Convention on Biological Diversity and the Framework Convention on Climate Change.[30] While neither of these agreements incorporates explicit mechanisms to deter free riding, they do distinguish between developed and developing countries, and require that the former compensate the latter for the 'incremental costs' of implementing the obligations under these conventions. It is in this sense that these agreements appear 'fair'.

Exactly what constitutes a 'fair' agreement will always be contentious, and I do not intend to offer any new insight into this concept. However, I do want to emphasise the importance of context when reflecting on the question of fairness. Several attempts have been made to articulate a fair resolution to the question of how the responsibility for abating carbon dioxide should be distributed among countries. Perhaps the best known attempt is by Grubb (1989). He argues that a global limt on CO_2 emissions should be negotiated, and that the allocation of this total limit should be fixed according to a rule of equal emissions per capita for all countries. He then argues that these permits should be tradable. The allocation rule is seen to be equitable. Trading is seen to ensure that the outcome is also achieved in a cost-effective manner. Grubb (1989, p. 37) sums up the proposal as follows:

The moral principle is simple, namely that every human being has an equal right to use the atmospheric resource. The economic principle follows directly – those who exceed their entitlement should pay for doing so. The practical effect is obvious: it would require the industrialised world, with high per capita energy consumption, to assist the developing world with efficient technology and technical services.

The main problem with this proposal, however, is that it polarises negotiations by favouring one group (the South) over another (the North). The North has much higher emissions per capita than the South. Any reduction in global emissions, however small, would therefore result in huge transfers of resources from North to South. This would not be acceptable to the North. But then no agreement is reached, and this outcome is not attractive to the South (or the North).

I have proposed an alternative allocation rule (grounded partly in game theory and partly in moral reasoning) that would seem to be acceptable to both types of country (Barrett (1992b)). This rule would require that each country choose an abatement level at least as large as the uniform abatement level it would like all countries, including itself, to undertake. Because each country takes account of both its own costs and the benefit it receives from global abatement, a country with high (marginal) abatement costs and low (marginal) abatement benefits, would not be required to undertake much abatement; a country with low (marginal) abatement costs and high (marginal) abatement benefits would be required to undertake more abatement. As a result, the allocation can be shown to be 'acceptable' to both North and South in the sense that each country would be better off as a party to such an agreement than it would be in the absence of any agreement (in this sense the approach is similar to Chander and Tulkens (1994, 1995)).

27 Applications

A number of papers have applied the apparatus of game theory to the study of different environmental problems. One of the first of its kind was Mäler's (1989) superb analysis of 'the acid rain game'. In this paper (and its longer versions), Mäler lays out the theory of games as applicable to acid rain, and builds into this strucutre some specific features of the acid rain problem and estimates of damages and abatement costs to calculate the non-cooperative and fully cooperative outcomes for Europe. Descendants of Mäler's paper include include Kaitala, Pohjola and Tahvonen (1992), Kaitala, Mäler and Tulkens (1992) and Mäler and de Zeeuw (1995).

Much attention has been devoted to the study of international interactions relating to global climate change. In addition to some papers already cited, examples include Kosobud and Daly's (1984) analysis of climate change as a North–South problem, Fankhauser and Kverndokk's (1992) more detailed model, Hoel's (1992b, 1993c) analyses of a carbon tax as a differential game, Barrett's (1992a) analysis of the economic aspects of negotiating a climate change treaty, and Barrett's (1992c) analysis of a carbon tax policy for the European Union.

Further research has applied the theory of games to the study of protecting the stratospheric ozone layer (in addition to the papers cited previously, see Heister (1993)), the management of fisheries (see, for example, Kaitala and Munro (1993)), the conservation of whales (Hämäläinen, Haurie and Kaitala (1984)), and the preservation of biodiversity (Barrett (1994a)). Sandler and Sargent (1995) apply their analysis of mixed strategy equilibria to a number of environmental problems, including tropical deforestation.

28 Conclusion

In pretty short time, economists have made considerable advances in understanding the management of transboundary resources, thanks largely to the availability of game theoretic techniques and their previous application to related phenomena in subjects like industrial organisation theory. If the literature can be characterised by a single theme it is that the global commons is not destined to 'ruin', as famously predicted by Hardin (1968). This is partly because the structure of some interactions imply that the full cooperative and non-cooperative outcomes are not very far apart. It is also because of clever institutional design, as in the use of 'carrots' (side payments) and 'sticks' (for example, trade restrictions) in international agreements. However, the literature does not convince me that cooperation is inevitable or that ruinous outcomes can always be avoided even when their avoidance is feasible.

Notes

Between drafts of this paper, I was invited to participate in the Workshop on Coalitions in Environmental Games and in Other Economic Applications, organized by Claude d'Apremont and Henry Tulkens at the Center for Operations

Research & Econometrics, Université Catholique de Louvain. Discussions with a number of colleagues at this workshop compelled me to rewrite sections of the first draft. I am especially grateful to Carlo Carraro, who provided helpful comments on the first draft. Financial support from the Fondezione ENI E. Mattei is gratefully acknowledged.

1 Even the fairly recent *Handbook of Natural Resource and Energy Economics* (see Kneese and Sweeney (1985–93)), which is intended to 'examine the current theory' in 30 chapters, spread over three volumes, makes barely a reference to international aspects of environmental policy.

2 I have borrowed this approach of graphical representation from Schelling (1978).

3 I should emphasise that it is the description of the game which is deficient and not its analysis.

4 Notice from the figure that if three other countries choose Abate, an additional country is indifferent between abating and polluting. I assume that where there is this indifference, a fourth country will choose to abate.

5 Local pollutants may also be reduced if CO_2 emissions are abated, but the benefits of the reduction in local pollutants can be subtracted from the gross cost of CO_2 abatement.

6 This observation was perhaps first made by Dasgupta (1982) and can be found in virtually every paper on the subject.

7 Chander and Tulkens (1994) consider two other kinds of behaviour by non-cooperating countries: a 'pessimistic' behaviour in which these countries undertake zero abatement and an 'optimistic' behaviour in which non-cooperating countries choose their abatement levels *jointly*, taking as given the abatement by cooperating countries. Neither form of behaviour is individually rational, and it is interesting to note that Chander and Tulkens label the behaviour assumed in the model above 'individually reasonable'.

8 Of course, an agreement could specify that signatories play q^u. But such an agreement would not add value to any country.

9 Notice that these are not the only possibilities. For example, Heal (1993) considers functional forms which imply $\partial Q_n/\partial Q_s > 0$.

10 This condition was first employed by d'Apremont *et al.* (1983) as a condition of cartel stability. It has been employed in the case of IEAs in a number of papers, including Hoel (1992a,b), Carraro and Siniscalco (1993) and Barrett (1994b).

11 For a recent review of this literature, see Roginko (1994).

12 For example, four years after the Montreal Protocol was signed, only about half of all signatories had complied fully with the treaty's reporting requirements. However the reason for non-compliance was not individual gain. According to Chayes and Chayes (1993, p. 194), 'the great majority of the nonreporting states were developing countries that for the most part were simply *unable* (emphasis added) to comply without technical assistance from the treaty organization'.

13 See, however, the discussion of Chander and Tulkens (1994, 1995) in section 18.

14 Obviously, we could rescale the measure of abatement in such a way that $a=1$.

15 The parameter a does not affect k^*.

16 Similarly, for specification (12) one finds that, for $\gamma=10$, $k^+=1.065$ for $N=3$ and $k^+=1.099$ for $N=100$. It is only when γ is very small that k^+ (and k^*) differ substantially with changes in N.

17 More generally, $0\leq q_n\leq q^{\mathrm{max}}$. However, to simplify, I shall assume that the constraint $q_i\leq q^{\mathrm{max}}$ never bites.

18 Commitment may also serve to *reduce* the aggregate payoff. Hoel (1991) shows that a commitment to reduce emissions unilaterally may only lead other countries to reduce their emissions by less than they otherwise would have done, with the result being that aggregate emissions are actually higher than would otherwise have been the case.

19 Using an alternative equilibrium concept, Bauer finds that the number of countries can be increased.

20 Suppose that damage is constant for all countries per unit of GDP. Then absolute damage will be greater for countries with higher income levels, all else being equal. Suppose, too, that marginal abatement costs are the same for all countries in terms of percentage abatement, but that emissions are much greater for the large countries. Then the marginal cost of abating any given quantity of emissions will be lower for the larger countries.

21 Unfortunately, they could as well reflect a multiplicity of other equilibria. This is a common criticism of the supergame literature.

22 The analysis is drawn from Barrett (1994b).

23 Farrell and Maskin (1989) refer to such an equilibrium as being strongly perfect.

24 For a similar analysis applied to the convention on biological diversity, see Barrett (1994a). This analysis reaches a similar conclusion, but the solution to the maximal N in this case cannot be solved analytically.

25 They also consider a 'suasion' game, but I shall not discuss this here.

26 Notice that with marginal benefits being constant, $\partial Q_n/\partial Q_s=0$. Hence, in the context of a stage game, there is no need to model the abatement choices of signatories and non-signatories in separate stages.

27 Bohm (1993) considers an alternative means of reducing leakage in the case of climate change. This would involve supplementing a carbon tax with a policy of reducing the supply of fossil fuels in non-cooperating countries.

28 This point is also made by Bhagwati (1993).

29 An example of an unfair agreement is the 1959 Nile Waters Agreement between Egypt and Sudan. This agreement did not reserve any water for upstream riparians – notably, Ethiopia. So far, Ethiopia has not claimed any rights to a portion of Nile waters, but such a claim is inevitable, and it is likely that the 1959 agreement will be renegotiated to include Ethiopia.

30 For game-theoretic analyses of these issues, see, respectively, Barrett (1994a) and (1992a).

References

d'Apremont, C.A., J. Jacquemin, J. Gabszeweiz and J.A. Weymark (1983), 'On the Stability of Collusive Price Leadership', *Canadian Journal of Economics*, 16, 17–25.

Barrett, S. (1990), 'The Problem of Global Environmental Protection', *Oxford Review of Economic Policy*, 6, 68–79.

—— (1992a), *Convention on Climate Change: Economic Aspects of Negotiations*, Paris: OECD.

—— (1992b), '"Acceptable" Allocations of Tradeable Carbon Emission Entitlements in a Global Warming Treaty', in UNCTAD (ed.), *Combating Global Warming: Study on a Global System of Tradeable Carbon Emission Entitlements*, New York: United Nations.

—— (1992c), 'Reaching a CO_2 Emission Limitation Agreement for the Community: Implications for Equity and Cost-Effectiveness', *European Economy*, Special Edition No. 1, pp. 3–24.

—— (1992d), 'International Environmental Agreements as Games', in R. Pethig (ed.), *Conflicts and Cooperation in Managing International Environmental Resources*, Berlin: Springer-Verlag, pp. 11–36.

—— (1994a), 'The Biodiversity Supergame', *Environmental and Resource Economics*, 4, 111–22.

—— (1994b), 'Self-Enforcing International Environmental Agreements', *Oxford Economic Papers*, 46, 878–94.

—— (1994c), 'Heterogeneous International Environmental Agreements', mimeo, London Business School and Centre for Social and Economic Research on the Global Environment.

—— (1994d), 'Trade Restrictions in International Environmental Agreements', CSERGE Working Paper GEC 94–12, Centre for Social and Economic Research on the Global Environment.

Bauer, A. (1992), 'International Cooperation over Environmental Goods', mimeo, Volkswirtschaftliches Institut, University of Munich.

Bhagwati, J. (1993), 'Trade and the Environment: The False Conflict?', in D. Zaelke, P. Orbuch and R.F. Housman (eds.), *Trade and the Environment: Law, Economics, and Policy*, Washington, DC: Island Press.

Black, J., M.D. Levi and D. de Meza (1993), 'Creating a Good Atmosphere: Minimum Participation for Tackling the "Greenhouse Effect"', *Economica*, 60, 281–93.

Bohm, P. (1993), 'Incomplete International Cooperation to Reduce CO_2 Emissions: Alternative Policies', *Journal of Environmental Economics and Management*, 24, 258–71.

Carraro, C. and D. Siniscalco (1993), 'Strategies for the International Protection of the Environment', *Journal of Public Economics*, 52, 309–28.

—— (1994a), 'Transfers and Commitments in International Negotiations', in K.G. Mäler (ed.), *International Environmental Problems: An Economic Perspective*, Dordrecht: Kluwer.

—— (1994b), 'R&D Cooperation and the Stability of International Environmental Agreements', Working Paper 65.94, Fondazione ENI Enrico Mattei.

Cesar, H. and A. de Zeeuw (1994), 'Issue Linkage in Global Environmental Problems', Working Paper 56.94, Fondazione ENI Enrico Mattei.

Chander, P. and H. Tulkens (1994), 'The Core of an Economy with Multilateral Environmental Externalities', Working Paper 69.94, Fondazione ENI Enrico Mattei.

(1995), 'A Core-Theoretic Solution for the Design of Cooperative Agreements on Transfronteir Pollution', Working Paper 22.95, Fondazione ENI Enrico Mattei.

Chayes, A. and A.H. Chayes (1991), 'Compliance Without Enforcement: State Regulatory Behavior Under Regulatory Treaties', *Negotiation Journal*, 7, 311–31.

(1993), 'On Compliance', *International Organization*, 47, 175–205.

Dasgupta, P. (1982), *The Control of Resources*, Cambridge, MA: Harvard University Press.

Fankhauser, S. and S. Kverndokk (1992), 'The Global Warming Game: Simulations of a CO_2 Reduction Agreement', GEC Working Paper 92–10, Centre for Social and Economic Research on the Global Environment (CSERGE), University College London and University of East Anglia.

Farrell, J. and E. Maskin (1989), 'Renegotiation in Repeated Games', *Games and Economic Behavior*, 1, 327–60.

Grubb, M. (1989), *The Greenhouse Effect: Negotiation Targets*, London: Royal Institute of International Affairs.

Hämäläinen, R.P., A. Haurie and V. Kaitala (1984), 'Bargaining on Whales: A Differential Game Model with Pareto Optimal Equilibria', *Operations Research Letters*, 3, 5–11.

Hardin, G. (1968), 'The Tragedy of the Commons', *Science*, 162, 1243–8.

Heal, G. (1993), 'Formation of International Environmental Agreements', in C. Carraro (ed.), *Trade, Innovation, Environment*, Dordrecht: Kluwer.

Heister, J. (1993), 'Who Will Win the Ozone Game?', Kiel Working Paper No. 579, Kiel Institute of World Economics.

Hoel, M. (1991), 'Global Environmental Problems: The Effects of Unilateral Actions Taken by One Country', *Journal of Environmental Economics and Management*, 20, 55–70.

(1992a), 'International Environment Conventions: The Case of Uniform Reductions of Emissions', *Environmental and Resource Economics*, 2, 141–59.

(1992b), 'Emission Taxes in a Dunamic International Game of CO_2 Emissions', in R. Pethig (ed.), *Conflicts and Cooperation in Managing International Environmental Resources*, Berlin: Springer-Verlag, pp. 39–68.

(1993a), 'Efficient Climate Policy in the Presence of Free Riders', mimeo, Department of Economics, University of Oslo.

(1993b), 'Should a Carbon Tax be Differentiated Across Sectors?', mimeo, Department of Economics, University of Oslo.

(1993c), 'Intertemporal Properties of an International Carbon Tax', *Resource and Energy Economics*, 15, 51–70.

Kaitala, V., K.-G. Mäler and H. Tulkens (1992), 'The Acid Rain Game as a Resource Allocation Process with an Application to the Cooperation Among Finland, Russia, and Estonia', CORE Discussion Paper No. 9242, Center for Operations Research & Econometrics, Université Catholique de Louvain.

Kaitala, V. and G. Munro (1993), 'The Economic Management of High Seas Fishery Resources: Some Game Theoretic Aspects', Discussion Paper No. 93–41, Department of Economics, University of British Columbia.

Kaitala, V., M. Pohjola and Olli Tahvonen (1992), 'An Economic Analysis of Transboundary Air Pollution between Finland and the Former Soviet Union', *Scandinavian Journal of Economics*, 94, 409–24.

Kneese, A.V. (1971), 'Background for the Economic Analysis of Environmental Pollution', in P. Bohm and A.V. Kneese (eds.), *The Economics of Environment*, London: Macmillan, pp. 1–24.

Kneese, A.V. and J.L. Sweeney (eds.) (1985–93), *Handbook of Natural Resource and Energy Economics*, vols. I–III, Amsterdam: North-Holland.

Kosobud, R.F. and T.A. Daly (1984), 'Global Conflict or Cooperation over the CO_2 Climate Impact?', *Kyklos*, 37, 638–59.

Mäler, K.-G. (1989), 'The Acid Rain Game', in H. Folmer and E. van Ierland (eds.), *Valuation Methods and Policy Making in Environmental Economics*, Amsterdam: Elsevier, pp. 231–52.

——— (1990), 'International Environmental Problems', *Oxford Review of Economic Policy*, 6, 80–108.

Mäler, K.-G. and A. de Zeeuw (1995), 'Critical Loads in Games of Transboundary Pollution Control', Working Paper 7.95, Fondazione ENI Enrico Mattei.

Oliveira-Martins, J., J.-M. Burniaux and J.P. Martin (1992), 'Trade and the Effectiveness of Unilateral CO_2-Abatement Policies: Evidence from GREEN', *OECD Economic Studies*, 19, 123–40.

Olson, M. (1965), *The Logic of Collective Action*, Cambridge, MA: Harvard University Press.

Pezzey, J. (1992), 'Analysis of Unilateral CO_2 Control in the European Community and OECD', *The Energy Journal*, 13, 159–71.

Roginko, A. (1994), 'Domestic Compliance with International Environmental Agreements: A Review of Current Literature', Working Paper 94–128, IIASA, Laxenburg, Austria.

Samuelson, P. (1954), *Foundations of Economic Analysis*, Cambridge, MA: Harvard University Press.

Sandler, T. and K. Sargent (1995), 'Management of Transnational Commons: Coordination, Publicness, and Treaty Formation', *Land Economics*, 71, 145–62.

Schelling, T.C. (1978), *Micromotives and Macrobehavior*, New York: Norton.

Shapiro, C. (1989), 'Theories of Oligopoly Behavior', in R. Schmalensee and R. Willig (eds.), *Handbook of Industrial Organization*, vol. I, Amsterdam: North-Holland, pp. 329–414.

van Damme, C. (1989), 'Renegotiation-Proof Equilibria in Repeated "Prisoners' Dilemma"', *Journal of Economic Theory*, 46, 206–17.

van der Ploeg, F. and A.J. de Zeeuw (1991), 'A Differential Game of International Pollution Control', *Systems & Control Letters*, 17, 409–14.

9 Group formation in games without spillovers

Hideo Konishi, Michel Le Breton and Shlomo Weber

1 Introduction

In many social and economic situations individuals form groups rather than operate on their own. For example, individuals form communities in order to share the costs of production of local public goods, or workers join a labour union in order to attain a better working contract. In fact, firms are coalitions of owners of different factors of production, political life is conducted through a rather complicated structure of political parties and interest groups, and households are actually coalitions of individuals.

The reason for the existence of groups which contain more than one agent but less than the entire society lies in the conflict between increasing returns to scale provided by large groups, on the one hand, and heterogeneity of agents' preferences, on the other. Indeed, it is often the case that firms create joint research ventures rather than conducting R&D independently in order to extract the gains from cooperation and obtain access to a larger pool of resources. However, given the heterogeneity of agents' tastes, the decision-making process of a large group may lead to outcomes quite undesirable for some of its members. This observation supports the claim that, on many occasions, a decentralised organisation is superior to a large social structure. Instead of a grand coalition containing the entire population, we often observe the emergence of group structures which consist of groups smaller than the entire society. Another example is that of political games, where voters have preferences over the policies that will be chosen and parties pick their 'ideological positions' so as to attract voters. Each voter will choose that party which is most likely to promote her own interests. While a voter prefers that party whose political position is closest to her own, she realises that if this party is (too) small it may be ineffective, and thus will refrain from voting for it. This reaction of voters has to be taken into account by parties when they choose their political positions. It is evident that the analysis of group formation is important and, in fact, central to game theory. Given the complexity of the general problem, this analysis proved to be rather difficult, which accounts for the relatively slow progress in this area (see survey in Greenberg (1995)). This chapter can be considered a contribution to the brand of literature which identifies environments that yield the existence of a 'stable' group structure.

The formal framework chosen here is that of a normal form non-cooperative game G with a finite number of players. In order to introduce the elements of cooperative behaviour in our framework, we assume that all players have the same strategy set. The strategies chosen by the players in a non-cooperative game generate a partition of the set of players into groups of individuals, where the players in each such group make identical choices. Thus, an equilibrium choice of strategies gives rise to an endogenously determined equilibrium partition of the set of players.

As we mentioned above, in order to obtain existence of an equilibrium, one needs to impose some restrictions on the way in which the payoff of each player i depends on the other players' choices. In this chapter we will analyse the issue of stability of endogenously formed group structures in *games with no spillovers*, where the *no spillover* condition means that for every group of players choosing the same strategy, the payoff of its members is independent of choices made by players outside of the group. An example of an environment satisfying this condition is given by an economy with local public goods where the utility of individuals residing in jurisdiction A would not be affected when another individual moves from jurisdiction B to C.

Within this framework we are interested in which alternatives will be adopted by players and what will be the resulting group structure. The answer to this central question depends, of course, on the restrictions imposed by different stability and equilibrium notions. As our focus here is to study emerging group structures, we shall be interested only in equilibria in pure strategies. The first notion is, naturally, that of a Nash equilibrium of game G. This is the weakest stability notion and can be interpreted as *free mobility*: each player is free to join the group which adopts the alternative she likes best from those offered by the *existing* groups.

Another equilibrium notion examined in this chapter is that of a strong Nash equilibrium introduced by Aumann (1959). Unlike a Nash equilibrium, which is immune only to individual deviations, a strong Nash equilibrium is immune to deviations by any group of players. Using the terminology of Greenberg and Weber (1993), a strong Nash equilibrium requires, in addition to free mobility, *free entry*: every group S of players is free to form and to choose any alternative its members desire. In the context of public goods economies, no new 'city manager' can offer a bundle of public goods that will attract a set of individuals S that will enable her to deliver the promised bundle which would make all individuals in S better off than they currently are. Though it is widely accepted that strong Nash equilibria very rarely exist, we shall show that there are interesting classes of no spillover games which admit a strong Nash equilibrium.

The third notion of equilibrium employed in this chapter is that of a coalition-proof Nash equilibrium. Introduced by Bernheim, Peleg and Whinston (1987), a coalition-proof Nash equilibrium makes use of only credible coalitional deviations. Since its introduction, the notion has become an attractive solution concept in non-cooperative game theory. As Bernheim, Peleg and Whinston point out, the concept of coalition-proof Nash equilibrium

is designed to capture the notion of an efficient self-enforcing agreement for environments with unlimited, but non-binding precommunication. An agreement is coalition-proof if and only if it is Pareto efficient within the class of self-enforcing agreements. In turn, an agreement is self-enforcing if and only if no proper subset (coalition) of players, taking the actions of its complement as fixed, can agree to deviate in a way that makes all its members better off. However, in contrast to the strong equilibrium concept, we do not entertain all possible deviations by such coalitions. Internal consistency requires us to judge the validity of deviations by the same criteria which we use to judge the original agreement – a valid deviation must be self-enforcing, in the sense that no proper sub-coalition can reach a mutually beneficial agreement to deviate from the deviation. Likewise, any potential deviation by a sub-coalition must be judged by the same criterion, and so on.

Although Bernheim, Peleg and Whinston argue that 'Coalition-Proof Nash equilibria certainly exist in a larger number of games than strong Nash equilibria. Further, examination of a number of examples indicates that coalition-proof equilibria do exist quite frequently'; we shall demonstrate that for many classes of no spillover games the sets of coalition-proof and strong Nash equilibria coincide and, in terms of existence, there is no advantage to using a coalition-proof rather than a strong Nash concept.

The main focus of this chapter is to examine those no spillover games where the payoff functions satisfy the *Population monotonicity* property.[1] *Population monotonicity* implies that the payoff of a player changes monotonically when the size of the group of players choosing the same strategy increases. This class of games consists of two types: those with *positive externality* and *negative externality*.

Games with *positive externality* ($\mathcal{PE}$) satisfy the following condition: the payoff of every player i would increase if more players choose a strategy identical to that of i. One of the natural examples which satisfies this condition is an environment with 'network externalities' where the utility that a given user derives from a good depends upon the number of other users who are in the same 'network' as she. Consider, for example, the choice of word processors in a department. If there are many users of *Word*, it might be beneficial to 'join the crowd' and become a *Word* user, a decision to be welcomed by other *Word* users. As Katz and Shapiro (1985) pointed out, there are several possible sources of positive consumption externalities.[2] It could be through a *direct* physical effect of the number of purchasers on the quality of the product, where the utility that a consumer derives from purchasing a telephone, for example, depends on the number of other households or businesses that have joined the telephone network. There may be *indirect* effects that give rise to consumption externalities as well. For example, an individual purchasing a personal computer is affected by the number of other individuals or firms purchasing similar hardware because the amount and variety of software supplied for use with a given computer is usually an increasing function of the number of hardware units that have been sold.

Another natural example of an environment with positive externality and the no spillover condition is a local public goods economy without congestion (Guesnerie and Oddou (1981), Greenberg and Weber (1986)). In such an economy an alternative or strategy represents a public good provision vector or a tax schedule adopted by a jurisdiction, and each player is free to make her residential choice by comparing population composition and policy in each jurisdiction. The conflict between agglomeration and diversification in a large group arises very naturally in the context of an economy with local public goods. Indeed, the cost of provision of a given level of public good declines with the number of residents in the jurisdiction. On the other hand, some residents may regard public education as quite important, while others might put a higher priority on police and fire protection services. The heterogeneity of agents' preferences for public services may explain the emergence of a large number of different jurisdictions in the society.

It turns out that if either the set of alternatives or the set of players consists of two elements, there exists a strong Nash equilibrium (propositions 4.1.1 and 4.1.2). This result, however, cannot be extended to the case where both the number of alternatives and the number of players are more than two. Thus, we introduce two additional assumptions. *Anonymity* ($\mathcal{AN}$) requires that the payoff of each individual depends on the *number* rather than on the *set* of players choosing every alternative. The *Order preservation* property, which, together with anonymity, implies that every player's ranking of any two alternatives x, y remains the same if an equal number of individuals joins the set of players choosing each of these two alternatives. We then prove (proposition 4.1.6) in a no spillover game that anonymity, order preservation and positive externality yield the existence of a Nash equilibrium in pure strategies. We show that this result is tight in the sense that if any of these three conditions is dropped, then the set of pure strategy Nash equilibria of a no spillover game might be empty. We also show (proposition 4.2.1) that the positive externality assumption guarantees the sets of coalition-proof and strong Nash equilibria coincide.

Games with *negative externality* ($\mathcal{N}\mathcal{E}$) represent decreasing returns to size: each player i is worse off if more players make an identical choice to that of i and thus join i's group. An example of an environment satisfying this condition is given by a public goods economy with 'congestion', where agents residing in a certain jurisdiction could be worse off when other individuals move in and consume public goods. A special example of this type of environment is given by the 'highway game' (Rosenthal (1973)), where each driver has to decide which of the existing roads to take while taking into account that her utility is a decreasing function of the number of individuals who choose the same road. 'Congestion games' in biology are another example, where the food supply in every habitat decreases with the number of its users and each individual is free to enter any habitat (see, for example, the experiment of Milinsky (1979) with sticklebacks). Another interesting example, studied by Haltiwanger and Waldman (1985), is a model with two types of agents distinguished by their ability to process information and form expectations: 'sophisticated' and 'naive'. Each agent is faced with the problem of choosing a single path among the given two, where the paths exhibit congestion effects, i.e., for any agent, the higher is the number of other agents who choose the same path as the one chosen by her, the less well off is she.

Propositions 5.1.1, 5.1.2 and 5.2.1 show that under $\mathcal{N}\mathcal{E}$ and $\mathcal{A}\mathcal{N}$, there exists a Nash and even a strong Nash equilibrium, and, moreover, that the sets of coalition-proof and strong Nash equilibria coincide. It is also demonstrated that if either of these two assumptions is violated, then even a pure strategy Nash equilibrium may fail to exist. We also prove that, though a Nash equilibrium fails to exist, there always exists an approximate strong Nash equilibrium in the case where the set of alternatives is an infinite compact set (proposition 5.1.9).

Finally, we consider games for which the population monotonicity assumption is dropped and neither $\mathcal{P}\mathcal{E}$ nor $\mathcal{N}\mathcal{E}$ is satisfied. The natural extension of these conditions is the assumption of the single-peaked preferences with respect to the population size. This would imply that there exists an optimal group size, such that the payoff of each player is increasing with the size of the group as long as it is smaller than the optimal size and is decreasing when it is larger than the optimal size. In other words, the congestion effect becomes a factor only if the group becomes large. It is not surprising that in this case one requires very strong conditions (propositions 6.1, 6.2 and 6.6) in order to guarantee the existence of an equilibrium.

The chapter is organised as follows. In section 2 we present the model.

The definitions of solution concepts employed in this chapter are given in section 3. Section 4 is devoted to games with positive externalities. Subsection 4.1 examines the existence of Nash and strong Nash equilibria and subsection 4.2 deals with the equivalence of the sets of coalition-proof and strong Nash equilibria. In subsection 4.3 we consider a special case of games satisfying *intermediate preferences* property. The *party formation game* is studied in subsection 4.4. Section 5 is devoted to games with negative externalities. Subsection 5.1 examines with the existence of Nash and strong Nash equilibria, and subsection 5.2 deals with the equivalence of the sets of coalition-proof and strong Nash equilibria. In section 6 we study games for which neither positive nor negative externality is satisfied.

2 The model

In order to study different notions of stability of group structures we consider a game in normal form, similar in spirit to that studied by von Neumann and Morgenstern (1944),[3] where players' choices determine their partition into different groups so that players in the given group choose the same strategy. We shall then derive the conditions which yield the existence of a pure strategy Nash equilibrium and its modifications. Let N be a finite set of players and X be a (finite or infinite) set of alternatives, which is assumed to be a compact subset of the m-dimensional Euclidean space $\mathfrak{R}^m (m \geq 1)$.

Each player i in N chooses an alternative x^i from the common strategy set X. The players' choices constitute a strategy profile $\mathrm{x} = (x^1, x^2, \ldots, x^n)$. The set of all strategy profiles is, therefore, given by the product $X^N = X \times X \times \ldots \times X$. Each player $i \in N$ has a preference ordering over strategy profiles which is represented by utility function $U^i : X^N \rightarrow \mathfrak{R}$. The noncooperative game G is therefore represented by the triple (N, X, U) where $U = \{U^i\}_{i \in N}$ is the profile of players' preferences.

It is useful to observe that every strategy profile $\mathrm{x} = (x^1, x^2, \ldots, x^n)$ generates the partition of the set of players N over the alternative set according to their choices at x. Denote this partition by $P(\mathrm{x})$. Since the set of alternatives X is common for all players, we may represent this partition as

$$P(\mathrm{x}) = (N_x(\mathrm{x}))_{x \in X}$$

where for each $x \in X$, $N_x(\mathrm{x})$ denotes the collection of those players who choose alternative x under the strategy profile x. Obviously, the partition $P(\mathrm{x})$ is uniquely determined by the strategy profile x. It is important to note that the correspondence between strategy profiles and the associated partitions is one-to-one, and from given partition $P(\mathrm{x})$ one can reproduce the strategy profile x.

We shall restrict our attention to *no spillover* games, where for each player

i her payoff is not affected by the choices of players which are different from her strategy x^i. That is, if the choice of player j, x^j is different from x^i, the payoff of i would not be affected if j switches her choice to any alternative x different from x^i. Formally, for any strategy profiles $\mathbf{x}, \mathbf{y} \in X^N$ and an alternative $x \in X$ such that $N_x(\mathbf{x}) = N_x(\mathbf{y}) \neq \emptyset$, the payoff of every player $i \in N_x(\mathbf{x})$ is the same at $\mathbf{x}$ and $\mathbf{y}$, that is, $U^i(\mathbf{x}) = U^i(\mathbf{y})$. It is useful to note that no spillover games allow for the following representation of the payoff function of player i when she chooses alternative x given the strategy profile $\mathbf{x}$

$$u^i(\mathbf{x}) = u^i(x, N_x(\mathbf{x}))$$

We assume that for each player $i \in N$ and every coalition S which contains i, the payoff function $u^i(\cdot, S)$ is continuous with respect to the first argument. We shall impose this continuity assumption, which is trivially satisfied if the set of alternatives X is finite, through the rest of the chapter.

Many of the results described below employ the *anonymity* assumption which requires the utility of individual i to depend only on her strategy and the number of individuals who choose the same alternative. That is, the payoff of each individual depends on the 'aggregate' or 'average' action of all other players (see Schmeidler (1973), Mas-Colell (1984) and Green (1984)). The anonymity assumption implies that for any three different players, i, j and k, the payoff of player i would not be affected if k and j switch their strategies while all other individuals do not alter their choices!

Assumption: *Anonymity* $(\mathcal{AN})$ *Let* $\mathbf{x} = (x^1, \ldots, x^n)$ *and* $\mathbf{y} = (y^1, \ldots, y^n)$ *be two strategy profiles such that* $|N(z, \mathbf{x})| = |N(z, \mathbf{y})|$ *for all* $z \in X$, *where* $|A|$ *stands for the cardinality of the set* A. *Then for each* $i \in N$ *with* $x^i = y^i$ *we have* $U^i(\mathbf{x}) = U^i(\mathbf{y})$.

The anonymity assumption implies that the payoff function of player i when she chooses alternative x given the strategy profile $\mathbf{x}$ can be represented by

$$U^i(\mathbf{x}) = u^i(x, |N_x(\mathbf{x})|)$$

The next two assumptions play the crucial role in our analysis as they specify how the payoff of player i making the choice x^i would be affected when the set of players choosing x^i is expanded. One possible effect is that of a *positive externality*, which requires that player i's payoff increases if another player j, who previously chose $x^j \neq x^i$, changes her strategy to x^i:

Assumption: *Positive Externality* $(\mathcal{PE})$ *For any two players* $i, j \in N$, *for any subset of players* $S \subset N$ *with* $i \in S$, $j \notin S$ *and alternative* $x \in X$, *we have* $u^i(x, S) \leq u^i(x, S \cup \{j\})$.

Another possibility is the *negative externality* case, where the payoff of any player i declines when an additional player j chooses player i's strategy:

Assumption: *Negative Externality* $(\mathcal{NE})$ *For any two players* $i,j \in N$, *for any subset of players* $S \subset N$ *with* $i \in S$, $j \notin S$ *and alternative* $x \in X$, *we have* $u^i(x,S) \geq u^i(x,S \cup \{j\})$.

3 Solution concepts

Let us now introduce some notation. For each vector of strategies $\mathbf{x} \in X^N$ and each coalition $S \subset N$ denote by $\mathbf{x}^S = (x^i)_{i \in S} \in X^S$ and $\mathbf{x}^{N \setminus S} = (x^i)_{i \in N \setminus S} \in X^{N \setminus S}$, the vector of strategies of players in S and outside of S, respectively. Thus, for every $\mathbf{x}^S = (x^i)_{i \in S} \in X^S$ and $\mathbf{y}^{N \setminus S} = (y^i)_{i \in N \setminus S} \in X^{N \setminus S}$, the strategy profile $(\mathbf{x}^S, \mathbf{y}^{N \setminus S})$ assigns the strategy x^i to every $i \in S$ and the strategy x^i to every $i \in N \setminus S$. If S is a singleton, say, $S = \{i\}$, then for every $x \in X$ and $\mathbf{y} \in X^{N \setminus \{i\}}$, we simply write $(x, \mathbf{y}^{N \setminus \{i\}})$ instead of $(\mathbf{x}^S, \mathbf{y}^{N \setminus \{i\}})$. We shall focus on the notions of a pure strategy Nash equilibrium and its refinements. A Nash equilibrium represents a relatively weak stability requirement which, in the context of a local public goods economy, for example, would correspond to a vector of individuals' residential choices so that no one would find it beneficial to move to another jurisdiction. Since our primary interest is in the study of group structures generated by unambiguous pure strategy individual decisions (such as jurisdictional choice or selection of word processor), we consider in this chapter Nash equilibria in pure strategies only. As usual:

Definition 3.1: *A strategy profile* $\mathbf{x} = (x^1, x^2, \ldots, x^n)$ *is a Nash equilibrium of game* G *if* $U^i(\mathbf{x}) \geq U^i(y, \mathbf{x}^{N \setminus \{i\}})$ *for each* $i \in N$ *and each* $y \in X$. *The set of all Nash equilibria of the game* G *is denoted by* $\mathcal{NE}(G)$.

We shall also make use of the notion of a strong Nash equilibrium, which states that a n-tuple of strategies x is a strong Nash equilibrium if there is no group of individuals which can benefit each of its members by deviating from x. Since a strong Nash equilibrium is immune to any group deviation, it is a much stronger equilibrium concept than a Nash equilibrium which allows only for individual deviations. To recall:

Definition 3.2: *A strategy profile* $\mathbf{x} = (x^1, x^2, \ldots, x^n)$ *is a strong Nash equilibrium of game* G *if for any subset* S *of* N *and any strategy profile* $y \in X^S$ *there exists a player* $j \in S$ *such that such* $U^i(\mathbf{x}) \leq U^i(\mathbf{y}^S, \mathbf{x}^{N \setminus S})$. *The set of all Nash equilibria of the game* G *is denoted by* $S\mathcal{NE}(G)$.

We shall also consider the notion of a *coalition-proof Nash equilibrium*, denoted $\mathscr{CPNE}$. The novelty of the concept of $\mathscr{CPNE}$ is highlighted by the fact that is immune only to *credible* coalitional deviations. This is in contrast to a strong Nash equilibrium which is immune to *any* coalitional deviation.

To introduce the notion of a coalition-proof Nash equilibrium, for each coalition S and each vector of strategies $x \in X^N$ define a reduced game G_x^S:

Definition 3.3: *For each coalition $S \subset N$ and each vector of strategies* $=(x^i)_{i \in N} \in X^N$, *a reduced game for S at x, denoted G_x^S, is the triple* $(S, X, (U^i(\cdot, x^{N\backslash S})_{i \in S}))$. *In other words, the reduced game for S at x is restricted to members of S only, assuming that players outside of S would still choose the strategies given by vector x.*

We are now in position to recall the recursive definition of coalition-proof Nash equilibrium:

Definition 3.4: A coalition-proof Nash equilibrium of game G *is defined recursively:*
(1) *In a one-player game, $x \in X$ is a coalition-proof Nash equilibrium if $h^i(x) \geq h^i(y)$ for any $y \in X$.*
Let the number of players n be greater than 1. Suppose that the notion of coalition-proof Nash equilibrium has been defined for any game with fewer than n players. Then:
(2) *For any G with n players, a vector of strategies $x \in X^N$ is* self-enforcing *in G if for all subsets S of N, $S \neq N$, x^S is a coalition-proof Nash equilibrium of the reduced game G_x^S;*
(3) *For any game G with n players, x is a coalition-proof Nash equilibrium of the game G if $x \in X^N$ is self-enforcing and there is no other self-enforcing vector of strategies $y \in X^N$ such that $U^i(y) > U^i(x)$ for every $i \in N$.*
The set of all coalition-proof Nash equilibria of the game G is denoted by $\mathscr{CPNE}(G)$.

Obviously, the three notions of equilibria introduced in this section are linked by the following set inclusion $\mathscr{SNE}(G) \subset \mathscr{CPNE}(G) \subset \mathscr{NE}(G)$

4 Positive externality

In this section we study a subclass of environments, satisfying *positive externality*, which reflects increasing returns to the size of groups, i.e., each player would enjoy a higher payoff from a given alternative in a larger group.

4.1 Existence

First we consider the cases where either the set of pure strategies for each player consists of two alternatives, as in many models with network externalities (Farrell and Saloner (1985,1988), Tirole (1988), Arthur (1989)), or the game contains only two players. We show then that the $\mathcal{PE}$ assumption alone guarantees the existence not only of a Nash equilibrium but even a strong Nash equilibrium. The results are quite strong since they yield the existence of a stable group structure while using a very demanding notion of stability:

Proposition 4.1.1: (Konishi/Le Breton/Weber (1997c) *Let $|X|=2$. Under $\mathcal{PE}$, the game G admits a strong Nash equilibrium.*

Proposition 4.1.2: *Let $N=2$. Under $\mathcal{PE}$, the game G admits a strong Nash equilibrium.*

Proof of proposition 4.1.2: Let $N=\{1,2\}$. We shall show first that the game G admits a Nash equilibrium. Continuity of the payoff functions $u^i(\cdot,S)$ for all coalitions S containing i and compactness of X imply that there exist alternatives x^1 and x^2 which maximise the payoff of players 1 and 2, respectively, when the other player makes a different choice, i.e., $x^1=\arg\max_{x\in X} u^1(x,\{1\})$ and $x^2=\arg\max_{x\in X} u^2(x,\{2\})$. If $u^1(x^1,\{1\})\geq u^1(x^2,N)$ and $u^2(x^2,\{2\})\geq u^2(x^1,N)$ then the pair (x^1,x^2) is, obviously, a Nash equilibrium. Suppose now that at least one of these two inequalities is violated, say, $u^1(x^1,\{1\})<u^1(x^2,N)$, then (x^2,x^2) is a Nash equilibrium.

Now take any Nash equilibrium **x**. If it is strong we are done. Suppose, therefore, that the strategy profile **x** is not strong. Since it guarantees each player i at least her 'individually rational level' $u^i(x^i,\{i\})$, the profile **x** is Pareto dominated by another profile at which both players choose the same alternative, i.e., the set $\overline{X}=\{x\in X|u^i(x,N)>U^i(\mathbf{x})i=1,2\}$ is non-empty. Define $y=\arg\max_{z\in\overline{X}} u^1(z,N)$. Continuity of the payoff functions and compactness of X guarantee that y is well-defined. Since every strategy profile in $\overline{X}$ guarantees both players their individually rational levels, $\mathcal{PE}$ implies that the profile (y,y) is not a strong Nash equilibrium if and only if there is an alternative $z\in X$ with $u^i(z,N)>u^i(y,N)$ for $i=1,2$. This would imply that there is an alternative $z\in\overline{X}$ with $u^1(z,N)>u^1(y,N)$, a contradiction to the choice of y. Thus, the strategy profile (y,y) is, indeed, a strong Nash equilibrium.□

However, propositions 4.1.1 and 4.1.2 cannot be extended to the case where the set of alternatives and set of players each contain more than two elements. Indeed, consider the following game with three players and three alternatives:

Example 4.1.3: *The set of players is given by* $N = \{1,2,3\}$, *and the set of alternatives is given by* $X = \{a,b,c\}$. *The players' payoff functions satisfy the anonymity assumption* $\mathcal{AN}$, $\mathcal{PE}$ *and, in addition, the following inequalities:*

$$u^1(b,2) > u^1(a,2) > u^1(a,1) > u^1(b,1) > u^1(c,3);$$

$$u^2(c,2) > u^2(b,2) > u^2(b,1) > u^2(c,1) > u^2(a,3);$$

$$u^3(a,2) > u^3(c,2) > u^3(c,1) > u^3(a,1) > u^3(b,3).$$

Then the game G does not admit a Nash equilibrium.

Proof: Suppose, in negation that game G in this example possesses Nash equilibrium (x^1, x^2, x^3). Since player 1 would never choose c, it suffices to consider two cases: $x^1 = a$ and $x^1 = b$.

Let $x^1 = a$. Then player 3 also chooses a whereas player 2 would consequently choose b. The triple (a,b,a) is not, however, a Nash equilibrium as player 1 would be better off by switching to b.

Let $x^1 = b$. Then either player 2 or 3 chooses b, too. (Otherwise, player 1 would select a.) Thus $x^2 = b$, and, consequently, $x^3 = c$. However, the strategy profile (b,b,c) is not a Nash equilibrium as player 2 would rather switch to c. Thus, there is no Nash equilibrium in this game. $\square$

This rather simple example shows that one has to impose much more demanding conditions to guarantee the existence of a Nash equilibrium in games with more than two players and more than two alternatives. One of the features of example 4.1.3 is that the players' preferences do not satisfy *order-invariance* which requires that every player i would make the same choice over any two alternatives x, y as long as the set of players choosing these alternatives is the same. Indeed, player 1 would prefer a over b if alone but shall reverse her choice if each alternative is chosen by two players. In the context of the example of a word processor choice in the department, mentioned in the introduction, order invariance implies that if an individual prefers *Word* over *Word Perfect* when she is the only word processor user, then she would still prefer *Word* over *Word Perfect* if both processors are used by the same group of faculty members. Formally:

Assumption: *Order-Invariance* ($\mathcal{OI}$) *For any player* $i \in N$, *for any* $S \subset N$ *with* $i \in S$ *and any two alternatives* $x, y \in X$, *the inequality* $u^i(x,S) \geq u^i(y,S)$ *holds if and only if* $u^i(x,\{i\}) \geq u^i(y,\{i\})$.

292   Hideo Konishi, Michel Le Breton and Shlomo Weber

Note that the $\mathcal{OS}$ is stronger than the no spillover condition. Thus, the set of games satisfying $\mathcal{OS}$ belongs to the class of no spillover games.

One may point out that the players' preferences in our example fail to satisfy *single-peakedness* which is commonly used in local public good economies where the individuals' preferences are often assumed to be single-peaked with the respect to the quantities of public goods produced in a given jurisdiction.

Definition 4.1.4: *Let ordering $\leqslant$ on the set of alternatives X be given. The preferences of player $i \in N$ are* singled-peaked *with respect to $\leqslant$ if for $S \subset N$ with $i \in S$, there exists an alternative x_S^i such that for any pair of alternatives x, $y \in X$ with either $x \leqslant y \leqslant x_S^i$ or $x \geqslant y \geqslant x_S^i$ it follows that $u^i(x,S) \leqslant u^i(y,S) \leqslant u^i(x_S^i,S)$. The preferences of players $i \in N$ are* singled-peaked *if there exists an ordering $\leqslant^*$ on X such that the preferences of every player $i \in N$ are singled-peaked with respect to $\leqslant^*$ over the set of alternatives X.*

Assumption: *Single-Peakedness ($\mathcal{SP}$) The preferences of all players are single-peaked.*

It turns out, however, that even assumptions $\mathcal{PE}$, $\mathcal{AN}$, $\mathcal{SP}$ and $\mathcal{OS}$ do not guarantee the existence of a Nash equilibrium. Indeed:

Proposition 4.1.5: (Konishi, Le Breton and Weber (1997c)) *There is a game G with six players and three alternatives, satisfying $\mathcal{PE}$, $\mathcal{AN}$, $\mathcal{SP}$ and $\mathcal{OS}$, which does not admit a Nash equilibrium.*

Thus, assuming that $\mathcal{PE}$, $\mathcal{AN}$ and $\mathcal{SP}$ hold, the condition $\mathcal{OS}$ does not yield the existence of a Nash equilibrium. One needs, therefore, to introduce an even stronger condition than $\mathcal{OS}$ on the individuals' preferences. The condition we employ here is that of *Order preservation* which implies that if player i prefers alternative x to alternative y when players in N_x choose x and players in N_y choose y, then she would still prefer x over y if N_x and N_y are both expanded by an additional player j. Similarly, she would still prefer x over y if a common player k withdraws from both N_x and N_y. To compare $\mathcal{OP}$ with $\mathcal{OS}$ recall that $\mathcal{OS}$ is equivalent to the following condition: for any $i, j \in N$, for any $S \subset N$ with $i \in S$ and $j \notin S$ for any two alternatives $x, y \in X$, $u^i(x,S) \geqslant u^i(y,S)$ if and only if $u^i(x,S \cup \{j\}) \geqslant u^i(y,S \cup \{j\})$. $\mathcal{OP}$ strengthens this requirement by removing the requirement that the coalitions on two sides of the inequality are the same:

Assumption: *Order Preservation ($\mathcal{OP}$) For any $i, j \in N$, for any S, $T \subset N$ with $i \in S \cap T$ and $j \notin S \cup T$, for any two alternatives $x, y \in X$, $u^i(x,S) \geqslant u^i(y,T)$ if and only if $u^i(x,S \cup \{j\}) \geqslant u^i(y,T \cup \{j\})$.*

As we mentioned above, setting $S = T$ for $\mathcal{OP}$ implies that $\mathcal{OP}$ is stronger than $\mathcal{OS}$. In fact, $\mathcal{OP}$ together with $\mathcal{AN}$ implies that, for any three positive integers l, m and r, whenever player i prefers alternative x chosen by l players over alternative y chosen by m players, then she would still prefer x chosen by $l+r$ players over y chosen by $m+r$ players.

The main result of this subsection is:

Proposition 4.1.6: (Konishi, Le Breton and Weber (1997c)) *Under* $\mathcal{PE}$, $\mathcal{AN}$ *and* $\mathcal{OP}$, *the game G admits a Nash equilibrium.*

Note that we do not impose single-peakedness of individuals' preferences, which is frequently used in order to prove the existence of an equilibrium in local public good economies and models of multiparty electoral spatial competition.

The proof of this proposition consists of two major steps. The first takes advantage of the result, due to Konishi and Fishburn (1996), implying that assumptions $\mathcal{PE}$, $\mathcal{AN}$ and $\mathcal{OP}$ allow for a convenient quasi-linear utility representation of each player i's payoff function. We then construct a real-valued function on the set of strategy profiles so that every local maximum of this function (the existence of which is guaranteed by our assumptions) corresponds to a Nash equilibrium of the game G. The method of the proof of the second part of proposition 4.1.5 is similar to the one used by Rosenthal (1973) who introduced the class of 'potential games' studied in Monderer and Shapley (1996). It is also important to note that this technique could be used to prove the existence of a Nash equilibrium in games with a more general class of players' preferences (see Konishi, Le Breton and Weber (1997d) for their study of economies with club or local public goods).

Proposition 4.1.5 shows that a Nash equilibrium might fail to exist if $\mathcal{OP}$ is relaxed. Konishi, Le Breton and Weber (1997c) have also pointed out that the same situation may occur if the anonymity assumption $\mathcal{AN}$ is dropped:

Proposition 4.1.7: (Konishi, Le Breton and Weber (1997c)) *There is a game G with six players and three alternatives, satisfying $\mathcal{PE}$, $\mathcal{SP}$ and $\mathcal{OP}$, which does not admit a Nash equilibrium.*

The next question which arises naturally is whether, similarly to Greenberg and Weber (1986,1993), the existence of a strong Nash equilibrium is guaranteed under the same assumptions which yield the existence of a Nash equilibrium. Weber and Zamir (1985) show that in the second-best local public good economy of Guesnerie and Oddou (1981) a strong Nash equilibrium may fail to exist.[4] Since the Weber and Zamir example violates $\mathcal{OP}$ there is still a question whether the condition $\mathcal{OP}$, together with $\mathcal{AN}$, $\mathcal{PE}$ and $\mathcal{SP}$, would yield an existence of a strong Nash equilibrium. The negative answer to this question is given by the following:

Proposition 4.1.8: (Konishi, Le Breton and Weber (1997c)) *There is a game G with seven players and three alternatives, satisfying $\mathcal{PE}$, $\mathcal{AN}$, $\mathcal{SP}$ and $\mathcal{OP}$, which does not admit a strong Nash equilibrium.*

4.2 *Equivalence of $\mathcal{CPNE}$ and $\mathcal{SNE}$*

Regardless of its appeal, the restrictions on coalitional deviations imposed by $\mathcal{CPNE}$ have come under certain criticism. As indicated by Ehud Kalai (Greenberg (1989)):

The concept of $\mathcal{CPNE}$ does not go far enough in its analysis of stability. When considering a deviating coalition, the validity of the deviation is checked against further deviations of subcoalitions of the deviating coalition. However, members of the deviating coalitions could also deviate by convincing other players (from non-deviating coalitions) to deviate provided they improve their payoff. In other words, the concept may not go far enough.

Bernheim, Peleg and Whinston (1987) were aware of the limitations of the $\mathcal{CPNE}$ concept:

when deviation occurs, only members of the deviating coalition may contemplate deviations from the deviation. This rules out the possibility that some member of the deviating coalition might form a pact to deviate further with someone not included in this coalition. Such arrangements are clearly much more complex than those made entirely by the members of coalition itself. In particular, coalition members have observed the original deviation firsthand. In contrast, nonmembers lack verifiable information on prior deviations. At times, the willingness of some party to form a coalition may reveal his agreement to some prior deviation (in the absence of a prior deviation, it would not be in his interests to join the coalition) but may identify that deviation. Similarly, the unwillingness of some party to join a coalition may also be informative. Further, there may be times when one player wishes to convince another that a prior deviation exists, in order to secure cooperation in deviating further. Implicitly, we assume that these information problems cripple any attempt to form coalitions consisting of both members and nonmembers from some other deviating coalition. Clearly, further work is required to resolve this issues in a fully satisfactory way.

In this subsection we demonstrate that this criticism does not apply to an important class of games with positive externalities by showing the equivalence of the sets of its coalition-proof and strong Nash equilibria. We have the following result:

Proposition 4.2.1: (Konishi, Le Breton and Weber (1997b)) $\mathcal{PE}$ *implies the equivalence of the sets $\mathcal{SNE}(G)$ and $\mathcal{CPNE}(G)$.*

Proposition 4.2.1 is an extension of theorem 3 in Greenberg and Weber (1993), who studied a model of political economy with *free mobility* (see subsection 4.4). Since their feasible agenda correspondence satisfies a *monotonicity* property and the payoff function of individual i, U^i, depends only on the agenda chosen by her party, $\mathcal{PE}$ is satisfied in the Greenberg and Weber (1993) model. This assumption is also satisfied in economies with public goods (Kalai, Postlewaite and Roberts (1979), Greenberg and Weber (1986)), voting models (Greenberg and Weber (1985)), industrial organisation models (Demange and Henriet (1991), Demange (1994)). Although not all these papers examine normal form games, proposition 4.2.1 could be used to establish the equivalence of coalition-proof and strong Nash equilibria for non-cooperative games associated with these models.

Proposition 4.2.1 is also related to the Borm and Tijs (1992) and Borm, Otten and Peters (1992) analysis of strong and coalition-proof implementability of the core of NTU (cooperative) games by using strategic claim games introduced in Borm and Tijs (1992). Borm, Otten and Peters (1993) also prove the equivalence of $\mathcal{CPNE}$ and $\mathcal{SNE}$ in strategic claim games. To relate proposition 4.2.1 to their results, construct a *(modified) strategic claim game*. First let an NTU game (N,V) be given, where N is the set of players and V is a mapping which assigns to each coalition $S \in 2^N \setminus \{\emptyset\}$ a non-empty, bounded from above, and closed subset $V(S)$ of $\mathfrak{R}^S$. For each player $i \in N$ denote by $v_i = \max\{t | t \in V(\{i\})\}$ the so-called 'individually rational' payoff each player can guarantee to herself. Let $\Omega^c = 2^N \setminus \{\emptyset\}$ be the set of all non-empty coalitions. Each player's strategy is a $2n$-dimensional vector which, for every player $i \in N$, contains both the non-negative payoff and the assignment to one of the coalitions. Thus, the (common) strategy set for each player can be represented by $X = \Pi_{i \in N}(X^c \times \mathfrak{R}_+)$. Let the representative element of Ω be $x^i = (S_1^i, t_1^i, S_2^i, t_2^i, \ldots, S_n^i, t_n^i)$, where S_j^i and t_j^i represent the assignment and payoff, respectively, offered to player j by player i and let $\mathbf{x} = (x^1, x^2, \ldots x^n)$. Player i enjoys her own offer t_i^i if and only if she assigns herself to the coalition of which she is a member, all the members of that coalition choose the same strategy and the offered payoffs are feasible in terms of the game (N,V). Otherwise the player i receives the minimum either t_i^i or her individually rational payoff v_i, whichever is less. That is, for each $i \in N$, the payoff function U^i is given by:

$$U^i(x) = \begin{cases} t_i^i & \text{if} \\ \min\{t_i^i, v_i\} & \text{otherwise} \end{cases} \quad i \in S_i^i, x^i = x^j \text{ for all } j \in S_i^i \text{ and}$$

$$(t_j^i)_{j \in S} \in V(S_i^i)$$

Obviously, $\mathcal{P}\mathcal{E}$ is satisfied. Since this modified strategic claim game and the strategic claim game in the Borm and Tijs paper yield the same equilibrium payoffs (the sets of $\mathcal{S}\mathcal{N}\mathcal{E}$ and $\mathcal{C}\mathcal{P}\mathcal{N}\mathcal{E}$ generated by these two games are the same), the equivalence results of Borm, Otten and Peters (theorem 4) and Wako (1994) in a model with indivisible goods can essentially be obtained from proposition 4.2.1.

4.3 Intermediate preferences

It is important to mention that all assumptions in this chapter are imposed directly on individual preferences and we do not impose any conditions on the *profiles* of individuals' preferences. In our view, given a specific economic or political environment, it would be more convenient to verify the applicability of our results by simply checking whether the preferences of every individual satisfy positive externality, anonymity or other assumptions rather than deal with intricate conditions on profiles of preferences.

We would like however to briefly survey a technique employed in the brand of literature which mainly deals with the existence of stable coalition structures by imposing various restrictions on profiles of preferences. First, Guesnerie and Oddou (1981) have derived the conditions on profiles of individuals' preferences which yield the existence of the core of the associated game in characteristic function form. Greenberg and Weber (1986) prove the existence of a strong Nash equilibrium in a game with linearly ordered players whose preferences satisfy a kind of *single crossing property*. Demange (1994) considered a more general framework where the hierarchical structure of the game is represented by a *tree* rather than a straight line as in the Greenberg and Weber (1986) model. In addition, the existence of a strong Nash equilibrium for various classes of games, satisfying $\mathcal{P}\mathcal{E}$, has been studied by Greenberg and Weber (1985) and (1993) in voting models, Demange and Henriet (1991), Demange (1994) in industrial organisation and location models, and Wako (1994) in a market with indivisible goods. In most of these papers the existence of a strong Nash equilibrium was linked to the non-emptiness of the core of a NTU cooperative game derived from the original normal form game. It is worthwhile pointing out that a similar technique has been used by Ichiishi (1993) to derive sufficient conditions for existence of a strong Nash equilibrium.

To illustrate the application of that technique consider a normal form game G, satisfying $\mathcal{P}\mathcal{E}$, given by the triple $(N, X, (u^i)_{i \in N})$, where $N = \{1, 2, \ldots, n\}$ is a finite set of players, X is a common strategy set for all players, $u^i : X \times S_i \to \Re$ is the payoff function of player $i \in N$, and S_i denotes the set of all coalitions containing player i. Assumption $\mathcal{P}\mathcal{E}$ implies that for each i, the function u^i is increasing in the second argument with respect to inclusion. Let us construct the following coalitional form game without side payments (N, V), where the characteristic function of V is given by

$$V(S) = \{z \in \mathbf{R}^N | \exists x \in X \text{ s.t. } u^i(x,S) \geq z^i \forall i \in S\}$$

for each non-empty coalition $S \subset N$. The game (N, V) is not necessarily super-additive. To introduce the superadditive cover of this game, denote by $\mathcal{P}(S)$ the set of all partitions of S. For each partition $P = (S_1, \ldots, S_K) \in \mathcal{P}(S)$, let V^P (S) be the intersection of all $V(S_k)$, $k = 1, \ldots, K$, i.e.

$$V^P(S) = \bigcap_{k=1}^{K} V(S_k)$$

Then the superadditive cover of the game (N, V), denoted by $(N, \overline{V})$ is defined by

$$\overline{V}(S) = \bigcup_{P \in \mathcal{P}(S)} V^P(S)$$

It is straightforward to verify that the non-emptiness of the core of the cooperative game $(N, \overline{V})$ yields the existence of a strong Nash equilibrium of the game G. Thus, one may use sufficient conditions for non-emptiness of the core of a cooperative game in order to derive the existence of a strong Nash equilibrium. In particular, if the game $(N, \overline{V})$ is balanced, by Scarf's theorem (1967), its core is non-empty.

It is well known, however, that the balancedness condition is too demanding for the existence of the core as reflected for instance in some studies of strong Nash equilibria of normal form voting games (e.g., Peleg (1984)). We would like now to briefly present an approach that combines arguments from cooperative game theory with other techniques. Let $\mathcal{C}$ be a non-empty family of coalitions which contains all one-person coalitions. For any coalition S, denote by $\mathcal{P}_{\mathcal{C}}(S)$ the set of all partitions of S into elements of $\mathcal{C}$. Define the game $(N, \overline{V}_{\mathcal{C}})$ by

$$\overline{V}_{\mathcal{C}}(S) = \bigcup_{P \in \mathcal{P}_{\mathcal{C}}(S)} V^P(S)$$

Given the family of coalitions $\mathcal{C}$, the natural question is whether the core of the game $\overline{V}_{\mathcal{C}}$ is non-empty. Kaneko and Wooders (1982) and Le Breton, Owen and Weber (1992) have derived the necessary and sufficient conditions to yield the non-emptiness of the core of the game $\overline{V}_{\mathcal{P}}$.

Consider, for instance, the case where the family of coalitions $\mathcal{P}$ has the 'no holes' property, namely, a coalition S belongs to C if and only if for every three players $i < j < k, i, k \in S$ implies $j \in S$. It has been shown (Greenberg and Weber (1986)) that in this case the core of the game $\overline{V}_{\mathcal{C}}$ is non-empty regardless of V. Since deviations by coalitions outside of $\mathcal{C}$ are ruled out, this type of result can not be used to directly obtain the existence of a strong Nash equilibrium. However, it is interesting to point out that any core imputation of the game $\overline{V}_{\mathcal{G}}$ induces a strong Nash equilibrium of the game G if the following 'intermediate preferences' property (called 'consecutiveness' in Greenberg and Weber (1986)), is satisfied:

Assumption: *Intermediate Preferences* $(\mathcal{IP})$ *For every three players $i<j<k$, two coalitions S, T with $i,j,k \in N\backslash(S\cup T)$, and two alternatives $x,y \in X$ the following two inequalities*

$$u^i(x,S\cup\{i\})>u^i(y,T\cup\{i\}) \text{ and } u^k(x,S\cup\{k\})>u^k(y,T\cup\{k\})$$

imply

$$u^j(x,S\cup\{j\})>u^j(x,T\cup\{j\})$$

Then

Proposition 4.3.1: (Greenberg and Weber (1986)) *Under $\mathcal{PE}$ and $\mathcal{IP}$, the game G admits a strong Nash equilibrium.*

The interpretation of this result is that if there exists a *single* parameter that orders individuals' preferences, then the $\mathcal{PE}$ yields the existence of a strong Nash equilibrium. The ranking of individuals obviously depends on the particular model and could be chosen according to income, marginal utility of money, degree of risk aversion, etc.

4.4 Party formation game

An interesting class of non-cooperative 'party formation' games was studied in Greenberg and Weber (1985, 1993). In their model the set of feasible alternatives of every group of players would expand with an increase in the number of its members. The feasibility constraints are given by the correspondence ϕ which assigns to each non-empty subset of N, S, a subset of X, denoted by $\phi(S)$, which consists of alternatives available to members of S, if and when S forms. This framework includes, in particular, all *simple games*. Indeed, such games are characterised by a set of *winning coalitions*, W, and the set of feasible alternatives, $\phi(S)$, available to coalition S is given by

$$\phi(S)=\begin{cases}X & \text{if } S \text{ belongs to } W \\ \varnothing & \text{if } S \text{ does not belong to } W\end{cases}$$

Thus, a winning coalition can choose, for its members, any alternative in X it desires, while a non-winning coalition 'has no say' whatsoever.

To define the players' payoffs, assume that for each $i \in N$ there exists a continuous utility function $h^i : X \to \Re$ over the set of alternatives X. Compactness of X implies that we may assume, without loss of generality, that $h^i(x) > 0$ for every $i \in N$ and $x \in X$. Thus, given the strategy profile $\mathbf{x} = (x^1, x^2, \ldots, x^n)$, the payoff of player i is determined by

$$u^i(x^i, N_{x^i}(\mathbf{x})) = \begin{cases} h^i(x^i) & \text{if } x^i \in \phi(N_{x^i}(\mathbf{x})) \\ 0 & \text{if } x^i \notin \phi(N_{x^i}(\mathbf{x})) \end{cases}$$

That is, if alternative x^i is feasible for the group of players $N_{x^i}(\mathbf{x})$ who choose it in the strategy profile $\mathbf{x}$ all players in $N_{x^i}(\mathbf{x})$ derive positive utility level, $h^i(x^i)$, otherwise, all of them obtain zero utility levels. Thus, the players' utilities are not directly affected by the number of players in a group, although the set of players choosing a given alternative affects its feasibility. We assume that the correspondence ϕ is (weakly) monotone, that is, if an alternative x is feasible for a coalition S, then it also feasible for all coalitions that contain S:

Assumption: *Monotonicity of Feasibility Correspondence ($\mathcal{MFC}$) If $S \subset T \subset N$ and $x \in \phi(S)$, then $x \in \phi(T)$. Moreover, $\phi(N)$ coincides with the set of alternatives X and for each $S \subset N$, $\phi(S)$ is a closed subset of X.*

Obviously, under $\mathcal{MFC}$, the Greenberg and Weber model is a special case of the games with positive externalities examined in this chapter.

The first result in this subsection makes use of *Anonymity of Feasibility correspondence* assumption:

Assumption: *Anonymity of Feasibility Correspondence ($\mathcal{AFC}$) For every coalition S and every two players i, j with $i \in S$ and $j \notin S$ and every alternative $x \in X$, $x \in \phi(S)$ implies $x \in \phi(T)$ where $T = (S \cup \{j\}) \setminus \{i\}$.*

That is, if an alternative x is feasible for coalition S then it should be feasible for coalition T where a member of S is replaced by a non-member of S. In other words, the feasibility correspondence is anonymous and depends only on the *number of players* who choose a given alternative. The example of an environment satisfying this assumption is 'the fixed standard method' (Greenberg and Weber (1985)), where there is an exogenously given quota, m, such that a group of voters is recognised as 'a political party' if and only if it contains at least m members and a political party is free to adopt any position it wishes.

We have

Proposition 4.4.1: $\mathcal{MFC}$ *and* $\mathcal{AFC}$ *yield the existence of a Nash equilibrium of the party formation game G.*

Proof: Denote by $\overline{X}$ the set of those alternatives in X which are feasible for a single player, or, equivalently, by $\mathscr{AFC}$, for every single player

$$\overline{X} = \{x \in X \mid x \in \phi(\{i\}) \text{ for all } i \in N\}$$

Suppose first that the set $\overline{X}$ is empty. Compactness of the set $\phi(N)$ and continuity of the function $h^1(\cdot)$ imply that there is a top alternative y for player 1, i.e., $y = \arg \max_{z \in X} h^i(y)\}$. Consider the strategy profile $\mathbf{y}$ which assigns y to every player. Then no player would deviate from $\mathbf{x}$, since the emptiness of $\overline{X}$ implies that no alternative would be feasible for a single player. Suppose now that the set $\overline{X}$ is non-empty. By $\mathscr{AFC}$, the set $\overline{X}$ coincides with $\phi(\{i\})$ for every $i \in N$ and, hence, is compact. For each player i denote $x^i = \arg \max_{x \in \overline{X}} h^i(x)$ for each $i \in N$. Then the strategy profile $\mathbf{x} = (x^1, \dots, x^n)$ is a Nash equilibrium. Indeed, every player i may switch to any alternative in $\overline{X}$ but since x^i is her optimal choice, she would not benefit by deviating from $\mathbf{x}$.$\square$

Let us show now that if $\mathscr{AFC}$ is dropped then a Nash equilibrium of the party formation game may fail to exist:

Example 4.4.2: *Consider the party formation game G with three players $N = \{1,2,3\}$ and three alternatives $X = \{x,y,z\}$, which satisfies*

$$h^1(x) > h^1(y) > h^1(z)$$

$$h^2(y) > h^2(z) > h^2(x)$$

$$h^3(z) > h^3(x) > h^3(y)$$

and whose feasibility correspondence is given by

$x \in \phi(S)$ *iff player 3 belongs to S*

$y \in \phi(S)$ *iff player 1 belongs to S*

$z \in \phi(S)$ *iff player 2 belongs to S*

Then the game G does not admit a Nash equilibrium. (Obviously, $\mathscr{MFC}$ holds whereas $\mathscr{AFC}$ does not. Indeed, alternative x is feasible for player 3 but not feasible for player 1.)

Proof: Note that for each player her second-best alternative is feasible and each alternative in X is the worst for some player. Thus, a strategy profile, for which all players are assigned the same alternative, cannot be a Nash equilibrium. Also, given the profile (y,z,x), player 1 would rather switch to her best choice x. Thus, it remains to show that no strategy profile, offering two different alternatives, could be a Nash equilibrium. Consider, without loss of generality, a profile where players 1 and 2 choose the same alternative whereas player 3 selects a different one. Then it could be either (y,y,x) or (z,z,x). In both cases, however, player 1 would switch to her best choice x. Thus, the game G does not admit a Nash equilibrium.☐

Greenberg and Weber (1993) showed that if the set of alternatives X is uni-dimensional and the utility functions of the individuals are single-peaked then there exists even a strong Nash equilibrium:

Proposition 4.4.3: (Greenberg and Weber (1993)) *Let the set of alternatives X be a subset of the real line* R. *Then the assumptions $\mathcal{MFC}$ and $\mathcal{SP}$ yield the existence of a strong Nash equilibrium of the party formation game G.*

The party formation game has been also studied in Demange (1994). By imposing a tree structure on the set of individuals, she was able to show the existence of a strong Nash equilibrium under an assumption which is weaker than $\mathcal{SP}$ introduced in the previous subsection. The following is, therefore, a corollary of Demange (1994):

Proposition 4.4.4: *Under $\mathcal{MFC}$ and $\mathcal{SP}$, the party formation game G admits a strong Nash equilibrium.*

5 Negative externality

In this section we impose the assumption of *negative externality*, which implies that the payoff of every player increases as the number of players who choose the same strategy declines.

5.1 Existence

We shall prove that if the individuals' payoff functions satisfy $\mathcal{NE}$ and $\mathcal{AN}$, then, whenever the set of alternatives X is finite, game G admits not only a Nash equilibrium but also a strong Nash equilibrium.

The first result of this subsection establishes conditions for non-emptiness of the set of Nash equilibria:

Proposition 5.1.1: (Milchtaich (1996) Quimt and Shubik (1995), Konishi, Le Breton and Weber (1996a)) *If the set of alternatives X is finite, the assumptions $\mathcal{NE}$ and $\mathcal{AN}$ yield the existence of a Nash equilibrium of the game G.*

We now show that the same assumptions which guarantee the existence of a Nash equilibrium also yield the existence of a strong Nash equilibrium.

Proposition 5.1.2: (Konishi, Le Breton and Weber (1997a)) *If the set of alternatives X is finite, the assumptions $\mathcal{N}\mathcal{E}$ and $\mathcal{A}\mathcal{N}$ yield the existence of a strong Nash equilibrium of the game G.*

The proof of this result is based on the following lemma which is useful for an examination of the set of Nash equilibria:

Lemma 5.1.3: *Suppose that $\mathcal{N}\mathcal{E}$ and $\mathcal{A}\mathcal{N}$ hold. If $\mathbf{x}$ is a Nash equilibrium of the game G, then there exists $\mathbf{y} \in \mathcal{S}\mathcal{N}\mathcal{E}(G)$ such that $U^i(\mathbf{y}) \geq U^i(\mathbf{x})$ for all $i \in N$.*

It is worthwhile to point out that, unlike games with a continuum of players where under assumptions $\mathcal{A}\mathcal{N}$ and $\mathcal{N}\mathcal{E}$ the set of strong Nash equilibria coincides with the set of Nash equilibria (Konishi, Le Breton and Weber (1997a)), this equivalence does not hold for the finite games. Thus, proposition 5.1.2 represents a non-trivial extension of proposition 5.1.1:

Example 5.1.4: *Consider the 'anti-coordination' game, given by the following matrix, with two players and two pure strategies, which admits two Nash equilibria, only one of which is strong*

	Strategy x	Strategy y
Strategy x	(0,0)	(1,1)
Strategy y	(2,2)	(0,0)

Note also that in games with two players since the assumption $\mathcal{A}\mathcal{N}$ is trivially satisfied, we have:

Corollary 5.1.5: *If the set of alternatives X is finite and the set N consists of two players, the assumption $\mathcal{N}\mathcal{E}$ yields the existence of a strong Nash equilibrium of the game G.*

Konishi, Le Breton and Weber (1997a) have shown that the results stated in propositions 5.1.1 and 5.1.2 are 'tight' in the sense that if $\mathcal{A}\mathcal{N}$ is dropped, then even Nash equilibrium may fail to exist:

Proposition 5.1.6: (Konishi, Le Breton and Weber (1997a)) *There is a game with three players and two alternatives, satisfying $\mathcal{N}\mathcal{E}$, which does not admit a Nash equilibrium.*

The second part of this section examines games where the set of alternatives is infinite. It turns out that in this case the assumptions $\mathcal{A}\mathcal{N}$ and $\mathcal{N}\mathcal{E}$ do not guarantee the existence of a Nash equilibrium. The reason for non-existence of a Nash equilibrium in the following example is that, under $\mathcal{N}\mathcal{E}$, the individuals' payoff functions are lower semicontinuous in their own strategies:

Example 5.1.7: *There are two individuals $N=\{1,2\}$, and the set of alternatives X is given by the interval $I=[0,1]$. Given a pair of strategies $\mathbf{x}=(x,y)$, the indirect utilities of individuals 1 and 2 are given by $u^1(x,|N_x(\mathbf{x})|)=x-|N_x(\mathbf{x})|$ and $u^2(y,|N_y(\mathbf{x})|)=y-|N_y(\mathbf{x})|$, respectively. Then the game G does not admit a Nash equilibrium.*

Proof: Suppose that the strategy profile $\mathbf{x}$ is a Nash equilibrium. Since the best possible outcome for both players is to choose 1 alone, then, in equilibrium, 1 would be chosen by at least one of the players. However, they cannot both choose 1, as each of them would be better off by choosing, say, 0.9 alone. However, no pair $(1,x)$ or $(x,1)$ with $x<1$ constitutes a Nash equilibrium, as the player choosing x would be better off by moving closer to 1, say, to $\dfrac{1+x}{2}$. Thus, this game does not admit a Nash equilibrium.$\square$

The existence of an equilibrium, however, can be rescued if we consider instead an 'approximate' Nash equilibrium. We then show that for every positive ϵ there exists a strong Nash ϵ equilibrium. Formally:

Definition 5.1.8: *Let $\epsilon>0$ be given. A strategy profile $\mathbf{x}=\{x^i\}_{i\in N}$ is a strong Nash ϵ equilibrium of the game G if there exist no group of individuals $S\subset N$ and S-tuple of strategies $\mathbf{y}\in X^S$ such that $u^i(\mathbf{x}^{N\setminus S},\mathbf{y}^S)>u^i(\mathbf{x})+\epsilon$ for all $i\in S$.*

We have the following result:

Proposition 5.1.9: (Konishi Le Breton and Weber (1997a)) *Let $\epsilon>0$ be given. Under $\mathcal{A}\mathcal{N}$ and $\mathcal{N}\mathcal{E}$, the game G admits a strong Nash ϵ equilibrium.*

5.2 Equivalence

Unfortunately, we cannot extend the result of proposition 4.2.1 to the games satisfying $\mathcal{N}\mathcal{E}$. Indeed, if $\mathcal{P}\mathcal{E}$ is replaced by $\mathcal{N}\mathcal{E}$ in the statement of proposition 4.2.1, Konishi, Le Breton and Weber (1997b) have shown that the equivalence of the sets of strong and coalition-proof Nash equilibria does not necessarily hold:

Proposition 5.2.1: (Konishi, Le Breton and Weber (1997b)) *There is a game G with six players and three alternatives, satisfying $\mathcal{N}\mathcal{E}$, for which the set $\mathcal{S}\mathcal{N}\mathcal{E}(G)$ is empty, whereas the set $\mathcal{C}\mathcal{P}\mathcal{N}\mathcal{E}(G)$ is not.*

However, equivalence can be rescued if $\mathcal{A}\mathcal{N}$ is added:

Proposition 5.2.2: (Konishi, Le Breton and Weber (1997b)) *Under $\mathcal{N}\mathcal{E}$ and $\mathcal{A}\mathcal{N}$, the sets $\mathcal{S}\mathcal{N}\mathcal{E}(G)$ and $\mathcal{C}\mathcal{P}\mathcal{N}\mathcal{E}(G)$ coincide.*

6 Extensions

In this section we shall study the environments in which both assumptions $\mathcal{P}\mathcal{E}$ and $\mathcal{N}\mathcal{E}$ could be violated.

Imposing assumption $\mathcal{A}\mathcal{N}$, the natural generalisation of both positive and negative externality is the *Single-Peaked Externality* of the payoff function with respect to the number of players who choose the same strategy:

Assumption: *Single-Peaked Externality ($\mathcal{S}\mathcal{P}\mathcal{E}$) Let $\mathcal{A}\mathcal{N}$ be satisfied. Then for each $i \in N$ and each $x \in X$, the payoff function $u^i(x,\cdot)$ is single-peaked in its second argument.*

Relaxation of the $\mathcal{P}\mathcal{E}$ and $\mathcal{N}\mathcal{E}$ assumptions will force us to impose additional conditions in order to still guarantee either the existence of an equilibrium or the equivalence of the sets of coalition-proof and strong Nash equilibria. We shall introduce the following assumptions:

Assumption: *Symmetry ($\mathcal{S}\mathcal{Y}$) For every two players $i, j \in N$ and every coalition S, which contains both i and j, we have $u^i(x,S) = u^j(x,S)$ for every $x \in X$.*

Condition $\mathcal{S}\mathcal{Y}$ is apparently stronger than $\mathcal{A}\mathcal{N}$ and generates a symmetric game where all players have identical payoff functions. It allows us to obtain the following result:

Proposition 6.1: (Rosenthal (1973)) *Under $\mathcal{S}\mathcal{Y}$, the game G admits a Nash equilibrium*

Proof: the method of the proof is actually the same as in the proof of proposition 4.1.6. Indeed, recall that every strategy profile **x** generates the unique partition $P(\mathbf{x}) = (N_x(\mathbf{x}))_{x \in X}$ of the set of players N, where for each $x \in X$, $N_x(\mathbf{x})$ denotes the collection of those players who choose alternative x under the strategy profile $\mathbf{x}$. Construct the following function $\Psi: X^N \to \mathfrak{R}$ given by

$$\Psi(\mathbf{x}) = \sum_{x \in X} \sum_{k=1}^{|N_x(\mathbf{x})|} u(x,k)$$

Compactness of X and continuity of the payoff functions $u(\cdot,k)$ for every $k = 1,\ldots,n$ imply that there is a strategy profile $\mathbf{x}^* = \arg\max_{x \in X^N} \Psi(\mathbf{x})$. It is easy to verify that $\mathbf{x}^*$ is a Nash equilibrium of the game G.□

If, in addition to $\mathcal{SU}$, we impose either $\mathcal{PE}$ or $\mathcal{NE}$ we can even prove the existence of a strong Nash equilibrium.

Proposition 6.2: *Under $\mathcal{SU}$ and $\mathcal{PE}$, the game G admits a strong Nash equilibrium.*

Proof: The regularity assumptions imply that there exists an alternative $y = \arg\max_{x \in X} u(\mathbf{x},n)$. Then the strategy profile $(y,\ldots,y)$ which assigns y to every player, is, obviously, a strong Nash equilibrium.□

Since condition $\mathcal{SU}$ is stronger than $\mathcal{AN}$, proposition 5.2.2 implies that proposition 6.2 would still hold if we replace $\mathcal{PE}$ by $\mathcal{NE}$:

Corollary 6.3: *Under $\mathcal{SU}$ and $\mathcal{NE}$, the game G admits a strong Nash equilibrium.*

If we, however, replace $\mathcal{PE}$ and $\mathcal{NE}$ in propositions 6.2 and 6.3, respectively, by a weaker assumption $\mathcal{SPE}$, then a strong Nash and even a coalition-proof equilibrium may fail to exist:

Example 6.4: *Consider the following game G with three players $N = \{1,2,3\}$ and two alternatives $X = \{x,y\}$, where the all three players have the same payoff function satisfying*

$$u(x,2) = u(y,2) > u(x,3) = u(y,3) > u(x,1) = u(y,1)$$

Then though game G satisfies $\mathcal{SU}$ and $\mathcal{SPE}$, it does not admit a coalition-proof Nash equilibrium or, hence, a strong Nash equilibrim.

Proof: The game G admits two Nash equilibria, (x,x,x) and (y,y,y). However, both these equilibria allow for a deviation by two-person coalitions. Since all deviations are credible, the set $\mathcal{CPNE}(G)$ is empty, implying that the set $\mathcal{SNE}(G)$ is empty as well.□

Propositions 4.2.1 and 5.2.2 provide us with equivalence of the sets of strong and coalition-proof Nash equilibria if either $\mathcal{PC}$ and $\mathcal{NC}$ is imposed. But again, these results might not hold if these assumptions are weakened:

Example 6.5: (Konishi, Le Breton and Weber (1997b)) *There exists a game G with four players and three alternatives, satisfying $\mathcal{PQ}$ and $\mathcal{PPC}$, for which the set $\mathcal{SNC}(G)$ is empty while the set $\mathcal{CPNC}(G)$ is not.*

Let us examine now games which satisfy a *neutrality* condition where the payoff of every player is not affected by her strategy but depends only on the set of players who choose it:

Assumption: *Neutrality ($\mathcal{NT}$) For every player $i \in N$ and every coalition S, which contains i, we have $u^i(x,S)=u^i(y,S)$ for every two alternatives $x,y \in X$.*

Imposing this assumption, we immediately have the following:

Proposition 6.6: *Under $\mathcal{NT}$ and $\mathcal{PC}$, the game G admits a strong Nash equilibrium.*

Proof: Since, by $\mathcal{NT}$, the players' payoffs are independent of their strategies and depend only on the set of players who choose it, $\mathcal{PC}$ implies that for every alternative $x \in X$, the strategy profile $(x,x,...,x)$ which assigns x to every player is, obviously, a strong Nash equilibrium.□

The existence of even a Nash equilibrium is not guaranteed if $\mathcal{PC}$ in the statement of proposition 6.6 is replaced by $\mathcal{NC}$:

Example 6.7: *Consider the following game G with three players $N=\{1,2,3\}$ and two alternatives $X=\{x,y\}$, which satisfies $\mathcal{NC}$ and where*

$$u^1(z,\{1,2\})>u^1(z,\{1,3\})$$

$$u^2(z,\{2,3\})>u^2(z,\{1,2\})$$

$$u^3(z,\{1,3\})>u^3(z,\{2,3\})$$

for every $z \in X$. ($\mathcal{NT}$ obviously holds.) Then the game G does not admit a Nash equilibrium.

Proof: Obviously no strategy profile which assigns the same alternative to all players is a Nash equilibrium, as every player would be better off by choosing a different alternative alone. Moreover:

players 1 and 2 cannot choose the same alternative since player 2 would rather join player 3,
players 1 and 3 would not choose the same alternative since player 1 would rather switch to the alternative selected by player 2,
players 2 and 3 would not choose the same alternative since player 3 would rather join player 1.
Thus, indeed, the game G does not admit a Nash equilibrium.☐

Note that since the game in example 6.4 satisfies $\mathcal{NT}$, it follows that the assumptions $\mathcal{PU}$ and $\mathcal{NT}$, even together with $\mathcal{PPE}$, do not, in general, yield the equivalence of the sets $\mathcal{CPNE}$ and $\mathcal{SNE}$. Nevertheless, provided that the strategy set is large enough, we can obtain the equivalence result under $\mathcal{PU}$ and $\mathcal{NT}$ without imposing $\mathcal{PP}$. A large number of strategies is required so that coalitional deviations do not interfere with the choices of other players.

Proposition 6.8: (Konishi, Le Breton and Weber (1997b)) *Suppose that $\mathcal{PU}$ and $\mathcal{NT}$ hold. If the cardinality of the strategy set X (finite or infinite) is at least n, then $\mathcal{SNE}(G)=\mathcal{CPNE}(G)$.*

Notes

We are grateful for a financial support of Fondazione ENI Enrico Mattei in preparing this manuscript. We wish to thank Charles Blackorby, Kim Border, John Conlon, Rajat Deb, Jim Dolmas, Peter Fishburn, Jean Gabszewicz, Douglas Gale, Paolo Ghirardato, Piero Gottardi, Ed Hopkins, Michihiro Kandori, Mamoru Kaneko, Aki Matsui, Hervé Moulin, Jean-Francois Mertens, Frederic Palomino, Laura Razzolini, Marci Rossell, Don Saari, Suzanne Scotchmer, Tomoichi Shinotsuka, Benyamin Shitovitz, Tayfun Sönmez, Kotaro Suzumura, William Thomson, Takashi Ui for their fruitful discussions and valuable suggestions. Parts of the research in this chapter have been presented at the Economic Theory Meetings in Cephalonia, Gargnano and Milan, Game Theory Conference in Toronto, SETIT Conferences, Charlottesville and Dallas, the Fourth TCER Summer Conference on Economic Theory, Tateshina (Nagano-Ken), Public Choice Society Meeting, Austin, ASSET Meeting, Lisbon, the seminars at Caltech, CORE, European University Institute, CentER, TCER, Universities of Brussels, Illinois, Minnesota, Mississippi, Pennsylvania, Rochester, Toulouse, Venice, Vienna, and Kansai, Kyoto, Osaka, Stanford, Tezukayama and Tsukuba Universities and we are grateful to their participants for their comments.

1 The concept of *population monotonicity* has been introduced by Thomson (1994) who used it in terms of social choice correspondence rather than, as in this chapter, a condition on payoff functions.
2 Liebovitz and Margolis (1994) referred to these circumstances as *network effects*.
3 See also Kalai, Postlewaite and Roberts (1979), Hart and Kurz (1983), Borm and

Tijs (1992), Borm, Otten and Peters (1992), Greenberg and Weber (1993), Wako (1994), Konishi, Le Breton and Weber (1997a,1997b,1997c).
4 It is easy to verify that the Weber and Zamir example admits a Nash equilibrium. Konishi, Le Breton and Weber (1995e) demonstrate, however, that the existence of a pure strategy Nash equilibrium is not, in general, guaranteed in the Guesnerie and Oddou economy with four or more agents.

References

Arthur, W.B. (1989), 'Competing Technologies, Increasing Returns, and Lock-in by Historical Events', *The Economic Journal*, 99, 116–31.

Aumann, R.J. (1959), 'Acceptable Points in General Cooperative *n*-Person Games', *Contributions to the Theory of Games*, Vol. IV, Princeton: Princeton University Press.

Bernheim, D., Peleg, B. and M. Whinston (1987), 'Coalition-Proof Nash Equilibria: I Concepts', *Journal of Economic Theory*, 42, 1–12.

Borm, P., Otten G-J. and H. Peters (1993), 'Core Implementation in Modified Strong and Coalition Proof Nash Equilibria', Tilburg University Discussion Paper.

Borm, P. and S.H. Tijs (1992), 'Strategic Claim Games Corresponding to *NTU*-Games', *Games and Economic Behavior*, 4, 58–71.

Demange, G. (1994), 'Intermediate Preferences and Stable Coalition Structures,' *Journal of Mathematical Economics*, 23, 45–58.

Demange, G. and D. Henriet (1991), 'Sustainable Oligopolies', *Journal of Economic Theory*, 54, 417–28.

Farrell, J. and G. Saloner (1985), 'Standardization, Compatibility, and Innovation', *Rand Journal of Economics*, 16, 70–83.

(1988), 'Coordination through Committees and Markets', *Rand Journal of Economics*, 19, 235–52.

Green, E.G. (1984), 'Continuum and Finite-Player Noncooperative Models of Competition', *Econometrica*, 52, 975–94.

Greenberg, J. (1989), 'Deriving Strong and Coalition-Proof Nash Equilibria from an Abstract System', *Journal of Economic Theory*, 49, 195–202.

(1994), 'Coalition Structures', in *Handbook of Game Theory with Economic Applications*, R.J. Aumann and S. Hart (eds.), Amsterdam: Elsevier.

Greenberg, J. and S. Weber (1985), 'Multiparty Equilibria under Proportional Representation', *American Political Science Review*, 79, 693–703.

(1986), 'Strong Tiebout Equilibrium under Restricted Preferences Domain', *Journal of Economic Theory*, 38, 101–17.

(1993), 'Stable Coalition Structures with Unidimensional Set of Alternatives', *Journal of Economic Theory*, 79, 693–703.

Guesnerie, R. and C. Oddou (1979), 'On Economic Games which are not Necessarily Superadditive', *Economics Letters*, 3, 301–6.

(1981), 'Second Best Taxation as a Game', *Journal of Economic Theory*, 25, 67–91.

Haltiwanger, J. and M. Waldman (1985), 'Rational Expectations and the Limits of

Rationality: An Analysis of Heterogeneity', *American Economic Review*, 75, 326–40.

Hart, S. and M. Kurz (1983), 'Endogenous Formation of Coalitions', *Econometrica*, 51, 1047–64.

Ichiishi, T. (1993), *The Cooperative Nature of the Firm*, Cambridge University Press.

Kalai, E., A. Postlewaite and J. Roberts (1979), 'A Group Incentive Compatible Mechanism Yielding Core Allocations', *Journal of Economic Theory*, 20, 13–22.

Kaneko, M. and M. Wooders (1982), 'Cores of Partitioning Games', *Mathematical Social Sciences*, 3, 313–27.

Katz, M. L. and C. Shapiro (1985), 'Network Externalities, Competition, and Compatibility', *American Economic Review*, 75(3), 424–40.

Konishi, H. and P. Fishburn (1996), 'Quasi-Linear Utility in a Discrete Choice Model', *Economics Letters*, 51, 197–200.

Konishi, H., M. Le Breton and S. Weber (1995a), 'Equilibrium in a Model with Partial Rivalry', *Journal of Economic Theory*, 72, 225–37.

(1997b), 'Equivalence of Strong and Coalition-Proof Nash Equilibria in Games without Spillovers', *Economic Theory*, 9, 97–113.

(1997c), 'Pure Strategy Nash Equilibrium in a Game with Positive Externalities', *Games and Economic Behaviour*, forthcoming.

(1997d), 'Free Mobility Equilibrium in an Economy with a Public Good', *Ricerche Economiche*, forthcoming.

(1997e), 'Equilibrium in e Finite Local Public Goods Economy', Southern Methodist University Working Paper.

Le Breton, M. (1989), 'A Note on Balancedness and Nonemptiness of the Core in Voting Games', *International Journal of Game Theory*, 18, 111–17.

Le Breton, M., G. Owen and S. Weber (1992), 'Strongly Balanced Cooperative Games', *International Journal of Game Theory*, 20, 419–27.

Liebowitz, S.J. and S.E. Margolis (1994), 'Network Externality: An Uncommon Tragedy', *Journal of Economic Perspectives*, 8(2), 137–51.

Mas-Colell, A. (1984), 'On a Theorem of Schmeidler', *Journal of Mathematical Economics*, 13, 201–6.

Milchtaich, I. (1996), 'Congestion Games', *Games and Economic Behavior*, 13, 111–24.

Milinsky, M. (1979), 'An Evolutionary Stable Feeding Strategy in Sticklebacks', *Zeitschrift für Tierpsychologië*, 51, 36–40.

Monderer, D. and L. Shapley (1996), 'Potential Games', *Games and Economic Behaviour*, 13, 124–43.

Moulin, H. and B. Peleg (1982), 'Cores of Effectivity Functions and Implementation Theory', *Journal of Mathematical Economics*, 10, 115–45.

von Neumann, J. and O. Morgenstern (1944), *Theory of Games and Economic Behaviour*, Princeton: Princeton University Press.

Peleg, B. (1984), *Game Theoretic Analysis of Voting in Committees*, Cambridge University Press.

Quint, T. and M. Shubik (1995), 'A Model of Migration', mimeo, Yale University.

Rosenthal, R.W. (1973), 'A Class of Games Possessing a Pure-Strategy Nash Equilibrium', *International Journal of Game Theory*, 2, 65–7.

Scarf, H. (1967), 'The Core of an N-person Game', *Econometrica*, 35, 50–69.
Schmeidler, D. (1973), 'Equilibrium Points in Nonatomic Games', *Journal of Statistical Physics*, 7, 295–300.
Thomson, W. (1994), 'Population Monotonic Allocation Rules', in A. Barnett, M. Salles, H. Moulin and N. Schofield (eds.), *Social Choice, Welfare and Ethics*, Cambridge University Press.
Tirole, J. (1988), *Industrial Organization*, Cambridge, MA: MIT Press.
Wako, J. (1994), 'Coalition ????? of the Competitive Allocations in a Model with Indivisible Goods', Gakushuin University Discussion Paper.
Weber, S. and S. Zamir (1985), 'Proportional Taxation: Nonexistence of Stable Structures in an Economy with a Public Good', *Journal of Economic Theory*, 35, 178–85.

10 Non-cooperative models of coalition formation in games with spillovers

Francis Bloch

1 Introduction

Since the publication of *Theory of Games and Economic Behavior* by von Neumann and Morgenstern (1944), the study of coalition formation has been one of the central questions in game theory. In the words of its founders, one of the purposes of game theory is to 'determine everything that can be said about coalitions between players, compensations between partners in every coalition, mergers or fights between coalitions. . .' (von Neumann and Morgenstern (1944, p. 240)). This quotation clearly poses the three basic questions of endogenous coalition formation: Which coalitions will be formed? How will the coalitional worth be divided among coalition members? How does the presence of other coalitions affect the incentives to cooperate?

As noted by Maschler (1992) in his survey on bargaining sets, cooperative game theory has focused mostly on the second question – the division of the payoff between coalition members. In fact, it is even surprising to note that the first question has been assumed away in most cooperative game theory. Even the Aumann–Maschler (1964) bargaining set, which was specially designed to analyse the formation of coalitions, specifies an exogenous coalition structure and falls short of determining which coalition struture will form.[1] Finally, the third question, dealing with competition between coalitions, is simply ignored in traditional cooperative game theory, since the coalitional function cannot take into account externalities among coalitions.

In recent years, the limitations of cooperative game theoretic solution concepts has led to the emergence of a new strand of the literature describing the formation of coalitions as a non-cooperative process. This reformulation of the old problem of endogenous coalition formation in non-cooperative terms can actually handle the issue of competition between coalitions which was ignored in traditional cooperative game theory. In this survey, my aim is to review those recent contributions and to discuss their applications to various economic problems.

In fact, the study of specific economic models is what prompted the renewed interest in coalition formation. In international trade, the formation of competing customs unions and the question of 'regionalism' in trade is one of the foremost current topics of debate. In environmental economics, international cooperation to control cross-border pollution (and the possibility that cooperation would only take place among a small subset of countries) has recently become an important subject of discussion. In industrial organisation, the study of cartels of firms, strategic alliances or standardisation committees are also examples of the application of endogenous coalition formation. Finally, in local public finance, the financial difficulties faced by large cities have led to a spur of interest in the study of spillovers between jurisdictions, and the taxation of neighbouring communities for local public goods provided by one jurisdiction.

While the previous examples are taken from various fields of economics and deal with very different problems, they all share a common structure. In all these applications, the coalitions formed are smaller than the grand coalition, and the spillovers between coalitions are important. The presence of spillovers and the lack of superadditivity of the underlying coalitional game require the use of a framework which is more general than classical cooperative game theory. The appropriate framework to deal with spillovers are *games in partition function form* where the worth of a coalition depends on the entire coalition structure.

In the next section of this survey, I analyse precisely the role of spillovers and the different representations of games with externalities. I first emphasise the limits of the classical approach and show how various partition function games can be defined. This leads me to define a general structure of payoffs for games with spillovers.

In section 3, I discuss a first class of non-cooperative games of coalition formation, where all agents announce *simultaneously* their decision to cooperate. I analyse various outcome rules for the simultaneous announcement games, and discuss different solution concepts. In particular, I show that, in order to select among the Nash equilibria of these games, more restrictive solution concepts must be used, such as coalition-proof Nash equilibria (CPNE) or strong Nash equilibria (SNE).

Section 4 is devoted to a second class of games, where agents announce *sequentially* their decision to participate in the coalition. These extensive-form games are meant to capture the 'forward looking' aspects of coalition formation: Each agent is aware that her decision to form a coalition might affect the behaviour of other agents, and takes into account the final consequences of her decision. I analyse different specifications of the extensive-form games which reflect differences in the procedures of coalition formation.

In section 5, I study some *cooperative* solution concepts which were proposed to analyse the stability of coalition structures in games with spillovers. While those stability concepts are not based on non-cooperative processes, they often provide interesting benchmarks, and give some new insights into the study of coalition formation with spillovers.

In the last sections of the survey, I discuss applications of the different models of coalition formation to economic problems. It turns out that most economic situations can be classified into two categories: games with *positive spillovers* where the formation of a coalition by other players increases the payoff of an agent, and games with *negative spillovers* where the formation of a coalition decreases the payoff of agents who are not members of the coalition. In section 6, I discuss games with positive spillovers, and compare the outcomes of the different models of coalition formation in that setting. In section 7, I perform the same analysis for games with negative spillovers.

In the last section, I conclude by mentioning the problems attached to the various games of coalition formation, and by providing some directions for future research.

While most of this survey is devoted to theoretical models of coalition formation, I believe that the results obtained should be viewed as *operational tools* which can be used in the study of coalition formation in various economic settings. Hence, rather than emphasising the theoretical aspects of the research, I have tried to give examples in order to show how the theory can be applied to specific economic models.

Finally, it is important to mention the exact range of questions covered by this survey. I have chosen to focus on models of coalition formation *in games with spillovers*, thereby excluding the large literature on games without spillovers. For cooperative solution concepts on games without spillovers, the reader is referred to the excellent survey on coalition structures by Joseph Greenberg in the *Handbook of Game Theory* (Greenberg (1994)). Simultaneous games of coalition formation in games without spillovers have recently been surveyed by Konishi, Le Breton and Weber (1996). Finally, the large (and growing) literature on sequential games of coalition formation in cooperative situations has not been surveyed yet. The reader is encouraged to go back to the original articles by Chatterjee *et al.* (1993) and Perry and Reny (1994) for a rapid introduction to this literature.

2 Games with spillovers and the partition function form

2.1 The classical approach

The classical representation of gains from cooperation does not allow for spillovers between coalitions. A *game in coalitional function form* is characterised by a coalitional function $v(\cdot)$, assigning to each coalition C a real number $v(C)$ representing the worth of the coalition.[2] The absence of spillovers is implicit in the derivation of the coalitional function: the set $v(C)$ represents whatever the coalition can get irrespective of the behaviour of other players.

Clearly, depending on the meaning assigned to 'irrespective of the behaviour of other players', various definitions of coalitional function games can be obtained. Following von Neumann and Morgenstern (1944), the primitive description of a game is a *strategic form* $\Gamma = \{N, \{S_i\}_{i \in N}, \{u_i\}_{i \in N}\}$ where N is the set of players, S_i the strategy space of player i and u_i the payoff function of player i, assigning to each profile of strategies s a real number. The different coalitional functions $v(C)$ are then derived by different *conversions* of the non-cooperative game into a game in coalitional function form.

In von Neumann and Morgenstern's (1944) analysis of n-person, zero-sum games, the coalitional value $v(C)$ is obtained as follows. Consider the two 'composite' players C and $N\backslash C$. (The 'composite' player C is defined to have a strategy set given by $S_C = \times_{i \in C} S_i$ and a payoff function $u_C = \Sigma_{i \in C} u_i$.) The two-person zero-sum game Γ' with players C and $N\backslash C$ possesses a value defined by

$$v = \max_{s_C} \min_{s_{N\backslash C}} u_C(s_C, s_{N\backslash C}) = \min_{s_{N\backslash C}} \max_{s_C} u_C(s_C, s_{N\backslash C})$$

and the coalition worth $v(C)$ is simply the value v of the game Γ'.

In non-zero-sum games, the minimax is not necessarily equal to the maximin, and hence, two different conversions are possible. These conversions have been labelled by Aumann (1967) the α and β conversions, and are defined as follows

$$v^\alpha(C) = \min_{s_{N\backslash C}} \max_{s_C} u_C(s_C, s_{N\backslash C}),$$

$$v^\beta(C) = \max_{s_C} \min_{s_{N\backslash C}} u_C(s_C, s_{N\backslash C})$$

In the α framework, a coalition C obtains the worth it can guarantee itself, irrespective of the strategy choice of the other players; in the β conversion, the coalition C obtains the worth it cannot be prevented from getting by players in $N\backslash C$. Clearly, both conversions embody a very pessimistic conjecture on the part of the members of coalition C on the behaviour of the complementary coalition. Hence, although this formulation might be adequate for very competitive situations, such as two-person zero-sum games, it is less convincing for general games, where players' interests may coincide. Why should the players in $N\backslash C$ behave in such an aggressive way if it is against their interest?

In order to mitigate this aggressivity, Harsanyi (1959) has proposed a different conversion of non-cooperative games, based on Nash's (1950) bargaining solution. In this formulation, we will let $A = \max_{s_N} u_N(s_N)$ denote the total gains from cooperation of the grand coalition. Define then $v(C)$ to be the maximiser of the Nash product

$$\Pi = (x - \min_{s_{N\setminus C}} \max_{s_C} u_C(s_C, s_{N\setminus C}))(A - x - \min_{s_C} \max_{s_{N\setminus C}} u_{N\setminus C}(s_C, s_{N\setminus C}))$$

Clearly, Harsanyi's (1959) conversion supposes a less extreme behaviour on the part of players outside the coalition. However, it still rests on two very specific assumptions: (i) players outside the coalition behave as a single complementary coalition and (ii) the two coalitions C and $N\setminus C$ bargain over the total gains from cooperation and obtain shares corresponding to Nash's (1950) bargaining solution.

In essence, all the conversions described above assume away externalities among coalitions and are ill-suited to handle situations where the actions of other players may affect the worth of the coalition. In Shubik's (1982) terminology, the coalitional function seems well suited to handle 'competitive games' (or c-games) where coalitions have antagonistic interests, or 'orthogonal' games where each coalition's worth is genuinely independent of the actions of the other players.[3] In any other situation, the description of the economic situation requires a more complete specification of the interactions between coalitions.

2.2 Partition function games

The earliest attempt to generalise coalitional functions to the case of externalities among coalitions is the introduction of *partition function games* by Thrall and Lucas (1963). In their original definition, Thrall and Lucas (1963) only considered TU games and simply proposed to extend coalitional functions, by making the worth of a coalition a function of *all* the coalitions formed in the game. Before stating the formal definition recall that a *coalition structure* π is a partition of the set N of players, $\pi = \{C_1, C_2, ..., C_m\}$, representing all the coalitions formed in the game.

Definition 2.1: A partition function v *is a mapping which associates to each coalition structure π a vector in $\Re^{|\pi|}$, representing the worth of all the coalitions in π.*

It is easy to see that partition function games are a generalisation of coalitional function games. If the worth of a coalition C is independent of the coalitions formed by the other players, the two definitions coincide. If, on the other hand, the formation of coalitions affect all the players in the game, there is no univocal relationship between partition functions and coalitional functions, and a game in partition function form carries more information about the underlying situation than a game in coalitional function form.

While partition function games may appear to be a natural extension of coalitional games, their interest is undermined by some conceptual difficulties in the definition and use of partition functions. First of all, partition functions have proved difficult to handle, and the extensions of cooperative solution concepts to partition functions due to Thrall and Lucas (1963) and Lucas and Maceli (1978) have yielded mixed results.

Second, and more importantly, the derivation of partition functions from games in strategic form poses some difficulties. To understand these problems, consider a game in strategic form and a coalition structure π. The given coalition structure imposes a fixed pattern of coalitions of players and, in particular, may include more than two coalitions. With more than two coalitions being formed, the minimax conversion of Aumann (1967) and the bargaining conversion of Harsanyi (1959) are not valid any longer. Rather, one needs to specify exactly how the various coalitions compete with one another.

Perhaps the most natural conversion is to suppose that, inside each coalition, players act cooperatively in order to maximise the coalitional surplus, but that coalitions compete in a non-cooperative way. This formalisation was originally proposed by Ichiishi (1983), and later used by Ray and Vohra (1995). The partition function is then obtained as a Nash equilibrium payoff of the game played by the coalitions.

Formally, for a fixed coalition structure $\pi=\{C_1,C_2,\ldots,C_m\}$, let s^* be a vector of strategies such that

$$\forall C_i \in \pi^i, \sum_{j \in C_i} u_j(s^*_{C_i}, s^*_{N \setminus C_i}) \geq \sum_{j \in C_i} u_j(s_{C_i}, s^*_{N \setminus C_i}), \forall s_{C_i} \in \times_{j \in C_i} S_j$$

Then define $v(C_i \pi) = \Sigma_{j \in C_i} u_j(s^*)$.

This approach is clearly more satisfactory than the classical conversions based on *ad hoc* assumptions on the behaviour of the complementary coalition, but it also raises new difficulties. First, this approach cannot easily be extended to NTU games, since, in that case, 'cooperative' behaviour inside each coalition is not well defined.[4] Second, even in the case of TU games, if the Nash equilibrium of the game played by coalitions is not unique, the partition function is not well defined.[5]

A third difficulty is linked to the interpretation of transferable utility in partition function games. The definition implicitly supposes that utility is transferable inside each coalition, but not across coalitions. The lack of transferability of utility across coalitions is in fact the defining feature of the partition function approach. In order to model cooperative situations with spillovers by partition function, one thus needs to justify this lack of transferability on either institutional or conceptual grounds.

Finally, it is useful to study how the classical properties of coalitional functions can be extended to partition functions. First of all, partition functions should satisfy *superadditivity* since, as in the case of coalitional functions, whatever strategies chosen by two coalitions A and B can be replicated by the coalition $A \cup B$. However, in partition function games, the definition of superadditivity needs to be qualified: for superadditivity to hold, it must be that the coalition structure formed by players in $N \backslash (A \cup B)$ remains constant.

Definition 2.2: *A partition function v is* superadditive *if and only if, for any coalition structure π and any two coalitions A and B in π, $v(A \cup B, \pi \backslash \{A,B\} \cup \{A \cup B\}) \geq v(A, \pi) + v(B, \pi)$.*

By a similar extension, one can define *monotonicity* of a partition function as follows.

Definition 2.3: *A partition function v is* monotonic *if for any two coalitions A and $B \subset A$, for any partition π containing A and any partition π' containing B such that π and π' coincide on $N \backslash A$, $v(A, \pi) \geq v(B, \pi')$.*

The following lemma is easily established

Lemma 2.4: *If a partition function v is superadditive, then it is monotonic.*

Proof: Consider two sets A, $B \subset A$ and two partitions π and π' coinciding on $N \backslash A$ such that $A \in \pi$ and $B \in \pi'$. Since π' and π coincide on $N \backslash A$, there must exist a collection $\{C_1, C_2, ..., C_m\}$ in π' such that $B \cup C_1 \cup C_2 \cup ... \cup C_m = A$. By superadditivity

$$v(B \cup C_1, \pi' \backslash \{B, C_1\} \cup \{B \cup C_1\}) \geq v(B, \pi')$$

and by a repeated application of this inequality, $v(A, \pi) \geq v(B, \pi')$. $\square$

Note that the monotonicity of partition functions implies that the grand coalition is always an efficient coalition structure. Hence, in any game of coalition formation, the formation of a fragmented coalition structure is an inefficient outcome.

The additional information contained in the partition function allows us to describe new properties which cannot be defined in games in coalitional function form. In particular, the effect of the formation of a coalition on external players can be precisely described. Depending on whether the formation of a coalition is beneficial or harmful to external players, the two concepts of positive and negative spillovers can be defined.

Definition 2.5: *A partition function v exhibits* positive spillovers *if, for any partition π, and any two coalitions A and B in* $\pi, v(C, \pi\backslash\{A,B\} \cup \{A \cup B\}) \geq v(C, \pi)$, *for all coalitions* $C \neq A, B$ *in π.*

Definition 2.6: *A partition function v exhibits* negative spillovers *if, for any partition π, and any two coalitions A and B in* $\pi, v(C, \pi\backslash\{A,B\} \cup \{A \cup B\}) \leq v(C, \pi)$, *for all coalitions* $C \neq A, B$ *in π.*

2.3 Valuations

While the partition function represents the natural extension of coalitional functions to games with externalities, most economic applications yield a specific representation of gains from cooperation, called a *valuation*. As opposed to a partition function, a valuation assigns to each coalition structure, not a vector of coalitional worths but a vector of individual payoffs.[6] The term 'valuation' indicates that each agent is able to evaluate directly the payoff she obtains in different coalition structures.

Valuations thus emerge when the rule of division of the payoffs between coalition members is fixed. Arguably, this assumption is a severe restriction on the cooperative situations which can be represented by valuations. However, fixed rules of division appear naturally in many economic applications and in theoretical studies of coalition formation based on a two-stage structure.

Many studies of coalition formation distinguish between two stages: a first stage of coalition formation and a second stage in which payoffs are distributed among coalition members. Hence, at the time the coalition is formed, players evaluate the payoff they obtain in different coalition structures according to a fixed sharing rule. This is the structure adopted by Shenoy (1979) and Hart and Kurz (1983) in their study of endogenous coalition formation, by Myerson (1978) in his 'threats and settlement game' and by Aumann and Myerson (1988) in their analysis of the endogenous formation of links between players. The valuations used by these authors differ. Shenoy (1979) adopts Aumann and Drèze's (1974) extension of the Shapley value to games with fixed coalition structures, Hart and Kurz (1983) consider Owen's (1977) extension of the Shapley value to games with groups of players and Aumann and Myerson (1988) use Myerson's (1977) value for games with graphs of players.

In economic applications, valuations emerge as the outcome of a two-stage process where coalitions are formed in the first stage and agents make decisions, given a fixed coalition structure, in the second stage. For example, firms form cartels or associations in the first stage of the game and then compete on the market in the second stage. Similarly, countries form customs unions in the first stage of the game, abolishing tariffs among themselves and selecting jointly an external tariff, thereby affecting the environment in which firms compete in the second stage of the game. In these economic applications, if individual decisions in the second stage of the game give rise to a unique payoff to all agents, the cooperative situation can be represented by a valuation mapping coalition structures into vectors of individual payoffs.[7]

Definition 2.7: *A valuation v is a mapping which associates to each coalition structure π a vector of individual payoffs in $\Re^n$.*

The description of gains from cooperation by a valuation thus assumes away one of the original problems of endogenous coalition formation: the distribution of the coalitional surplus among coalition members. On the other hand, this formulation allows us to analyse more precisely the role of spillovers between coalitions, and, in most of this survey, I will be working with valuations.

Importantly, it should be noted that *valuations are not necessarily super-additive nor monotonic*. Since the rule of payoff division is fixed, the usual reasoning showing that, in the coalition $A \cup B$, agents necessarily obtain higher payoffs than in the separate coalitions A and B, does not hold. As a consequence, an agent might receive a lower payoff in the coalition A than in a subset B of that coalition. Hence, in games described by a valuation, *the grand coalition is not necessarily efficient* and games of endogenous coalition formation might yield fragmented coalition structures.[8]

Finally, I just mention that positive and negative spillovers can easily be defined in the context of valuations, and the formal definitions are given below.

Definition 2.8: *A valuation v exhibits* positive (resp. negative) spillovers *if, for any partition π, and any two coalitions A and B in π, $v_i(\pi\backslash\{A,B\}\cup\{A\cup B\})\geq(\text{resp.}\leq) v_i(\pi)$, for all players $i\notin A\cup B$.*

3 Simultaneous games of coalition formation

The first class of simultaneous games I consider are *simultaneous games* where all players announce at the same time their decision to form coalitions. In such games, it appears that the set of Nash equilibria is often quite large – forcing the analyst to use some refinements in order to make interesting predictions. These refinements, in turn, are usually of a cooperative nature, involving joint moves on the part of players. Hence, the study of simultaneous games of coalition formation is at the frontier between cooperative and non-cooperative game theory, borrowing ideas and results from the two fields. Following Yi and Shin (1995), I separate simultaneous games of coalition formation into two types: (i) open membership games and (ii) exclusive membership games. Open membership games are games where players are free to join or leave any coalition. Exclusive membership games are games where outsiders are not free to join a coalition. In both cases, I start the analysis with the simplest games, the open membership game proposed by d'Aspremont *et al.* (1983) and the exclusive membership game due to von Neumann and Morgenstern (1944). The study is then extended to more complex processes of coalition formation, and various refinements of Nash equilibrium are introduced.

3.1 Open membership games

In open membership games, any player is free to join or leave a coalition. Accordingly, players cannot specify in advance the coalition they wish to form. Rather, players announce a message (for instance their willingness to participate in a coalition), and coalitions are formed by all players who make the same announcement. We will discuss two such games: the cartel formation game of d'Aspremont *et al.* (1983) and the open membership game proposed by Yi and Shin (1995).

3.1.1 The cartel formation game

The cartel formation game of d'Aspremont *et al.* (1983) is the simplest example of an open membership game. All players in N simultaneouly announce a choice in the set $\{Y,N\}$. Let C be the set of all players who announce Y. This set is the coalition formed in the game, the coalition structure formed is $\pi = C \cup \{j\}_{j \notin C}$ and each player receives a payoff given by $v_i(C \cup \{j\}_{j \notin C})$.

This simple participation game has been used by d'Aspremont *et al.* (1983) to analyse the formation of a 'dominant' cartel on a market. They analyse the *Nash equilibria* of the game and show that the Nash equilibrium outcomes correspond to the two intuitive concepts of *internal stability* (no player who announces Y has an incentive to announce N) and *external stability* (no player who announces N has an incentive to announce Y). It is important to note that, in this game, membership to the cartel is open, but individual players cannot be forced to accept the formation of a cartel, i.e., by announcing N, individual players commit to remain independent in the game.

It is easy to see that the cartel formation game always has a Nash equilibrium where no coalition is formed. In fact, if all $n-1$ other players announce N, announcing N is obviously a best response. Whether or not this game possesses a non-trivial equilibrium is a more difficult question.[9]

In general, there is no guarantee that a non-trivial equilibrium exists, and if it exists, that it is unique.[10] This, of course, may force us to consider refinements of the set of Nash equilibria.

Another obvious defect of the cartel formation game is that it only allows for the formation of *one* coalition on the market. The next game I present retains the features of open membership while allowing for an arbitrary coalition structure to form.

3.1.2 *The open membership game*

The general open membership game I discuss below was suggested by Yi and Shin (1995). In this game, the strategy space of the players is a message space $\mathcal{M}$ with $|\mathcal{M}|{\geq}n$. (There are at least as many different messages as players.) All players simultaneously announce a message in $\mathcal{M}$. Coalitions are then formed by all players who have announced the same message, $C(m)=\{i{\in}N, m_i{=}m\}$ for all $m{\in}\mathcal{M}$. The coalition structure formed is then given by $\pi=\{C(m)\}$, $\forall m, C(m){\neq}\emptyset$, and each player obtains a payoff $v_i(\{C(m)\})$.

It turns out that this game is not a direct generalisation of the cartel formation game of d'Aspremont *et al.* (1983) because individual players cannot commit to remain independent in the game. In fact, in the general open membership game, any player can form a coalition with another player simply by announcing the same message.[11] Since players can thus 'force' the formation of coalitions with other players, it is not necessarily true that the trivial coalition structure consisting of singletons is a Nash equilibrium of the game.[12] On the other hand, since entry into a coalition is free, it is easy to obtain a condition under which the only Nash equilibrium outcome of the game is the grand coalition.

Proposition 3.1 (Yi (1995a)): *Suppose that, for any two coalitions A and B with $|A|{\geq}|B|$, any player i in B and any partition π containing A and B, $v_i(\pi\backslash\{A,B\}\cup\{A\cup\{i\},B\backslash\{i\}\})>v_i(\pi)$, then the only Nash equilibrium outcome of the open membership game is the grand coalition.*

Proof: First note that, if all other players announce a message m, by the hypothesis, player i obtains a higher payoff in the grand coalition than in the coalition structure $\pi=\{N\backslash\{i\}, \{i\}\}$ so that it is a best response to announce the same message m. On the other hand, for any other coalition structure, it is possible to find a player who belongs to a small coalition and who would benefit from joining a larger coalition.□

Proposition 3.1 shows that, under a rather mild monotonicity requirement, the only Nash equilibrium outcome of the open membership game is the grand coalition.[13] In fact, since coalition members cannot prevent the entry of outsiders into the coalition, the coalition structures formed under open membership can be expected to be larger than under exclusive membership.

3.2 Exclusive membership games

In exclusive membership games, players are not free to join an existing coalition. The composition of coalitions is announced in advance and only those coalitions which are announced can be formed. Two situations may arise: either coalitions are formed as soon as some of their members agree to join (this is the case in the game Δ) or the formation of a coalition requires the unanimous agreement of its members (this is the case in the game Γ). In both cases, Nash equilibria are usually not unique, and refinements need to be imposed in order to obtain a sharp prediction on the equilibrium coalition structures.

3.2.1 The game Γ

The first example of a simultaneous game of coalition formation is the game originally proposed by von Neumann and Morgenstern (1944, pp. 243–4). This game was later reintroduced by Hart and Kurz (1983) as the game Γ. In this game, the strategy (or message) space of any player i is the set of all coalitions to which she belongs

$$S_i = \{C \subset N, i \in C\}$$

A coalition C is formed if and only if all members i of C have chosen $s_i = C$. Hence, in the game Γ, a coalition can only be formed if all its members unanimously agree to participate.

Intuitively, in the game Γ, membership is exclusive because all members announce beforehand the list of potential coalition members. Furthermore, for a coalition to form, unanimous agreement of all potential members is required. This definition implies that, whenever a member deviates and leaves a coalition, the coalition breaks apart, and all former coalition members form singletons.

3.2.2 The Game Δ

Hart and Kurz (1983) propose an alternative exclusive membership game, called the game Δ. In this game, the strategy space of agent i is the same as in game Γ ($S_i = \{C \subset N,\ i \in C\}$), but the outcome function is different. In the game Δ, coalitions are formed by all players who have announced the same coalition, whether or not the formation of the coalition has been approved unanimously by all its members. Formally, for any possible message (i.e., coalition) m, let $C(m) = \{i, s_i = m\}$ denote the coalition formed by all players who have announced m. Notice that, as in the case of open membership games, messages in the game Δ are used as coordination devices. However, as opposed to the case of open membership, messages also carry an important restriction on the coalitions that can be formed. Only those coalitions that are announced by the players are feasible in the game.

Intuitively, in the game Δ, membership is exclusive because players announce beforehand the list of coalition members. However, for a coalition to form, the participation of all listed members is not needed: all those agents who agree to participate form a coalition. This definition implies that, whenever a member leaves a coalition, she assumes that all other coalition members remain together as in the open membership games.

3.2.3 Cooperative refinements of Nash equilibrium

In both the game Γ and the game Δ, as in the case of cartel formation, the trivial coalition structure with singletons is a Nash equilibrium outcome: if all other players announce singletons, it is a best response for a player to announce a singleton as well. It thus appears that the set of Nash equilibria is too large to allow for sharp predictions.

In order to refine the set of equilibria, Yi and Shin (1995) and Hart and Kurz (1983) propose to consider cooperative refinements: coalition-proof Nash equilibria in the case of Yi and Shin (1995) and strong Nash equilibria in Hart and Kurz (1983). I recall here the definitions of these two solution concepts due to Bernheim, Peleg and Whinston (1987) and Aumann (1959) respectively.

In order to define coalition-proof Nash equilibria some preliminary notation is needed. For any strategic game $G = \{N, \{S_i\}_{i \in N}, \{u_i\}_{i \in N}\}$, and any fixed strategy profile σ define the reduced game for coalition C given σ as follows

$$G_\sigma^C = \{C, \{S_i\}_{i \in C}, \{\tilde{u}_i\}_{i \in C}\}$$

where $\tilde{u}_i(s) = u_i(s_C, \sigma_{N \backslash C})$. In words, the reduced game is obtained by fixing the strategies of all the players outside C, and defining the utility of every player given this fixed strategy choices. Coalition-proof Nash equilibria are then defined recursively.

Definition 3.2 (Bernheim, Peleg and Whinston (1987)): *For $n = 1$, σ_i is a coalition-proof Nash equilibrium (CPNE) if and only if σ_i is a maximiser of u_i over S_i. Let $n > 1$ and assume that CPNE have been defined for all $m < n$. Then*

    $-\sigma$ is self-enforcing for G if and only if, for all $C \subset N$, $C \neq N$, σ_C is a CPNE of G_σ^C.

    $-\sigma$ is a CPNE if and only if it is self-enforcing and there does not exist another self-enforcing strategy σ' such that $u_i(\sigma') > u_i(\sigma)$ for all $i \in N$.

Definition 3.3 (Aumann (1959)): *A* strong Nash equilibrium (*SNE*) *is a strategy profile σ for which there does not exist a coalition $C \subset N$ and a strategy profile σ'_C for players in C such that $u_i(\sigma'_C, \sigma_{N \setminus C}) > u_i(\sigma)$.*

Very briefly, these two solution concepts introduce a cooperative element in the analysis of the game. A SNE is not only immune to unilateral deviations, but also to deviations by coalitions. In a CPNE, the only coalitional deviations which are considered are those which satisfy a 'consistency' requirement – coalitional deviations must themselves be immune to further deviations by subcoalitions.

In their study of the SNE of the games Γ and Δ, Hart and Kurz (1983) only prove, by a counterexample, that SNE may fail to exist.

Proposition 3.4: *The games Γ and Δ may not admit SNE.*

Proof: See the counterexample in Hart and Kurz (1984).

For CPNE, Yi and Shin (1995) do not prove any general result. They characterise the CPNE of the games Δ and Γ for the specific case of cartel formation in Cournot oligopolies.[14] The existence of CPNE of the games Γ and Δ in general settings is still an open question.

As a final remark, the non-existence of SNE and CPNE may be due to the fact that *any coalition* is allowed to propose a deviation. In many applications, such as local public finance, the creation of new coalitions may be prohibitively costly. In that case, the right equilibrium concept should only involve individual moves. However, since individual players move from one coalition to another, the approval of the coalitions which are left or joned may be required. This in turn induces a restriction on the set of coalitions who may propose a deviation which might lead to an existence result.[15]

4 Sequential games of coalition formation

The study of simultaneous games of coalition formation raises three important difficulties (i) the set of Nash equilibria is usually very large, (ii) this multiplicity of equilibria imposes the use of a selection mechanism which might be too stringent (as in the case of SNE studied by Hart and Kurz (1983)) and (iii) in simultaneous games, players cannot be 'farsighted' in the sense that individual deviations cannot be countered by subsequent moves. I view this last difficulty as the most disturbing feature of simultaneous coalition formation games. For example consider the departure of a player from a coalition. In the simultaneous games of coalition formation, either the other coalition members remain together (in the open membership games and in the game Δ) or the coalition breaks apart (in the game Γ). But in both these formulations, members of the coalition which was left by the deviator respond in an *ad hoc* fashion; they are not allowed to react to the move of the deviator.

The problems of simultaneous games of coalition formation have led to the formulation of *sequential games of coalition formation* where the process is described by an explicit extensive form non-cooperative game. The earliest extensive form game was proposed by Aumann and Myerson (1988) in a setting slightly different from the classical coalition formation problem.[16] Aumann and Myerson (1988) explicitly emphasise that they want to study farsighted players, who take their actions envisioning the final consequences of their decisions.

In the context of games without spillovers, sequential processes have been proposed by Selten (1981), Chatterjee *et al.* (1993), Moldovanu (1992) and Perry and Reny (1994) among others. In most of these games, the basic structure is an extension to n players of Rubinstein's (1982) alternative-offers bargaining model. This structure was extended to games with spillovers by Bloch (1996) and Ray and Vohra (1996). These are the two models which will be presented here.

4.1 Sequential coalition formation with fixed payoff division

In the first paper, Bloch (1996) studies a sequential game of coalition formation when the rule of payoff division is fixed so that the underlying cooperation structure is represented by a valuation. The exact specification of the extensive form borrows from Rubinstein's (1982) bargaining game and its extension by Chatterjee *et al.* (1983).

The game proceeds as follows. Players are ordered according to a fixed rule. The first player starts the game by proposing the formation of a coalition C to which she belongs. Each prospective member responds to the proposal in the order determined by the fixed rule. If one of the players rejects the proposal, she must make a counteroffer and propose a coalition C' to which she belongs. If all members accept, the coalition is formed. All members of C then withdraw from the game, and the first player in $N\backslash C$ starts making a proposal.

This game describes in the simplest way a procedure where coalitions are formed *in sequence*. The main characteristic of the game is that, once a coalition has been formed, the game is only played among the remaining players. The extensive form thus embodies a high degree of commitment by the players. When players agree to join a coalition, they are bound to remain in that coalition. They can neither leave the coalition nor propose to change the coalition at later stages of the game.

It is assumed that players do not discount the future. Rather, in the case of an infinite play, the players who are still in the game receive a payoff of zero. Otherwise, if the game finishes in finite time, a coalition structure is formed, and players receive their payoff according to the underlying valuation.

As is well known, infinite-horizon games based on an alternating-offers scheme may have a multiplicity of subgame perfect equilibria. It is thus important to restrict the set of subgame perfect equilibria, by considering *stationary* strategies, which only depend on the current state of the game. The first result in Bloch (1996) shows that a stationary perfect equilibrium may fail to exist. This result is based on the following example.

Example 4.1: $N = \{a,b,c\}$, and ρ defines $a < b < c$

π	$v_a(\pi)$	$v_b(\pi)$	$v_c(\pi)$
$a\|b\|c$	1	1	1
$ab\|c$	3	2	1
$ac\|b$	2	1	3
$a\|bc$	1	3	2
abc	1	1	1

In this example, player a wants to form a coalition with player b, player b with player c, and player c with player a.

To show that the game does not admit any stationary equilibrium coalition structure, observe first that the three coalition structures $\{\{a,b,c\}\}$, $\{\{a\},\{b\},\{c\}\}$ and $\{\{a\},\{b,c\}\}$ cannot be supported by any equilibrium since player a would benefit from deviating and offering the formation of the coalition $\{a,c\}$ which player c would accept. The two other coalition structures $\{\{a,b\},\{c\}\}$ and $\{\{a,c\},\{b\}\}$ can be supported by equilibria in non-stationary strategies but not by a stationary perfect equilibrium.

For $\{\{a,b\},\{c\}\}$ to be supported by a stationary perfect equilibrium, it must be that player c rejects the offer $\{b,c\}$. But, in equilibrium, player c will only reject the offer $\{b,c\}$ if player a accepts the offer $\{a,c\}$. By stationarity, player b accepts the offer $\{a,b\}$ irrespective of the history of rejections which have preceded it. Hence, since player b always accepts the offer $\{a,b\}$, player a cannot accept the offer $\{a,c\}$.

Similarly, the coalition structure $\{\{a,c\},\{b\}\}$ is only supported by a strategy prescribing that player b rejects the offer $\{a,b\}$, implying that player c accepts the offer $\{b,c\}$. Since by stationarity, player a always accepts the offer $\{a,c\}$ player c should reject the offer $\{a,c\}$. Hence, the game does not admit any stationary perfect equilibrium.

Even when they exist, stationary perfect equilibria of the sequential game differ in general from the SNE of the simultaneous games, as the following proposition shows.

Proposition 4.2 (Bloch (1996)): *The coalition structures generated by the stationary perfect equilibria of the sequential game may differ from the coalition structures generated by SNE of the games Γ and Δ.*

Proof: See the example in Bloch (1996).

However, Bloch (1996) shows that there exists a specific class of valuations for which stationary perfect equilibria exist and are easily characterised. These are *symmetric* valuations where the value of a coalition structure only depends on the size of coalitions and not on the identity of coalition members.[17] For symmetric valuations, a simple finite procedure is defined to characterise the symmetric stationary perfect equilibria of the game.

The finite procedure runs as follows. Player 1 starts the game and chooses an integer k_1 in the interval $[1,n]$. Player k_1+1 then moves and chooses an integer k_2 in the set $[1,n-k]$. Player k_1+k_2+1 chooses at the next stage an integer k_3 in the set $[1,n-k_1-k_2]$. The game continues until the sequence of integers $(k_1,k_2,\ldots,k_j,\ldots,k_J)$ satisfies $\Sigma k_j=n$.

The exact equivalence between symmetric stationary perfect equilibria of the sequential game and the coalition structures obtained as outcome of the finite procedure is described in the following two propositions.

Proposition 4.3 (Bloch (1996)): *For any coalition structure generated by a symmetric stationary perfect equilibrium of the sequential game, there exists an equivalent coalition structure which is obtained as a subgame perfect equilibrium of the finite procedure.*

Proposition 4.4 (Bloch (1996), Ray and Vohra (1996)): *Consider a coalition structure π obtained as a subgame perfect equilibrium of the finite procedure with the property that payoffs are decreasing in the order in which coalitions are formed. Then there exists a symmetric stationary perfect equilibrium of the sequential game generating a coalition structure equivalent to π.*

Proof: See Bloch (1996).

Since the finite procedure described above always yields a subgame perfect equilibrium, and this equilibrium is generically unique, the equivalence result of propositions 4.3 and 4.4 imply the following corollary.

Corollary 4.5: *For symmetric valuations, when the finite procedure yields a coalition structure with the property that payoffs are decreasing in the order in which coalitions are formed, there exists a symmetric stationary perfect equilibrium of the sequential game. Furthermore, this equilibrium is generically unique.*

To conclude, for a specific class of valuations (symmetric valuations with the additional property that payoffs are decreasing in the order in which coalitions are formed), the sequential game proposed by Bloch (1996) yields a particularly sharp prediction. A symmetric stationary equilibrium always exists and is (generically) unique. This result should be contrasted to the multiplicity of Nash equilibria (and the possible non-existence of SNE) in the simultaneous case.[18] In applications, the sequential game might thus prove to be more useful than the simultaneous games.

4.2 Sequential coalition formation and bargaining

In a recent paper, Ray and Vohra (1996) have generalised the game proposed by Bloch (1996) by allowing for an *endogenous distribution of coalitional gains*. This paper represents a very important step in the study of endogenous coalition formation, since it is the first paper to tackle simultaneously the three questions posed in the Introduction.

In Ray and Vohra (1996), the underlying cooperative situation is represented by a *TU partition function game* rather than a valuation. The main difference between the game proposed by Bloch (1996) and the game studied by Ray and Vohra (1996) stems from the strategy spaces of the players. In Bloch (1996), players simply announce the coalition they want to form; in Ray and Vohra (1996), players simultaneously announce a coalition and the division of the coalitional worth.[19]

Ray and Vohra's (1996) first result shows the existence of a stationary perfect equilibrium of the bargaining game (in mixed strategies). An important feature of their existence result is that players only need to use a mixed strategy in their choice of coalitions (and not in their offer of division of the coalitional worth).

In symmetric games, where the partition function only depends on the size composition of the coalition structures, Ray and Vohra (1996) analyse in depth the stationary perfect equilibria of the bargaining game. They introduce the notion of *proposer-symmetric* equilibria, where at any stage of the game, the payoff of player i as a proposer is identical to the payoff of player j as a proposer.

Ray and Vohra (1996) introduce a finite algorithm to compute coalition structures, which is almost equivalent to that proposed in Bloch (1996).

(The only difference is that, in case of indifference between two strategies, Ray and Vohra (1996) assume that a player selects the *largest* coalition size.) They show that the coalition structure generated by proposer-symmetric equilibria must be equivalent to those obtained in the finite algorithm. Ray and Vohra (1996) also study no-delay equilibria and prove that, if an equilibrium does not involve delay, it must be proposer-symmetric.

The results in Ray and Vohra (1996) can be summarised by the following list of inclusions.

Proposition 4.6: *Let $\mathscr{E}_1$ be the set of stationary perfect equilibria (SPE) of the bargaining game, $\mathscr{E}_2$ the set of SPE yielding the coalition structure obtained by the finite algorithm, $\mathscr{E}_3$ the set of proposer-symmetric SPE and $\mathscr{E}_4$ the set of no-delay SPE. Then*

$$\mathscr{E}_1 \supset \mathscr{E}_2 \supset \mathscr{E}_3 \supset \mathscr{E}_4$$

Proof: See Ray and Vohra (1996).

In their paper, Ray and Vohra (1996) present examples to show that these inclusions may be strict. Furthermore, it is important to observe that the existence of SPE (non-emptiness of the set $\mathscr{E}_1$) does not guarantee that a SPE yielding the same coalition structure as the finite algorithm always exists (i.e., that the set $\mathscr{E}_2$ is non-empty.) In the paper, Ray and Vohra (1996) propose a stronger requirement, in order to show that the set $\mathscr{E}_4$ is non-empty. The sufficient condition they define can be intuitively interpreted as the fact that, in a constrained version of the finite algorithm, the payoffs obtained by coalition members are always decreasing in the order in which coalitions are formed.

In the second part of their paper, Ray and Vohra (1996) generalise their results to all TU partition function games and provide a general algorithm for computing the no-delay SPE of the bargaining game. I would like to emphasise what I believe are the two most important contributions of Ray and Vohra (1996): (i) they show that, in symmetric games, the assumption of equal division can be supported in a bargaining game, and that the coalition structures formed can be obtained by the same finite algorithm as in the fixed payoff division case and (ii) they provide a generalisation of the finite algorithm to the non-symmetric case.

5 Stable coalition structures

In this section, I turn my attention to *cooperative* concepts of stability which have been proposed for games with spillovers. Unfortunately, most of these stability concepts lack clear non-cooperative foundations. Nevertheless, they provide useful benchmarks and have been used extensively in economic applications. I first describe the most elementary stability concepts, which are based on two extreme notions of core stability. I then describe various restrictions on the set of deviations and deviating coalitions which have been proposed in the literature.

5.1 Core stable coalition structures

As noted by Greenberg (1994), in games without spillovers, the most natural concept of stability is directly derived from the core: a coalition structure is said to be *core stable* if there does not exist a group of agents who would obtain a higher payoff by forming another coalition. Unfortunately, this simple definition does not easily generalise to games with spillovers. In a game represented by a valuation, or a partition function, the payoff obtained by a deviating coalition is not well defined. This payoff depends on the *reaction of external players* to the deviation.

Two extreme solution concepts have been proposed to deal with this issue. The first solution concept, initially proposed by Shenoy (1979) and termed 'core stability' supposes that, following a deviation, external players react as if they were *maximising* the payoff of the deviating coalition. This is clearly a very optimistic conjecture on the part of members of the deviating coalition. On the other hand, Hart and Kurz (1983) suggest to look at α and β stability concepts where members of the deviating coalition expect the worst from external players. As in the definitions of the α and β core, in an α stable coalition structure, it is assumed that there does not exist a group of players who could obtain a higher payoff irrespective of the behaviour of the external players; in a β stable structure, there is no group of players who are guaranteed to obtain a higher payoff whatever the behaviour of the external players.

Formally, we define core stable, α stable and β stable coalition structures below. We assume that the underlying cooperative situation is represented by a valuation, but similar definitions could be given for partition function games.

Definition 5.1: *A coalition structure π is* core stable *if there does not exist a group C of players and a coalition structure $\pi' \supset C$ such that $\forall i \in C$, $v_i(\pi') > v_i(\pi)$.*

Definition 5.2: *A coalition structure π is α stable if there does not exist a group C of players and a partition π'_C such that, for all partitions $\pi_{N\backslash C}$ formed by external players, $\forall i \in C$, $v_i(\pi'_C \cup \pi_{N\backslash C}) > v_i(\pi)$.*

Definition 5.3: *A coalition structure π is β stable if there does not exist a group C of players such that, for all partitions $\pi_{N\backslash C}$ of external players, there exists a partition π_C of C such that $\forall i \in C$, $v_i(\pi_C \cup \pi_{N\backslash C}) > v_i(\pi)$.*

From the definitions, it is easy to see that deviations occur more frequently under core stability than under β stability and under β stability than under α-stablity. Hence, letting C_c, C_β and C_α denote the set of core stable, β-stable and α-stable coalition structures, one easily obtains the following inclusions: $C_c \subset C_\beta \subset C_\alpha$. Furthermore, as we have noted, the SNE of the games Γ and Δ can also be analysed as cooperative concepts of stability, where the external players behave according to an *ad hoc* rule. In the game Δ, members of a coalition left by some player stick together, whereas in the game Γ, coalitions left by some player dissolve. Since these *ad hoc* rules of behaviour can be viewed as intermediate assumptions on the behaviour of external player, we obtain the following list of inclusions.

Proposition 5.4: (Hart and Kurz (1983) and Kurz (1988)) *Let C_c, C_γ, C_δ, C_β and C_α denote the stable coalition structures under core stability, the Γ game, the Δ game, β-stability and α-stability respectively. Then*

$$C_c \subset (C_\gamma \cup C_\delta) \subset C_\beta \subset C_\alpha$$

Proof: Immediate from the definitions.

It thus appears that all concepts of stability proposed in Hart and Kurz (1983) can be ranked by inclusion. Unfortunately, even the largest solution concept C_α may be empty, as Hart and Kurz (1984) show in an example of a ten-player symmetric majority game.

Proposition 5.5 (Hart and Kurz (1984)): *There exist valuations v for which the set C_α is empty.*

5.2 Equilibrium binding agreements

The possible emptiness of the set of α stable coalition structures may indeed be due to the fact that *all* coalitional deviations are allowed. Ray and Vohra (1995) propose a new solution concept which, as the CPNE of Bernheim, Peleg and Whinston (1987) for non-cooperative games, rules out coalitional deviations which are not themselves immune to further deviations by sub-coalitions. This solution concept – termed 'Equilibrium Binding Agreements' (EBA) – can be viewed as the most sophisticated notion of stability for games with spillovers. It is defined for games in strategic form, and EBA are strategy profiles. A coalition structure will be termed 'stable' if it can be supported by an EBA.

Intuitively, in their analysis of stable coalition structures, Ray and Vohra (1995) restrict the set of possible deviations by imposing a consistency requirement on the deviation. Furthermore, rather than postulating a fixed rule of behaviour on the part of external players, Ray and Vohra (1995) propose an ingenious definition of the reaction of external players to a deviation.

The formal definition of Equilibrium Binding Agreements is recursive and goes as follows. For the finest partition, consisting only of singletons, the set of EBA is simply the set of Nash equilibria of the game. Suppose now that EBAs have been defined for all partitions finer than a fixed partition π. Take a strategy profile x for the coalition structure π which is obtained as a Nash equilibrium of the game between coalitions, and cooperative play inside each coalition.

We say that (π,x) is *blocked* by (π',x') if π' is a refinement of π and there exists a collection of agents in the move from π to π' such that:

x' is an EBA for π'.

There exists a group of agents C such that $\forall i \in C$, $u_i(x') > u_i(x)$.

Any remerging of other agents is also blocked by (π',x').

Now x is an EBA for π if there does not exist any (π',x') which blocks (π,x).

In words, for a strategy profile to be an EBA, it must be immune to a coalitional deviation which (i) is consistent in the sense that no further deviations will occur inside the coalition and (ii) can be supported by external players in the sense that if some external players were to remerge, this remerging would again be blocked by the same deviation.

In spite of its apparent complexity, the definition of EBA thus corresponds to natural consistency requirements on coalitional deviations. Clearly, as in other cooperative notions of stability, the process analysed by Ray and Vohra (1995) does not generally yield a unique stable coalition structure. Rather, the focus of the analysis in Ray and Vohra (1995) is on *efficiency* of the coalition structures supported by EBAs.

5.3 Membership rights

The last class of cooperative stability concepts is closer in spirit to traditional solution concepts. In this class, it is the set of *deviating coalitions* which is restricted rather than the set of *coalitional deviations*. In particular, it is assumed that only individual players can deviate and that the only coalitions which may have a say are the coalitions left and joined by the player.

The motivation for restricting attention to individual moves comes from some economic applications, where the creation of new coalitions is prohibitively costly and movements of players only take place across existing coalitions. For example, in the studies inspired by Tiebout (1956) on the provision of local public goods, jurisdictions are usually assumed to be fixed, and economic agents can only move from one jurisdiction to another.

Formally, there exists a variety of solution concepts based on individual moves depending on which coalitions can object to the move of the player. In Greenberg's (1977) original concept of *individually stable coalition structures*, agreement was required from the coalition joined by the individual player. The concept of *individually stable contractual coalition structures* later proposed by Drèze and Greenberg (1980) requires agreement both from the coalition left and the coalition joined by the player. Recently, Sertel (1993) and Eren (1993) have generalised these solution concepts by defining *property rights* for coalitions. These property rights are money transfers which need to be paid for participation in a coalition or departure from a coalition.

It should be noted that, in the context of games without spillovers, the existence of individually stable coalition structures has been proved for a large class of models (see Greenberg, 1994). In fact, it turns out that by only allowing deviations by a group formed by an individual and a coalition, this solution concept is much less demanding than concepts based on core stability. It thus seems that the existence of individually stable coalition strutures in games with spillovers could be obtained for some classes of games. But the study of existence of stable coalition structures with property rights in games with spillovers still remains to be done.

6 Games with positive spillovers

In this section, I present and discuss the outcome of several models of coalition formation in situations where the underlying cooperative game exhibits positive spillovers. Positive spillovers arise in a number of economic models, where outsiders benefit from the formation of a coalition. In these models, coalition members provide some type of public good which benefits all the players, and external members enjoy the public good without supporting its cost. The two most studied examples of coalition formation with positive spillovers are the formation of cartels on oligopolistic markets and of coalitions providing pure public goods. I will study both of these models in turn. However, before entering into the details of the models, I first present some general results on games with positive spillovers due to Yi (1995b).

6.1 Games with positive spillovers: general results

In his study of games with positive spillovers, Yi (1995b) compares the outcomes of different games of coalition formation for a class of symmetric valuation satisfying three properties: (i) positive spillovers, (ii) negative association between coalition size and payoff and (iii) inverse monotonicity for small coalitions. Before I can formally list these three axioms, I need to define Yi and Shin's (1995) concept of *concentration* which is not to be confused with the more classical notion of coarsening.

Definition 6.1: *A coalition structure $\pi=\{n_1,n_2,...,n_m\}$ is a concentration of a coalition structure $\pi'=\{n'_1,n'_2,...,n'_{m'}\}$ if there exist two subcoalition structures, D and D' of π and π', $D=\{k_1,k_2,...,k_s\}$ with $k_1 \geq k_2 \geq ... \geq k_s$ and $D'=\{k'_1,k'_2,...,k'_{s+t}\}$ with $k'_1 \geq k'_2 \geq ... \geq k'_{s+t}$ such that (i) $\pi \backslash D = \pi' \backslash D'$ and (ii) $\Sigma^{j}_{i=1}k_i > \Sigma^{j}_{i=1}k'_i$ for all $j=1,2...,s$.*

In words, a coalition structure π is a concentration of π' if it can be obtained by picking members of some coalitions in π' and adding those members to larger or equal sized coalitions in π'. Not that this definition *is not* equivalent to the more classical definition of a coarsening. It is easy to see that any coarsening is a concentration, but the following example shows that the reverse implication is not necessarily true. The coalition structure $\pi=\{3,3\}$ is a concentration of the coalition structure $\pi'=\{2,2,2\}$ but it is not a coarsening. The three axioms can then be expressed as follows.

Axiom 6.2 (Positive spillovers): *Consider two coalition structures π and π' such that $C \in \pi'$ and $\pi \backslash C$ is a concentration of $\pi' \backslash C$ then $v_i(\pi) > v_i(\pi')$ for all $i \in C$.*

Axiom 6.3 (Negative association): *For any coalition structure π and any two coalitions C and D in π, for all $i \in C, j \in D, v_i(\pi) < v_j(\pi)$ if and only if $|C| > |D|$.*

Axiom 6.4 (Inverse montonicity): *Consider two coalitions C and D in π with $|C| > |D|$. Then $\forall i \in D, v_i(\pi) > v_i(\pi \backslash \{C,D\} \cup \{C \backslash \{j\}, D \cup \{j\}\})$.*

Under these three axioms, Yi and Shin (1995) and Yi (1995b) study the outcomes of the open membership game, the games Γ and Δ, the sequential game of coalition formation and Ray and Vohra's (1995) equilibrium binding agreements. The results are as follows.

Proposition 6.5 (Yi and Shin (1995) and Yi (1995b)): *Suppose that the three axioms of positive spillovers, negative association and inverse monotonicity hold. The coalition structures obtained as a CPNE of the open membership game are always less concentrated than any CPNE of the game* Δ. *All SNE of the game* Γ *give rise to coalition structures which are more concentrated than in the CPNE of the game* Δ. *The unique SPE of the sequential game gives rise to a coalition structure which is more concentrated than the coalition structures obtained as CPNE of the game* Δ. *Finally, the EBA can support coalition structures which are more concentrated than those obtained as CPNE of the game* Δ.

Proof: See Yi and Shin (1995) and Yi (1995b).

The studies by Yi (1995b) and Yi and Shin (1995) thus provide a general ordering on the coalition structures obtained under various games of coalition formation. In order to obtain a complete characterisation of the coalition structures, one needs to go back to specific economic models.

6.2 Cartel formation in a homogeneous Cournot oligopoly

The most famous economic model in which the issue of coalition formation with positive spillover arises is the model of cartels on oligopolistic markets. I consider here the simplest version of the model, where firms compete in quantities, produce a homogeneous good and face a linear demand schedule. Formally, let the inverse demand be given by

$$P = 1 - \Sigma q_i$$

I assume that all firms are identical, and may produce the homogeneous good at a constant marginal cost equal to zero. In this framework, fix a cartel structure $\pi = \{C_1, C_2, \ldots, C_k\}$ consisting of k different cartels. Given the assumption made on cost and demand structures, it is easy to see that competition between cartels gives rise to the same output as competition between k independent firms. Hence, each cartel will produce a quantity $q = \dfrac{1}{k+1}$ and obtain a profit $Pr = \dfrac{1}{(k+1)^2}$. The valuation (which gives the profit a firm obtains in any cartel structure) can thus be defined for any firm i in cartel C_j as

$$v_i(\pi) = \frac{1}{(k+1)^2 |C_j|}.$$

It appears that the profit obtained by a firm only depends on (i) the size of the cartel to which it belongs and (ii) the total number of cartels formed on the market. Furthermore, it is easy to check that the valuation satisfies the three axioms defined above. In fact, when the other players form a more concentrated coalition structure, the total number of cartels k goes down, thus increasing the payoff of an outside firm. It is also clear that, for a fixed coalition structure, members of smaller cartels obtain a higher payoff. Finally, it is easy to check that, if one firm leaves a cartel C to join a cartel D, all members of the cartel D are worse off. Using the valuation defined above, I can now characterise the outcome of various games of coalition formation.

First, I need to define, following Salant, Switzer and Reynolds (1983) the *minimal profitable coalition size*. This is the smallest coalition size for which a coalition member obtains a higher payoff than if all firms are independent, i.e.

$$k^* = \min \left\{ k, \frac{1}{k(n-k+1)^2} \geq \frac{1}{(n+1)^2} \right\}.$$

It is easy to see that

$$k^* = \frac{2n+3-\sqrt{4n+5}}{2},$$

a value which is never smaller than $0.8n$, namely 80 per cent of the firms on the market. Table 10.1 summarises the outcomes of the games of coalition formation.

The precise proofs of these statements can be found in the papers by Yi and Shin (1995). Bloch (1996) and Ray and Vohra (1995). The intuition underlying the results is easy to grasp. In the game Δ and the open membership game, following the departure of one firm, members of a cartel remain together. This assumption makes it easy for a firm to leave the cartel and free-ride on the output reduction of other cartel members. Hence, in the only Nash equilibrium (and CPNE) of the game, firms remain independent and no cartel is formed.[20] In the game Δ and under the α and β stability concepts, following the departure of a firm, the cartel breaks down. This assumption clearly makes deviations more difficult and in fact any cartel of size greater than k^* can be supported as a SNE. In the sequential game, firms commit to stay out of the cartel until the number of remaining firms equals the minimal profitable cartel size. At that point, the remaining firms form a cartel. Finally, EBAs exhibit an interesting cyclical pattern, whereby the grand coalition $\pi = \{n\}$ is sometimes supported as a stable coalition structure, sometimes not, depending on the number of firms on the market.[21]

Table 10.1. *Cartels*

Open membership	$\{1,1,\ldots,1\}$
Game Γ	$\{k,1,\ldots,1\}$ for any $k \geq k*$
Game Δ	$\{1,1,\ldots,1\}$
Sequential game	$\{k*,1,\ldots,1\}$
α stability	$\{k,1,\ldots,1\}$ for any $k \geq k*$
β stability	$\{k,1,\ldots,1\}$ for any $k \geq k*$
Equilibrium binding agreements	Cyclical pattern for n to be stable.

6.3 Pure public goods

The second application of games with positive spillovers are economies with pure public goods. In these economies, agents have an incentive to form coalitions in order to benefit from increasing returns to size in the production of public goods, but also have an incentive to leave the coalition and free ride on the provision of public goods by coalition members. Recently, models inspired by pure public goods economies have been proposed to study the formation of International Environmental Agreements (IEA). Carraro and Siniscalco (1993), Barrett (1994) and Tulkens and Chander (1992) study the participation of countries to IEAs by which they commit to reduce (or abate) the pollution they emit. In that case, pollution abatement is viewed as a pure public good provided by the signatories of the IEA. I analyse here a simple public good model inspired by Barrett's (1994) study of IEAs.

I consider an economy with n identical agents. Each agent benefits from the public good, and obtains a utility which is assumed to be linear in the total amount of public good provided

$$U_i(x) = x.$$

I also assume that each agent owns a technology to produce the public good, and that the cost of producing the amount x_i of the public good is given by

$$C_i(x_i) = \frac{1}{2}x_i^2.$$

Note that, since individual cost functions are convex and exhibit decreasing returns to scale, it is cheaper to produce an amount x of public goods using all n technologies than using a single technology. Hence, coalitions benefit from increasing returns to size in the production of the public good.

Next, I suppose that, once the coalition structure $\pi = \{C_1, C_2, \ldots, C_m\}$ is formed, each coalition of agents acts non-cooperatively, and chooses a level of public good in response to the contributions of the other coalitions. However, inside every coalition, agents act cooperatively and the level of public good is chosen to maximise the sum of utilities of the coalition members.

Hence, for any coalition structure π, the level of public good x_i chosen by the coalition C_i solves

$$\max |C_i| \left(x_i + \sum_{j \neq i} x_j - \frac{1}{2} \left(\frac{x_i^2}{|C_i|} \right) \right),$$

yielding a total level of public good provision for the coalition $x_i = |C_i|^2$.

In equilibrium, any member of the coalition C_i thus provides an amount $|C_i|$ of the public good, and receives a utility

$$v_i(\pi) = \sum_{j=1}^{m} |C_j|^2 - \frac{1}{2} |C_i|^2.$$

Again, it is easy to see that whenever the coalition structure formed by other agents is more concentrated, the payoff $v_i(\pi)$ increases. It is also immediate to note that larger coalitions receive lower payoffs and that the arrival of a new member decreases the payoff of members of smaller cartels. Hence, the three axioms defined by Yi (1995b) are satisfied.

In order to characterise the outcomes of the various games of coalition formation, it appears to be useful to recall the definition of the sequence of *Fibonacci numbers*, $f_0 = 1$, $f_1 = 2$ and $f_n = f_{n-1} + f_{n-2}$. Next consider, for any integer n, the following partition. In the first step, select the largest Fibonnaci number f^1 smaller than n. At any step k, select the largest Fibonacci number f^k smaller than $n - \sum_{i=1}^{k-1} f^i$. This is a finite procedure, and it yields a unique result that we call the *Fibonacci decomposition of n*, denoted $\Phi(n)$.

The computations underlying the construction of table 10.2 can be found in the appendix. It appears that, as opposed to the case of cartel formation, in a public good economy, agents have an incentive to form coalitions of at least two players. Hence, even in the open membership game and in the game Δ, there exist non-trivial coalition structures emerging as Nash equilibrium outcomes. (Note however that there does not exist any SNE for these games, since in any coalition structure obtained in equilibrium, members of two coalitions have an incentive to merge.) It is also worthwhile to note that the sizes of the coalitions formed is rather small (2 or 3). This result is reminiscent of Barrett's (1994) observation that International Environmental Agreements typically have only group a small number of signatories. The game Γ admits a large number of SNE, all characterised by

Table 10.2. *Coalitions providing public goods*

Open membership	$\{c_1,c_2,...,c_m\}$ with $c_i \leq 3$ for all i and $c_j = 1 \Rightarrow c_i \neq 1$ for all $i \neq j$
Game Γ	$\{c_1,c_2,...,c_m\}$ with $c_1 < c_2 < ... < c_m$ and $c_i \leq \frac{c_{i+1}}{2}$ for all i.
Game Δ	$\{c_1,c_2,...,c_m\}$ with $c_i \leq 3$ for all i and $c_j = 1 \Rightarrow c_i \neq 1$ for all $i \neq j$
Sequential game	$\Phi(n)$
α stability	$\{c_1,c_2,...,c_m\}$ with $c_1 < c_2 < ... < c_m$ and $c_i \leq \frac{c_{i+1}}{2}$ for all i.
β stability	$\{c_1,c_2,...,c_m\}$ with $c_1 < c_2 < ... < c_m$ and $c_i \leq \frac{c_{i+1}}{2}$ for all i.
Equilibrium binding agreements	Cyclical pattern for n to be stable.

a wide variation in the sizes of the coalitions formed. For a coalition structure to emerge as a SNE of the game Γ, it must contain coalitions such that,
for any two consecutive coalitions, the smaller contains fewer than half the
number of players of the larger. Now it is clear that in games with positive
spillovers, the three concepts of α, β and γ stablity coincide, so that there
also exist a large number of α and β stable coalitions. The most intriguing
result is obtained for the sequential game. Following Ray and Vohra (1996),
I assume that whenever an agent is indifferent between forming two coalitions of different sizes, she chooses the largest coalition size. It then appears
that the coalitions formed in equilibrium follow a simple recursive structure
(given by Fibonacci numbers), and can be viewed as the 'most concentrated' coalitions satisfying the property that, for any two consecutive coalitions, the size of the smaller is less than half that of the larger. Finally, for
EBAs, Ray and Vohra (1995) prove, in a different public good economy,
that a cyclical pattern emerges, in which the grand coalition is sometimes,
but not always, supported by an EBA.

7 Games with negative spillovers

In games with negative spillovers, the formation of a coalition by external
players has an adverse effect on the profit of a player. Negative spillovers
arise naturally in many oligopolistic games where the formation of a coalition leads to a decrease in the production cost of member firms. For
example, the formation by firms of associations or of Research Joint
Ventures (RJVs) leads to a decrease in production costs, which makes

coalition members behave more aggressively on the market. Similarly, the formation of customs unions enables firms of member states to benefit from increasing returns to scale and to exploit that cost advantage on the world market. More generally, these examples suggest that negative spillovers emerge in two-stage games where cooperation improves the position of players who compete against each other in the second stage of the game. I first present some general results on games with negative spillovers due to Yi (1995a) before analysing in detail models of associations of firms and of customs unions.

7.1 Games with negative spillovers: general results

As in his study of games with positive spillovers, Yi (1995a) first introduces three general axioms which can be shown to be satisfied by most economic examples of games with negative spillovers.

Axiom 7.1 (Negative spillovers): *Let π and π' be two coalition structures such that $C \in \pi$, $C \in \pi'$ and $\pi' = \pi \backslash \{D_1, D_2\} \cup \{(D_1 \cup D_2)\}$ for some coalitions D_1 and D_2, then, for all $i \in C$, $v_i(\pi) > v_i(\pi')$.*

Axiom 7.2 (Monotonicity for small coalitions): *Let π and π' be two coalition structures such that $\pi' = \pi \backslash \{C_1, C_2, ..., C_k\} \cup \{C_1 \cup C_2 \cup ... \cup C_k\}$ where $c_1 \geq c_2 \geq ... \geq c_k$ then for all $i \in C_k$, $v_i(\pi') > v_i(\pi)$.*

Axiom 7.3 (Individual monotonicity): *Let π and π' be two coalition structures such that $\pi' = \pi \backslash \{C, D\} \cup \{C \cup \{i\}, D \backslash \{i\}\}$ for some $i \in D$ and $c \geq d$, then $v_i(\pi') > v_i(\pi)$.*

The three axioms can easily be interpreted. The first axiom states that, whenever two coalitions of external players merge, the payoff of a player decreases: this is the negative spillovers axiom. The second and third axioms introduce a monotonicity requirement on the valuation v. The axiom of monotonicity of small coalitions states that, whenever a group of coalitions merge, members of the smallest coalition benefit from the merger. The axiom of individual monotonicity indicates that an individual player always has an incentive to leave a coalition in order to join a coalition of equal or larger size.

It is easy to see that, under the individual monotonicity axiom, the only Nash equilibrium of the open membership game is the grand coalition. Yi (1995a) states and proves a more general proposition, comparing the outcomes of the open membership game, the sequential game of coalition formation and EBAs.

Proposition 7.4 (Yi (1995a)): *In games satisfying individual monotonicity, the NE outcome of the open membership game is more concentrated than the SPE outcomes of the sequential game or any of the EBAs. Under some additional conditions, the SPE outcome of the sequential game is more concentrated than any of the EBAs.*

Proof: See Yi (1995a).

7.2 Associations of firms

Cooperation among competing firms is increasingly common on oligopolistic markets. More and more often, competing firms agree to share information, build common facilities or launch common research programmes, in order to decrease their production costs. Bloch (1995) studies the formation of these associations of firms in a very simple model where the benefits from cooperation increase linearly in the size of the association (see also Yi (1995c)).

I assume that demand is linear and given by $P = \alpha - \sum_{i=1}^{n} q_i$. Firms have a constant marginal cost of production, which is decreasing in the size of the association they belong to. The cost of a firm i in an association A of size a is thus given by: $c_i = \lambda - \mu a$. Finally, I suppose that the parameter values α, λ and μ are chosen in such a way that for any coalition structure, all firms are active in a Cournot equilibrium.

Once associations are formed on the market, firms select non-cooperatively the quantities they offer on the market. For a coalition structure $\pi = \{A_1, A_2, \ldots, A_k\}$, it is easy to see that there exists a unique Cournot equilibrium on the market, and that each firm's profit is a monotonically increasing function of the following valuation

$$v_i(\pi) = \frac{\alpha - \lambda}{n+1} + \mu a(i) - \mu \frac{\sum_{j=1}^{k} a_j^2}{n+1},$$

where $a(i)$ denotes the size of the association firm i belongs to. It is easy to check that this valuation satisfies the three axioms in Yi (1995a). Negative spillovers arise because the merger of two outside associations leads to a decrease in the valuation. The two monotonicity axioms can also easily be shown to hold for the valuation v defined above. I describe the outcomes of the various games of coalition formation for associations of firms in table 10.3.

It turns out that, with the exception of the open membership game and the game Γ, all models of coalition formation give the same solution: a dominant association grouping around three quarters of the industry

Table 10.3. *Associations of firms*

Open membership	$\{n\}$
Game Γ	No SNE. All π are NE.
Game Δ	$\{k^*, n-k^*\}$ where $k^* = \frac{3n+1}{4}$
Sequential game	$\{k^*, n-k^*\}$ where $k^* = \frac{3n+1}{4}$
α stability	$\{k^*, n-k^*\}$ where $k^* = \frac{3n+1}{4}$
β stability	$\{k^*, n-k^*\}$ where $k^* = \frac{3n+1}{4}$

forms, and the remaining firms form a smaller association. This result can be understood by recalling the following two observations, which are proved in Bloch (1995): (i) an association has an incentive to accept new members until its size reaches $\frac{n}{2}$ and (ii) when two associations form, the size $k^* = \frac{3n+1}{4}$ is the optimal size from the viewpoint of the first association. From these two observations, it is easy to check that the only α and β stable coalition structure is $\pi = \{k^*, n-k^*\}$ which is also immune to deviations by coalitions in the game Δ. Bloch (1995) shows that this coalition structure is also the unique SPE outcome of the sequential game. Note however that this structure is not a SNE in the game Γ: firms obtain a higher payoff in the structure $\pi' = \left\{\frac{n}{2}, 1, \ldots, 1\right\}$ and hence the coalition structure $\pi = \{k^*, n-k^*\}$ is not immune to a coalitional deviation in the game Γ. Since, in the game Γ, individual players never have an incentive to leave any coalition and are not free to join the coalition they want, any coalition structure is a NE outcome of the game.

7.3 Customs unions

The second example I present is the formation of customs unions in international trade. The emergence of three regional trading blocks, in North America, Europe and Asia has prompted considerable interest in the study of the formation of customs unions. Recent contributions to the study of trading blocs have focused on cooperative solution concepts (Riezman (1995) and Macho-Stadler *et al.* (1994)) on symmetric trading blocs (Krugman (1991) and Bond and Syropoulos (1993)) or on very specific coalition structures (Baldwin (1993) and Haveman (1995)).[22] I consider here a simplified version of Yi's (1995d)'s model of customs unions formation, which does not impose any restriction on the coalition structure formed.[23]

Following Krugman (1991), a customs union is modelled as a coalition of countries which eliminate tariffs among themselves and impose a common external tariff. In a model of imperfect competition with increasing returns to scale, it turns out that firms in larger trading blocs have a lower production cost and behave more aggressively on the world market. Hence, the game exhibits negative spillovers and the formation of customs unions can be viewed as special case of games with negative spillovers.

More precisely, let there be n countries. The utility function of a representative consumer in country i is quasi-linear and quadratic in the consumption of the good

$$u_i = aq_i - \frac{1}{2}q_i^2 + M_i,$$

where q_i is the consumption of the good and M_i the numeraire good consumption.

In each country, the good is produced by a monopolistic firm at a constant marginal cost (measured in the numeraire good) equal to c. Letting τ_{ij} denote the tariff imposed by country i on goods from j, firm j's effective cost of production in country j is $c + \tau_{ij}$. Hence, the firm of country j chooses a production q_{ij} in order to maximise its profit

$$P_{ij} = (a - \sum_{k=1}^{n} q_{ik} - c - \tau_{ij})q_{ij}.$$

In a Nash equilibrium of the model, the quantity offered by firm j on market i is thus given by

$$q_{ij}^* = \frac{1 + \sum_{k=1}^{n} \tau_{ik} - (n+1)\tau_{ij}}{n+1}.$$

Next suppose that a customs unions structure $\pi = \{C_1, C_2, ..., C_m\}$ forms. Each customs union abolishes tariffs inside the union and selects a common external tariff in order to maximise the sum of welfare of its members. Simple computations show that the optimal tariff only depends on the size c_i of the customs union, and is given by

$$\tau = \frac{2c_i + 1}{n + 1 + (c_i + 1)(2c_i + 1)}.$$

One can then compute the total welfare of country i in customs union C_i as

$$W_i = u_i + \sum_{j=1}^{n} P_{ji},$$

and replacing by the equilibrium values of τ and q_{ij}^*, we obtain the valuation

$$v_i(\pi) = \frac{1}{2} - \frac{1}{n+1+(c_i+1)(2c_i+1)} + \sum_{j=1, j \neq i}^{m} \frac{c_j}{((n+1)+(c_j+1)(2c_j+1))^2}.$$

This valuation has been studied by Yi (1995d) who shows in particular that it satisfies the three axioms of games with negative spillovers. Table 10.4 reproduces some of Yi's (1995d) results for 'reasonable values' of the number n of countries.[24]

The complexity of the valuation does not permit a full characterisation of the coalition structures emerging as the outcomes of the various games of coalition formation. In particular, nothing is known about the outcomes of the games Δ and Γ in that model. For the open membership game and the sequential game of coalition formation, Yi (1995d) only obtains the partial characterisation given above (see table 10.4).

8 Conclusion and open questions

In this survey, I have described some recent contributions to the theory of endogenous coalition formation. I have discussed various representations of games with externalities among coalitions and presented some non-cooperative procedures which were recently proposed to analyse cooperation situations with spillovers. I have also shown how these models can be applied to address various economic problems, taken from public economics, industrial organisation and industrial economics. As I conclude this survey, I would like to mention what I view as important open problems in the area.

Cooperative study of partition function games. The study of partition function games is still very rudimentary. The following questions should be addressed: (i) conversion of strategic form games into partition function games, (ii) extension of classical cooperative concepts to partition function games, (iii) non-emptiness of the core in partition function games and (iv) relation between the core and the various Shapley values for games with fixed coalition strutures. Some properties of partition function games also need to be studied (e.g., convexity, negative and positive spillovers) and used to prove results on cooperative solution concepts.

Efficiency and transfers across coalitions All the solution concepts studied in this survey prohibit transfers across coalitions. Since transfers across coalitions are not allowed, the coalition structures obtained might be inefficient. Games with transfers among coalitions could be defined both

Table 10.4. *Customs unions*

Open membership	$\{n\}$
Sequential game	$\{k^*, n-k^*\}$ where k^* maximises $v_i(\{k, n-k\})$
α stability	$\{k^*, n-k^*\}$ where k^* maximises $v_i(\{k, n-k\})$
β stability	$\{k^*, n-k^*\}$ where k^* maximises $v_i(\{k, n-k\})$

in the simultaneous and sequential cases. Simultaneous games with transfers should be developed along the lines of Kamien and Zang's (1990) acquisition game. (See also Carraro and Siniscalco (1993) for a discussion of the role of transfers in the formation of coalitions.) Alternatively, one could analyse games with additional players acting as 'developers' of coalitions, as in Perez-Castrillo (1994). The issue of competition to attract members inside a coalition, and of the existence of a 'market' for coalitions is still understudied and should be investigated further. In the sequential setting, the extensive form could embody different rounds of negotiations, as in Gul (1989). It would then be interesting to study how players form temporary coalition structures in order to increase their bargaining power in future negotiations.

Applications While some economic applications have been discussed in the survey, there is still need for further studies of economic models of coalition formation. The inherent difficulty of computing stable coalition structures may prevent a general characterisation of coalitions in economic models, but some simple illustrative examples could provide additional insights into many areas. For instance, in public economics, the study of the provision of local public goods with spillovers is still very rudimentary. Another important area of application is the formation of coalitions of countries (for instance customs unions or signatories of different treaties) and the interrelation between the various issues over which those countries (or coalitions of countries) bargain. Finally, in political science, the models described above could be used and tested against data on the formation of coalitional governments in democratic countries.

Appendix: Equilibrium coalition structures for public goods

I start by establishing three simple facts, which will be used repeatedly in the computations. Note that whenever we compare the payoffs in two different coalition structures, it is enough to consider those coalitions which have changed from one structure to the other, since the payoff is an additive function of the sizes of external coalitions.

Fact 1   If $c \geq 4$ and members of coalition C remain together after the departure of an agent, then it pays to leave the coalition.

To establish this fact, notice that the inequality $1 + (k-1)^2 - \frac{1}{2} \geq \frac{1}{2} k^2$ is true for all $k \geq 4$. Hence, it always pays to leave a coalition of more than four members, if the remaining coalition members remain together.

Fact 2   For any two coalitions C and D with $c \geq d$, members of D have an incentive to merge if and only if $d \geq \frac{c}{2}$.

Note that the payoff to a member of D before the merger is $c^2 + \frac{1}{2} d^2$, to be compared with the payoff after the merger of $\frac{1}{2}(c+d)^2$. The latter is larger than the former if and only if $d \geq \frac{c}{2}$.

Fact 3   Suppose that, following the departure of some member, the coalition C breaks off, then it never pays to any subcoalition D of C to deviate.

In coalition C, the payoff is given by $\frac{1}{2} c^2$. After the deviation of the subcoalition D, its members receive $\frac{1}{2} d^2 + (c-d)$. Since $c \geq d$ and $c \geq 2$, the latter payoff is higher than the former, and the deviation does not benefit members of D.

Using facts 1 and 2, the Nash equilibrium outcomes of the open membership game and the game Δ can easily be derived. By fact 1, coalitions cannot contain more than three members, and by fact 2, there cannot exist two coalitions of size 1. Note however that the coalition structures found as NE outcomes cannot be strong Nash equilibria: as soon as it contains more than one coalition of size 2 or 3, members of these coalitions have an incentive to merge by fact 2.

To compute the SNE of the game Γ, first note that, when coalitions left by some member dissolves, it never pays for a player to leave a coalition, because $c - \frac{1}{2} \leq \frac{1}{2} c^2$ for all coalition sizes c. Furthermore, by fact 2, two coalitions C and D in a SNE coalition structure must satisfy the following condition: if $d \leq c$, then $d \leq \frac{c}{2}$.

It remains to show that any such coalition forms a SNE. Consider then a deviation by a coalition D. By fact 3, it never pays for a subcoalition to deviate. Hence the only candidates for deviations are supercoalitions, consisting of members of k different coalitions $C_1, C_2, \ldots, C_k$. However, by a repeated application of fact 2, it appears that members of the smaller coalition never gain by merging successively with members of larger coalitions.

Finally, I establish that the coalition structure Φ is the unique subgame perfect equilibrium of the sequential game, when ties are broken by making players choose the largest coalition when they are indifferent between two coalitions. The proof is by induction on the number n of players. First, it is easy to see that, for $n = 1$, the characterisation of equilibrium is correct.

Now pick $n > 1$ and consider the Fibonacci decomposition of $n = f_1 + f_2 + \ldots + f_K$ with $f_k > f_{k-1}$ for all k. The induction hypothesis is written as follows: for any $m < n$, in the unique SPE, the first player chooses f_K, the smallest coalition size in the Fibonacci decomposition.

I now prove that the induction hypothesis is true for n. Consider first a choice of coalition size $c > f_K$. Let the Fibonacci decompositions of $n - c$ and $n - f_K$ be denoted by $\mathcal{F}$ and $\mathcal{F}'$ respectively. Since $c > f_K$, $v_i(\mathcal{F}) < v_i(\mathcal{F}')$, $\forall i \in C$ and $v_i(\mathcal{F}') < v_j(\mathcal{F}')$ for all $i \in C$, $j \in F_K$. Hence, choosing a coalition of size $c > f_K$ cannot be a profitable deviation.

Suppose now that there exists a profitable deviation, by choosing a coalition size $c < f_K$. By fact 2, it must have $c < \dfrac{f_K}{2}$. But then, by the definition of Fibonacci numbers, and calling f^1 the number preceding $f_K = f^0$ in the Fibonacci sequence, I must have

$$f^0 - c > f^1,$$

so that, following the departure of c members, the coalition structure formed is of the form $\pi = \{f_1, \ldots, f_{K-1}, f^1, \ldots, f^L\}$. Now, I claim that c must be less than $\dfrac{1}{2} f^1$. If not, by fact 2, members of C have an incentive to merge with the coalition of size f^1, thus forming a coalition of size greater than $\dfrac{1}{2} f^0$. But then, by fact 2, members of C obtain a higher profit in the coalition of size f_K than in C and the deviation cannot be profitable. Repeating the argument, it turns out that, for a deviation to be profitable, the deviating coalition C must have a size satisfying: $c < \dfrac{f}{2}$ for all Fibonacci numbers f. In particular, $c < \dfrac{1}{2}$, a contradiction.

To conclude, I have shown that in a game with n players, the first player's optimal strategy is to choose a coalition size f_K. Now it is clear that, in a game with $n - f_K$ players, the last term of the Fibonacci decomposition is

f_{K-1}, so that the next coalition formed is the size of coalition f_{K-1}. A repeated application of this argument gives the desired result.□

Notes

I owe a great debt to Debraj Ray, Rajiv Vohra and Sang-Seung Yi for the ideas contained in this paper. My thoughts on coalition formation have been shaped by the numerous discussions I had with them over time. Part of this survey is based on work I did during my Ph.D. dissertation at the University of Pennsylvania and later as a post-doctoral fellow at CORE. I have greatly benefitted from discussions with Beth Allen, George Mailath, Andrew Postlewaite and Yves Younès at Penn and with Claude d'Aspremont, Jean Gabszewicz, Heracles Polemarchakis and Jacques Thisse at CORE. Finally, I gratefully acknowledge the financial support of the Fondazione ENI Enrico Mattei in the preparation of this survey.

1   More recent definitions of the bargaining set due to Mas-Colell (1989) and Zhou (1994) allow for the possibility that the coalition structure be endogenously formed. However, these bargaining sets were never used to build a general theory of endogenous coalition formation.

2   This definition corresponds to games with transferable utilities (TU games). In the case of NTU games, $v(C)$ is a subset of the Euclidean space $\mathfrak{R}^{|C|}$. For most of the discussion, I will focus on TU games.

3   As an example of a situation where the worth of a coalition is independent of the action of other players, consider an exchange economy. The worth of a coalition C of agents who form an exclusive trading group is independent of the actions of the other traders.

4   In order to deal with that problem, Zhao (1992) suggests to use the α core allocations inside each coalition.

5   In that case, Ray and Vohra (1995) suggest to take the best Nash equilibrium payoff from the coalition's point of view. But this might be unfeasible, since the best equilibrium might be different for different coalitions. Other selection devices could be used as well.

6   In that sense, a valuation can be viewed as a specific example of an NTU partition function, where each player gets a rectangular utility set.

7   The differences between these different values will not be discussed here. Kurz (1988) contains an excellent survey of the various extensions of the Shapley value to games with coalition structures.

8   The lack of superadditivity of valuations is of course linked to the existence of a fixed division rule. In the literature the possible lack of superadditivity of cooperative games has always been problematic. Aumann and Drèze (1974) discuss at length the reasons for which a cooperative game may not be superadditive. (See also Greenberg (1994), pp. 1308–9.) Guesnerie and Oddou (1981) give a public goods example of a game with a fixed division rule, which is not superadditive.

9   In their model of a 'dominant' cartel, d'Aspremont et al. (1983) show that the answer is always affirmative. However, in the traditional model of Cournot oli-

gopoly with homogeneous goods studied by Salant, Switzer and Reynolds (1983) and more recently by Thoron (1994), the answer is negative: there is no stable cartel of firms on the market.

10 See Donsimoni, Economides and Polemarchakis (1986) for examples where there exist multiple equilibria in the cartel formation game.

11 A generalisation of the cartel formation game would be obtained if individual players had the opportunity to announce a message by which they commit to remain independent.

12 In fact, the existence of a Nash equilibrium in pure strategies is not guaranteed in this open membership game.

13 It will be seen in section 7 that this monotonicity requirement is satisfied in many economic games with negative spillovers.

14 These results will be discussed in section 6.

15 These ideas are pursued in more detail in section 5 on stable coalition structures.

16 Aumann and Myerson (1988) study the formation of *bilateral links* between players yielding a *cooperation graph* rather than a coalition structure. For recent studies of link formation games see Qin (1996) and Dutta, Tijs and van Nouweland (1995).

17 Symmetric valuations are obtained when all players are *ex ante* identical.

18 In fact, the example used by Hart and Kurz (1984) to show inexistence of a SNE for the two games Γ and Δ involves precisely a symmetric valuation where the payoffs are decreasing in the order in which coalitions are formed. See Bloch (1996) for details.

19 There is another difference in the way the future is discounted. In Ray and Vohra (1996), as opposed to Bloch (1996), players discount the future at a constant rate δ. The game proposed by Ray and Vohra (1996) is thus a direct generalisation of the game in Chatterjee *et al.* (1993) to the case of games with spillovers.

20 It is worthwhile to note that this Nash equilibrium is not a SNE. All firms obtain a higher profit under the grand coalition $\pi = \{n\}$.

21 See Ray and Vohra (1995) for details.

22 The literature on customs unions formation is already very large – and growing rapidly. I have only mentioned here those papers which deal explicitly with the theoretical issue of coalition formation.

23 The formulation I use is identical to that proposed by Krishna (1995).

24 Yi (1995d) shows that the results are true for $n \leq 2^{18} = 262144$! Beyond that limit, the characterisation of the SPE of the sequential game does not hold any longer.

References

Aumann, R. (1959), 'Acceptable Points and General n-Person Cooperative Games', *Annals of Mathematical Studies*, 40, 287–324.

— (1967), 'A Survey of Games without Side Payments', in M. Shubik (ed.), *Essays in Mathematical Economics*, Princeton: Princeton University Press, pp. 3–27.

Aumann, R. and J. Drèze (1974), 'Cooperative Games with Coalition Structures', *International Journal of Game Theory*, 3, 217–37.

Aumann, R. and M. Maschler (1964), 'The Bargaining Set for Cooperative Games', in M. Dresher, L. Shapley and A. Tucker (eds.), *Advances in Game Theory*, Princeton: Princeton University Press, pp. 443–70.

Aumann, R. and R. Myerson (1988), 'Endogenous Formation of Links Between Players and of Coalitions: An Application of the Shapley Value', in A. Roth (ed.), *The Shapley Value: Essays in Honor of Lloyd Shapley*, Cambridge University Press, pp. 175–91.

Baldwin, R. (1993), 'A Domino Theory of Regionalism', NBER Working Paper 4465.

Barrett, S. (1994). 'Self-Enforcing International Environmental Agreements', *Oxford Economic Papers*, 46, 878–94.

Bernheim, D., B. Peleg and M. Whinston (1987), 'Coalition-Proof Nash Equilibria. I. Concepts', *Journal of Economic Theory*, 42, 1–12.

Bloch, F. (1995), 'Endogenous Structures of Association in Oligopolies', *Rand Journal of Economics* 26, 537–56.

(1996), 'Sequential Formation of Coalitions in Games with Externalities and Fixed Payoff Division', *Games and Economic Behaviour*, 14, 90–123.

Bond, E. and C. Syropoulos (1993), 'Optimality and Stability of Regional Trading Blocs', mimeo, Department of Economics, Pennsylvania State University.

Carraro, C. and D. Siniscalco (1993), 'Strategies for the International Protection of the Environment', *Journal of Public Economics*, 52, 309–28.

Chander, P. and H. Tulkens (1992), 'Theoretical Foundations of Negotiations and Cost Sharing in Transfrontier Pollution Problems', *European Economic Review* 36, 388–98.

Chatterjee, K., B. Dutta, D. Ray and K. Sengupta (1993), 'A Noncooperative Theory of Coalitional Bargaining', *Review of Economic Studies*, 60, 463–77.

d'Aspremont, C., A. Jacquemin, J.J. Gabszewicz and J. Weymark (1983), 'On the Stability of Collusive Price Leadership', *Canadian Journal of Economics*, 16, 17–25.

Donsimoni, M.P., N. Economides and H. Polemarchakis (1986), 'Stable Cartels', *International Economic Review*, 27, 317–27.

Drèze, J. and J. Greenberg (1980), 'Hedonic Coalitions: Optimality and Stability', *Econometrica*, 48, 987–1003.

Dutta, B., S. Tijs and A. van Nouweland (1995), 'Link Formation in Cooperative Situations', mimeo, CentER, Tilburg.

Eren, N. (1993), 'Coalitional Structural Form Games and Stability under Property Rights', mimeo, Bogazici University.

Greenberg, J. (1977), 'Pure and Local Public Goods', in A. Sandmo (ed.), *Public Finance*, Lexington, MA: Heath and Co.

(1994), 'Coalition Structures', in R. Aumann and S. Hart (eds.), *Handbook of Game Theory with Applications,* vol. II, Amsterdam: North-Holland, pp. 1305–37.

Guesnerie, R. and C. Oddou (1981), 'Second Best Taxation as a Game', *Journal of Economic Theory*, 25, 67–91.

Gul, F. (1989), 'Bargaining Foundations of the Shapley Value', *Econometrica,* 57, 81–95.

Harsanyi, J. (1959), 'A Bargaining Model for the Cooperative n-Person Game', in A. Tucker and D. Luce (eds.), *Contributions to the Theory of Games*, Princeton: Princeton University Press, pp. 324–56.

Hart, S. and M. Kurz (1983), 'Endogenous Formation of Coalitions', *Econometrica*, 51, 1047–64.

(1984), 'Stable Coalition Structures', in M. Holler (ed.), *Coalitions and Collective Action*, Vienna: Physica Verlag, pp. 236–58.

Haveman, J. (1995), 'Some Welfare Effects of Sequential Customs Union Formation', mimeo, Department of Economics, Purdue University.

Ichiishi, T. (1983), 'A Social Coalitional Equilibrium Existence Lemma', *Econometrica*, 49, 369–77.

Kamien, M. and I. Zang (1990), 'The Limits of Monopolization through Acquisition', *Quarterly Journal of Economics*, 105, 465–99.

Konishi, H., M. Le Breton and S. Weber (1996), 'Group Formation in Games without Spillovers: A Noncooperative Approach', Chapter 9 in this book.

Krishna, P. (1995), 'Regionalism and Multilateralism: A Political Economy Approach', mimeo, Department of Economics, Columbia University.

Krugman, P. (1991), 'Is Bilateralism Bad?', in E. Helpman and A. Razin (eds.), *International Trade and Trade Policy*, Cambridge, MA: MIT Press, pp. 9–24.

Kurz, M. (1988), 'Coalitional Value', in A. Roth (ed.), *The Shapley Value: Essays in Honor of Lloyd Shapley*, Cambridge University Press, pp. 155–73.

Lucas, W. and J. Maceli (1978), 'Discrete Partition Function Games', in P. Ordeshook (ed.), *Game Theory and Political Science*, New York: Academic Press, pp. 191–213.

Macho-Stadler, I., D. Perez-Castrillo and C. Ponsati (1994), 'Stable Multilateral Trade Agreements', mimeo Department of Economics, University Autonoma Barcelona.

Mas-Colell, A. (1989), 'An Equivalence Theorem for a Bargaining Set', *Journal of Mathematical Economics*, 18, 129–39.

Maschler, M. (1992), 'The Bargaining Set, Kernel and Nucleolus', in R. Aumann and S. Hart (eds.), *Handbook of Game Theory with Applications, Volume I*, Amsterdam: North-Holland, pp. 591–667.

Moldovanu, B. (1992), 'Coalition-Proof Nash Equilibria and the Core in Three-Player Games', *Games and Economic Behaviour*, 4, 565–81.

Myerson, R. (1977), 'Graphs and Cooperation in Games', *Mathematics of Operations Research*, 2, 225–9.

(1978), 'Threat Equilibria and Fair Settlements in Cooperative Games', *Mathematics of Operations Research*, 3, 265–74.

Nash, J. (1950), 'The Bargaining Problem', *Econometrica*, 28, 155–62.

Owen, G. (1977), 'Value of Games With A Prori Unions', in R. Hein, and O. Moeschlin (eds.), *Essays in Mathematical Economics and Game Theory*, New York: Springer-Verlag, pp. 76–88.

Perez-Castrillo, D. (1994), 'Cooperative Outcomes through Noncooperative Games', *Games and Economic Behaviour*, 7, 428–40.

Perry, M. and P. Reny (1994), 'A Noncooperative View of Coalition Formation and the Core', *Econometrica*, 62, 795–817.

Qin, C. Z. (1996), 'Endogenous Formation of Cooperation Structures', *Journal of Economic Theory*, 69, 218–26.

Ray, D. and R. Vohra (1995), 'Equilibrium Binding Agreement', mimeo. Department of Economics, Boston University and Brown University, to appear in *Journal of Economic Theory*.

— (1996), 'Binding Agreements and Coalitional Bargaining', mimeo, Department of Economics, Brown University and Boston University.

Riezman, R. (1995), 'Customs Unions and the Core', *Journal of International Economics*, 19, 355–66.

Rubinstein, A. (1982), 'Perfect Equilibrium in a Bargaining Model', *Econometrica*, 50, 97–109.

Salant, S., S. Switzer and R. Reynolds (1983), 'Losses from Horizontal Mergers: The Effects of an Exogenous Change in Industry Structure on Cournot-Nash Equilibrium', *Quarterly Journal of Economics*, 98, 185–99.

Selten, R. (1981), 'A Noncooperative Model of Characteristic Function Bargaining', in V. Bohm and H. Nachtkamp (eds.), *Essays in Game Theory and Mathematical Economics in Honor of Oskar Morgenstern*, Mannheim: Bibliographisches Institut Mannheim, pp. 131–51.

Sertel, M. (1993), 'Membership Property Rights, Efficiency and Stability', mimeo, Bogazici University.

Shenoy, P. (1979), 'On Coalition Formation: A Game Theoretical Approach', *International Journal of Game Theory*, 8, 133–64.

Shubik, M. (1982), *Game Theory in the Social Sciences*, Cambridge, MA: MIT Press.

Thoron, S. (1994), 'Formation of a Coalition-Proof Stable Cartel', mimeo, GREQAM Marseille.

Thrall, R. and W. Lucas (1963), 'N-Person Games in Partition Function Form', *Naval Research Logistics Quarterly*, 10, 281–98.

Tiebout, C. (1956), 'A Pure Theory of Local Expenditures', *Journal of Political Economy*, 64, 416–24.

Von Neumann, J. and O. Morgenstern (1944), *Theory of Games and Economic Behavior*, Princeton: Princeton University Press.

Yi, S.S. (1995a), 'Stable Coalition Structures with Negative External Effects', mimeo, Department of Economics, Dartmouth College.

— (1995b), 'Stable Coalition Structures with Positive External Effects', mimeo, Department of Economics, Dartmouth College.

— (1995c), 'Endogenous Formation of Research Coalitions with Efficiency Gains', mimeo, Department of Economics, Dartmouth College.

— (1995d), 'Endogenous Formation of Customs Unions under Imperfect Competition: Open Regionalism is Good', mimeo, Department of Economics, Dartmouth College, to appear in *Journal of International Economics*.

Yi, S.S. and H. Shin (1995), 'Endogenous Formation of Coalitions in Oligopoly', mimeo, Department of Economics, Dartmouth College.

Zhao, J. (1992), 'The Hybrid Solutions of an n-Person Game', *Games and Economic Behaviour*, 4, 145–60.

Zhou L. (1994), 'A New Bargaining Set of an n-Person Game and Endogenous Coalition formation', *Games and Economic Behaviour*, 6, 512–26.

Index

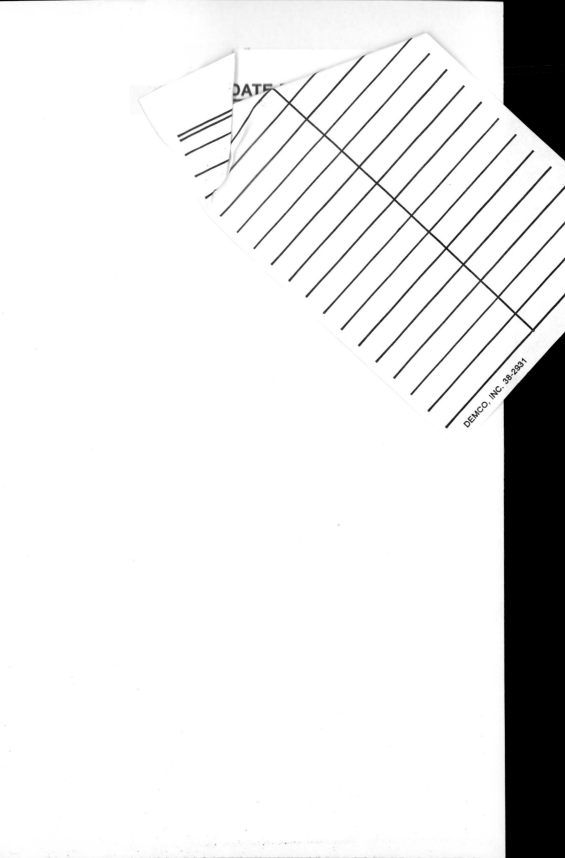

DATE

DEMCO, INC. 38-2931